S0-AUE-091

WORLD REPORT

2007

EVENTS OF 2006

ISBN-10: 1-58322-740-7   ISBN-13: 978-1-58322-740-4

Front cover photo: *An internally displaced man holds his sick infant son at a clinic in Tawila, North Darfur.* © 2004 James Nachtwey/VII Photos

Back cover photo: *Djorlo in eastern Chad was attacked by Chadian Arab militia on November 8, 2006. The militia burned huts and destroyed the storage for the harvest. In the background the village Damri is burning after being attacked on November 12.* © 2006 Kadir van Louhizen/Agence VU

Cover design by Rafael Jiménez

Human Rights Watch

350 Fifth Avenue, 34th floor
New York, NY 10118-3299 USA
Tel: +1 212 290 4700, Fax: +1 212 736 1300
hrwnyc@hrw.org

1630 Connecticut Avenue, N.W., Suite 500
Washington, DC 20009 USA
Tel: +1 202 612 4321, Fax: +1 202 612 4333
hrwdc@hrw.org

2-12 Pentonville Road, 2nd Floor
London N1 9HF, UK
Tel: +44 20 7713 1995, Fax: +44 20 7713 1800
hrwuk@hrw.org

Avenue des Gaulois, 7
1040 Brussels, Belgium
Tel: + 32 (2) 732 2009, Fax: + 32 (2) 732 0471
hrwbe@hrw.org

9 rue Cornavin
1201 Geneva
Tel: +41 22 738 0481, Fax: +41 22 738 1791
hrwgva@hrw.org

Poststraße 4-5
10178 Berlin, Germany
Tel: +49 30 2593 06-10, Fax: +49 30 2593 0629
berlin@hrw.org

www.hrw.org

Human Rights Watch is dedicated to protecting the human rights of people around the world.

We stand with victims and activists to prevent discrimination, to uphold political freedom, to protect people from inhumane conduct in wartime, and to bring offenders to justice.

We investigate and expose human rights violations and hold abusers accountable.

We challenge governments and those who hold power to end abusive practices and respect international human rights law.

We enlist the public and the international community to support the cause of human rights for all.

HUMAN RIGHTS WATCH

Human Rights Watch conducts regular, systematic investigations of human rights abuses in some seventy countries around the world. Our reputation for timely, reliable disclosures has made us an essential source of information for those concerned with human rights. We address the human rights practices of governments of all political stripes, of all geopolitical alignments, and of all ethnic and religious persuasions. Human Rights Watch defends freedom of thought and expression, due process and equal protection of the law, and a vigorous civil society; we document and denounce murders, disappearances, torture, arbitrary imprisonment, discrimination, and other abuses of internationally recognized human rights. Our goal is to hold governments accountable if they transgress the rights of their people.

Human Rights Watch began in 1978 with the founding of its Europe and Central Asia division (then known as Helsinki Watch). Today, it also includes divisions covering Africa, the Americas, Asia, and the Middle East. In addition, it includes three thematic divisions on arms, children's rights, and women's rights. It maintains offices in Berlin, Brussels, Chicago, Geneva, London, Los Angeles, Moscow, New York, San Francisco, Toronto, and Washington. Human Rights Watch is an independent, nongovernmental organization, supported by contributions from private individuals and foundations worldwide. It accepts no government funds, directly or indirectly.

ACKNOWLEDGMENTS

A compilation of this magnitude requires contribution from a large number of people, including most of the Human Rights Watch staff. The contributors were:

Fred Abrahams, Brad Adams, Ranee Adipat, Chris Albin-Lackey, Joe Amon, Assef Ashraf, Leeam Azulay-Yagev, Clarisa Bencomo, Nicholas Bequelin, Olivier Bercault, Andrea Berg, Nehal Bhuta, Michael Bochenek, Nicolette Boehland, Carroll Bogert, Peter Bouckaert, Sebastian Brett, Celeste Bruff, Jane Buchanan, David Buchbinder, Maria Burnett, Holly Cartner, Dominique Chambless, Christine Chiu, Grace Choi, Sandy Colliver, Sara Colm, Andrea Cottom, Zama Coursen-Neff, Steve Crawshaw, Sara Dareshori, Jennifer Daskal, Rachel Denber, Alison Des Forges, Thodleen Dessources, Richard Dicker, Bojan Djuric, Corinne Dufka, Elizabeth Evenson, Jamie Fellner, Conor Fortune, Loubna Freih, Bill Frelick, Georgette Gagnon, Arvind Ganesan, Meenakshi Ganguli, Erika George, Hadi Ghaemi, Allison Gill, Anna Goldin, Eric Goldstein, Rachel Good, Steve Goose, Ian Gorvin, Mariette Grange, Brian Griffey, Inara Gulpe-Laganovska, Julia Hall, Ali Dayan Hasan, Marianne Heuwagen, Peggy Hicks, Ethel Higonnet, Andrea Holley, Hameeda Hossain, Nadim Houry, Chris Huggins, Sarah Jackson, Rachel Jacobson, LaShawn Jefferson, Nerma Jelacic, Tiseke Kasambala, Steven Kass, Elise Keppler, Juliane Kippenberg, Norma Kriger, Katie Lane, Leslie Lefkow, Lotte Leicht, Hillel Levine, Iain Levine, Diederick Lohman, Scott Long, Jamie Loxton, Maira Magro, Lucy Mair, Tom Malinowski, Joanne Mariner, Paula Martins, David Mathieson, Veronica Matushaj, Nobuntu Mbelle, Maria McFarland, Anna McTaggart, Lisa Misol, Amha Mogus, Charmain Mohamed, Marianne Mollmann, Ella Moran, Hania Mufti, Sahr MuhammedAlly, Ashoka Mukpo, Jim Murphy, Katherine Newell Bierman, Joe Pace, Jagdish Parikh, Alison Parker, Tafadzwa Pasipanodya, Sasha Petrov, Sunai Phasuk, Carol Pier, Dinah PoKempner, Vitalii Ponamarev, Tom Porteous, Lutz Prager, Clara Presler, Tarek Radwan, Ben Rawlence, Aisling Reidy, Sophie Richardson, Katinka Ridderbos, Mihra Rittmann, Jemera Rone, James Ross, Kenneth Roth, Joe Saunders, Rebecca Schleifer, Halyna Senyk, Kay Seok, Steve Shapiro, Sofia Sharova, Dustin Sharp, Bede Sheppard, Elizabeth Siegel, Lee Sigal, Carmen Silvestre, Charles Sims, Anna Sinelnikova, Param-Preet Singh, Peter Smith,

Eugene Sokoloff, Mickey Spiegel, Joe Stork, Jonathan Sugden, Rania Suidan, Judith Sunderland, Veronika Szente Goldston, Peter Takirambudde, Tamara Taraciuk, Wilder Taylor, Sarah Tofte, Anneke Van Woudenberg, Nisha Varia, Hannah Vaughan-Lee, José Miguel Vivanco, Nicholas Vysny, Danielle Wainer, Janet Walsh, Ben Ward, Lois Whitman, Sarah Leah Whitson, Christoph Wilcke, Daniel Wilkinson, Beth Wolfram, Minky Worden, Elijah Zarwan, Sam Zia-Zarifi, and Iwona Zielinska.

Joe Saunders, Ian Gorvin, and Iain Levine edited the report; Leeam Azulay-Yagev coordinated the editing process. Layout and production were coordinated by Andrea Holley and Rafael Jiménez, with assistance from Grace Choi, Veronica Matushaj, Jim Murphy, Amha Mogus, and Jagdish Parikh.

Ranee Adipat, Assef Ashraf, Leeam Azulay-Yagev, Nicolette Boehland, Christine Chiu, Thodleen Dessources, Conor Fortune, Brian Griffey, Rachel Jacobson, Katie Lane, Clara Presler, Elizabeth Siegel and Rania Suidan proofread the report.

For a full list of Human Rights Watch staff, please go to our website: www.hrw.org/about/info/staff.html.

TABLE OF CONTENTS

FILLING THE LEADERSHIP VOID: WHERE IS THE EUROPEAN UNION?

By Kenneth Roth

What government is today's champion of human rights? Washington's potentially powerful voice no longer resonates after the US government's use of detention without trial and interrogation by torture. The administration of President George W. Bush can still promote "democracy"—the word it uses to avoid raising the thorny subject of human rights—but it cannot credibly advocate rights that it flouts.

As America's influence wanes, China's waxes. Yet China is hardly a leader on human rights. Its growing economic power has enhanced its global influence, but it remains at best indifferent to the human rights practices of others. Unwilling to permit political pluralism or the rule of law at home, Beijing pretends that human rights are an internal affair when dealing with others abroad.

Russia, with its internal crackdown on independent voices and its dirty war in Chechnya, is going down the same perverse path. Its goal seems to be rebuilding a sphere of influence, especially among the nations of the former Soviet Union, even if that means embracing tyrants and murderers. Attempting to deflect criticism, President Vladimir Putin went so far as to dismiss human rights as "artificial 'standards.'"

In this bleak environment, the European Union and the world's emerging democracies could provide potential sources of human rights leadership. Each has made important contributions, but none is performing with the consistency or effectiveness needed to fill the leadership void.

With Washington's voice diminished, the European Union today should be the strongest and most effective defender of human rights. It is founded on human rights principles and aspires to greatness in global affairs. But as the EU grapples with its enlarged membership, it is punching well below its weight. Its effort to achieve consensus among its diverse members has become so laborious that it yields a faint shadow of its potential. Union was supposed to enhance Europe's influence. Instead, when it comes to promoting human rights, the whole has been less than the sum of its parts.

The democracies of Latin America, Africa, and Asia, some long established but many new and insecure, have begun to stand up for human rights in certain international dealings. Despite moments of promise, however, these governments have yet to cooperate across regional boundaries to find an effective common voice. Too often, they show greater allegiance to their regional blocs than to their human rights ideals, greater solidarity with neighboring dictators than with the people whose rights they have pledged to uphold. This tendency played a particularly pernicious role in the United Nations' new Human Rights Council, which, far from improving on the discredited Commission on Human Rights, is threatening to repeat its disappointing ways, damaging the credibility of the entire UN system.

Every government these days seems to have a ready excuse for ignoring human rights. High-minded pronouncements occasionally ring from capitals or from ambassadors to the United Nations, but without the sustained follow-through needed for real leadership or change. Commitments are crabbed by caveats, engagements by escape clauses. Whether it is the lack of punitive consequences for Sudan's criminal campaign in Darfur, the EU's requirement of consensus before taking collective action, China's proclaimed deference to national sovereignty, Washington's preoccupation with Iraq and terrorism, or the developing world's sacrifice of human rights principles to regional solidarity, the excuses for inaction overwhelm the imperative of decisive action.

The trend is bleak, but not irreversible. Whether Washington's credibility gap is the temporary consequence of a particularly lawless administration or a long-term problem that will plague US standing for years depends in part on the new Congress—and whether it repudiates past abuses, presses for policy change, and seeks accountability for those responsible. No one pretends that such a turnaround will be easy when the architects of those abuses still control the executive branch, but it is essential if the United States is to redeem its tarnished reputation as a defender of human rights.

Leadership will also be needed to steer China and Russia toward more responsible behavior. To a large extent, Beijing and Moscow are the beneficiaries of low expectations. As long as few insist that they uphold international standards at home or abroad, they have little incentive to do so. Their new economic strength—China's booming market, Russia's energy reserves—only reinforces their ability to resist what meager pressure is directed their way while discouraging other governments from even exerting such pressure. Meanwhile, China's growing foreign aid program creates new options for dictators who were previously dependent on those who insisted on human rights progress. Changing this dynamic depends on treating China and Russia like countries that aspire to global leadership—on insisting that they respect human rights in their treatment of their people and their peers, and holding them accountable if they fall short. They must be convinced that the route to influence and respect is not through callousness and thuggery but through responsible global citizenship. But they can hardly be expected to improve if other governments' commitment to human rights is so cheaply sold for energy contracts or investment opportunities.

In Latin America, while a few countries have actively resisted human rights scrutiny, others have played an increasingly important role in promoting the application of international standards. Rare glimmers of hope can be found in Africa and Asia as well. The world needs a true Southern defender of human rights—a nation that rejects reflexive regionalism as an anachronism, a throwback to an era in which authoritarian governments joined hands to deflect human rights pressure. Today, as a growing number of governments stand for periodic election and speak for the aspirations of their people, they should be guided in their dealings with other governments by concern for the same rights that their own citizens embrace.

As for the European Union, many of its members recognize the paralysis and are searching for solutions. The European experiment has helped to bring peace and prosperity to those lucky enough to live inside its borders, but the EU is falling woefully short of its promise as a defender of rights around the world. Some needed changes might be relatively straightforward and swiftly implemented, such as modifying the flurry of rotating six-month presidencies to permit better accumulation of expertise and pursuit of long-term strategies. Some would require a change in tradition and bad habits, such as making EU institutions more transparent in order to minimize the gap between popular values and governmental action. Some changes are more fundamental, such as easing the requirement of unanimity for collective action in the sphere of human rights, to permit more timely and effective action around the world. All require EU governments to recognize that the status quo reflects an unacceptable abdication of leadership at a time when such leadership is in dangerously short supply.

The Human Rights Challenges

There is no shortage of serious challenges to human rights requiring more effective global leadership. As recently as September 2005, the governments of the world, in an historic declaration, embraced the doctrine of the responsibility to protect people facing mass atrocities. That commitment has rung hollow, however, as Darfur remains synonymous with mass murder, rape, and forcible displacement while the international community has managed little more than to produce reams of unimplemented UN resolutions. The usual political cowardice when it comes to military deployments to prevent mass murder accounts for some of the inaction, but there has also been far too little pressure on the Sudanese government to accept a real protection force. Predictably, Khartoum responds to such spinelessness with rejectionism. As this report went to press in November, there were signs that the Sudanese government might relent somewhat, partly in response to new and welcome pressure from China, but it remained far from clear that Khartoum would permit the deployment of troops with sufficient mandate and capacity to stop the killings or that it would end its own murderous policies.

Part of the problem is that the US invasion of Iraq and the Bush administration's belated attempts to justify it as a humanitarian intervention made it easier for governments like Sudan's to build opposition to any forceful effort to save the people of Darfur. Similarly, the promotion of democracy, a central human rights goal, risks being discredited by the administration's equating it with regime change through military force.

Meanwhile, the importance of bringing mass murderers to justice is under attack, particularly in Uganda, where the murderers are trying to trade impunity for an end to their killing. Terrorism—the dangerous view that civilians can be legitimately murdered for political ends—remains acceptable in too many parts of the world. Iraq has degenerated into massive sectarian blood-letting, with civilians the principal victims. Ruthlessly repressive governments impose enormous cruelty on their people in North Korea, Burma, and Turkmenistan. Closed dictatorships persist in Vietnam, Saudi Arabia, and Syria. China is slipping backwards. Russia and Egypt are cracking down on nongovernmental organizations (NGOs), and Peru and Venezuela are considering similar steps. Iran and Ethiopia are silencing dissident voices. Uzbekistan is crushing dissent with new vigor while refusing to allow independent investigation of its May 2005 massacre in its eastern city of Andijan. In Zimbabwe, President Robert Mugabe would rather drive his country to ruin than tolerate a political opposition. Civil war is reigniting in Sri Lanka, intensifying in Afghanistan, continuing in Colombia, and threatening in Nigeria. Israel launched indiscriminate attacks in Lebanon during its war with Hezbollah, while Hezbollah often targeted Israeli cities with no military objective in sight.

The intergovernmental institution devoted to addressing these problems—the new UN Human Rights Council—has yet to show any real improvement over its ineffectual predecessor, the Commission on Human Rights. A central duty of the council is to pressure highly abusive governments to change. That requires a series of graduated steps that can lead to the deployment of human rights monitors or public condemnation. Yet in a mockery of the high principles of its founding, the council has so far failed to criticize any government other than Israel. The most it has managed to muster is an "interactive dialogue" with UN investigators and a planned "peer review," forsaking its most powerful tool—collective condemnation by fellow governments. This failure threatens to call into question whether the United Nations is capable of upholding global human rights standards. Proponents of "coalitions of the willing"—the antithesis of the UN ideal of universal standards—will have gained the upper hand unless remedied by governments supportive of human rights.

The US Government: Compromised Credibility

In the past, many would have looked to the United States to take the lead in addressing these challenges. Though never a consistent promoter of human rights, Washington has been a prominent and influential one. Yet its voice now rings hollow—an enormous loss for the human rights cause. Quite apart from the fallout of its ill-fated Iraq invasion, its credibility as a proponent of human rights has been tarnished by the abuses it practices in the name of fighting terrorism. Few US ambassadors dare to protest another government's harsh interrogations, detention without trial, or even "disappearances," knowing how easily an interlocutor could turn the tables and cite US misconduct as an excuse for his government's own abuses. The cheapness of that excuse does not diminish its embarrassing effectiveness. Nor can consolation be taken in the fact that the United States is far from the world's worst rights violator. The abuses it has committed have done damage enough.

The last year dispelled any doubt that the Bush administration's use of torture and other mistreatment was a matter of policy dictated at the top rather than the aberrant misconduct of a few low-level interrogators. The administration claimed to foreswear torture but refused to classify mock execution by drowning—the classic torture technique now known as water-boarding—as prohibited torture. Despite the absolute treaty prohibition on cruel, inhuman, or degrading treatment, the administration claimed it could impose such abuse so long as the victim was a non-American held outside the United States—a position it abandoned only after the US Congress adopted the Detainee Treatment Act of 2005 by a veto-proof majority. Perhaps the low point came in September 2006, when President Bush offered a full-throated defense of torture, referring to it euphemistically as "an alternative set of [interrogation] procedures."

In the face of these developments and of growing resistance to these illegal techniques by the uniformed members of the US military, the Pentagon in September adopted a new Army Field Manual on Intelligence Interrogation which prohibits coercive interrogation by its own forces. Yet the administration continues to insist on granting Central Intelligence Agency (CIA) interrogators the power to use these coercive techniques. The Military Commissions Act, adopted by Congress in September, reaffirmed the absolute ban on cruel, inhuman, or degrading treatment but undermined enforcement by denying detainees the right to challenge their detention and treatment in court.

Of parallel concern is the administration's continued use of arbitrary detention as a tool of counterterrorism. It has distorted beyond all proportion the traditional power of warring parties to detain enemy combatants until the end of an armed conflict. Wielding the concept of a "global war on terrorism," the administration claims the power to detain, without judicial supervision, any non-American any-where in the world as an "enemy combatant" and to hold him without charge or trial as long as it wants—even until the end of his life. The administration denies the need to establish any link between the detainee and actual participation in an armed conflict—a traditional restraint on this wartime power to limit due process rights. The most basic rights are in jeopardy when a government asserts such extraordinary power.

Indeed, the administration's arrogation of power extends even to the claimed authority to "disappear" people—to seize them surreptitiously without any acknowledgment, any lawyer, any Red Cross visit, any contact with the outside world. This odious practice, widely and correctly condemned by the United States in the past when practiced by other governments, leaves friends and family guessing why their loved one has disappeared and whether he or she is even alive.

These abuses committed in the name of counterterrorism have only aggravated the terrorist threat. The use of torture and arbitrary detention spurs terrorist recruitment in communities that identify with the victims. It alienates those com-munities from law enforcement officials who are trying to reach out to them for tips about suspicious activity—a far more important source of intelligence than statements squeezed abusively from a suspect. And it sacrifices the moral high ground while eroding the principle that laudable ends cannot justify despicable means.

This catastrophic path has left the United States effectively incapable of defend-ing some of the most basic rights. The United States can still promote freedom of expression, association, or religion—where it largely practices what it preaches. But when it comes to such fundamental rights as freedom from torture and arbi-trary detention, the hypocrisy renders effective advocacy all but impossible.

Chinese President Hu Jintao's April 2006 visit to Washington made this limitation evident. In a rare exception to his usual practice, President Bush mentioned the phrase "human rights," but he quickly specified that he meant "the freedom to assemble, to speak freely, and to worship"—all worthy goals, all freedoms that the United States itself respects, but hardly a direct confrontation of the Chinese government's use of arbitrary detention and abusive prison conditions to enforce its grip on power.

One might hope that this effective silencing of America's voice on human rights would be short-lived—the product of a particular administration's contempt for any constraint on its power. Much will depend on steps taken by a new Congress to remedy the administration's worst excesses and by a successor administration to reverse and punish them.

But the damage done is also more fundamental. Abusive governments now conveniently equate the advancement of human rights with "regime change" and the invasion of Iraq—an equation that Sudan has used with deadly effect to ward off pressure regarding Darfur. Some Americans are doing the same. Sustaining American will and capacity to promote human rights will require divorcing the militarism of the neo-conservative vision from the laudable quest for democratic governance. Popular support for defending human rights is likely to depend on separating the administration's imperial indifference to national boundaries—ostensibly in the name of human rights but in situations that fall far short of those justifying humanitarian intervention—from the essential duty to stand up for victims of political repression and other abuses.

China

As US credibility on human rights diminished, China has often made matters worse. Its burgeoning economy and thirst for natural resources have led it to play a more assertive international role, but it has studiously avoided using that influence to promote human rights. Instead, it insists on dealing with other governments, in the words of President Hu Jintao, "without any political strings." Indeed, China's position on human rights ranges from indifference to hostility.

Concerns about hypocrisy and blowback might lie behind China's reluctance to defend rights that it routinely violates at home—such as those that sustain an independent civil society and the rule of law. Yet there are areas where such fears are less acute and should not constrain China. At least since the repression of the Tiananmen Square democracy movement, China has eschewed mass murder, let alone mass ethnic cleansing and crimes against humanity. China thus could credibly defend people facing such severe oppression, such as the people of Darfur or ethnic minorities in Burma. Yet it has done too little too late. Part of the explanation is its expressed ideological discomfort with what it calls "interference in the internal affairs" of other countries. Part is prioritization of its own quest for natural resource over the survival of people whose land yields those resources. Whatever the balance of considerations, China has done far less than it should.

There are signs that on certain matters, not always involving human rights, China's reluctance to meddle in others' affairs might be easing somewhat. In September, China seemed temporarily to suspend oil deliveries to North Korea because of Pyongyang's testing of a long-range missile. In October, after North Korea's first nuclear test, China reportedly threatened additional fuel suspensions until Pyongyang returned to the negotiating table. In November China's permanent representative to the UN, Wang Guangya, applied some, though insufficient, pressure on Sudan to agree to the deployment of a UN peacekeeping force in Darfur. China is also increasing the number of troops it offers to UN peacekeeping efforts.

Yet even though a UN Security Council resolution authorizing the deployment of a protection force in Darfur was premised on Khartoum's consent, China could bring itself only to abstain on the resolution, not support it. It is bad enough that China joined with other council members to reduce the international "responsibility to protect"—a doctrine aimed at preventing mass atrocities—to asking the murderers' permission to protect their victims. But China has made matters worse by refusing to use, or blocking, key sources of leverage to secure that consent.

Because China purchases a reported two-thirds of Sudan's oil exports and is the largest investor in its oil industry, Sudan's economy is booming, emboldening Khartoum to pursue its slaughter in Darfur and leaving it flush with funds to purchase arms (sometimes Chinese) for the fighting. Cutting off that revenue would make Khartoum far more susceptible to pressure to stop the killing in Darfur and allow the deployment of a protection force. Yet while China has now shown itself willing to invoke oil sanctions with respect to North Korea, it is not known to have done anything of the kind for Darfur. Indeed, it has allowed the UN Security Council only to ban travel and freeze assets for four individuals—two rebel commanders, a Janjaweed militia leader, and a former army officer—none of them a senior government official. If China wants to avoid the impression that it is more interested in continuing the flow of oil to its growing economy (some 4 to 7 percent of which comes from Sudan) than in staunching the flow of blood in Darfur, it should step up its public efforts to press Khartoum to cooperate.

The problem extends beyond Darfur:

- China remains a source of investment and military supplies for Zimbabwe despite President Mugabe's war on his people—the mass eviction of some 700,000 urban poor perceived as potential supporters of the political opposition, the bulldozing of their homes, the routine arbitrary detention and torture of opposition supporters, and the destruction of the country's economy. By disrupting their access to treatment, the evictions have had a particularly devastating impact on tens of thousands of people living with HIV/AIDS.

- By making some US$5 billion in no-strings-attached loans to Angola, China effectively undermined efforts by the International Monetary Fund to promote greater budgetary transparency to stop the government's looting of the national treasury—some $4 billion from 1997 to 2002, the equivalent of Angola's entire budget for social programs during that period.

- After Uzbekistan's government forces massacred hundreds of demonstrators in Andijan in May 2005, China greeted the country's president, Islam Karimov, with a 21-gun salute and announced a US$600 million oil deal. In 2006 China participated in joint military exercises with Uzbekistan and signed a two-year cooperation protocol.

- China is more concerned about stemming the flow of refugees from North Korea than stopping the grave threats to their lives caused by the ruthless and economically incompetent government of Kim Jong Il. Despite North Korea's pervasive repression, China pretends that those fleeing North Korea are all economic migrants and refuses even to cooperate with the UN special rapporteur investigating human rights conditions in North Korea or to allow the UN High Commissioner for Refugees access to refugees congregating near the North Korean border. There is no evidence that China has exerted pressure on Pyongyang for its repression comparable to the pressure apparently exerted with respect to its nuclear and long-range missile tests. China does look the other way as some refugees flee through it to third countries, but it could do much more.

- China is the most generous supporter of the Burmese military government, showing more interest in securing access to a deep water port and Burmese natural resources than in supporting the rights of the long-suffering Burmese people. In many parts of southeast Asia, China is showering aid on rights-abusing governments.

China is not the first government to place its own economic and political interests above those of the world's poor and unfortunate. Imperial powers have long done the same and worse. But the Chinese Communist Party is, at least in theory, built on an ideology of looking out for everyone's basic needs. Beijing cultivates a profile of friend to the developing world. It prides itself on creating jobs and relieving poverty. Increasingly it is contributing foreign assistance. But some of its behavior runs counter to those principles.

The repressive governments it supports are crushing and impoverishing their people. Newly rich oil magnates in Khartoum may toast the Chinese from their posh cafes along the banks of the Nile, but the uprooted and destitute people of Darfur do not. Robert Mugabe may thank the Chinese government for his ability to cling to power, but the hundreds of thousands of Zimbabweans rendered homeless by his Operation Clean the Filth do not. The Burmese military, with Chinese help, is building a splendid new capital and enjoys access to a vast array of weapons, but the Burmese people live in squalor and fear. If China is to gain the international respect it craves, it must shun—not subsidize—these governments.

It is hard to believe that the Chinese government wants to be known as the supporter of tyrants, the exploiter of the impoverished. We would hope a government that eagerly sought the symbol of international fair play and cooperation—the Olympic Games—would not dispense with international solidarity when it comes to the victims of its tyrannical partners. But change will come only if China is called to task for its ugly actions. For decades, the Chinese government was so repressive, its global role so limited, that few looked for anything from Beijing but hostility toward human rights. China did not disappoint. Today, we can hardly expect better if no government is willing even to ask.

When pointedly confronted on human rights, the Chinese government has made some concessions. At his meeting with President Bush in April, President Hu said that, "on the basis of mutual respect and equality," the Chinese government would be "ready...to promote the world's cause of human rights." By abstaining on Darfur, China allowed passage of UN Security Council resolutions authorizing the deployment of a UN protection force in Darfur and the investigation of atrocities by the International Criminal Court. It also, as noted, has applied some limited pressure on Khartoum.

Yet governments that are the traditional proponents of human rights are so busy cutting their own trade deals with China that they rarely voice concern about Beijing's inhumane behavior at home or abroad. If they were true to their principles, they would condemn China's rising role in global repression. Only by ensuring that China pays with its reputation for its misconduct is there any chance of encouraging better behavior.

Russia

Russia has followed a similar trajectory. After the collapse of the Soviet Union, Russia was in too much disarray at home to play much of a role abroad. But as the value of its gas and oil reserves has soared and President Putin has consolidated power by neutralizing most other domestic centers of power, the Kremlin is flexing its muscles. Determined to reassert its dominance within the former Soviet Union, Putin's Russia has cozied up to entrenched dictators such as Uzbekistan's Islam Karimov, Belarus's Alexander Lukashenko, and Turkmenistan's Saparmurat Niazov, and done much to undermine democratic government in Ukraine and Georgia.

For example, on the eve of the first anniversary of Uzbekistan's Andijan massacre, President Putin demonstrated his political support of President Karimov by inviting him to Putin's holiday residence. At about the same time, the lower house of the Russian parliament ratified a military alliance treaty with Uzbekistan.

Similarly, despite its considerable influence, Russia has not lifted a finger to ease repression in Turkmenistan, even when the victims are Russian citizens.

This behavior abroad is matched by Putin's conduct at home. He presides over military forces in Chechnya that continue to use pervasive torture and to "disappear" more people than security forces in just about any other country. He has the power to rein in his Chechen proxies who are behind most of these abuses, but instead he supports them unconditionally and heaps praise on their leader. His Kremlin has transformed most competing centers of power—the Duma, the provincial governors, the electronic media, the business community—into pliant partners. Nongovernmental organizations, one of the few remaining independent sectors, are threatened by new regulations that invite meddling and closures. Unidentified assailants have murdered high-profile independent journalists, such as Anna Politkovskaia, who was investigating atrocities in Chechnya, without any successful prosecution of the perpetrators.

Like China, Putin has paid little price for dancing with dictators. Few other governments refer publicly to his misdeeds. Their occasional grumbling is barely heard over their groveling for energy deals.

Russia will persist in its misconduct if it continues to get away with it. The Russian government aspires to global citizenship. Its membership in the G8 matters to it. But the world's most powerful democracies have not insisted that it earn its seat at the table. They rewarded Russia with the G8 chairmanship in July and let it host the G8 summit in St. Petersburg without any positive movement on its human rights record at home or abroad. Its desire to join the World Trade Organization, which seemed to be nearing fulfillment as this report went to press, depends on a willingness to play by global economic rules. But it is wrong for the world to accept Russia as a closed, authoritarian country so long as its markets are open. Turning Russia around will hardly be easy, but it will be impossible if no one even tries, and those in a position to speak out remain mute.

Democracies in the Global South

One potential source of human rights leadership might be some of the democracies, both new and established, in the global South. Because these governments are non-Western, their rights advocacy could help to reinforce the fact that human rights are universal values. Because they often live in the neighborhood of abusive governments, their proximity could give them added clout. And because many have emerged from periods of extreme repression, whether colonialism, apartheid, or dictatorship, they could have special moral authority on human rights. Some Southern governments have begun to live up to their leadership potential, but principled stands for human rights have been too sporadic to fill the leadership void.

Latin American countries have generally supported efforts to strengthen international human rights mechanisms. Nearly all countries in the region ratified the Rome statute and joined the International Criminal Court, and many have resisted intense US pressure, including the threatened loss of substantial US assistance, to sign bilateral agreements that exempt US citizens from the ICC's jurisdiction. More recently several countries, most notably Argentina, Chile, and Mexico, actively supported the creation of the UN's new Human Rights Council. Mexico was then chosen to serve as the council's first president, largely because of the vocal role it has played in recent years in the international promotion of human rights. The Mexican government has been a forceful advocate for protecting human rights while fighting terrorism, drafting a resolution on the issue that the UN General Assembly unanimously adopted and pressing successfully for the creation of a post on human rights and terrorism within the Office of the UN High Commissioner for Human Rights. Argentina has also supported human rights protections within the UN system, using its seat on the Security Council to address human rights crises in Darfur and Burma.

However, there are important exceptions in Latin America. Cuba has categorically rejected all efforts to hold it accountable for its dismal human rights record. The Colombian government has campaigned aggressively to undercut the authority of the representative in Colombia of the UN High Commissioner for Human Rights. Venezuela has championed the view that national sovereignty trumps international human rights obligations.

Positive developments in Africa include Liberian President Ellen Johnson Sirleaf's call for the surrender for trial on charges of war crimes and crimes against humanity of former Liberian President Charles Taylor, to which Nigeria's President

Olusegun Obasanjo ultimately acquiesced; and Senegal's President Abdoulaye Wade's belated agreement, at the request of the African Union, to begin moving toward prosecution for systematic torture of former Chadian President Hissène Habré. The African Union—an institution built on a commitment to democracy, human rights, and the rule of law—has also played an important role in Darfur, although its protection force of 7,000 was inadequate to the task without UN help which Khartoum has blocked. In addition, in June the African Peer Review Mechanism of the New Economic Partnership for Africa completed a report that was surprisingly critical of several aspects of Rwanda's poor human rights record—the beginning of what is supposed to be regular African commentary on African human rights problems. Ghana's human rights record has also been reviewed.

In Asia, South Korea has emerged as a consistent supporter of human rights efforts, so long as they are not directed toward North Korea, where Seoul seems more interested in averting a governmental collapse than precluding crushing repression of the North Korean people. Even there, in a significant shift, Seoul voted in November in favor of a UN General Assembly resolution on human rights in North Korea.

However, these governmental efforts on behalf of human rights remain the exception rather than the rule. At the Human Rights Council, an outdated sense of regional loyalty led several African and Asian governments that are ostensibly committed to human rights—Ghana, Mali, Senegal, South Africa, as well as India and Indonesia—to allow their positions to be dictated by the likes of Algeria and Pakistan.

India, the world's largest democracy and a potential leader, remains mired in a Cold War-era antipathy to the promotion of human rights abroad. It has not forcefully condemned Burma's dismal human rights record. It went so far, during a summit with China in November, to order Tibetan refugees not to publicly protest on pain of deportation. However, on the positive side, India overcame its longstanding allergy to outside involvement in South Asia and supported the deployment of a successful UN human rights monitoring mission which helped halt Nepal's slide toward disaster.

South Africa, having seemingly forgotten that it was the beneficiary of strong public campaigns against apartheid, continues to insist that only quiet diplomacy is appropriate for addressing Robert Mugabe's devastation of Zimbabwe's people. Mugabe himself was a strong opponent of apartheid, but South African President Thebo Mbeki seems to be putting respect for his former political ally ahead of respect for the human rights principles they fought for.

In sum, while democracies of the global South should be key partners in protecting human rights, they have yet to show themselves ready to fill the leadership void.

The European Union

With the United States having largely disqualified itself from human rights promotion, China and Russia effectively undermining the effort, and the global South not yet bearing its share of the burden, it is imperative that the European Union rise to the occasion and assume a leadership role. After all, the EU is the world's leading collection of democracies, founded on a commitment to human rights and the rule of law. Yet the sad truth is that the EU is nowhere near picking up the leadership mantle. All too often, when the EU musters a statement about a human rights problem, it is delivered by a Brussels bureaucrat or takes the form of a written EU Presidency press release rather than a forceful public pronouncement by a head of state or foreign minister. Such statements are rarely followed by firm action or pressure to protect human rights. Due in part to structural problems and in part to a lack of political will, the EU's underperformance on human rights has left a gaping leadership hole.

The EU role at the UN Human Rights Council illustrates the problem. The United States did not even seek election to the council, a decision apparently based in large part on fear that it would lose. Much of the burden for making the new council live up to its ideals thus rests on the EU and its closest partners—governments like Australia, Canada, New Zealand, Norway, and Switzerland.

The council is evenly divided between traditional supporters and opponents of human rights enforcement, with several democracies in Asia and Africa holding the swing votes. By working with Latin American governments to join forces with these undecided voters, European governments could muster a working majority to address such problems as the crimes against humanity in Darfur, the Uzbek government's murderous impunity, and Sri Lanka's reviving civil war. But the sad truth is that the spoilers—the abusive governments that, despite pledges to the contrary, seem to have joined the council to undermine it—have run circles around the Europeans and their allies. In a seeming daze, the supporters of human rights offered mainly defeatism and feeble excuses.

The EU and other governmental supporters of human rights never put forward a compelling vision for the council's treatment of abusive governments. They never did the needed outreach and lobbying to dissuade swing voters from following their spoiler-led regional blocs rather than their own stated human rights principles. They never called for a special session on Darfur or the deteriorating situation in Sri Lanka to expand the spoilers' fixation on Israel. Many supporters went so far as to take up the spoilers' refrain, "cooperation, not condemnation," as if the threat of condemnation for gross abuses had nothing to do with securing governmental cooperation in overcoming them. For these and other reasons, the council left an awful first impression.

Making Decisions

The EU's clumsiness can be attributed in part to its cumbersome decision-making process. The need to cobble together a consensus among its 25 members (due to be 27 when this appears in print) tends to yield delays and a lowest-common-denominator position. It takes only one government with deeply felt parochial interests—Cyprus on Turkey, Germany on Russia, France on Tunisia—to block an effective EU position.

For example, Germany's new *Ostpolitik* is undermining a strong EU human rights position on Central Asia. In November 2006 Germany succeeded in its aggressive push to ease even the modest sanctions imposed on Uzbekistan following the Andijan massacre of May 2005 even though the Uzbek government took no meaningful steps to meet the conditions originally set for lifting the sanctions. Rather than allow an independent investigation into the massacre, as required, Uzbekistan has offered only "dialogue" and an "expert seminar" on Andijan. Meanwhile, its crackdown on those who dare to voice their dissent has been ruthless, with a dozen human rights defenders convicted and imprisoned on politically motivated charges in 2006 alone.

To support its stance toward Uzbekistan, a country with huge gas reserves and a useful airbase to German troops in Afghanistan, Germany has argued that sanctions had failed to produce positive results—despite Germany having done everything in its power to undermine the sanctions from the moment of their adoption. The EU travel ban on high-ranking Uzbek government officials had barely been announced when Berlin permitted entry into Germany for medical treatment one of the architects of the Andijan massacre—former Uzbek Interior Minister Zokir Almatov—who topped the EU's travel-ban list. When several of his victims' families sought his prosecution at great personal risk, the German federal prosecutor refused to arrest him and would not even open a criminal investigation. Nothing that Uzbekistan has done justifies Germany's capitulationist approach, yet Germany seems to be dragging the EU along, despite resistance from a sizeable group of member-states.

Germany has also taken the lead in presenting a weak EU position on Kazakhstan by lending unequivocal support to the country's bid to chair the Organization for Security and Cooperation in Europe in 2009, rather than using Kazakh President Nursultan Nazarbaev's desire for the leadership post as an opportunity to press for long-overdue, concrete reforms.

Similarly in Nepal, following the February 2005 royal coup, the Nordic governments wanted to condemn the coup forcefully and stop the military government from using EU aid. While Denmark in particular played a positive role, other EU governments, including France and Germany, weakened the EU consensus. Britain also pursued an independent, at times accommodationist policy, citing a historic relationship with Nepal. The result was that in the immediate aftermath of the coup the EU adopted a less than vigorous stance that left Nepali civil society feeling unsupported and discouraged.

The EU's tilt toward the lowest common denominator reflects a preference for unity over effectiveness. Achieving a common position is understandably important for building a community of European nations. In addition, by banding together, EU governments have more clout, and face less risk of retaliation, than if they proceed individually. But if the EU never acts beyond the wishes of its most reluctant member, it will most often end up doing little or nothing. Some more nimble and reasonable decisional process is needed. One option would be to allow a supermajority rather than unanimity to achieve a common foreign policy. But that would require each EU government giving up its prized veto over EU action and the sovereign prerogative that it implies. Yet the status quo also exacts a high price in terms of the repressed people of the world whose pleas for help the EU leaves unanswered.

Even within the requirement of unanimity, improvements are possible. For one, at the Human Rights Council, the EU seems to demand a consensus at an absurdly petty level. Rather than signing off on a strategy and having faith in EU representatives to pursue it wisely, EU members insist on signing off on each proposed resolution word by word. This micromanagement makes it impossible for the EU to respond effectively to changing circumstances or to engage in the quick diplomatic give-and-take needed to build majority alliances.

When human rights are at stake, the EU could also treat its common position as a floor rather than a ceiling. It is appropriate to insist that no government do less than the common EU position on key human rights issues, but why should no government—or group of governments—do more? There is no formal bar, and occasionally it happens, for example with respect to treaties on the International Criminal Court, anti-personnel landmines, and enforced disappearances. Denmark even suggested this approach with respect to Darfur. But too often EU governments use the lack of a strong common position to justify the lack of a strong national one. That may make sense on, say, a tax or trade issue, but to preclude national action for human rights, or action by a group of nations, beyond a minimal consensus is callous—a prioritization of the collective over the effective. It suggests that the EU, despite its ideals, despite its lofty pledges, has ultimately decided that a weak uniform defense of human rights is more important than a vigorous varied one.

One welcome exception to the unanimity rule was the decision in November 2006 by 14 EU member-states to co-sponsor a resolution on Uzbekistan at the UN General Assembly after attempts to reach an agreement among all 25 failed. More such initiatives are needed.

Our aim is not to return to a pre-EU era of 25 separate foreign policies. There is strength in numbers. The relative weakness of the European presence in Afghanistan—where many governments pursue their own bilateral projects without the leverage and reinforcement that would come from a more coordinated approach—highlights the costs of such disarray. Although the EU mission in Kabul is well informed, its member-states hardly use it. As a result, Germany's police reform was not coordinated with Italy's judicial reform (the latter ended in 2006). Governments with provincial reconstruction teams do not synchronize their development work. EU participants in NATO's military operations impose their own bilateral restrictions—German troops will not directly engage insurgents to protect civilians, British troops will not take action against drug runners even if they are supporting the insurgency, Dutch troops are reluctant to hold detainees—that stymie efforts to provide a secure environment for the Afghan people. Yet there are times when strong action by few would be better than weak or no action by many.

Even when a common position is reached, the EU's insistence on speaking and working almost exclusively through its "presidency" often undermines its clout. At the Human Rights Council, the tradition of the EU speaking once through its presidency, rather than allowing member governments to chime in to second the common position, leaves spoiler nations who have learned the value of repetition to dominate the debate.

More fundamentally, it is difficult to imagine a less effective way to maintain continuity or build expertise than the EU's rotating blur of six-month leaders. Sometimes, as in the case of Finland's presidency during the critical first six months of the Human Rights Council, the government seems to be in over its head and to view its job as consensus-forging rather than leadership. Other times, better resourced governments take the reins, but even they must squeeze an agenda into an abbreviated six-month period. The tradition of the incoming presidency as well as the European Council and Commission maintaining a role in a presidential "troika" mitigates this self-imposed handicap somewhat, but not nearly enough. Leadership rotation reaffirms the equality of all EU members, but the refusal to assign long-term responsibility to governments—thus undercutting the possibility of their developing expertise and long-term strategies—is a recipe for dysfunction. In some cases, such as negotiations with Iran over its nuclear program, the EU has taken steps to overcome this disability by appointing a permanent strong troika of Britain, France, and Germany to represent the EU. But similar steps have not been taken with respect to important human rights issues.

To overcome this liability, the EU should recognize that its diverse membership could be an asset rather than a procedural problem. Its 25 members have a diversity of experiences and relations with the rest of the world which could be harnessed through long-term "troikas of expertise" or "troikas of effectiveness" rather than rotating "troikas of the recently arrived." The EU's clout would be greatly enhanced if, rather than sending a new generation of fresh faces every six months, the same three governments kept showing up at a trouble spot year after year, representing a continuity of concern and a determination to follow through.

EU effectiveness on human rights is also hampered by a lack of transparency. The promotion of human rights will often bump up against other governmental interests. Developing and pursuing a human rights strategy in the back room makes it difficult for the public to know how the EU resolves such clashes—particularly since so many key decisions are taken in Brussels rather than national capitals, and so few involve open parliamentary debate. Governments may find it convenient to avoid embarrassing public scrutiny, but the consequences are felt in the EU's weak human rights commitments and mediocre performance.

These procedural failings cannot fully explain the EU's failure of leadership on human rights. Much of the problem is due to a simple lack of political will. Promoting human rights can be costly and difficult, and many governments do not want to bother—at least beyond lip service. But whether procedure or commitment is to blame, the EU's credibility as a principled promoter of human rights is at stake.

To examine EU leadership on human rights in more detail, it is useful to look at its response to several sets of challenges: the major powers of China, Russia, and the United States; crises such as Darfur; other human rights problems; and human rights issues within the EU itself.

On China

With respect to China, the EU has steadily muted its human rights critique, rele-
gating most public comments to bland written statements that are easily ignored.
The EU maintains a periodic human rights "dialogue" with China, but mid-level
officials carry it out, headed each time by a representative of a new presidency,
with no apparent benchmarks to measure progress from meeting to meeting, and
no tangible results. By contrast, Beijing has developed a team of dialogue specialists to deflect criticism and obstruct any impetus for reform. As a result, dialogue remains ensconced in the foreign ministry without the public airing that
might jeopardize China's reputation and spur change.

The dialogue's insignificance was highlighted at the time of the most recent EU-
China summit, held in Helsinki in September 2006, with Chinese Prime Minister
Wen Jiabao in attendance. On behalf of the EU presidency, Finland's ambassador
to Beijing, Antti Kuosmanen, stated that human rights would "not be a dominant
point" at the summit and that human rights were a "sensitive and delicate issue
... because we are dealing with values." In a stroke, the EU relegated universal
human rights standards to the realm of subjectivity. Predictably, business and
security issues dominated the agenda, as they did during Wen's later visits with
British Prime Minister Tony Blair and German Chancellor Angela Merkel, as well as
French President Jacques Chirac's subsequent visit to Beijing.

Similarly, in October the EU's External Relations Commissioner Benita Ferrero-
Waldner and Trade Commissioner Peter Mandelson urged a "comprehensive
reframing" of the EU's relations with China but never mentioned human rights.
Their proposal could be summed up as putting profits ahead of principles.

One area where this lack of pressure on human rights has been felt is internet
freedom. With no help from the EU (or, for that matter, the United States) to resist
Chinese pressure, internet companies have engaged in a race to the bottom,
doing the Chinese government's dirty work as web censors.

There have been a few bright spots in EU-China relations on human rights.
German Chancellor Merkel, in Beijing for her first summit with Chinese leaders,
took time out to meet with Chinese activists addressing the problems and unrest
of the countryside. Despite Chinese lobbying, the EU resisted lifting its arms

embargo on China imposed after the bloody crackdown in Tiananmen Square in 1989—a rare case in which the consensus rules facilitated a strong human rights position because the embargo, originally imposed without an end date, requires a common position to lift. But with China eager to have the embargo ended before the 2008 Olympic Games, the EU still has not articulated the conditions that must be met—such as a transparent and credible investigation into the Tiananmen killings—and thus has squandered a potential source of influence.

On Russia

EU policy toward Russia is dominated by Germany, which will assume the EU presidency in the first half of 2007. Berlin's new *Ostpolitik* reflects an apparent determination to engage at any cost, with no strings attached. As Russia's most important and respected interlocutor, the German government squanders its influence by seeming to assume that achieving energy security—a major European priority—is incompatible with challenging Russia's disturbing human rights record. German reluctance to engage critically with the Russian government may also be influenced by feelings of guilt due to the millions of Russians who died because of the German invasion of World War II, although why today's victims of Russian oppression should suffer because of their ancestors' plight is never explained. The EU has held semi-annual human rights "consultations" with Russia, also at a low diplomatic level, but human rights have not featured prominently on the broader EU-Russia agenda. As with China, the EU periodically responds to individual cases or events such as the new Russian law on NGOs, but human rights rarely enter the public discourse of senior officials. Atrocities in Chechnya have essentially been forgotten, with no public demands for accountability or even a word on the fate of the "disappeared."

As during her trip to China, German Chancellor Merkel made a point of visiting Russian human rights defenders at the time of her first summit with President Putin. She has also spoken about the importance of human rights and the rule of law in Russia. But no other European leader matched her statements or gestures, and they were not reflected in any common EU position. France's President Chirac even awarded Putin the Grand Cross of the Legion of Honor. By contrast, on four occasions in 2006, the European Court of Human Rights found Russia responsible for violating the right to life because of the role of Russian troops and their proxies in the forced disappearance of people in Chechnya. European leaders are missing an enormous opportunity presented by these court rulings to press Russia to curb abuses and end impunity.

On the United States

As for the United States, the EU has a mixed record. US detainee operations in Europe made European governments complicit in torture, arbitrary detention, and forced disappearance. Evidence suggests that Poland and Romania allowed the secret detention of "disappeared" suspects on their soil. While the US Congress did nothing to investigate these operations, the European Parliament launched an inquiry. The temporary parliamentary committee (TDIP) found it "utterly implausible" that these activities could have occurred without the knowledge of European intelligence or security services. It found similar official complicity in the apprehension of suspects on European soil and their rendition to governments that systematically torture, while also finding the US Central Intelligence Agency "clearly responsible." But Poland has stonewalled in the face of revelations of its complicity, refusing to cooperate with various investigations into the secret detention centers.

An Italian court, by contrast, has been more vigorous, issuing arrest warrants for CIA agents and their Italian accomplices who were allegedly responsible for the 2003 abduction of Osama Mustafa Hassan Nasr, known as Abu Omar, and his rendition to torture in Egypt. In November, in what it described as a "natural rotation," the new government of Prime Minister Romano Prodi replaced the head of the military intelligence services SISMI, who is under investigation for his role in the abduction. But the real test for Italy will be whether the government forwards the court's extradition requests to the United States, and whether it releases information regarding its possible prior knowledge of the kidnapping.

As for US conduct outside of Europe, the EU has not offered any high-level public comment on the findings of the UN Committee against Torture about US complicity in torture and other abusive interrogation. And it took the EU years—not until the EU-US summit in June 2006—to call collectively for the closure of the US detention facility at Guantanamo Bay. That appeal was preceded by similar ones from Britain, Germany, and Spain. Yet the EU has refused to make the humanitarian gesture of taking in Guantanamo detainees whom the US is willing to release but who cannot be returned to their native lands for fear that they might be tortured there. It was only non-EU member Albania that ultimately agreed to resettle five Uighur detainees who were freed from Guantanamo but could not safely be returned to China, as well as allowing Egyptian, Algerian, and Uzbek detainees.

On Darfur

In addressing the enormous crisis in Darfur, the EU likes to trumpet the funds it has sent to support the underequipped and understaffed African Union force (AMIS). However, it has done little to persuade Khartoum to accept the better equipped and staffed UN protection force that the UN Security Council approved in August. The EU imposed an arms embargo on Sudan during the north-south civil war, but has done nothing to enforce the embargo since the Darfur conflict began. Preferring engagement, EU members have resisted freezing assets and banning travel for senior Sudanese officials responsible for the Darfur slaughters. Far from matching US trade sanctions toward Sudan, the EU has seen its, and particularly France's, trade with Sudan increase sharply. That Khartoum has made no progress in disarming the murderous Janjaweed militias or holding accountable those responsible for atrocities, as the EU and UN have demanded, has done nothing to spur the EU to a more vigorous response.

Part of the problem is that Britain and France, as permanent members of the UN Security Council, have insisted that EU policy on Darfur be set in New York rather than Brussels. To its credit, the EU—especially Germany and France—played the key role in the Security Council's establishment of a commission of inquiry to examine atrocities in Darfur and the later referral of Darfur to the International Criminal Court. But the important task of achieving justice for victims is no substitute for immediate action to stop today's murder, rape, and forced displacement. As for enlisting others to pressure Khartoum, the EU raised Darfur with China in advance of the China-Africa summit in November 2006, and German Chancellor Merkel discussed Darfur in her meetings with Chinese and Russian leaders, but the effort to enlist China and Russia in pressing Khartoum to accept a UN protection force and reverse its brutal policies in Darfur has not been sufficiently sustained or intensive to make a difference on the ground, where Khartoum and its Janjaweed proxies persist in attacking civilians with impunity.

On Other Human Rights Issues

There are many other countries where the EU has dropped the ball on human rights. Sometimes business interests have played an important role.

- In Burma, the EU provides assistance to the democracy movement in exile. It is also a critic of the Burmese government and has imposed limited sanctions. However, several EU members—Britain, France, Germany, the Netherlands—have sizeable trade and investment interests in Burma, a disturbing fact given the Burmese military's use of forced labor in many sectors of the economy. At a time when Burma's neighbors have become outspoken critics, many powerful EU states are relatively passive. EU countries even saw fit to invite the Burmese foreign minister to the Asia-Europe (ASEM) summit in September.

- In Thailand, the EU responded firmly to the military coup in September 2006 that overthrew Prime Minister Thaksin Shinawatra. But during Thaksin's five-year tenure, the EU expressed concern only quietly about deteriorating rights conditions—including some 2,500 extrajudicial executions in Thaksin's war on drugs, the suppression of media freedom, abrutal counter-insurgency in the south, and the downgrading of refugee protection. Meanwhile, the EU sought a free trade agreement with Thailand.

- In the Middle East, the EU, which has human rights clauses in its trade and cooperation agreements with most countries, should have played a more active role on human rights. The main exception has been its support for an international investigation into the 2005 car-bombing murder of former Lebanese Prime Minister Rafik Hariri.

- In Ethiopia, the EU strongly protested government abuses in the course of the hotly contested 2005 elections in Ethiopia. It also backed those words with some action, withholding or re-channeling more than US$375 million in direct multilateral budget support to the Ethiopian government. However, there has been no visible EU follow-up in addressing Ethiopia's continuing major human rights problems such as the repression of political opponents and the beating, rape, and extrajudicial killing of members of the Anuak ethnic group in the Gambella region of Ethiopia.

- The EU played a positive role in pressing Nigeria to surrender former Liberian President Charles Taylor for trial before the Special Court for Sierra Leone, based on charges that he committed war crimes and crimes against humanity by supporting the murderous Revolutionary United Front in Sierra Leone. But when the Special Court for Sierra Leone asked that the trial be moved to The Hague because of security concerns associated with Taylor's being held in Freetown—a concern seconded by Liberia—the EU dawdled. The International Criminal Court promptly offered its facilities, and the Netherlands agreed on the condition that another government commit to detain Taylor if convicted. But at a time of potential instability in West Africa, Taylor's transfer was held up for weeks while the EU sought such a government. Britain finally stepped forward.

- The government of Tunisia, intolerant of any entity that criticizes its record, has for years blocked a series of grants that the EU approved to the independent Tunisian Human Rights League, as well as grants that the EU wishes to make to other independent organizations. Yet the EU has failed to publicly protest this ongoing practice except in the mildest terms.

None of this is to deny that sometimes the EU plays a positive role, especially when it comes to fielding operational missions.

- It has played a key part in forging a peace agreement in Aceh and mobilizing a monitoring team, although it has not pressed the Indonesian government to leave open the option of bringing those responsible for atrocities during the war to justice.

- A European force sent to the Democratic Republic of Congo in advance of the October 2006 elections provided an important boost to the efforts of the UN peacekeeping force to maintain security, although Germany's insistence on bringing soldiers home for Christmas risked reducing troop strength at a time when political tensions over disputed election results remained high. The risks were underscored by a new revolt in eastern Congo at the end of November 2006.

- In October 2006 a European Parliament committee rejected a proposal put forward by the European Commission for an interim trade agreement with Turkmenistan, stressing that the parliament would approve such an agreement only when "clear, tangible, and sustained progress on the human rights situation is achieved" in Turkmenistan.

- Six thousand EU troops keep the peace in Bosnia, where the EU is expected to take sole responsibility for a scaled-down international civilian presence in mid-2007.

- In Kosovo, the EU is planning to take the lead in the international civilian mission that is expected to deploy in 2007 when the territory's status is determined. Its focus will include justice and policing.

Similarly, the EU can be a strong force for human rights through the accession process, where the requirement of unanimity for action tends to raise the bar for the candidate state—since any EU member can object that the candidate has not done enough to improve its human rights record—rather than stymie the projection of EU influence. That positive influence was felt most forcefully over the past year in the Balkans, notwithstanding Brussels's failure to focus sufficiently on domestic accountability for war crimes in the region. In the recent past, it has been felt in Turkey as well, although the increasing reluctance of several EU governments to admit Turkey on any terms has now undermined much of the power of the stated human rights criteria for accession.

But these positive exceptions do not substitute for the lack of policy coherence that handicaps the EU's response to some of the most important human rights challenges of our time. Finding a firmer and more consistent voice on human rights is essential if the EU is to play a much-needed global leadership role.

On Human Rights at Home

Policy on human rights issues within the EU has been particularly disappointing when it comes to the treatment of migrants and asylum seekers. The EU's determination to stem the flow of migrants at all costs has led it to ignore migrants' rights and narrow their right to seek asylum in Europe from persecution in their homelands. In January 2006, the Asylum Procedures Directive entered into force with its requirement that all member-states turn back asylum seekers from an EU list of "safe countries of origin." Lack of consensus about which countries should figure on the list—many of the proposed ones offer dubious safety—has so far held up implementation, but several member-states already follow their own national lists of safe countries.

In its effort to "internationalize" migration management, the EU has allied itself with repressive regimes such as Libya, a launching pad for thousands of migrants seeking protection and work in Europe. Libya-EU cooperation on migration is one-dimensional, focusing exclusively on blocking access to Europe, with little concern for the rights or refugee claims of migrants. On the eastern border, the EU signed a readmission agreement with the Ukraine in October requiring it to readmit third-country nationals seeking protection in the EU, despite continuing concerns about Ukraine's abusive detention practices and barely functioning asylum system. The two-year "grace period" before such returns commence is hardly enough time to set the Ukraine's beleaguered system right. Spain, which in 2006 received the lion's share of arrivals by sea, is pursuing readmission agreements with countries such as Senegal and Mauritania.

Most EU governments appropriately address terrorism offenses through the normal criminal justice system, but their cutting away at procedural guarantees for terrorism suspects risks damaging the entire edifice of the rule of law. The UK passed a law that increased pre-charge detention from 14 to 28 days, and is debating whether to try again to increase it to 90 days. The Netherlands, in pending counterterrorism legislation, is poised to increase its pre-charge detention from three to 14 days. As of January 2006, terrorism suspects in France may be held up to six days in police custody with extremely limited access to counsel while police interrogators can question detainees at will.

Some EU members seek to avoid criminal prosecutions at home by deporting or extraditing terror suspects, often to places where they are at risk of torture. The UK has insisted on detaining suspects without charge and attempting to send them back to countries such as Libya and Jordan on the basis of flimsy promises of humane treatment from those governments. It justifies this breach of international law as necessary to fight terrorism, yet it has not empowered its prosecutors to introduce court-authorized wiretap evidence at trial—one of only two Western democracies (the other being Ireland) to take this extreme view. The British government has never explained why the sacrifice of fundamental rights should be considered before widely accepted law enforcement tools are even tried.

The Netherlands continues to seek to extradite certain terrorism suspects to Turkey, based on similarly unreliable promises against ill-treatment. Other governments, including Switzerland, are now poised to adopt this dubious practice. It is ironic that while the European Parliament rightly investigates European complicity in CIA renditions to countries presenting a risk of torture, some EU member-states have embraced transfers to similar countries as a counterterrorism measure at home.

Conclusion

Governments the world over will always be tempted to sidestep human rights, whether in their treatment of their own people or their relations with other governments. If their own values and institutions do not restrain them, external pressure is needed. Those who indulge this temptation must be made to pay a price until human rights are respected at home and find their proper place in the conduct of foreign policy.

But unless a new leader emerges in this time of diminished US credibility, the tyrants of the world will enjoy free rein. Both EU members and democratic governments of the developing world have found safety in numbers, the ease of hiding in the pack when the going gets rough. EU governments retreat behind consensus rules, other democratic governments behind regional networks. Neither technique for evading the burdens of leadership should be accepted, particularly at a time when China and Russia are mostly leading in the wrong direction.

It is time to transcend these excuses. New leadership on human rights could come from visionary governments of the developing world, a more nimble European Union, or if the new Congress finds its voice, a US government that recovers its ideals. One way or the other, the people of the world need meaningful leadership on human rights. The urgency of this need should not be underestimated—if the great treaty commitments of the twentieth century are not to give way to hypocrisy and empty promises in the twenty-first.

This Report

This report is Human Rights Watch's 17th annual review of human rights practices around the globe. It summarizes key human rights issues in more than 70 countries worldwide, drawing on events through mid-November 2006.

Each country entry identifies significant human rights issues, examines the freedom of local human rights defenders to conduct their work, and surveys the response of key international actors, such as the United Nations, European Union, Japan, the United States, and various regional and international organizations and institutions.

This report reflects extensive investigative work undertaken in 2006 by the Human Rights Watch research staff, usually in close partnership with human rights activists in the country in question. It also reflects the work of our advocacy team, which monitors policy developments and strives to persuade governments and international institutions to curb abuses and promote human rights. Human Rights Watch publications, issued throughout the year, contain more detailed accounts of many of the issues addressed in the brief summaries collected in this volume. They can be found on the Human Rights Watch website, www.hrw.org.

As in past years, this report does not include a chapter on every country where Human Rights Watch works, nor does it discuss every issue of importance. The failure to include a particular country or issue often reflects no more than staffing limitations and should not be taken as commentary on the significance of the problem. There are many serious human rights violations that Human Rights Watch simply lacks the capacity to address.

The factors we considered in determining the focus of our work in 2006 (and hence the content of this volume) include the number of people affected and the severity of abuse, access to the country and the availability of information about it, the susceptibility of abusive forces to influence, and the importance of addressing certain thematic concerns and of reinforcing the work of local rights organizations.

The World Report does not have separate chapters addressing our thematic work but instead incorporates such material directly into the country entries. Please consult the Human Rights Watch website for more detailed treatment of our work on children's rights, women's rights, arms and military issues, business and human rights, HIV/AIDS and human rights, international justice, terrorism and counterterrorism, refugees and displaced people, and lesbian, gay, bisexual, and transgender people's rights, and for information about our international film festivals.

Kenneth Roth is executive director of Human Rights Watch.

Principled Leadership: A Human Rights Agenda for UN Secretary-General Ban Ki-moon

By Peggy Hicks

The post of United Nations (UN) secretary-general has been called "the most impossible job on earth" by both the first secretary-general, Trygve Lie, and the most recent, Kofi Annan. During his tenure, Annan made the position even more arduous than it had been before by treating human rights as an integral part of his job. There is no turning back: there is an urgent need today for the new Secretary-General Ban Ki-moon to speak out forcefully in defense of human rights and give substance to the United Nations' now extensive human rights commitments.

Ban comes to the job with a stated predisposition to support human rights, but a limited track record that can be used to assess the strength of that commitment. As South Korea's foreign minister, he was willing to subordinate human rights concerns to other objectives in his country's dialogue with North Korea. In his new position, he will need to take on those who want to overlook human rights for the sake of political expediency and confront those responsible for human rights abuses.

The UN secretary-general's role is barely defined by the United Nations Charter, the scope of potential work is vast, and his or her power is ambiguous. The secretary-general is the world's chief diplomat, manager of some 30,000 staff, and public face of the United Nations. As an international civil servant, the UN leader is responsible to the 192 members of the United Nations collectively and must count on members' support individually to implement his or her agenda. While diplomatic skills are a must, successful officeholders also are remembered for their vision and leadership.

Annan's most important contribution as secretary-general was the recognition that human rights must be respected as the "third pillar" of the UN's work alongside development, and peace and security, and that the UN's efforts in these areas will not be successful so long as human rights are neglected and marginalized. Within the UN system, the reality remains far removed from Annan's vision.

As the scope of human rights protections has grown, so has the gap between the UN's human rights aspirations and its ability to act on them.

Ban's success as secretary-general will depend in part on his ability to address that void. Doing so successfully will take vision, drive, and a clear agenda for strengthening the UN's human rights performance. His agenda should include the following:

- Exercising leadership for human rights protection;
- Strengthening UN institutions and integrating human rights;
- Building a "new UN for women"; and
- Addressing the human rights aspects of peace and security.

While putting an ambitious agenda in place will not be easy, Ban should keep in mind the perils of putting human rights on the back burner. As Annan emphasized in his 2005 report "In Larger Freedom: Towards Development, Security and Human Rights for All" (General Assembly document A/59/2005), "we will not enjoy development without security, we will not enjoy security without development, and we will not enjoy either without respect for human rights. Unless all these causes are advanced, none will succeed." But the risks of ignoring human rights are even greater than that, as Annan's own record demonstrates. Ban, like his predecessor, will be judged at least in part by the UN's response to the most horrendous crimes it faces during his tenure. Annan has been haunted by the UN's failures in Rwanda, and has played a vocal—but as yet unsuccessful—role in trying to see that they were not repeated in Darfur. Ban will need to do better.

Annan's Legacy

Annan's human rights legacy provides both a solid foundation and an enormous challenge for the new secretary-general. The most significant achievements under Annan's leadership include:

Acting as a moral voice: Annan's willingness to speak out on human rights issues and to be the conscience of the world has been critical and has given greater courage to human rights defenders worldwide. His advocacy on Darfur since 2004 has been crucial to the limited successes the United Nations has achieved in that crisis to date.

Strengthening the Office of the High Commissioner for Human Rights (OHCHR): Annan successfully pushed for expansion both of the high commissioner's staff and of her influence within the UN system with important results. The OHCHR's monitoring mission in Nepal is a telling example of what timely human rights work can achieve.

Human security: During Annan's tenure, the Security Council has made real if inconsistent progress in integrating the impact of conflict on civilians in its work, including through adoption of resolutions on protection of civilians, women and armed conflict, and children and armed conflict.

Responsibility to Protect: Annan put response to grave human rights violations at the center of his agenda. His work culminated in the recognition by leaders at the 2005 World Summit and later the General Assembly and the Security Council of a "responsibility to protect" populations from mass atrocities.

Human Rights Council: Annan initiated the idea of replacing the Commission on Human Rights with the Human Rights Council, a permanent, standing body that would raise the profile of inter-governmental human rights activity. Although the Human Rights Council is off to a rocky start, the resolution establishing the council provides the foundation for the stronger, more effective institution that Annan envisioned.

Mainstreaming: From the outset of his first term, Annan emphasized that human rights was a cross-cutting issue that is the "common thread" running through all the UN's other activities. He worked to make that understanding operational through the "mainstreaming" of human rights, incorporating a rights-based approach within all aspects of the UN's work.

Engaging with civil society: Recognizing that expanded civil society involvement would both strengthen the UN's work and enhance its credibility, Annan opened up new opportunities for civil society organizations to contribute to the UN's work.

Key Human Rights Challenges

Ban assumes the post of secretary-general at a pivotal moment for human rights within the UN system. The key pieces of Annan's human rights legacy—the Human Rights Council and the "responsibility to protect" doctrine—are not just incomplete, but endangered. The Human Rights Council has failed to take action to address the world's human rights crises, and has adopted a one-sided approach to abuses in Israel and Lebanon. States with poor human rights records have dominated the council's deliberations, and supporters of human rights have failed to exercise leadership to put this new body on course. The situation in Darfur is deteriorating, exposing the absence of a mechanism to put the principle of responsibility to protect into practice. Annan's efforts to mainstream human rights are also incomplete: human rights frequently remain a secondary—and often unwelcome—consideration in the UN's work.

At the same time, given the failure of governmental leadership detailed in the Introduction to this volume, the UN's role in human rights protection has never been more important. Of course, there is reason to question whether the United Nations—which is composed of those same governments—will be willing to do more than its members individually. While these constraints should temper expectations, the United Nations has shown the ability to do more for human rights than the sum of its parts, particularly when it has had a committed secretary-general at the helm. For example, the Security Council was able to refer the situation in Darfur to the International Criminal Court, although the United States (US), Russia, and China were all potentially opposed to that action.

The period since the adoption of the Universal Declaration of Human Rights has witnessed an impressive growth in human rights standards. The development of norms, however, has not been matched by effective means for their implementation. Today, the accumulated body of human rights law faces another great challenge—adapting and responding to the dual threats of terrorism and the abuse of human rights in counterterrorism efforts.

Addressing terrorism as a human rights abuse is at once both simple and inordinately complex. Simple, as terrorist attacks breach the most basic human rights—the rights to life and security of the person. Complex, as the organizations responsible for human rights violations are not states or traditional "non-state actors" like rebel groups, and treating their actions as human rights abuses raises important questions concerning the nature of these groups and our response to them. The erosion of human rights in the "war on terror" is the flip side of this coin. In the post-September 11 world, some of those threatened by terrorism have suggested that human rights are neither universal nor absolute, and that the rights of some can somehow be effectively traded for more security for all. The suggestion that terrorism creates a perpetual state of emergency in which derogation from basic rights is permitted has already undermined human rights protection worldwide, and the threat to human rights continues to grow. While Ban's primary challenge will be implementing norms already developed, this new context requires continuing diligence to defend fundamental human rights standards.

Leadership

Faced with these challenges, the most important single element in Secretary-General Ban's human rights agenda should be public advocacy for human rights. While some of the secretary-general's work will involve private diplomacy, he must also be the United Nations' most prominent human rights defender. Ban should follow Annan's example in using the "bully pulpit" of the secretary-general's office to take on those responsible for human rights abuses and to push the UN system to be stronger in the defense of human rights. To demonstrate the universal basis of human rights, he should be willing to speak out even when the offender is a powerful government.

Ban should move quickly upon assuming his office to make public statements on human rights issues. Ban's early attention to human rights is essential to send a signal to abusive governments that the UN secretary-general will continue to be a vocal advocate for victims of human rights violations worldwide. Such statements would also make clear to those resisting change within the United Nations that human rights mainstreaming will accelerate. He should also recognize the critical role of civil society in the UN's work, and step in as needed to protect human rights defenders. Ban should pay careful attention as well to selecting senior staff who are seriously committed to human rights, particularly in key Secretariat posts such as the under-secretary-general for political affairs and in peacekeeping missions.

Further, the secretary-general must be a forceful advocate for the importance of human rights in the achievement of the Millennium Development Goals. In particular, Ban should emphasize that failures to respect freedom of speech and association undermine the participation and accountability essential to drive development processes and attack corruption.

Like his predecessor, Ban should also speak out on the importance of justice and accountability in the protection of human rights. In addition, the new secretary-general should address head on other challenges to the universality of human rights, including claims that human rights standards are imposed values from developed, Western states. In particular, Ban should engage in ongoing discussions about religion and human rights in ways that reinforce fundamental human rights principles.

Strengthening UN Institutions and Integrating Human Rights

The Human Rights Council

Annan's effort to replace the UN Commission on Human Rights with a stronger and more credible body—the Human Rights Council—is off to a rocky start. The council, which began work in June 2006, has quickly fallen prey to some of the same problems that doomed its predecessor. It has failed to take concrete action regarding human rights abuses in places like Darfur, Burma, Uzbekistan, and Colombia. During the same period, the council has adopted three resolutions condemning Israeli human rights violations, none of which even mentions abuses by Palestinian armed groups or Hezbollah.

States with poor human rights records are working to render the new institution impotent, including through seeking to do away with its ability to criticize governments for their human rights abuses. States ordinarily supportive of human rights have been ineffective in responding, and have displayed a conspicuous lack of leadership.

This reform cannot be allowed to fail. Despite its shortcomings, the Commission on Human Rights, particularly its system of independent experts, played an important role in spotlighting abuses and pushing governments to address human rights violations. The Human Rights Council must build on the commission's successes, not repeat its mistakes. The UN needs a strong, effective intergovernmental body to carry forward its human rights agenda. The council's work is also seen as an indicator of the seriousness of UN reform more generally. The council's missteps have given succor to UN detractors, and the credibility of the UN as a whole has been damaged. Ban will need to make getting this fledgling institution on track a priority, both for its own sake and for the sake of the UN as a whole.

While the majority of the action on the Human Rights Council will take place in Geneva, the council also needs strong support from the United Nations in New York and from foreign ministries in capitals. Ban should exert his leadership to rally support for a broad cross-regional coalition of "friends of human rights" within the council that would take action on pressing issues and act as a counterweight to those states that are seeking to weaken the new body. He should plan on attending the March 2007 session of the Human Rights Council, and should engage actively with council members and other interested governments to strengthen this fledgling institution.

The UN High Commissioner for Human Rights

The United Nations' ability to move from rhetorical support for human rights to real strengthening of human rights protection on the ground is dependent upon the Office of the UN High Commissioner for Human Rights. Under General Assembly resolution 48/141, OHCHR has "principal responsibility" for the UN's human rights activities, yet OHCHR received only 1.8 percent of the UN budget in 2005, and lacks operational capacity, particularly in the field. The World Summit recognized this gap, and called for doubling OHCHR's budget in five years. The high commissioner is now implementing a plan to strengthen her office. Ban should make full implementation of this plan a priority.

Two crucial elements of the OHCHR plan are a substantial strengthening of its field presence and an expansion of its New York office. Both will be critical to the

UN's ability to meet the challenges it faces in the coming decade. A broader field presence will allow OHCHR to serve the United Nations and its members more effectively in many ways through more effective mainstreaming, improved monitoring of abuses, and strengthened technical assistance and capacity building. For example, by more closely monitoring human rights situations, field-based staff are more likely to be able to identify impending political and security crises. Monitoring missions are also a proven means of improving human rights protection, as OHCHR's recent deployment in Nepal has again shown. An enhanced field presence will also enable OHCHR to play a stronger role within UN country teams.

In addition, the role of the high commissioner's office in New York must be enhanced. Given the interdependent relationship between peace and security, development, and human rights, OHCHR must be able to engage frequently and at the right level with the UN's institutions and agencies that are based in New York. This requires not only a much larger office, but also a more powerful one. The office should be headed by an assistant secretary-general, and the head of office should be able to represent the high commissioner in meetings of the new secretary-general's cabinet (the UN's Senior Management Group).

Secretary-General Ban should also make clear that he will stand behind the high commissioner and defend the independence of her office at all costs. The high commissioner must be able to speak frankly about any government, even the most powerful, without repercussions. An important case study for Ban can be found in Annan's response to a broadside launched by US Ambassador John Bolton against the high commissioner in 2005. Bolton called High Commissioner Louise Arbour's comments on secret detention and rendition of suspects to governments that routinely practice torture "inappropriate and illegitimate for an international civil servant." Annan quickly responded by publicly reaffirming his "absolute full confidence" in Arbour and noting that he intended to take up the issue with Bolton "at an early date." Ban should similarly be vigilant in his defense of the independent operations of OHCHR, and of the high commissioner's ability to speak freely about human rights abuses wherever and whenever they occur.

Mainstreaming Human Rights

As secretary-general, Kofi Annan emphasized mainstreaming of human rights as a centerpiece of his UN reform agenda. While some progress has been made, the high commissioner for human rights recently noted that conceptual and methodological advances in mainstreaming are "well ahead of actual results on the ground." Human rights may be at the table, but it does not yet have an equal voice in the discussion. In many circumstances, human rights protection is an afterthought or, worse, is seen as an unnecessary obstacle in the path of other objectives such as stability or reconciliation. For example, when the United Nations engaged in Afghanistan, those who expressed concern for human rights and cautioned against relying on warlords were overruled for the sake of political expediency. Sidelining human rights was justified as the pragmatic view, but Afghanistan is paying the price today. As is often the case, what its practitioners describe as "pragmatism" proved to be shortsightedness.

More effective integration of human rights at an operational level in UN country work is the chief outstanding element of the mainstreaming effort. This will require a much greater role for OHCHR in the selection, support, and evaluation of the heads of UN country teams, including the addition of dedicated capacity on human rights. It also means that senior UN officials, including heads of country teams, must be held accountable for their performance on human rights.

Effective mainstreaming of human rights also requires leadership, not just from the secretary-general himself, but from other senior UN staff. As noted, Ban's senior staff should be truly committed to human rights, and they should be held accountable when they fail to uphold the human rights standards of the United Nations in their interactions with national actors.

Building a "New UN for Women"

In no area has the UN's promise on human rights fallen as far short as it has on women's rights. The first target within the Millennium Development Goals to go unmet was the objective of eliminating gender disparity in primary and secondary education by 2005. As Stephen Lewis, the UN special envoy for HIV/AIDS in Africa, recently noted, "A destructive pattern has taken hold of landmark agreements on women's rights: gender equality advocates work tirelessly to gain international consensus, only to see their hard-won declarations and resolutions reach dead ends for lack of expertise and operational capacity at the country level."

The limitations of gender mainstreaming efforts have been widely recognized. In its November 2006 report, the secretary-general's High-Level Panel on UN System-Wide Coherence in the Areas of Development, Humanitarian Assistance and the Environment acknowledged "a strong sense" that the UN's contribution to achieving gender equality "has been incoherent, under-resourced and fragmented." The panel concluded that the United Nations needs to pursue gender equality "far more vigorously" and that it requires "a much stronger voice on women's issues to ensure that gender equality and women's empowerment are taken seriously throughout the UN system and to ensure that the UN works more effectively with governments and civil society in this mission."

To address these needs, the panel recommended the creation of "a dynamic gender entity responsible for gender equality and women's empowerment." The new entity would consolidate the Office of the Special Advisor on Gender Issues, the Division for the Advancement of Women, and the Development Fund for Women, and would have policy, advocacy, and operational functions. The panel also found that the new entity should be headed by an under-secretary-general and have stable funding that is substantially greater than that accorded to its three constituent components.

While there may be debate about the details of this prescription, the panel's diagnosis is widely accepted: the United Nations is substantially underperforming on women's human rights, and tinkering with current approaches will not remedy the problem. As with human rights generally, the major challenge faced today in women's human rights is not in standard-setting but rather, implementation. The United Nations is ill-equipped to meet that challenge, as the coherence panel concluded. Despite Annan's strong commitment to women's human rights, the panel's report has laid bare the deficiencies of the existing system and placed this issue squarely on the new secretary-general's plate. Creating an improved framework for the UN's women's human rights work—a "new UN for women"— should be a signature effort for Ban.

Human Rights and Peace and Security

Secretary-General Annan made a compelling case for the interrelationship of human rights and the UN's work on peace and security. In his "In Larger Freedom" report (2005), Annan stated:

> It would be a mistake to treat human rights as though there were a trade-off to be made between human rights and such goals as security or development. We only weaken our hand in fighting the horrors of extreme poverty or terrorism if, in our efforts to do so, we deny the very human rights that these scourges take away from citizens. Strategies based on the protection of human rights are vital for both our moral standing and the practical effectiveness of our actions.

The Responsibility to Protect

One of the UN's greatest challenges and its best known failures involve its response to mass atrocities. Annan's legacy here is substantial. Growing out of his own experiences as head of the Department of Peacekeeping Operations during the Rwandan genocide, Annan made a priority of improving the UN's response to future genocides. In a 1999 speech to the UN General Assembly, Annan argued that "the core challenge to the Security Council and to the United Nations as a whole in the next century" would be "to forge unity behind the principle that massive and systematic violations of human rights—wherever they may take place—should not be allowed to stand."

Six years later at the 2005 World Summit, leaders from some 150 nations agreed to recognize a "responsibility to protect populations from genocide, war crimes, ethnic cleansing, and crimes against humanity." The primary burden to protect falls upon individual states, which must prevent such crimes "through appropriate and necessary means." When states are unable or unwilling to protect their population, however, the responsibility to protect holds that other states, through the United Nations, should use "appropriate diplomatic, humanitarian, and other peaceful means" to help protect those in danger and should take collective action, including the use of force, "should peaceful means be inadequate and national authorities manifestly fail to protect their populations from genocide, war crimes, ethnic cleansing and crimes against humanity."

Recognition of this multifacted Responsibility to Protect (or "R2P" as it has come to be known in UN circles) was in some sense the culmination of Annan's tenure as secretary-general. He has left the new secretary-general, however, the thorny task of making the agreed principle a reality. Ban must pick up this gauntlet, and work within the UN system to create a framework for implementation of R2P. Of course, it will be up to states themselves whether they act in the face of mass atrocities. But the secretary-general can play a crucial role as an educator, organizer, and catalyst.

As an educator, Ban should work to build understanding of R2P among member states. While R2P is mistakenly often seen as synonymous only with intervention by force, in fact R2P encompasses a continuum of actions where forcible intervention is at one end of the spectrum. Short of such intervention, R2P requires that states take other measures such as technical assistance, diplomatic initiatives and sanctions to protect endangered populations. The new secretary-general and his staff should work with member states to explain this continuum, and to identify opportunities where strategies short of military intervention are required because of the responsibility to protect.

Secretary-General Ban should also work to put in place a framework to make the concept of R2P operate in practice. This effort will have many parts, some of which are still to be agreed. At a minimum though, the secretary-general should be the focal point for efforts to see that the UN's institutions bring R2P into their work systematically and with effect. He should also make recommendations as to the role of other UN actors regarding implementation of R2P. In particular, the Security Council, the Peacebuilding Commission, and the Human Rights Council must all play a part in implementing R2P, and Ban should work with those institutions to build a consistent approach to addressing R2P within the United Nations.

One part of that effort should be the development of guidelines for when situations rise to the level demanding Security Council attention and, in particular, for when intervention by force is required. In addition, Ban should work with his special advisor for the prevention of genocide to prepare indicators that can be monitored to give early warning in situations where the responsibility to protect is implicated. Further, the new secretary-general should actively support Annan's request to create a permanent core of UN staff who would be available for deployment on urgent peacekeeping or special political missions. Ban should also push for serious dialogue concerning broader proposals to create a standing emergency peace service within the United Nations that could include a military component able to respond quickly when mass atrocities are threatening.

Finally, Secretary-General Ban needs to be willing to push both UN institutions and member states to live up to their commitments regarding the responsibility to protect. His office and the special advisor should act as watchdogs for situations in which R2P is implicated, and they should be willing to speak loudly and often when the responsibility to protect is not being met.

Darfur

The credibility both of the responsibility to protect doctrine and of Ban's leadership will depend at least in part upon how the United Nations responds to the Darfur crisis in which the Sudanese government and allied militias have forcibly displaced over two million people; over 200,000 have been killed and tens of thousands of women have been subject to sexual violence. The UN's apparent impotence in the face of the government of Sudan's barbarity and stubborn refusal to allow a UN peacekeeping force in Darfur raises justified concerns that the R2P is merely rhetoric.

In such a situation, the secretary-general must act as the conscience of the United Nations and its members. Ban should use the platform provided by his office to shine a sustained spotlight on the plight of the people of Darfur. He should also use his diplomatic role to conduct a persistent dialogue with UN member states that have shown a willingness to sacrifice the R2P for their own economic or energy interests, such as China. Ban also needs to encourage African and Arab states to set aside concerns of regional solidarity and put the principle of R2P into practice by being willing to condemn the Sudanese government, and call for stronger sanctions to stop its murderous policies.

The Security Council

Significant headway on human rights has been made in recent years within the UN Security Council, which has now taken up human rights matters in a range of guises (e.g.: the protection of civilians; women and peace and security; children and armed conflict; as well as country-specific discussions on places such as Darfur). The high commissioner for human rights has been invited to brief the Security Council, reflecting recognition of the interrelationship between human rights and peace and security, but this is still a rare occurrence. In his "In Larger Freedom" report, Annan called for this trend to be intensified, arguing that the high commissioner should play a more active role in the deliberations of the Security Council and of the Peacebuilding Commission.

Despite this progress, the Security Council's practices relating to human rights are still sporadic and inconsistent. Its ability to address human rights violations relates not as much to the level of abuses or their relationship to security, but rather to the weight and persistence of those countries who seek to place (or block) issues on the Security Council's agenda. The United Kingdom succeeded in 2005 in holding a private meeting of the Security Council for a briefing concerning housing evictions in Zimbabwe. During the same period, however, Russia was able to block the high commissioner from briefing the Security Council on the situation in Uzbekistan in the wake of the massacre of hundreds of civilians in Andijan.

Ban should push for integration of human rights in the Security Council's work in a more systematic manner, and should take up Annan's call for a greater role for the high commissioner in Security Council discussions. At the same time, the secretary-general should practice what he preaches by ensuring that a human rights analysis is an integral part of the reports that he presents to the Security Council.

The responsibility to protect also has a direct bearing on the Security Council's work, and on its consideration of human rights crises. As the 2005 World Summit outcome document makes clear, collective action should be taken through the Security Council when peaceful means have proven inadequate and national authorities are manifestly failing to protect their populations. To be able to exercise that power appropriately, the Security Council should be prepared to discuss situations implicating the responsibility to protect, regardless of where they fall on the R2P continuum discussed above. As part of his efforts to make R2P operational, Ban should encourage integration of R2P issues into the Security Council's agenda in a consistent and timely manner.

Annan's High-Level Panel on Threats, Challenges, and Change also called on the permanent members of the Security Council to "refrain from the use of the veto in cases of genocide and large scale human rights abuses." Ban should encourage Security Council members to commit themselves to that practice, as it is essential if the council is to live up to its commitment to the responsibility to protect.

Conclusion

Secretary-General Ban Ki-moon, like his predecessor, will have his hands full with UN reform and managing a large and complex organization. And human rights can be a messy business—placing the secretary-general into conflict with UN member states to whom he reports. But, despite the difficulties he may face in doing so, Ban needs to put human rights at the center of his agenda.

Progress on human rights is inextricably linked to the other core functions of the United Nations: development, and peace and security. By focusing needed attention on human rights, Ban will reap dividends in those areas as well. Ensuring that UN human rights institutions function effectively, and strengthening the work of the United Nations on women's rights, will significantly aid the UN's development efforts. Keeping a close eye on global human rights crises will aid the UN's peace and security efforts.

The reverse is also true: Ban should be very aware that failure to address human rights issues could place the rest of his agenda at risk. The legacy of Rwanda should not only haunt Annan, but his successor. Despite the limitations on any secretary-general's ability to take on a crisis like Darfur single-handedly, Ban's leadership and vision in responding to the most dire human rights situations will be critical to how his tenure as secretary-general is remembered.

Peggy Hicks is global advocacy director at Human Rights Watch

GLOBALIZATION COMES HOME:
PROTECTING MIGRANT DOMESTIC WORKERS' RIGHTS

By Nisha Varia

I decided to migrate for work because my parents do not have a home, we do not have any land of our own.... I just really want to build a house like my friend and give happiness to my family.

—Sumiyatun, a 24-year-old woman waiting to board a ferry to Singapore, where she had secured a job as a domestic worker, Batam, Indonesia, May 23, 2006

Introduction

Imagine working sixteen hours a day, every single day, for years, or perhaps getting one day off per month. Then, imagine being rarely allowed to leave your workplace, where you also sleep.

Suppose that to get this job, you will forgo seeing your family for months or years at a time. Furthermore, that you are forced to turn over the first ten months of your salary to pay off the expenses your employer incurred in recruiting you, or else spend years paying off loans with interest rates as high as 100 percent.

Welcome to life as a migrant domestic worker. In the hopes of earning money for a better life, and with few other alternatives, millions migrate to big cities or across borders to work as live-in nannies, caretakers for the elderly, and house-cleaners. Domestic workers around the world, predominantly women and girls, lack basic labor protections that most governments guarantee for other workers. Domestic workers are typically excluded from standard labor protections such as a minimum wage, regular payment of wages, a weekly day off, and paid leave.

The movement of people across borders promises new opportunities and has become extremely lucrative: the US$167 billion that migrant workers from developing nations sent home in 2005 exceeded foreign aid in many countries—and much of this money directly reaches poor households. Yet this money has often come at a profound human cost. Governments and employers interested in "flexible" labor have been quick to take advantage of a transnational workforce. But they often have turned their backs on labor and immigration protections for migrants and done little to establish a safety-net to address widespread abuses. The situation of migrant domestic workers is a particularly stark illustration of the need for transnational governance in an era of globalization.

In 2006, Hawazi Daipi, Singapore's Senior Parliamentary Secretary for Manpower, chose to celebrate International Women's Day by reiterating in Parliament his rejection of decent minimum employment terms for foreign domestic workers. Such labor protections would lead to "inconvenience for many households," he claimed.

Many employers treat their domestic workers well. But as Human Rights Watch investigations in countries as diverse as the United States, El Salvador, Guatemala, Saudi Arabia, Morocco, Indonesia, and Malaysia demonstrate, far too many others take advantage of inadequate labor protections to exploit domestic workers isolated behind the walls of private homes. Despite regional variations in domestic work, migration patterns, and recruitment systems, striking similarities exist among the abuses confronted by domestic workers around the world. The examples in this essay draw primarily on Asia and the Middle East.

Criminal abuses such as physical and sexual violence, food deprivation, and trafficking into forced labor take place with disturbing frequency. Moreover, labor recruitment systems and punitive immigration laws leave many workers highly indebted, out of legal status, and afraid to report abuse. These problems are made more difficult to address in the case of domestic workers by deep-seated, discriminatory norms about gender roles and the value of tasks considered to be women's work.

Despite this long catalog of abuses, however, concrete and feasible measures exist that could dramatically improve the working conditions of most migrant domestic workers. Many governments have argued that it is impossible to treat private homes like a workplace. Yet labor legislation in Hong Kong and South Africa has set positive examples: domestic workers have the right to a minimum wage, overtime pay, a weekly day of rest, maternity leave, and paid annual leave. While the domestic workers in these countries are not immune from abuse, they have legal remedies available, unlike their counterparts elsewhere. Combined with the freedom to form associations and trade unions, many of these domestic workers have greater awareness of their rights, an ability to negotiate better working conditions, and avenues for reporting labor exploitation.

Other important reforms include enhancing local economic and educational opportunities so that domestic workers can migrate based on informed choice; setting standards for and monitoring transnational labor recruitment systems, which are often a determining factor in how such migrants fare; amending restrictive immigration policies that leave such workers particularly at risk of exploitation; and promoting international cooperation between sending and receiving states to prevent and respond to abuse.

While some governments have already started making meaningful reforms to help domestic workers work in greater safety and dignity, others are pursuing superficial changes that fail to address the root causes of exploitation and abuse. Governments around the world have choices to make about the route they will take; this essay identifies some of the positive options available.

Migration Based on Informed Choice

I'm crying inside my heart.... If I can solve my financial problems this time, I will never migrate again.... If we have no money, we have no other choice but to go abroad. We have to get rid of this poverty.
—Chandrika Malkanthi, a 45-year-old woman preparing to migrate to the Middle East as a domestic worker for the ninth time, Kurunegala, Sri Lanka, November 4, 2006

One of the most overlooked and critically important responses to promoting safe migration is offering the choice of not migrating at all. While it is equally important that discriminatory restrictions not be placed on women's mobility, more can be done in countries of origin to provide migrants with alternatives to leaving their families behind and embarking on journeys that often involve a considerable gamble in terms of safety and success. Such a response includes creating viable local employment opportunities and providing children with accessible, quality education.

The numbers are astounding—and growing. Fifty to seventy-five percent of the legal migrants leaving Indonesia, the Philippines, and Sri Lanka are women, most of them hoping to earn money as domestic workers in the Middle East and other parts of Asia. The International Labor Organization (ILO) estimates there are more girls under age sixteen employed in domestic service than in any other form of child labor. Some of these children start working as domestics at the age of six or seven. In Indonesia alone, there are approximately 700,000 child domestic workers.

Access to education carries many important consequences for internal and international migration into domestic work. Prohibitive schooling costs and the need to supplement their families' incomes are key reasons for girls entering domestic work. Many international migrant domestic workers cite earning enough to provide their children or siblings with a decent education as one of the top reasons they chose to work abroad—an emotional sacrifice, since to do so, they must live apart from these family members for years. More could also be done to improve women's and girls' entrance into higher education and vocational training programs that would improve their skill sets and qualify them for better-paying jobs.

Current government policies often actively promote urban and international migration in order to relieve rural unemployment and generate income from remittances. For example, Indonesia sets targets of the numbers of migrant workers it hopes to send abroad in its five-year national economic development plans. Its target rose from 100,000 in 1979–84 to 2.8 million in 1999–2003.[1] Similarly, many other countries have started setting a target for the numbers of workers they hope to "export," arguably without a similar emphasis on how to create livelihoods at home.

The responsibility does not lie only with countries of origin. Foreign investment from wealthy countries has often focused on the exploitation of natural resources and labor without building local capacity or links to other domestic industries. International trade agreements have often failed to include adequate protections for workers' rights; for example, freedom from workplace discrimination. Such policies may particularly affect women's local employment opportunities and their pay. Destination countries often rely heavily on migrant labor without doing their part to ensure transparent and fair recruitment practices, or equal access to the law once migrants begin working.

Labor-sending governments, enamored with the promises of migration, must remember that it may involve profound social costs and that poorly-regulated sectors such as domestic work pose a wide range of risks. Governments should do more to ensure that migration occurs not out of desperation, but out of choice, in safety, and with full information and informed consent. Governments and international institutions have a responsibility to promote fair trade regimes, invest in education, and foster local employment opportunities so that potential migrants have real alternatives.

Good Business: Monitoring Labor Recruitment Systems

> *The broker brought me to the training center in Tanjung Pinang by ship…. I only paid 100,000 rupiah [US$12] to the broker but afterwards they deducted my full wages for four-and-a-half months [to repay what they said were up-front costs]…. I had to spend two months at the training center though I had expected to wait only a few days…. We were never allowed outside, there was a very high gate and it was always locked. They treated us poorly, always calling us names like "dog."*
>
> —Widyaningsih, a 35-year-old woman recently returned from Malaysia describing conditions she had faced while being recruited in Indonesia, East Java, Indonesia, May 21, 2006

Recruiting migrant domestic workers has become a profitable industry, with hundreds and sometimes thousands of licensed and unlicensed labor agencies and brokers in many countries. Local recruiters trawl through villages, painting rosy pictures of success in urban centers or rich countries abroad. They may promise women the income to help them build new homes for their families or girls the opportunity to continue their education. Labor recruiters and agencies undergo scant monitoring, and in most countries, few regulations exist to contain the recruitment fees charged to workers.

What happens during recruitment can influence a worker's fate heavily. If she is lucky, she will know how to discern a licensed agent from an unlicensed one,

55

obtain a copy of her employment contract, and learn about her rights before she leaves home. More likely, she will become heavily indebted due to huge recruitment fees, be promised certain working conditions but encounter something markedly different when she begins working, have her passport held by her agent, and never even see an employment contract in her own language. Deception or coercion used during the recruitment process sets workers up for abuse, and if they end up in extremely exploitative working conditions, these cases rise to the level of trafficking into forced labor.

Taking advantage of migrants' desperation to find work, agents and employers have shifted the burden of recruitment fees, including airfare, visas, and administrative fees on to the workers themselves, while employers pay nominal fees. This has led to an unreasonable debt burden on international migrant domestic workers. Many Indonesian domestic workers migrating to Persian Gulf countries take out loans from local moneylenders with interest rates as high as 100 percent to pay these fees, while those traveling to Asia typically use a "fly now, pay later" scheme. In Singapore and Hong Kong, Indonesian migrant domestic workers often spend up to 10 months out of a two-year contract without a salary since they must turn over these wages to repay their recruitment fees. The resulting financial pressure makes it difficult for workers to report abuse for fear of losing their jobs and having no way to pay off their debts.

International labor recruitment is a fast-growing industry that requires more stringent licensing requirements and more rigorous monitoring. If migrant domestic workers are to have a chance, governments need to acknowledge the unequal bargaining power between potential migrants, employers, and labor agents and shift the burden of recruitment costs back to employers. Reforming current practice means tough measures, including unannounced inspections of labor recruitment agencies and real penalties for those committing violations.

These steps have the added benefit of probably doing more to combat human trafficking than many other steps taken to date as they address the heart of what puts individuals at risk: misinformation from labor recruiters, heavy debts, passport confiscation, and improper immigration processing.

Transforming such ideals into actual practice may be simpler to implement than expected. Migrants and governments have some unlikely allies in the campaign to clean up the labor recruitment industry—labor agencies themselves. Far from being a monolithic group, they vary greatly in size, experience, and ethics. Among them are reformers operating legally and who view unlicensed, fly-by-night operations as unfair competition. Others take personal responsibility for the workers they place and become effective advocates on their behalf.

An interesting example is the Association of Employment Agencies of Singapore (AEAS) which has a mission to professionalize and raise the standards of labor agencies in Singapore. It has developed accreditation criteria that are slowly improving the accountability of labor agencies. The government supports the association's efforts by making accreditation a requirement for licensing. While it has yet to make important reforms like caps on recruitment fees, it has introduced incremental improvements and raised awareness about good practice.

Comprehensive Legal Protections and Enforcement

> *The government gets a good profit from us, they must take care of us. They must do more to protect us.*
> —Sitakumari, a 38-year-old woman who worked in Bahrain and Dubai as a domestic worker for a total of 10 years, Kurunegala district, Sri Lanka, November 6, 2006

Households turn to hiring migrant domestic workers to meet the demands of cleaning, child care, and elderly care, especially if they have little access to affordable day care or a flexible, family-friendly workplace.

For many families around the world, there is nothing more precious than their children and their homes. Yet the caretakers who clean, cook, feed, wash, and love these most valuable parts of our lives are singled out for exclusion from most countries' main labor laws. The current arrangement, leaving many domestic workers overworked and underpaid, is in the best interest of neither the worker nor the employer.

As already noted, governments in Hong Kong and South Africa are setting the standard by guaranteeing domestic workers equal protection under labor laws, providing them opportunities to form associations and trade unions and greater access to meaningful legal remedies in cases of abuse.

In the name of labor reform, many governments have begun introducing standard employment contracts for domestic workers. Although these represent a step forward by setting forth the terms of work, the elaborated conditions rarely meet the minimum standards guaranteed to other workers. These contracts also do not have the enforceability of provisions protected under labor laws.

While labor law reform can do much to address the labor exploitation confronted by migrant domestic workers, strong criminal laws and law enforcement are also essential to combat physical, psychological, and sexual abuse, forced labor, and forced confinement. In increasing the criminal penalties for certain abuses against migrant domestic workers by a factor of 1.5, Singapore has rightly acknowledged the particular risks faced by these workers. Good laws become meaningful when accompanied by public awareness campaigns and training of law enforcement, labor, and immigration officials. Laws that could be used to protect child domestic workers, such as Indonesia's Child Protection Act as well as minimum age for employment laws in most countries, are rarely invoked.

The domestic violence movement illustrates an important lesson learned: governments have an obligation to prevent and respond to abuses taking place in the private sphere. Currently, monitoring of workplace conditions—a critical element in enforcing domestic workers' rights—remains weak to non-existent in most countries, in part due to restrictions on the ability of labor inspectors to enter private households. Lawmakers should reform such policies and ensure that accessible complaint mechanisms and support services such as health care, shelter, and legal aid are available to survivors of abuse. These mechanisms and services should be especially sensitive to the needs of child domestics, whose age and curtailed education often make it even harder for them to escape abusive employers and gain access to the assistance they need.

Why Fair Immigration Policies Matter

Countries with a highly-educated, highly-skilled workforce often have difficulty finding local workers for low-paying jobs and have created special immigration schemes for domestic workers.

Despite the contributions these workers are making to destination countries, immigration policies may exacerbate conditions that put migrants at risk of abuse. For example, several countries impose "security bonds" on employers, penalizing them if their migrant domestic worker runs away. Such bonds appear to have little impact on the stated policy goal of staunching undocumented migration, whereas employers use the bonds as justifications for confining domestic workers to the workplace, holding their passports, and withholding their wages—conditions that are abusive and may rise to the level of forced labor.

In several countries, migrant domestic workers lose their legal status once they leave their employers, since their visas are tied to their employer. This makes it difficult for them to run away from abusive situations, change employers, or to negotiate their conditions of employment. The consequences may be dire: in Malaysia, punitive immigration laws mean that migrants can face up to five years' imprisonment, heavy fines, caning, and indefinite detention for an immigration offense.

Immigration policies often strip migrants of some of their fundamental civil and political rights—including the right to marry and the right to form associations. Inadequate government intervention with respect to labor rights pair with overly intrusive policies on other rights. The Singaporean government imposes a lifetime ban on foreign domestic workers marrying Singaporean citizens, even after they have finished their employment. Although exceptions to this policy can be made on application, the government treats these requests like job interviews. Those with less marketable skills and education may be rejected. As Mr. Hawazi Daipi explained, "Those who are financially self-reliant or who are better qualified should have no problem in securing permission to get married."

For those migrant domestic workers who enter the country as undocumented workers, or who lose their legal status while abroad, access to redress may become unattainable. Governments should promote immigration rules that permit migrants to report abuse without fear of imprisonment or criminal penalties. Coordination between labor and immigration ministries is essential.

Governments should tackle the links between poverty, unsafe migration, and inadequate labor standards by reforming immigration policies that drive migrants underground to unlicensed recruiters and smugglers. Anti-trafficking programs monitoring borders and women's mobility also threaten to compound the problem. Rather than restricting women's and girls' right to migrate and seek work, the real challenge lies in creating the guarantees for them to do so safely and with dignity.

Rights-Based International Cooperation

An increasingly mobile labor force is an ineluctable consequence of globalization. Humane treatment of such workers, however, requires that governments agree on ground rules and work together to enforce them. International treaties, like the Convention to Protect the Rights of Migrant Workers and Their Families and several ILO conventions, already embody the outlines of an international regulatory framework. But these instruments will only become more effective with widespread ratification and enforcement. Countries that host migrant workers have been particularly slow to ratify these conventions and have often used their positions of greater bargaining power to negotiate bilateral labor agreements that have largely avoided human rights protections.

More could be done for migrant domestic workers, for instance, multilateral agreements that establish minimum standards for recruitment and working conditions. Such agreements are needed to avoid a "race to the bottom," in which labor-sending countries compete for jobs by lowering their protections for their workers. The United Nations can support such efforts. To do so, it must expand from the politically cautious focus on the money migrants bring to economic development through their remittances, highlighted in the September 2006 UN High-Level Dialogue on Migration and Development. Instead it should centralize a rights-based approach to migration that seeks to end the abuses migrants confront and incorporates the kinds of ideas sketched here. A good time to start would be the next global meeting of governments on migration due to take place in Belgium in March 2007.

Conclusion

Millions of migrants labor as domestic workers—most of them women and girls. Rather than receiving the respect due them and a proper recognition of the critical role they play in supporting families and providing care for the young and elderly, such workers are met with disregard and, too often, neglect and abuse. Remedies are known and feasible, but action requires political will.

Experience shows that governments gain, not lose, by providing protections for such workers. Large-scale labor migration is a prominent feature of globalization today, but this force is best harnessed to serve economic growth through rules that respect the dignity and protect the basic rights of the workers, whatever job they perform.

Extending and enforcing the protections of existing labor laws, monitoring the labor recruitment industry, and reforming immigration policies are steps that successful governments are already taking which can be usefully emulated by others. Such changes not only encourage safe migration and safe work, but help reduce human trafficking and undocumented migration. Protecting the migrants' right to form associations and raising public awareness among employers can also facilitate passage of needed reforms and generate public pressure for accountability. Domestic workers should not have to gamble with their rights.

Nisha Varia is a senior researcher with the Women's Rights Division at Human Rights Watch.

[1] Graeme Hugo, Indonesian Overseas Contract Workers' HIV Knowledge: A gap in information (Bangkok: UNDP, 2000), p.3.

A SHRINKING REALM:
FREEDOM OF EXPRESSION SINCE 9/11

By Dinah PoKempner

When one speaks of the danger to the norm against torture since 9/11, it is fairly obvious what that means. Torture, after all, draws up rather specific images of the individual under assault, despite the Bush administration's attempts to muddy the issue. But the same is not true for freedom of expression, a norm that applies to an expansive range of human activity.

The right to free expression protects everyone from the man on the public soapbox to the anonymous blogger; from the woman who prefers hijab to the crossdresser; from the persecuted defender of human rights to the repellant genocide denier. The erosion of the norm against torture is alarming precisely because the norm is absolute: under the law, there are no other interests to balance. But the right to free expression can be qualified in light of public safety, national security, public order, morality, and the rights of others. The communities concerned with these many aspects are often fragmented, and the precise contours of the right are more fluid. It is easy to lose track of the whole picture.

This is why some five years after 9/11 it is especially important to try to take stock of the scope of free expression. The view is not reassuring. Responses to terrorism combined with dynamics that long predate 9/11 have produced an array of threats to free expression.

From Iraq to Russia to the Philippines, journalists are being treated as partisans, even combatants, and are now more frequently targeted for attack than at any time in recent memory. Global migration (witness the tensions surrounding the integration of Muslim immigrants in Europe) and the steady growth of civil society in many formerly closed countries (witness conditions in Russia and China) are fueling governmental urges to restrict expression. Counterterrorism has given new vigor to some old forms of censorship, and created new ones. Crimes of "glorification" of terrorism, once rare, are proliferating, and hate speech is increasingly becoming the rationale for imposing criminal or administrative sanctions against those thought to be extremists. Despite (or because of) the continuing cyber-revolution, states are also moving quickly to fence and filter the internet, and new technologies are fueling an explosion of state surveillance, often justified in the name of counterterrorism.

Cataloguing the new rents in the fabric of the right to free expression is important in itself but then we need to step back to understand better how these affect the cloth as a whole. When communications are subjected to unwarranted surveillance, or when new speech-based crimes are created, the entire context for deciding whether an article can be published, a sermon preached, or a certain garment worn is changed. Moreover, the effect of new restrictions in states with long records of protecting free expression is global; restrictive precedents give fresh cover and encouragement to states with a history of trammeling this right. The effect of these developments is greater than the sum of discrete instances.

With this in mind, it is plain that mending the fabric will require more than just a patch here and there. This essay sketches some of the damage and suggests ways to respond. We must overcome the tendency to look at each restriction in isolation from others and only in local context. And we must be vigilant in responding to each assault on this freedom, systematically and repeatedly, if we are to protect all other rights.

Frederick Douglass, the abolitionist and publisher, spoke to what is at stake:

> Liberty is meaningless where the right to utter one's thoughts
> and opinions has ceased to exist. That, of all rights, is the dread
> of tyrants. It is the right which they first of all strike down. They
> know its power.[1]

Journalists in the Crosshairs

The press has often been subject to attack, both physically and legally. But there is reason to believe that both contemporary armed conflicts and the so-called war on terror have rendered it more precarious than ever to be a journalist.

In Russia, it has become extremely dangerous to report on the conflict in Chechnya in any way. Most recently, the world was shocked by what seemed like the contract killing of investigative journalist Anna Politkovskaia on October 7,

2006, potentially in retaliation for her searching and critical writing on Chechnya. Earlier in the year, the government had convicted the director of the Russian-Chechen Friendship Society of "inciting racial hatred" through articles he published in the group's journal, and then shut down the nongovernmental organization itself for good measure.

Though war correspondents enjoy immunity under the laws of armed conflict, they work in precarious circumstances and are vulnerable. Even so, the toll on journalists in Iraq by any measure has been extraordinary, with 137 journalists and media assistants killed since March 2003, sometimes in attacks specifically directed at reporters and media organizations.[2] Also troubling is the frequency with which Iraqi and coalition forces have detained journalists without charge.[3]

In the larger view, it is undeniable that the overthrow of Saddam Hussein enabled independent journalism to become established in Iraq, despite general security conditions that make it a life-threatening enterprise. But even there the picture is mixed. During both coalition and subsequent Iraqi administrations, authorities have laid limits on reporting news that could in any way be seen as promoting the views of insurgents or adherents of Saddam Hussein.[4]

For the purpose of taking stock, the practices of the US with regard to press freedom are important to examine, as historically the US has often been on the cutting edge of legal protection for speech, its constitutional standards often exceeding other countries' legal safeguards. Unfortunately, under the Bush administration, there have been significant steps backwards.

The Bush administration was notably more hostile to releasing information to the press than prior administrations, moving to reclassify information that had been in the public domain, to reverse the presumption toward disclosure under the Freedom of Information Act, and to greatly restrict public access to presidential papers, an important source of information on public policy.[5] The government also showed an unusual determination to force investigative reporters to disclose confidential sources, while Congress yet again failed to create a federal "shield law."[6] When scandals surfaced that could impugn the administration, its first reaction was to retaliate by announcing leak investigations against the press, as when the *Washington Post* revealed the existence of secret Central Intelligence

Agency detention centers ("black sites"), and when the *New York Times* disclosed that the National Security Agency was illegally snooping on millions of domestic and international calls.

In the US, reporters on the receiving end of official leaks generally do not face prosecution, but there were signs that this may change. Figures in both the administration and the political right-wing press called for espionage prosecutions of newspapers in the wake of these scandals. In August 2005 the federal government indicted two former lobbyists for the American Israel Public Affairs Committee (AIPAC) for receiving leaked national defense information from a US official and then repeating it to foreign officials and reporters. The AIPAC case raised concern as a stepping stone to future prosecutions of journalists, as it involves a novel application of a 1917 law that has typically been interpreted as applying only to leakers, rather than recipient publishers, of national defense information.[7]

It is important to remember that apart from these particular fronts, the press remained in the crosshairs of rights-abusing governments the world over. Cuba in 2006 held some 25 journalists in prison for political crimes, and in Venezuela the Chavez administration further restrained critical reporting through "gag" laws and control of the courts.[8] In Sudan, security forces have been arresting and detaining journalists, banning newspaper editions and performing pre-print inspections—and this is apart from routine restrictions on media reporting on Darfur.[9] Burma, Turkmenistan, and North Korea continue to be black holes for press freedom (and many other freedoms besides) while Iran and Saudi Arabia have kept journalists on a tight leash even as online communications have taken off. The list of literal and legal attacks on the press goes on and on, with Reporters Without Borders listing, at this writing, 95 journalists and media assistants killed in 2006, an increase over the prior four years, and 135 imprisoned.[10] A rare bright spot was a decision by the UK House of Lords to restore a measure of balance to that country's notorious libel law by providing greater protections for information that is of public interest.[11]

New Offenses in the Age of Counterterrorism: "Glorification" or "Apologie" and "Indirect" Incitement

Incitement to commit a crime is an offense in many legal systems around the world, and specific laws prohibiting incitement to terrorist acts are increasingly common. Such conduct sometimes can be reached through accomplice liability and conspiracy laws as well. The crime of direct incitement generally requires that the message directly encourage the commission of a crime, and that the speaker intend this, whether or not a criminal act results. In the United States, constitutional jurisprudence requires that the incitement present a risk of "imminent" criminal action; in Europe, the courts tend to allow somewhat more latitude with respect to the risk of proximate causation.

What is new on the scene is the proliferation of crimes of "indirect incitement," that is, criminalization of speech which is thought to have some potential to incite criminal action, but which may be less targeted in message or audience and less obviously a proximate cause of actual criminal acts. These laws are often ambiguous on whether the proscribed speech must merely portray terrorism or terrorists—variously or vaguely defined—in a favorable light to an outside observer, or whether it must be specifically intended to spur violent criminal acts and present a real risk of doing so under the circumstances.

In 2004 only three European countries had laws against "apologie" or "glorification" of terrorism, but by mid-November 2006 some 36 countries had signed the Council of Europe Convention on Terrorism which requires states to criminalize "provocation" of terrorism, a crime that could include indirect incitement.[12] The new crime is catching on in domestic law. Spain and France had apologie laws on the books prior to 2001; the United Kingdom and Denmark have more recently adopted laws on promotion or glorification of terrorist acts, while Turkey and Russia in 2006 amended terrorism legislation in ways that would punish speech characterized, respectively, as "propaganda" for terrorism or support of "extremism."

Australia has been considering following the model of the UK Terrorism Act of 2006, which outlaws "glorification" where it is reasonable to infer that the audience would understand the speech as encouraging emulation of terrorist conduct.

There is no qualification in the UK law, however, for either imminent danger that a terrorist act would be committed, or the speaker's intention to cause such a result. It is important to recognize that acts of glorification or apologie are the basis for more than penal consequences: they also may lead to blacklisting of organizations for the purpose of halting fundraising or freezing assets, as in the UK, or to deportation of aliens, as in France.

The crime of indirect incitement has to be seen as an effort to go beyond situations where the evidence shows that the speaker clearly intends to provoke the audience to criminal conduct. There are strong reasons to question whether there is, in fact, room for principled distinction between controversial but protected political speech and indirect incitement.[13] In the UK, some have sought to distinguish between those who carry placards praising the perpetrators of the London 7/7 attacks and those whose placards urge murder of critics of Islam. Others have worried that glorification laws could be used against Muslims who speak in favor of armed resistance against occupation, expression which is typically viewed as a form of protected, if controversial, political speech. Prime Minister Tony Blair's statement that juries would understand glorification "when they see it" underscored the fears of minorities that the definition would be subject to the popular prejudices of the moment.[14]

If counterterrorism has been the motive for new speech-restrictive laws in Europe, it also has become a pretext for repression of political dissent in places such as Uzbekistan. Treated as an ally in the aftermath of the 9/11 attacks by Washington and Moscow, Uzbekistan significantly intensified its persecution of independent reporters and human rights monitors, justifying this crackdown as a legitimate counterterrorism response. And it did so with particular energy against those who contradicted the government's claims that Islamist terrorists, rather than government agents, were responsible for massacring hundreds of unarmed civilians in Andijan in May 2005.[15] Despite commitments to reform its laws, Jordan still prosecutes writers for criminal defamation of government leaders and officials or for material that endangers foreign relations. In June 2006 the state jailed four parliamentarians who paid a condolence call to the family of Abu Mus'ab al-Zarqawi; one of the four also allegedly called al-Zarqawi "a martyr and a fighter." The charge against the four was stirring up sectarian or racial tension or strife among different elements of the nation.[16]

But it is in Spain that one finds one of the stranger prosecutions for *apologie*, which ended in acquittal in November 2006. Impelled by the Association of Terrorism Victims, the government indicted a Basque punk rock band for allegedly praising separatist terrorism in the lyrics of its songs. The group denied supporting terrorists and explicitly disavowed supporting the armed ETA insurgency when it was alleged that their songs were hurtful to the ETA's victims. Under the European Court's jurisprudence, works of art and political speech are both to be given an extra degree of latitude. Even so, the prosecutor sought not only to imprison the band, but to bar them from working as musicians.[17]

New Twists on Old Offenses: Hate Speech and Blasphemy

As the examples above suggest, there is a good deal of blurring between the rationales of hate speech and of indirect incitement. The formulation of indirect incitement, praising terrorism as "just and necessary" or holding up for admiration known terrorists, is often intertwined with derision or denigration of victims or opponents. Although there are differences in the two types of proscriptions, both derive from an appreciation of the power of speech to facilitate mass violence.

The state has a legal option to limit speech to protect national security or other state interests. But prohibiting hate speech is obligatory under several major human rights treaties, including the International Covenant on Civil and Political Rights (ICCPR) and the later Convention on the Elimination of Racial Discrimination (CERD). The ICCPR does not require states to punish hate speech as a crime, but many states interpret CERD as requiring criminal proscription of hate speech. Many states have entered reservations or interpretations to these provisions in consideration of protecting the right to free expression.[18]

Hate speech is indeed hateful. It can also be deeply harmful, even when it does not incite imminent violence or criminal acts, in that it can provoke public and self-denigration, and a great deal of psychological pain. The point of freedom of expression, however, is to preserve space for highly controversial or even deeply offensive speech, as socially acceptable messages seldom need protection. The hate speech provisions of the ICCPR were negotiated by parties with fresh memories of the Holocaust, and their concern was less to spare group sensibilities from insult than to establish that hate speech, even when not direct incitement, often played a key role in facilitating violence and state discrimination against minorities.[19]

In the decades following the Holocaust, however, the goal of social equality became a more prominent rationale for hate speech prohibitions, particularly in Europe. Laws and prosecutions for hate speech often seemed focused on limiting certain content no matter the context, and seemed unmoored from hard analysis of whether the speech in question, however repugnant, had any potential actually to incite violence or any other criminal action by third parties. The shift to this rationale could be seen in the controversial trial court judgment of the International Criminal Tribunal for Rwanda in the *Nahimana* case, where the court construed hate speech as a basis for "persecution" as a crime against humanity. It wrote:

> Hate speech is a discriminatory form of aggression that destroys the dignity of those in the group under attack. It creates a lesser status not only in the eyes of the group members themselves but also in the eyes of others who perceive and treat them as less than human. The denigration of persons on the basis of their ethnic identity or other group membership in and of itself, as well as in its other consequences, can be an irreversible harm.[20]

The competition between two rationales—hate speech as a catalyst of criminal acts, versus hate speech as a harm to dignity in and of itself—has not always been obvious, nor have the problems of assessing harm to dignity in a democratic society or a world of global communications. The Danish cartoon scandal brought these tensions into vivid relief.

On September 30, 2005, the Danish newspaper *Jyllands-Posten* published twelve cartoon depictions of the Prophet Mohammed that it said were solicited in an effort to overcome self-censorship. The cartoons were highly offensive to Muslims, because Islam is frequently interpreted to prohibit depictions of the Prophet and some of the depictions were extremely derogatory, for example, by associating him, and by implication all Muslims, with terrorism. Denmark declined to take action against the publishers, citing its own obligations to protect free expression. Beyond this, it also declined to apologize for the cartoons. By February 2006, massive and often violent protests against the cartoons and against Denmark spread throughout the Muslim world.

The context for the protests included the invasions of Afghanistan and Iraq, tensions in Israel/Palestine, rising Western prejudice and suspicion against Muslims as "terrorists," and an associated sense of persecution and social alienation on the part of Muslim minorities in many parts of the world. Against the backdrop of travel restrictions, debates over the public acceptability of women in hijab, terrorism blacklists, deportations, and investigations of Muslim charities, the cartoons were felt as particularly denigrating, and to some Muslims may have conveyed a quality of threat.

Criticism of the cartoons, however, seldom focused on their directly provoking discrimination or violence against Muslim communities, but rather they focused on equality issues more generally. The unwillingness of Denmark to either take action against the newspaper or apologize was contrasted with the proliferation of Holocaust-denial laws and blasphemy laws protecting Christianity in Europe. The discourse on whether the media had a right to publish the cartoons became confused with whether the media were right to do so. While the European emphasis on equality and non-discrimination as values prompted much soul-searching as to whether Denmark had taken the proper course, Muslim states by and large did not respond to retorts that they permit abusive depictions of and speech about religious minorities in their jurisdictions; indeed, Iran sponsored an anti-Semitic Holocaust denial cartoon contest in response.

The after-effects of the controversy have been significant. Governments with large Muslim populations, including Jordan, Yemen, Syria, India, and Algeria, pressed charges against editors and journalists who reproduced the cartoons, and newspapers were censored, suspended or closed in Malaysia, Saudi Arabia, Yemen, Belarus, South Africa, and Russia. The Organization of the Islamic Conference criticized Denmark and has sought a UN General Assembly statement banning attacks on religious beliefs. On September 8, 2006, the United Nations General Assembly adopted a global counterterrorism strategy that contained the phrase, "and to promote mutual respect for and prevent defamation of religions." In a speech before the UN General Assembly on September 20, 2006, Pakistan's President Pervez Musharraf called for a ban on the "defamation of Islam."[21]

This response, in essence an international endorsement of blasphemy laws as part of counterterrorism strategy, is exactly the wrong direction for any state that values robust discourse and democratic values. While critics are right to point to the selectivity of existing European blasphemy laws in protecting only Christianity, the key question here is why any religious system should be legally shielded from criticism or even ridicule when political beliefs, aesthetic views, or cultural opinions are not. Speech which targets religious believers for criminal acts should not be protected, but speech which derides only religious ideas should not be punished.

This approach avoids imposing criminal penalties for either blasphemous or hateful speech that threatens dignity but not crime. It is more consistent with the primary articulation of the ban on hate speech in article 20 of the ICCPR than an approach which places whole categories of speech outside protection. Article 20 requires states to prohibit "any *advocacy* of national, racial or religious hatred that constitutes incitement to discrimination, hostility or violence" (emphasis added). The term "advocacy" implies that there must be a conscious intent to spur hatred, rather than just approval of or inadvertent contribution to hatred. The fact that the advocacy of hatred must additionally constitute *incitement* points to provocation of an action, rather than merely fostering negative feelings (since that is already specified by "hatred"), and violence and discrimination are two species of criminal acts. But what has never been clear is exactly what "hostility" entails, although the construction implies something beyond hatred, involving overt manifestation of hatred against another. An argument can be made that the sort of hostility that calls for imprisonment for speech in a democratic society must amount at minimum to a criminal level of harassment, and not to expression of repugnant opinions or impugning of reputation.[22]

Genocide Denial: Incitement or Hate Speech?

The rationale for genocide denial laws has undergone a shift similar to that for hate speech. In the wake of World War II, Germany's strict laws prohibiting the use of Nazi symbols or the promotion of Nazi ideology were designed to stifle any revival of the movement or the passions of anti-Semitism. But rather than fading away with the passage of time, Holocaust denial laws proliferated in Europe right through the 1990s, more as political statements against anti-Semitism than as responses to some genuine prospect of incitement to genocide. Indeed, it may have been the increasing marginality of Holocaust deniers that made laws somewhat easier to propose and pass than in the immediate aftermath of WWII.

In 2006 France's legislature considered criminalizing denial of the Armenian genocide, but hardly because there was a live prospect of repetition, much less in France. Also in 2006, a Belgian cabinet minister proposed a denial law for the Rwandan genocide. It is safe to assume this was more likely a political gesture in view of Belgium's historical role in Rwanda than an admission that Belgium is a serious incubator of renewed violence against Tutsi.

Joel Simon, executive director of the Committee to Protect Journalists, describes a dynamic common to many African countries since the International Criminal Tribunal for Rwanda convicted individuals of inciting genocide over the radio. Political parties are often organized along ethnic or tribal lines; reporting on government failings ignites political protests; and the government then takes action against the media on the basis of "incitement to rebellion" or "incitement to hatred," citing the need to avert large-scale ethnic violence. This dynamic is particularly evident in Rwanda, where charges of "divisionism" or "negationism" (the latter, in essence, genocide-denial) are frequently launched against perceived government opponents and critics, including Rwanda's one independent newspaper, *Umuseso.*[23]

The potential of genocide denial laws for abuse should make us think hard about their rationale. In Rwanda the blood of genocide is barely dry and there would seem to be a more compelling case for outlawing genocide denial. And yet the government's use of genocide denial laws to stifle critics is cautionary. Prosecuting genocide denial to protect victims from insult or the genuine harm that denial of their suffering inflicts can easily be taken to extremes. And taken to extremes, such laws can create new means of persecution that could well stifle political and social debate and undermine pluralism. The criminalization of genocide denial seems more plausibly grounded in concerns over inciting violence or even genocide, and the evaluation of whether speech should be suppressed should take into account the likelihood of inciting criminal acts in the particular context.

Making genocide denial a crime of political correctness has rather obvious deleterious effects. It makes martyrs of cranks, as has been the case with Austria's conviction of David Irving, a Nazi apologist whose fade into obscurity was only halted by his trial in February 2006. It invites expansive interpretations of "denial" and "genocide" and the slide into new crimes of ideological deviance, as governments are often eager to rally support by tarring critics as threats to national security or human rights. And it cheapens the concept of genocide in the process, arguably making governments less willing to intervene or call the deliberate destruction of peoples by its true name.

That said, genocide denial, even when not amounting to incitement to a crime, is often a type of hate speech that inflicts serious harm, both to the group and to individual members. The state's duty regarding genocide denial does not begin and end with the criminal law. Above all, the state should recognize the crime of genocide where the evidence establishes it, and provide appropriate avenues of reparation and prevention, including positive acts of acknowledgment, education, and debate. Genocide deniers should be marginalized, and even subject to other forms of sanction where they cause real harm, but they should not be subject to incarceration except where their actions amount to incitement to violence. In this regard, it is notable that Australia allows those harmed by public expression of racial hatred to apply to the Human Rights and Equal Opportunity Commission for conciliation and relief, and generally reserves criminal sanction for acts of racial vilification that intentionally cause criminal menace or harassment.[24]

The state's duty to recognize genocide and similar mass crimes where they have been committed flows not only from the harm done to individual or group survivors through denial, but the harm done to humanity itself. Denial is a form of desecration of the dead, a violation of one of the most basic human norms. It brutalizes us, and facilitates repetition of atrocity. As a corollary to the duty to recognize and remember genocide and crimes against humanity, the state should not do so selectively, favoring some victims and ignoring or denying others. In this context, it is particularly reprehensible that some Turkish writers continue to be prosecuted for "insulting Turkishness" under article 301 of the criminal code when they probe into the mass killing of Armenians in 1915 or suggest that those actions might have been genocide.[25]

Technology as a Restraint: Internet Censorship and Surveillance

Access to information is integral to free expression: speech is an empty right if it means talking into a box rather than communicating and sharing information and ideas with others.[26] The internet, in this sense, is a powerful engine for free expression, creating global audiences and global sources of information, and it is understandable that states have sought to monitor and restrict it for both good reasons and bad. Privacy plays a less obvious, but equally important role in free expression in a democracy. The inability to choose one's audience or to seek ideas and information without monitoring, inhibits thought, speech, and association. And even for those not easily inhibited, surveillance is invasive. For that reason alone, privacy merits protection to ensure human dignity and integrity.[27]

The "war on terror" did not cause, but did exacerbate, the trend towards restriction of the internet and the proliferation of surveillance through modern technology. Governments that once invoked child pornographers as a good reason to censor internet publications shifted emphasis to terrorism as a rationale. Corporations became willing assistants in the fencing and filtering of access, even while justifying their cooperation with repressive governments in terms of expanding public access to information (and of course, their own access to markets). Surveillance and data collection grew exponentially, not only because developments in modern technology made such practices more economically feasible, but also because security fears made them more politically palatable.

Some governments have been eager to grasp the internet as a tool for economic and educational development but are wary that losing control over information will also cause them to lose control over their population. A number of Middle Eastern governments have embraced the cause of improving public access to the internet, but at the same time use advanced filtering and surveillance technology to monitor online expression. Egypt, Tunisia, Iran, and Syria prosecute and imprison online writers for politically objectionable material, and these as well as many other countries in the Middle East block websites for political, human rights, or Islamist content in addition to pornography and gambling, and monitor internet cafes.

In 2005 Tunisia hosted the World Summit on the Information Society to showcase its commitment to internet access. What also fell into the global spotlight was the government's robust censorship, harassment, and prosecution of online critics for offenses such as false news, defamation, or terrorism, expansively defined and interpreted. Tunisia strictly controls internet service providers, regulates internet cafes, and uses filtering technology to block political, news, and human rights sites. It has cited counterterrorism and the need to curb incitement to hatred and violence as among its justifications for censoring information online. Yet tests that Human Rights Watch ran in September 2005 on 41 radical Islamist sites found only four blocked, and numerous sites relating to weapons manufacture and purchase were also readily available. In contrast, the website of Reporters Without Borders was blocked as were numerous opposition political and news sites, discrediting the government's justifications for censorship.[28]

The Great Firewall of China is a case of corporate collaboration in censorship. Press liberty has deteriorated since 2003 when President Hu Jintao took office, and the government has taken harsh steps to control and suppress peaceful political and religious dissent, including jailing journalists and bloggers. China operates the most sophisticated internet filtering and surveillance apparatus in the world, employing tens of thousands, but also relying on the active cooperation of major internet companies in proactive censorship. Yahoo! has provided user information to government authorities that enabled China to convict four government critics, and it has censored the results generated by its search engine to eliminate politically controversial terms and sites. Microsoft and Google also proactively censor their Chinese search engines, in anticipation of what the government would require them to block.

Censorship has not always been transparent, with companies sometimes providing minimal notice that results have been filtered, but no indication of what is missing or why. Skype also censored text-chats, but without notifying users that it was doing so.[29] Pressure is on internet companies to create a voluntary code of conduct to guide their dealings with governments that do not respect freedom of expression or information. It is unlikely, however, that this alone will avert a "race to the bottom" in human rights standards without government regulation to put the brakes on proactive censorship and the lack of transparency.

While China is probably the most advanced in filtering and monitoring its slice of the internet, it is hardly alone. China has exported its technology to censor and monitor electronic communications to Robert Mugabe's government in Zimbabwe. Other governments are trying to reproduce China's success in fencing in cyberspace and purging it of unwanted ideas, among them Iran, Yemen, Vietnam, and Tunisia. Burma monitors emails and uses software in internet cafes that records what is displayed on the screen every five minutes, while Uzbekistan fines cafe surfers for accessing banned political sites.[30]

As important as it is to free speech, the internet is only one arena for burgeoning state surveillance. The US requires telephone companies to have a surveillance capability, and has pressed for internet voice telephony to have surveillance capability embedded into the service as well.[31] In most jurisdictions, governments have easy access to both telephone traffic data and internet traffic data as collected by internet service providers, in distinction to the substantive content of calls, which usually requires judicial warrant. Internet traffic data, however, gives far more information than telephone traffic data—for example, websites and pages visited, chat partners, searches—enabling the monitor to create a thorough profile of individuals. EU nations have sometimes considered whether to require retention of electronic communications records for a period of time so that they may be searched, a measure the US supports.[32] Governments are creating enormous databases of personal information in many other ways (from data collected during travel, corporate records, national identity documents) that can be shared. These days, the person standing on the soapbox in Hyde Park is likely to be preserved by the government on film; London has one of the highest densities of public surveillance cameras in the world. Many are unaware of this surveillance explosion, which is likely to continue and deepen as technological ability to track people improves. But when surveillance pierces the consciousness, as the intensive monitoring of Muslim charities has in the US, it can have a profoundly intimidating effect.[33]

Assessing the Erosion

Cataloguing, even anecdotally, the many encroachments on free expression since 9/11 is a little like writing about global warming. The danger is real, catastrophic, accelerating, and yet almost invisible. So many things are going on at so many levels we fail to see the interconnections.

Among the interconnections is the chill that one instance of censorship throws upon other speakers (as, for example, in the selective prosecution of reporters) but also the pall that violations of related rights throw onto free expression. When it is unsafe to assemble, it is usually unsafe to speak as well, or even to express one's identity in other ways. When the internet is monitored, blogging becomes unsafe, and freedom of opinion and information suffer. And the repression of speech can swiftly lead to other rights violations, as when a controversial speaker is first arrested, imprisoned, and then tortured, or when candid messages on preventing AIDS through condoms and safe sex are banned, leading to more cases of risky sex, and ultimately more preventable deaths from the disease. Had the White House and Pentagon managed to suppress all photographs of Abu Ghraib, it is difficult to imagine that the issue of torture and permissible interrogation techniques would have received the Congressional or global attention it did.

National security anxiety also connects many of the new developments. Security has justified restrictions on what electronic information may be accessed, what headgear or facial hair can be worn, what scholars may be invited to speak, what political arguments can be voiced, and what newspapers will dare to publish. And this is no new phenomenon.

In 1995 a group of eminent scholars met in Johannesburg to consider the relation between national security and freedom of expression. The resulting Johannesburg Principles are often invoked as reflecting the best practices of many domestic jurisdictions. They define as a "legitimate" national security interest only those interests whose genuine purpose and demonstrable effect is to protect a country's existence or its territorial integrity against the use or threat of force, or its capacity to respond to the use or threat of force. Protecting the state against embarrassment, industrial unrest, exposure of wrongdoing, ideological deviance, or muckraking are not interests that can justify censorship.[34]

Our fragmented perspective on the problem is reinforced by the infrequency with which most people encounter new restrictions or perceive them. We do not suffer bullets or subpoenas, we are not accused of glorification of terrorism or hate speech, and we are mostly unaware of internet censorship or most forms of surveillance. That is, unless we are Muslims in Europe, Islamists in Egypt, journalists in Sudan, rights advocates in Uzbekistan, democracy activists in Vietnam, or Uighurs in China. Members of these targeted groups experience the full cumulative force of many forms of restriction and are painfully aware of the narrowing space they have for expression.

How can the rest of us be less like the frog placed in a pot on a stove that eventually boils to death because it fails to notice the gradual rise in the temperature? There is not just one practice to protest and reverse but a myriad of them, with each contributing to a new and more illiberal world.

One precept that has stood the test of time is, do not unto others as you would not have them do unto you. This works fairly well as a pocket "rule of engagement" to test our reactions. It is clarifying on the issue of torture to imagine how we would want our own troops treated as prisoners. Similarly, when evaluating concepts such as defamation of religion, we should imagine our co-religionists on trial for blaspheming another faith.

Another precept is that criminal penalties should be reserved for criminal actions and not for insults or falsehoods, however hurtful. Blasphemy laws should be repealed. There are other means to rectify many of the harms associated with hate speech than loss of liberty. A corollary is insisting on rigorous justification for each restriction of speech, with scrutiny of the magnitude and immediacy of the threats it presents, rather than opting for a categorical approach that lumps art along with incitement, debate with criminal demagoguery.

A third precept is that governments should cultivate a sense of global responsibility in policy. They should be mindful of how their own well-intentioned but restrictive laws and practices can take on a life of their own domestically, when different groups are perceived as threatening, pressure to censor spreads, or zealous prosecutors target types of expression not originally contemplated. Moreover, laws and policies that tread the margins of free expression can also wreak damage internationally, when removed from their domestic context and held up as a template by states that wish to justify crackdowns on critics or disfavored minority groups. Taking responsibility for policy also means not shifting blame— to unregulated corporations, answerable only for profits, or to multilateral fora, where broad mandates to combat support for terrorism can be translated domestically into laws that significantly encroach on free expression.

It is possible to repair the damage already done, but doing so will require a wide-angle perspective and a better appreciation that these days, silencing dissent in one group invariably imperils expression—and myriad other rights—worldwide.

Dinah PoKempner is general counsel of Human Rights Watch.

1 Frederick Douglass, speaking in the Boston Music Hall after an anti-slavery meeting had been broken up. David J. Brewer, *World's Best Orations* (St. Louis: Ferd. P. Kaiser, 1899), vol. 5, pp.1906-1909. Also at http://douglassarchives.org/doug_a68.htm.

2 Reporters Without Borders, "War in Iraq," undated, http://www.rsf.org/special_iraq_en.php3.

3 Ann Cooper, "Jailing Iraqi Journalists," *Dangerous Assignments,* October 4, 2005, http://www.cpj.org/Briefings/2005/DA_fall05/comment/comment_DA_fall05.html. Abdul Ameer Younis Hussein, a CBS cameraman, was held by US forces without charge for almost a year and his case ultimately dismissed in April 2006 for lack of evidence. Bilal Hussein, a photojournalist with Associated Press whose pictures of Fallujah won the Pulitzer Prize, is in his seventh month of detention by US forces at this writing.

4 See, for example, Mariah Blake, "From All Sides: In the Deadly Cauldron of Iraq, Even the Arab Media are Being Pushed Off the Story," *Columbia Journalism Review* (2005), http://www.cjr.org/issues/2005/2/onthejob-blake.asp, and Committee to Protect Journalists, "Iraq: Government instructs media to promote leadership's positions," November 12, 2004, http://www.cpj.org/news/2004/Iraq12nov04na.html. Most recently, the authorities closed two television stations for broadcasting images of Iraqis protesting the sentencing of Saddam Hussein to death, adding to the media blackout caused by temporary official suspension of the major newspapers. Reporters Without Borders, " http://www.rsf.org/article.php3?id_article=19599.

5 See Floyd Abrams, "The State of Free Speech," *New York Law Journal,* vol. 236 (2006).

6 Although a majority of states have enacted "shield laws" to protect reporters from having to disclose their confidential sources, various bills to provide a federal privilege have been stuck in both houses of Congress. For an account of both legislative developments and various reporters who have been jailed for refusing to divulge their sources, see Reporters Committee for Freedom of the Press, "Special Report: Reporters and Federal Subpoenas," October 13, 2006 http://www.rcfp.org/shields_and_subpoenas.html#shield.

7 Adam Liptak, "In Leak Cases, New Pressure on Journalists," *New York Times*, April 30, 2006.

8 "IAPA meeting ends with severe criticism of press freedom in the hemisphere," Inter American Press Association news release, March 14, 2005, http://www.sipiapa.org/pressreleases/chronologicaldetail.cfm?PressReleaseID=1336.

9 "Sudan: Press Under Pressure," Human Rights Watch news release, November 6, 2006, http://hrw.org/english/docs/2006/11/06/darfur14514.htm.

[10] Reporters Without Borders, "Press Freedom Barometer," covering data from January to October 2006, http://www.rsf.org/rubrique.php3?id_rubrique=113. The Committee to Protect Journalists lists 46 confirmed cases of journalists killed in 2006 as of November 7, 2006, http://www.cpj.org/killed/killed06.html.

[11] *Jameel v. Wall Street Journal Europe*, UKHL 44 (October 11, 2006).

[12] The treaty was adopted in May 2005. At this writing only Bulgaria and Russia have ratified it; the treaty requires six ratifications to enter into force. Article 5.1 of the treaty defines "public provocation to commit a terrorist offence" as making a message available to the public, through either direct or indirect advocacy, with the intent to incite the commission of a terrorist offense and causing a danger that such an offense be committed. Council of Europe Convention on the Prevention of Terrorism, May 16, 2005, CETS No. 196, http://conventions.coe.int/Treaty/EN/Treaties/Html/196.htm. Security Council Resolution 1624 adopted on September 14, 2005, also calls on states to legally prohibit "incitement" to commit terrorist acts, but with explicit reference in its preamble to the boundaries created by the international right of free expression.

[13] See Opinion of the Commissioner for Human Rights, Alvaro Gil-Robles, on the draft Convention on the Prevention of Terrorism, Strasbourg, February 2, 2005, BCommDH(2005), para. 26 (Gil-Robles notes, "The question is where the boundary lies between indirect incitement to commit terrorist acts and the legitimate voicing of criticism.").

[14] Jon Silverman, "Glorification law passes 'first test,'" *BBC News Online,* February 16, 2006, http://news.bbc.co.uk/2/hi/uk_news/4720682.stm.

[15] Human Rights Watch, *Burying the Truth: Uzbekistan Rewrites the Story of the Andijan Massacre*, vol. 15, no. 6(D), September 2005, http://hrw.org/reports/2005/uzbekistan0905/ and "Uzbekistan: Journalist Assaulted after Reporting on Massacre," Human Rights Watch news release, November 11, 2005, http://hrw.org/english/docs/2005/11/11/uzbeki12007.htm.

[16] "Jordan: Rise in Arrests Restricting Free Speech," Human Rights Watch news release, June 17, 2006, http://hrw.org/english/docs/2006/06/17/jordan13574.htm.

[17] "Band Sozidad Alkoholika denies lyrics aimed at praising terrorism," *EITB 24*, November 2, 2006, http://www.eitb24.com/portal/eitb24/noticia/en/politics/national-court-trial-band-soziedad-alkoholika-denies-lyrics-aimed?itemId=B24_18543&cl=%2Feitb24%2Fpolitica&idioma=en/.

[18] International Criminal Tribunal for the former Yugoslavia, *Prosecutor v. Kordi and Cerkez*, Case No. IT-95-14/2-T, Judgment (Trial Chamber) of 26 February 2001, sec. 209 n.272.

[19] See Manfred Nowak, *CCPR Commentary* (Kehl: N.P. Engel, 1993), p.366, para. 15.

[20] International Criminal Tribunal for Rwanda, *The Prosecutor v. Nahimana et al.*, Case No. ICTR-99-52-T, Judgment (Trial Chamber) of 3 December 2003, p.351, sec. 1072.

[21] Just as the original furor appeared to be quieting, a video came to light of activists from the far-right Danish People's Party at a summer camp drawing more derogatory images of the Prophet Muhammad. Iran and Indonesia summoned their Danish ambassadors to protest, and the Danish prime minister denounced the drawing of the cartoons, if not the airing of the video. Danish imams who had traveled abroad to rally support to protest the original cartoons, however, stated they would not let themselves be provoked this time. "Row over Danish cartoons escalates," BBC News Online, October 10, 2006, http://news.bbc.co.uk/2/hi/europe/6037597.stm. The action of Denmark in criticizing the cartoons was significant, and highlights the difference between the state moving to repress the publisher of offensive speech, and the state taking measures to repudiate the offensive and discriminatory message.

[22] Manfred Nowak has argued that article 20, while providing an additional basis for restricting free expression, cannot authorize restrictions beyond the terms of what article 19 allows, so that, for example, it would not permit punishing freedom of opinion, nor permit pre-censorship, nor would it allow for sanctions to attach without consideration of the interests enumerated in article 19.3 in respect of which speech may be restricted. Nowak, *CCPR Commentary*, pp. 368-369. This view finds support in the Human Rights Committee's General Comment 11 on article 20, which states, "In the opinion of the Committee, these required prohibitions are fully compatible with the right of freedom of expression as contained in article 19, the exercise of which carries with it special duties and responsibilities." UN Human Rights Committee, General Comment 11, Article 20 (Nineteenth session, 1983), Compilation of General Comments and General Recommendations Adopted by Human Rights Treaty Bodies, U.N. Doc. HRI\GEN\1\Rev.1 at 12 (1994). Although it is permissible under article 19 to enact laws against defamation, criminal penalties are strongly disfavored under international jurisprudence. Human Rights Watch's policy on hate speech treads a middle ground between US constitutional practice and article 20 of the ICCPR by accepting the criminalization of hate speech where there is a danger of inciting imminent violence, discrimination or hostility, with "hostility" understood to entail criminal harassment or intimidation.

[23] Joel Simon, "Hate Speech and Press Freedom in Africa" ("Simon Speech"), remarks at conference on "International Criminal Tribunals in the 21st Century," American University Washington College of Law, September 30, 2005, pp.1-2.

[24] Racial Vilification Law in Australia, Race Discrimination Unit, HREOC, October 2002, http://www.hreoc.gov.au/racial_discrimination/cyberracism/vilification.html#other.

[25] Orhan Pamuk, a Nobel Prize-winning author, for example, was charged with this crime in December 2005 after saying in a newspaper that 30,000 Kurds and one million Ottoman Armenians were killed in Turkey yet nobody in the Turkish population would dare talk about it. The trial was dismissed by the Turkish Ministry of Justice at the beginning of 2006. The novelist Elif Shafak was also indicted under this provision but charges were dropped in September 2006. Daniel Dombey and Vincent Boland, "Why Turkey's long journey west is in jeopardy," *Financial Times,* November 7, 2006.

[26] Indeed, the guarantee of free speech in the International Covenant on Civil and Political Rights provides so explicitly. Article 19(2) states, "Everyone shall have the right to freedom of expression; this right shall include freedom to seek, receive and impart information and ideas of all kinds, regardless of frontiers, either orally, in writing or in print, in the form of art, or through any other media of his choice."

[27] The protection of privacy in international law is from "arbitrary" or "unlawful" interference. See International Covenant on Civil and Political Rights, art. 17, and General Comment 16 of the United Nations Human Rights Committee, interpreting these qualifiers.

[28] Human Rights Watch, *False Freedom: Online Censorship in the Middle East and North Africa*, vol. 17, no. 10(E), November 2005, http://hrw.org/reports/2005/mena1105/index.htm.

[29] See Human Rights Watch, *Race to the Bottom: Corporate Complicity in Chinese Internet Censorship*, vol. 18, no. 8(C), August 2006, http://www.hrw.org/reports/2006/china0806/index.htm.

[30] Reporters Without Borders, The Internet Black Holes, "Burma," undated, http://www.rsf.org/int_blackholes_en.php3?id_mot=86&annee=2006&Valider=OK, and "Uzbekistan," undated, http://www.rsf.org/int_blackholes_en.php3?id_mot=105&annee=2005.

[31] Electronic Privacy Information Center, "Internet Telephony," undated, http://www.epic.org/privacy/voip/.

32 "US Data Access Proposal Shows Need for More Protection, EU Official Says," *Communications Daily*, May 15, 2000.

33 Neil Macfarquhar, "Fears of inquiry dampen giving by U.S. Muslims," *New York Times,* October 30, 2006.

34 The Johannesburg Principles on National Security, Freedom of Expression and Access to Information, adopted October 1, 1995, U.N. Doc. E/CN.4/1996/39 (1996), principle 2.

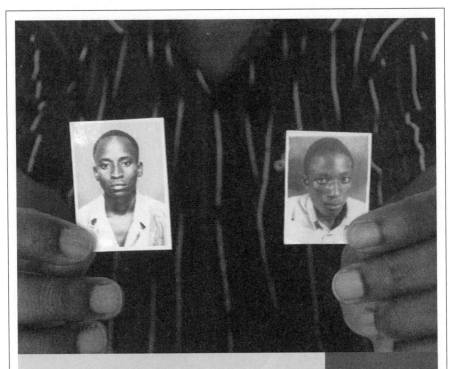

"We flee when we see them"

Abuses with impunity at the National Intelligence Service
in Burundi

WORLD REPORT

2007

AFRICA

ANGOLA

Planned national elections, Angola's first since 1992, were postponed yet again in 2006. Legislative elections are now scheduled for late 2007, but there is no indication whether the presidential election will also be held then.

Angola insulated itself in 2006 from international criticism concerning lack of transparency and good governance in managing public funds, in particular oil revenues, due to a combination of high oil prices and playing the "China card" against Western governments that had been critical in the past.

Economic prosperity and post-war rehabilitation is visible in the capital, Luanda, but it has not reached the rural provinces. Poor Angolans continue to be forcibly and violently evicted from informal settlements in Luanda to make way for development and "beautification" projects by the government and private companies.

Election Preparations

In August 2006 the Cabinet approved the voter registration period for the election to run from November 15, 2006, through June 15, 2007. However, the preparations for this process are plagued with deficiencies. The computer-based system designed to carry out the registration is not guaranteed to work effectively in all areas of the country, especially where there is limited infrastructure and power supply. As of early October 2006 the system had not been tested and the government had not provided an alternative in the event the system fails. Only 4,400 of the planned 14,000 members of the registration teams (*brigadas*) had been recruited and started training at this writing.

The National Electoral Commission is charged with supervising the registration process but its capacity to undertake this task is undermined by the limited resources in its provincial and municipal offices. Poor infrastructure and transportation risk excluding a large part of the population from the registration process, particularly in rural areas, where most of the returnee population is concentrated. Since the war ended in 2002, over 360,000 Angolan refugees have returned to the country.

Civic education for voter registration started on October 3, 2006, a mere 43 days before the start of the registration. This civic education campaign is led by the Ministry of Territorial Administration (MAT). Civil society organizations are allowed to conduct civic education for the registration only if it is an activity explicitly mandated in their statutes and once accredited for that purpose by the MAT. Accreditations were only issued a week before the start of the registration.

In early September 2006 Okutiuka, a local organization in Lobito, Benguela, was prevented by police officers from showing a documentary film on voter registration produced by journalism students, part of a week-long event authorized by the provincial delegations of two government ministries. After the screening of the first film in the program the police barred access to the movie theater for the rest of the week. Police and other authorities did not provide Okutiuka with formal notice or justification for canceling the event.

Cabinda

The 29-year conflict in the oil-rich enclave of Cabinda purportedly ended with the formal signing, on August 1, 2006, of a Memorandum of Understanding (MOU) between the government and representatives of Cabinda. However, controversy surrounding the negotiation and the terms of the MOU indicate that a long-lasting peace in Cabinda may not yet be ensured. The manner in which the peace agreement will be implemented is a crucial factor in the overall pre-electoral environment and is expected to remain a central human rights concern throughout 2007.

The MOU was signed for the Cabindan side by Bento Bembe, a former leader of the rebel Front for the Liberation of the Cabinda Enclave (FLEC) claiming to represent the Cabindan Forum for Dialogue (FCD). The FCD comprises members of FLEC, the Roman Catholic Church, and civil society groups. Several members of the FCD stated that they did not recognize Bembe's legitimacy to sign the memorandum on behalf of the FCD and, therefore, did not accept its terms, in particular the definite refusal of independence for the enclave.

The MOU was approved by the National Assembly in August 2006, but by early October its text had still not been made public. It reportedly includes a special (autonomy) status for Cabinda, as well as an amnesty for crimes committed during the conflict. It is not clear whether the amnesty applies to both parties to the conflict (Angolan government armed forces and rebel forces).

In June 2006 Mpalabanda, a Cabindan human rights NGO and a member of the FCD, was accused by the government of involvement in political activities and shut down by court order. Mpalabanda appealed the decision, but the organization cannot resume its activities until a final decision is reached on the appeal. Mpalabanda has documented human rights violations by both government and FLEC forces in Cabinda. On September 29 Mpalabanda's spokesman Raul Danda was arrested by border control officers at Cabinda airport, reportedly accused of instigating crimes against the security of the state for carrying pro-independence literature.

Media Freedom

The media environment in Angola remains poor. On May 15, 2006, a new press law was enacted that improves the legal framework governing media freedom but still falls short of fully ensuring the right to freedom of expression, as guaranteed in Angola's constitution.

Media coverage of news and events is still highly biased in favor of the government and the ruling party, the Popular Movement for the Liberation of Angola (MPLA). Access to information, in particular in rural areas, is very difficult. The only daily newspaper is owned by the state. Private newspapers are only published weekly and their circulation outside Luanda is extremely limited. Throughout 2006 television broadcasting continued to be a state monopoly and the government failed to authorize private radio outlets to broadcast nationwide. If maintained, this situation will seriously hinder the dissemination of diverse information in the pre-election period.

Housing Rights and Forced Evictions in Luanda

Forced evictions in Luanda in the past five years have undermined Angola's obligation in international law to progressively realize the right to adequate housing. Local authorities, acting with little or no notice, are forcibly and violently evicting hundreds of residents of low income neighborhoods, demolishing their homes and destroying their possessions. Many evictees are left without adequate shelter and sometimes with no possibility to care for themselves. Land that provided income and livelihood to entire families has been taken, in violation of the Angolan government's obligations under national as well as international law. Evictions documented by Human Rights Watch indicate that more than 3,000 houses were destroyed and approximately 500 cultivated land plots appropriated, affecting an estimated 30,000 people since 2002.

Gender Violence

Local human rights and women's organizations report an increase in domestic and sexual violence against women and girls in 2006, which extends to gender violence against girls in the school system. According to information provided by field-based NGOs, girls have been required to provide sexual favors in order to be approved to the subsequent grades, for example.

The Angolan government has not enacted specific legislation to protect women from domestic and sexual violence. It has also failed to provide adequate health care and emotional support services for the victims. Despite its obligations under the Convention on the Elimination of all forms of Discrimination against Women (CEDAW), the Angolan government has not developed or enacted comprehensive policies to address pervasive gender discrimination.

Key International Actors

In October 2006 the Angolan government called for international technical support for the electoral process, but the government has not indicated whether it intends to invite regional and international bodies to observe the elections.

An interim International Monetary Fund (IMF) report, issued in March 2006 subsequent to consultations between the IMF and the Angolan government, highlighted that the government had not fully responded to IMF recommendations for ensuring transparency in managing oil revenues, as contained in the "Oil Diagnostic Study" of 2004. Angola's increased ability to insulate itself from criticism by Western governments of its poor record of revenue governance was compounded by those governments' becoming more muted in such criticism in 2006.

China continues to make substantial financial investments in Angola, including loans of around US$5 billion in 2006. Angola in turn is one of China's largest oil suppliers. Chinese Prime Minister Wen Jiabao visited Luanda in June to push forward multifaceted cooperation between China and Angola. The presence of Chinese companies is very noticeable throughout the country, in particular construction companies working on the rehabilitation of major infrastructure such as railroads.

BURUNDI

Having come to power the previous year, in 2006 the government led by the National Council for the Defense of Democracy—Forces for the Defense of Democracy (CNDD-FDD) moved towards restoration of government services disrupted by more than a decade of civil war, but abuses by soldiers, police, and intelligence agents persisted, including torture and apparent extrajudicial executions. The August arrest by intelligence agents of opposition politicians accused of planning a coup, and government corruption allegations, threatened the country's fragile post-war stability. Other opposition figures and some journalists fled the country following the arrests, and at the beginning of September Second Vice President Alice Nzomukunda resigned, accusing the government of human rights violations and corruption.

In September the National Liberation Forces (FNL), the last active rebel group, signed a ceasefire with the government, but implementation of the agreement fell behind schedule, having missed a 30-day deadline for disarming and demobilizing some combatants and integrating others into government forces. FNL forces killed, raped and abused civilians in 2006, although there were fewer such incidents than in previous years. Since the ceasefire, combatants reportedly continued to rob and extort money and goods from civilians in and around the capital.

Human Rights Violations by Security Agents and Soldiers

In the months preceding the September 2006 ceasefire with the FNL, government soldiers and intelligence agents summarily executed some civilians and tortured others, most of whom were suspected of links with the FNL. Some 40 persons disappeared while in the custody of agents of the National Intelligence Service (SNR, the renamed Documentation Nationale), including around 30 who went missing in Muyinga province in July after being arrested by soldiers and interrogated by SNR agents. The Muyinga disappeared are presumed dead, based on local residents' reports of bodies and body parts in a nearby river. In past cases, SNR agents have acted with impunity but in a positive step the Muyinga prosecutor arrested two soldiers and the provincial head of the SNR in connection with the July disappearances. At this writing they were awaiting trial. The prosecutor reported receiving threats from the regional military commander after the arrests and soon after was moved to another province. Following investigation by a high-level judicial commission, another prosecutor issued a warrant for the arrest of the military commander, but execution of the warrant was interrupted, reportedly on orders from the executive branch.

Demobilization and Disarmament

Over 1,300 former members of the armed forces were demobilized in 2006, bringing the total since the program began in 2004 to over 21,000. However, the reintegration program for ex-combatants supported by the Multi-Country Demobilization and Reintegration Program had not yet begun in late 2006. In violation of international law, the government held dozens of children associated with the FNL, some in prison, some in a demobilization center. Lack of a clear government policy on the children hindered the delivery of international aid for them. Easy availability of weapons posed continuing risks to security. A series of apparently politically motivated grenade attacks killed 13 and wounded 122 persons in July and August.

Transitional Justice

An ad hoc commission, established under the terms of the Arusha peace accords of 2000, identified over 4,000 persons as "political prisoners" and in early 2006 ordered them freed. Most were convicted of crimes related to the violence following the assassination of President Melchior Ndadaye in 1993 or had been held for years without trial. Although the government said the releases were provisional and that the persons would face a proposed truth and reconciliation commission (TRC), some members of civil society brought a case before the Constitutional Court, arguing that the release violated the constitution. The court ruled in favor of the government.

Despite hopeful signs the previous year, efforts to deliver justice for crimes related to the civil war progressed little in 2006. In March 2005 the United Nations Security Council had recommended establishment of a TRC and a special chamber in the Burundian judicial system to try serious violations of international humanitarian law, both to be staffed by Burundian and international personnel.

After a first round of negotiations between Burundian officials and the UN Office of the Legal Advisor in March 2006, a second round planned for July did not take place, nor did consultations with the population about future judicial mechanisms, agreed to by both the UN and the government.

In general, Burundi's overburdened judicial system, hampered by limited resources, continues to function poorly. All prosecutors were replaced in March, many of them with young and inexperienced personnel.

Abuses against Government Critics and Opponents

Harassment and arrests of journalists and other members of civil society raised questions about the government's commitment to freedom of expression. In April 2006 parliamentarian Mathias Basabose called a press conference to discuss the political situation. Journalists who attended were detained for hours by police and some were beaten, and journalist Aloys Kabura was subsequently sentenced to five months in prison on charges of having insulted public authorities. In May Terence Nahimana, a former parliamentarian and head of the CIVIC peace group was detained, and at this writing was awaiting trial on charges of endangering state security, after he questioned delays in negotiations between the government and the FNL. In August Gabriel Rufyiri, president of the Organization for the Fight Against Corruption and Economic Embezzlement (OLUCOME), was imprisoned on charges of libel after denouncing corruption in the allocation of public tenders and government positions. He is awaiting trial.

Three of the eight opposition politicians arrested in August, including former Vice President Alphonse Marie Kadege, have filed complaints that they were tortured by the SNR. They have been transferred to a regular prison pending trial, and at this writing no action is known to have been taken to investigate their torture complaints. When the torture allegations first came to light Kadege's lawyer, Isidore Rufyikiri, asked the SNR to provide a medical report on the condition of his client, but in response he too was arrested by SNR agents and is still in prison.

Detention in Public Hospitals

With the health sector devastated by war and the government requiring citizens to pay the cost of health care, hospitals resorted to detaining indigent patients unable to pay their bills. During 2005 and 2006, hundreds who had completed treatment were prevented from leaving hospitals for this reason.

Rwandan Refugees Returned

In 2005, thousands of Rwandans sought asylum in Burundi, some fleeing a justice system in which they had no trust (see Rwanda chapter). Under pressure from Rwanda, Burundian authorities forcibly repatriated some 8,000 persons, violating international refugee law, but many of those repatriated as well as thousands of others crossed into Burundi later in 2005 and in 2006, making a total of some 20,000 persons seeking asylum by February 2006. In December 2005 Burundian authorities agreed to work with the Office of the United Nations High Commissioner for Refugees in determining whether the asylum claims were justified. Only some 3 percent of claimants were recognized as refugees. Discouraged by the low acceptance rate, asylum seekers boycotted the interview process meant to assess the validity of their claims, but eventually gave in when threatened with loss of food rations. In mid-2006 more than 13,000 of the total 20,000 Rwandans who had crossed into Burundi returned to Rwanda, some of them after credible complaints of intimidation by Burundian authorities. In November some 2,000 remained in Burundi, awaiting appeals of initially negative decisions.

Burundian Refugees Come Home

By November 2006 about 33,000 Burundian refugees returned from years in Tanzania, thousands fewer than in 2005, leaving roughly 400,000 Burundian refugees in Tanzania. Fear of food shortages and continued insecurity seem to account for the decline in returns. The return of refugees has multiplied conflicts over land ownership, flooding the justice system with land cases. A new land commission was announced in 2006 but has not yet begun work.

BURUNDI

A High Price To Pay

Detention of Poor Patients in Hospitals

HUMAN
RIGHTS
WATCH

Key International Actors

Donors pledged generous assistance to all aspects of Burundi's recovery from the war and have been reluctant to criticize the continuing human rights abuses.

On December 31, 2006, the United Nations Operation in Burundi (ONUB), a peacekeeping operation, was due to end operations, including its human rights section which played a particularly important role in denouncing and limiting abuses. ONUB will be replaced by an Integrated Office of the United Nations for Burundi (BINUB), focusing on security sector reform, institutional capacity building, and transitional justice. Along with Sierra Leone, Burundi will receive support from the new UN Peacebuilding Commission.

CHAD

In 2006, several separate but intertwined developments threatened the political stability of Chad: the effects of the influx of refugees and militias into eastern Chad due to the crisis in neighboring Darfur; efforts by Chadian rebel groups to oust President Idriss Déby's government; an acute fiscal crisis; and a protracted revenue dispute with the World Bank and international oil companies. The May 2006 presidential elections, won by Déby following a constitutional amendment permitting him to run for a third five-year term, contributed to domestic discontent.

Human rights abuses in eastern Chad worsened in the wake of Chadian government efforts to repel a Darfur-based Chadian insurgency. There were indiscriminate and targeted attacks by Sudanese militia on Chadian civilians left unprotected by the Chadian military, and Chadian officials were complicit in the forced recruitment of refugees, including children, by Sudanese rebel movements.

Domestic Political Instability

Chadian rebels hoping to oust Déby prior to the presidential elections scheduled for May 3 staged a failed attack on N'djamena on April 13, 2006. While civilians in N'djamena did not appear to have been specifically targeted or indiscriminately attacked by Chadian government or rebel forces, at least 291 people died in the fighting, including civilians, government soldiers and rebels.

An estimated 250 suspected Chadian rebels who were captured during the coup attempt were held at the Gendarmerie Nationale in N'djamena in inadequate detention facilities, and several detainees were subjected to torture or deliberately cruel treatment.

Government security forces have been guilty of violations including extrajudicial killings, torture, beatings, arbitrary arrests and rapes, which have been met by near total impunity. The government has placed limits on freedom of speech and the press; journalists who are critical of the government have been arrested on charges of defamation, and in some cases have been held in detention even after their charges have been dismissed.

Abuses Related to the Conflict in Darfur

Civilians in Chad have suffered human rights abuses as the conflict in Darfur has become increasingly cross-border and regional in scope. Chadian government security forces responded to the Chadian insurgency by redeploying troops away from long stretches of the Chad-Sudan border, leaving civilians exposed to raids by "Janjaweed" militias allied with the government of Sudan. Sudanese rebels, supported by a Chadian president desperate for allies among the many armed groups in the region, preyed upon Sudanese refugee camps in eastern Chad, forcibly recruiting civilians into their ranks.

Cross-border attacks on Chadian civilians by "Janjaweed" militias based in Darfur worsened in both scale and in intensity in 2006. In the first six months of the year, at least 50,000 Chadian civilians living in rural villages on or near the Sudan-Chad border were forced to leave their homes due to persistent attacks, which reached deeper into Chad than ever before.

In one of the worst known attacks, 118 civilians were killed on April 12-13 in the village of Djawara, approximately 70 kilometers west of the border with Sudan, simultaneous with the unsuccessful coup attempt by Chadian rebels. At the same time, Janjaweed militias reportedly killed 43 others in three villages in the Djawara vicinity: Gimeze, Singatao and Korkosanyo.

On March 17-19, a Sudanese rebel faction of the Sudan Liberation Army (SLA) lead by commander Khamis Abdullah and linked to the Chadian government forcibly recruited approximately 4,700 men and boys from UN-supervised refugee camps in Chad, many of them seized from schools. Many of the refugees were forcibly recruited and held in brutal conditions in training camps, and some individuals were exposed to torture and cruel treatment. Though most were eventually able to escape, some were integrated into rebel forces in Darfur.

Fiscal Crisis and Oil Revenue Disputes

Chad has been an oil producer since 2003, thanks in large part to financing provided by the World Bank, but the government ran a widening budget deficit in spite of high oil prices in 2006 and was often unable to pay salaries and pensions. In January, citing security needs, Déby pulled out of an unusual program designed by the World Bank to allocate the bulk of Chad's oil revenues to poverty-reduction projects, including priority sectors such as health, education and rural development. The World Bank froze the escrow account into which Chad's oil revenue flows, deepening the country's fiscal crisis.

President Déby has used much of the oil revenue that was supposed to help the poor on military hardware in a bid to bolster his regime against the threat of armed opposition groups. The government's lack of absorptive capacity and a high incidence of off-budget spending also raise concerns about corruption. The conflict with the World Bank was resolved in July with the government being accorded more discretion to spend oil income, but by August Chad was locked in another revenue dispute, this time with two foreign oil companies it accused of tax evasion.

The Trial of Hissène Habré

The long-standing campaign to bring Chad's former dictator Hissène Habré to justice reached a turning point in 2006 with Senegal's announcement that it would prosecute Habré on charges of torture and crimes against humanity. Habré, whose eight-year rule was marked by widespread atrocities, fled Chad following a 1990 *coup d'etat* and took refuge in Senegal, where he was indicted and placed under house arrest in February 2000. Senegal's highest court later ruled that Habré could not stand trial in Senegal for crimes allegedly committed elsewhere, leading the Senegalese government to ask the African Union (AU) to decide where Habré should be tried. In July, citing Senegal's obligation under the 1984 UN Convention against Torture to either prosecute or extradite alleged torturers who enter its territory, the AU asked Senegal to reverse itself and prosecute Habré.

Key International Actors

Sudan exacerbated political instability in Chad in 2006 by backing both Chadian rebel groups determined to topple Déby and "Janjaweed" militia groups responsible for depredation and death in the volatile east of the country. Chad and Sudan signed an agreement in February under which they promised not to interfere in each other's internal affairs and agreed not to host the opposition of one country in the other's territory; but Chad unilaterally severed relations with Sudan following the April 13 coup attempt, which it blamed on Khartoum. On August 28, the two countries signed an agreement in Khartoum almost identical to the one they signed in February but at year's end both governments continued to support rebel movements on either side of the border.

France has remained actively involved in Chadian affairs since Chad achieved independence from France in 1960, and has been a crucial ally to President Déby since he seized power in a 1990 *coup d'etat*. More than 1,000 French troops are permanently stationed in Chad under the terms of a military cooperation treaty.

During the April coup attempt, French Mirage fighter jets fired warning shots at an advancing rebel column. French jets made surveillance runs over rebel positions during the April coup attempt and once again during government combat operations in eastern Chad in late September; in both instances the French military shared intelligence on the disposition of the rebel forces with their Chadian counterparts.

CÔTE D'IVOIRE

The political and military impasse between the Ivorian government and northern-based New Forces rebels resulted in 2006 in continued human rights abuses by all sides, a further erosion of the rule of law, and yet another postponement of elections that were to have taken place in October. As the crisis continued through its fourth year the institutions that once provided benefits to ordinary Ivorians—the public education, healthcare, and judicial systems—deteriorated further, resulting in serious hardship particularly in the north, and in the entrenchment of impunity. There were persistent reports of extortion, torture, and arbitrary detentions by the Ivorian security forces, pro-government militias, and the New Forces.

Some 4,000 French troops continue to monitor a buffer zone between the government-controlled south and the rebel-controlled north. An 8,000-strong peace-keeping mission, the United Nations Operation in Côte d'Ivoire (UNOCI), established in April 2004, is deployed countrywide.

The problems underlying the Ivorian conflict—eligibility for citizenship of some three million immigrant residents, the exploitation of ethnicity for political gain, and competition for land resources between "indigenous" and immigrant communities in the volatile western region—remain unresolved.

Efforts to End the Political-Military Stalemate

Elections originally scheduled to be held in October 2005 were postponed for one year under Security Council Resolution 1633, which called for the appointment of a prime minister "acceptable to all" to lead the country to elections before October 31, 2006. Following his appointment in December 2005, Prime Minister Charles Konan Banny's efforts to implement the "roadmap" to elections soon deadlocked due to persistent squabbling between all sides about implementation of key areas. Citing the lack of political will as one of the principal reasons for the impasse, in September 2006 the International Working Group (IWG, composed of various government and international and regional organization representatives, and charged by the UN Security Council with monitoring implementation of its resolutions on Côte d'Ivoire) stated that holding elections in 2006 was impossible and called on the Security Council to establish a "new transitional framework."

In November the UN Security Council duly adopted resolution 1721 extending the mandates of President Laurent Gbagbo and Prime Minister Banny (in Gbagbo's case for a second time since the expiry of his constitutional mandate in October 2005). In the "new and final" 12-month transition period established by 1721, Banny is to wield enlarged powers to help lead the country to elections before October 31, 2007, including the ability to issue ordinances or decree laws, and to exert authority over the defense and security forces. Many political observers believe that Banny's increased powers are necessary if he is to successfully break deadlock in debates surrounding the sequencing and modalities of key prerequisites for elections, including disarmament of pro-government and rebel forces, identification of Ivorian citizens who hold no identity documents, and registration of eligible voters. However, as 2006 drew to a close Gbagbo and his ruling FPI party appeared determined to resist ceding any authority to Banny.

Abuses by State Security Forces

During 2006 the police, army, and the Security Operations Command Center (CECOS, an elite, rapid reaction force charged with fighting crime in the economic capital Abidjan) rounded up, illegally detained, and sometimes tortured scores of individuals, often with little or no explanation for the reasons behind their arrest and detention. In January, seven individuals, Malians and Ivorians of northern origin, were rounded up by CECOS, accused of being rebels, and tortured at the *Ecole de la Gendarmerie* in Abidjan; one of them was tortured to death, and the others were released. Police, army, and CECOS engaged in systematic and widespread extortion, racketeering, and intimidation of business people, street traders, and taxi drivers, among others. The majority of these violations appeared to target northerners, West African immigrants, and other perceived rebel sympathizers.

Abuses by Pro-Government Militias and Groups

Pro-government militias and groups regularly intimidated, harassed, and at times attacked and sexually abused perceived opposition party members and rebel

CÔTE D'IVOIRE

"Because they have the guns ... I'm left with nothing."

The Price of Continuing Impunity in Côte d'Ivoire

HUMAN
RIGHTS
WATCH

sympathizers. The groups most often associated with these attacks were the Young Patriots and a student group, the Students' Federation of Côte d'Ivoire (FESCI), which committed serious abuses, including torture, against students perceived to support the opposition. In January 2006 thousands of Young Patriots directed their violence against the international community, attacking vehicles and premises of the UN and international humanitarian agencies (resulting in heavy material losses); they also briefly took control of the national television station. The violence and associated incitement forced temporary retreat of some 400 UN and humanitarian personnel from parts of western Côte d'Ivoire. In April Young Patriots attacked a bus carrying UN staff in Abidjan's Yopougon neighborhood. In May militias trapped and stoned the cars of senior opposition figures, and in July they erected barricades, burned cars, and disrupted citizenship hearings in Abidjan and other places around the country after the head of Gbagbo's FPI party, Pascal Affi N'Guessan, declared that the hearings should be blocked by "all means necessary."

Abuses by the New Forces

New Forces rebels regularly extorted money and looted goods from civilians in areas under their control. Roadblocks erected by the New Forces were focal points for extortion and to a lesser extent rape and sexual harassment. New Forces police commissioners arbitrarily dispensed justice, acting in effect as investigator, prosecutor, judge, and jury for those individuals brought before them. As a result, numerous individuals accused of common crimes were arbitrarily detained in prisons, informal detention centers, and military camps for often extended periods. Some individuals are believed to be held incommunicado in secret detention centers.

Internal Displacement

An estimated 750,000 individuals have been displaced from their homes since the beginning of the crisis in 2002, causing dire economic hardship for thousands of families across Côte d'Ivoire. In 2006 continued human rights abuses contributed to ongoing displacement of individuals from their homes and prevented many individuals from returning, particularly in the volatile cocoa-producing regions of the west where the internally displaced are regularly subject to extortion and robbery by Ivorian security forces and pro-government militias.

Accountability

Throughout 2006 neither the government nor the rebel leadership took significant steps to discipline, investigate, or hold accountable those responsible for ongoing crimes, much less past atrocities during the 2002-2003 civil war. Despite repeated threats to impose sanctions on Ivorians who violate human rights, break the arms embargo, indulge in hate speech, or block the peace process, the UN Security Council has only imposed travel and economic sanctions against three mid-level individuals from the Young Patriots and New Forces. Subsequent attempts to impose sanctions against additional individuals (leaders in Gbagbo's FPI party) were stymied by China and Russia. The Security Council has yet to make public or discuss the findings of the Commission of Inquiry report into serious violations of human rights and international humanitarian law since September 2002, which was handed to the UN secretary-general in November 2004. The report contained a secret annex listing people accused of human rights abuses who could eventually face trial.

Although the Ivorian government lodged a declaration in September 2003 with the International Criminal Court (ICC) accepting the court's jurisdiction over serious crimes committed since September 2002, the prosecutor has not yet determined whether his office will open an investigation in Côte d'Ivoire. Although the ICC prosecutor indicated in early 2005 and then again in late 2005 that he intended to send a delegation to Côte d'Ivoire, this has yet to take place. The delay has been due in part to the Ivorian authorities.

Key International Actors

Although the African Union took the lead in attempting to resolve the Ivorian crisis in 2006, no one country or international body appeared willing or able to exert sufficient influence to move the two sides towards a settlement. Throughout the year, international actors attempting to mediate the conflict continued to be exasperated with the lack of political will by all parties, but particularly Ivorian government actors, to implement resolution 1633. Key international players were equally unprepared to take serious measures to combat impunity, although the UN Security Council on numerous occasions expressed serious concern at ongoing violations, and France, together with Denmark, Slovakia, and the United Kingdom, attempted to expand the list of individuals subject to sanctions. This reluctance appeared to embolden the perpetrators and fed into the intransigence of the Ivorian government and New Forces.

For their part, both sides to the conflict appear to have lost confidence in international actors that have in the past played an important role in attempting to achieve peaceful resolution of the crisis. In September 2006 Gbagbo's party called for the departure of all French troops and the dissolution of the IWG. In October the New Forces leadership pushed for replacement of AU mediator Thabo Mbeki, whom it accused of being too sympathetic to the government, resulting in Mbeki's withdrawal.

Although it failed to expand the list of persons subject to sanctions beyond three individuals, or take action to ensure accountability for current or past abuses, the UN Security Council in June 2006 authorized increasing UNOCI by some 1,025 additional military personnel.

DEMOCRATIC REPUBLIC OF CONGO

The Democratic Republic of Congo (DRC) held historic elections in 2006 bringing to power Joseph Kabila as the country's first democratically elected president in over 40 years. The electoral process marked the end of a three-year transitional government that followed five years of war. But both government soldiers and armed groups continued killing, raping, and otherwise injuring civilians, particularly in the east. Officials harassed, beat, and arrested journalists and members of civil society and the political opposition. Officials and a growing number of Congolese soldiers profited from the illegal exploitation of national resources, often in conjunction with foreign interests. The judicial system failed to keep up with recent cases and made little effort to address thousands of violations of international law stemming from the war. More than a dozen militia leaders credibly accused of war crimes were granted high rank in the national army.

Elections and Civil and Political Rights in the Pre-Election Period

Voting went relatively smoothly in presidential and legislative elections in July and in the presidential run-off vote in October 2006, but in the months before, security forces used excessive force against peaceful demonstrators of the political opposition and attacked journalists and human rights defenders. In July, when results were to be announced of the presidential contest, the Presidential Guard of incumbent President Joseph Kabila skirmished for three days with the security forces of Vice-President and presidential contender Jean-Pierre Bemba, leaving dozens dead and wounded.

The Haute Autorite des Medias, a government agency tasked with enforcing responsible journalistic behavior, denounced what it saw as a dangerous political environment and accused presidential candidates of using the media to demonize their opponents. It temporarily suspended political programs broadcast by numerous media outlets. Civil society groups reported an increase in ethnic hate speech, including against the Tutsi community and others thought to be linked to Rwanda.

Police officers used excessive force against members of the political opposition, including supporters of the Union for Democracy and Social Progress (UDPS) and other political parties. On March 10, for example, police broke up a peaceful UDPS demonstration in Kinshasa, beating demonstrators and briefly detaining 15 of them.

In April and May 2006 at least seven journalists were threatened or beaten in the course of their work. Another two were detained by security forces, and three others were arrested a few months earlier on charges of criminal defamation, an accusation frequently invoked by officials to restrict legitimate freedom of expression. On October 12 armed men destroyed essential broadcasting equipment at the office of Vice-President Bemba's private media station in Lubumbashi. On May 22, agents of the special police in plainclothes seized and destroyed broadcasting equipment of the Christian television station Radio Tele Message de Vie, which had broadcast a speech by Pastor Fernando Kutino critical of the political process.

On November 2, 2005, four armed men murdered journalist Franck Ngyke of the newspaper *La Reference Plus,* who was investigating a story potentially damaging to leading politicians, and his wife Hélène Mpaka. Two leading members of the nongovernmental organization Journaliste En Danger received death threats in January 2006 when they published results of their investigation into the murder. Impunity continues for the July 2005 murder of human rights defender Pascal Kabungulu. In one of the rare prosecutions of an attack on a human rights activist, men accused of the murder were brought to trial, but the proceeding stalled in 2006 following interference from political and military authorities.

Government Soldiers Attack Civilians

Government soldiers killed, raped, and tortured civilians in the provinces of Katanga, Ituri, and North and South Kivu. In central Katanga in late 2005 and early 2006 soldiers seeking to quell an insurgency rounded up hundreds of civilians suspected of being involved, and killed or tortured to death dozens of them. They gang raped scores of women alleged to have supported the rebel militia. More than 150,000 residents fled their homes in the zone of military operations, an area that became known as "the triangle of death." In a similar operation

DEMOCRATIC REPUBLIC OF CONGO

What Future?

Street Children in the Democratic Republic of Congo

HUMAN
RIGHTS
WATCH

against an insurgent militia group in Ituri in the first months of 2006, Congolese army soldiers deliberately killed more than 60 civilians accused of supporting the militia, raped women and girls, and burned homes, churches, schools, and health centers in communities suspected of harboring insurgents. In one incident on January 23, government soldiers fired into a church in the village of Nyata, killing seven people, including two babies.

Congolese government soldiers, including those from the old national army and combatants from disbanded rebel groups, are inadequately trained and disciplined. Paid little and sometimes at infrequent intervals, they subsist by exploiting the population.

Local and Foreign Armed Groups

Local armed groups opposed to the government continue to operate in eastern DRC killing, raping, and looting from civilians. In Ituri in 2006 combatants of the Revolutionary Movement of Congo (MRC) killed scores of civilians and arbitrarily detained and tortured others they believed opposed them. In Katanga, a local armed group known as the Mai Mai, commanded by Gédéon Kyungu Mutanga, killed, raped, and abused civilians. In some cases the Mai Mai publicly tortured victims before killing and cannibalizing them in ceremonies intended to terrorize the local population. In May Gédéon surrendered to United Nations peacekeepers in central Katanga. He was handed over to Congolese officials who have kept him in detention but not charged him with any crime.

Foreign armed groups from Rwanda and Uganda still account for pockets of insecurity, although they have been weakened by military operations against them over the past three years. Notably, remnants of Rwandan combatants from the Democratic Forces for the Liberation of Rwanda (FDLR) remain in Congo, though internal splits have contributed to weakening them militarily. They often prey upon civilians, using force to extort goods or money. In September 2005 combatants from the Ugandan rebel group the Lord's Resistance Army (LRA), moved across the border into Congo, heightening tensions between Uganda and the DRC. Following negotiations in September 2006 between the LRA and the Ugandan government many LRA combatants left Congo for assembly points in Sudan, though some of the leaders may have remained in Congo.

Delivering Justice

Despite national and international proclamations about the importance of accountability for past crimes, many persons suspected of violations of international human rights and humanitarian law continue in posts or were named to posts of national or local responsibility, including in the newly integrated army. For example, in July 2006 former MRC combatant Peter Karim, who in the previous month had killed a UN peacekeeper and taken seven others hostage, was named colonel in the Congolese army in an attempt to broker a peace deal.

In March the prosecutor of the International Criminal Court made his first arrest and initiated proceedings against Thomas Lubanga, a militia leader accused of ethnic massacres, torture, and rape in Ituri. The ICC charged Lubanga only with enlisting, conscripting, and using children as soldiers in armed conflict. No other militia leaders or soldiers from the Congolese, Ugandan, or Rwandan armies have been charged with any crimes despite their role in human rights abuses in Ituri, and there has been no action against those who armed and supported militia groups, which may extend to senior officials in Kinshasa, Kampala, and Kigali.

Congolese courts had some success in addressing a very few cases of war crimes. While such cases were few, they brought some hope to victims that perpetrators could be condemned for their crimes. In April 2006 a military court in Mbandaka found seven army officers guilty of mass rape of more than 100 women at Songo Mboyo in 2003, the first time rape was tried as a crime against humanity in Congo. In August 2006 militia leader Kahwa Mandro was found guilty by a military court in Ituri and sentenced to 20 years' imprisonment for war crimes committed in Ituri.

Illegal Exploitation of Resources

Armed groups, government officials and, increasingly, military officers continue to profit from the illegal exploitation of Congo's vast mineral wealth. At the Bavi mine in Ituri in late 2005 government soldiers used villagers as slave labor, forcing them under threat of death to dig for gold.

A Congolese parliamentary commission investigating contracts for the exploitation of resources signed during the war years reported many irregularities and recommended ending or renegotiating dozens of contracts. The commission's findings, which named senior Congolese politicians, were published in an unauthorized version on the internet in 2006. Hundreds of copies of the report destined for members of parliament disappeared and the report was not debated in parliament. Commission members received death threats. Some diplomats urged that the report's findings not be discussed before the elections because debate might trouble the electoral process.

Key International Actors

United Nations peacekeepers attempted to control sporadic violence in Kinshasa and parts of eastern Congo throughout 2006 and were reinforced briefly by troops from the UN peacekeeping mission in Burundi and others from the European Union. In September the UN Security Council extended the UN peacekeeping mission until February 2007.

Key international governments including the United States, France, the United Kingdom, and South Africa focused primarily on keeping the electoral process on track and largely ignored concerns about corruption, human rights abuses, or the need to disarm private militias.

ERITREA

Since 2001 the government of President Isayas Afewerki has carried out an unremitting attack on democratic institutions and civil society in Eritrea by arrest-ing political opponents, destroying the private press, and incarcerating anyone thought to challenge the government's policies. Almost no civil society institu-tions survive but the assault continued in 2006 on religious practitioners, military service evaders, and staff of international agencies.

A constitution approved by referendum in 1997 has never been implemented. No national elections have been held since independence in 1993. No opposition political party is allowed to exist. No independent labor organizations are permit-ted. Nongovernmental organizations have been systematically dismantled and their assets confiscated; those still operational are closely monitored. The govern-ment controls all access to information.

The border dispute with Ethiopia that led to the devastating 1998-2000 war con-tinues to fester, a circumstance the government uses to justify repressive poli-cies. Ethiopia has demanded "dialogue" with Eritrea about the border in the Badme sector (where the war began) before it will comply with the independent boundary commission decision on border demarcation, but Eritrea, having accepted the April 2002 commission decision, rejects further talks before full demarcation. In 2006 the threat of war resuming between Ethiopia and Eritrea waned temporarily, but Eritrea continued arming rebel forces in parts of Ethiopia. Eritrea denies reports by the United Nations and United States that in 2006 it sent arms and military trainers to assist the Islamic Courts movement that has taken power in Somalia's capital and is strongly opposed to Ethiopia.

Suppression of Political Dissent and Free Expression

Governing party and government leaders and journalists arrested in 2001 as alleged traitors, spies, and foreign agents continue to be held incommunicado in undisclosed prisons. In 2006 a website issued a detailed but unconfirmed report asserting that 31 prisoners, including the leaders and journalists, were being held in isolation cells in a remote jail built expressly to hold them. The report claimed that nine of the 31 had died in captivity (one by suicide).

Absent an independent press and with foreign broadcasts periodically jammed, Eritreans seldom have access to information other than from government-run media outlets. The government also takes pains to avoid information filtering out of the country. There are no domestic human rights groups; and no international human rights organizations are allowed to operate in Eritrea.

Freedom of Religion

The government closed all religious institutions in May 2002 except those affiliated with the Eritrean Orthodox, Roman Catholic, and Eritrean Evangelical (Lutheran) churches and with traditional Islam. Although the government claimed it would register other churches, it had not done so as of November 2006 despite having had applications pending for more than four years. Some religious groups have not applied, fearing that disclosing membership rolls will endanger their members. The government is reported to have confiscated all assets of the Kale Hiwot (Baptist) Church in 2006, including orphanages and kindergartens, even though the church had applied for registration.

In 2006 the government arrested members and clergy of religious groups that had not filed for registration, raiding homes during worship, including wedding ceremonies. Several hundred are in detention, and recantation of church membership is often imposed as a condition for release.

Jehovah's Witnesses have been especially mistreated. Some have been detained for more than a decade for refusing to participate in national military service even though the official penalty is a prison term of no more than three years (Eritrea does not provide for alternative service). Jehovah's Witnesses are precluded from government employment and from receiving many government services, including business licenses.

Religious persecution has not been limited to minority religions. The Orthodox patriarch was placed under house arrest in 2006 and his lifetime appointment was rescinded after he questioned the arrest of three reformist bishops. He had already been stripped of administrative functions in 2005 in favor of a government-appointed lay administrator.

Military Conscription Roundups and Arbitrary Arrest of Family Members

Eritrean men between the ages of 18 and 50 must perform two years of compulsory national service. In addition to military duties, conscripts are used for public works projects, but there have been repeated reports that they have also been used as laborers on military generals' personal properties. Spurred by the rigors and abuses of the national service system, draft-age Eritreans and high school seniors have been fleeing the country in the thousands over the past five years or have gone into hiding. Refugee agencies estimated that each month in 2006 about 700 Eritreans fled to Sudan and another 400 to Ethiopia.

Since mid-2005 the government has been arresting family members when a conscript fails to report for service. Relatives can buy their release by forfeiting the equivalent of about US$3,500, a huge penalty in a country where, according to the World Bank, the annual per capita income is around $220; there were reports in 2006 that the amount to be forfeited had doubled.

Prison Conditions, Torture, and Ill-Treatment

Ongoing political and religious persecution and the clampdown connected to evasion of national service have contributed to thousands of people being detained. Most of those arrested are held incommunicado indefinitely without formal charge or trial. Torture has frequently been reported. Detention facilities are severely overcrowded—because of the large number of arrests, less prominent prisoners (such as adherents to unregistered religious groups) are sometimes packed into cargo containers, located so as to be unbearably hot or cold. Other harsh detention conditions include starvation rations, lack of sanitation, and hard labor. Psychological abuse can include indefinite solitary confinement.

Information on abusive prison conditions emerges despite frequent warnings to prisoners who are released not to talk about their imprisonment or treatment.

Freedom of Movement

Eritreans must have exit visas to leave the country. These are rarely granted to men of military age. In 2006 government officials and members of sports teams defected when abroad, as others had in previous years. To discourage defections, the government reportedly began requiring the posting of bonds equivalent to US$7,000 for participants in sports teams traveling outside the country.

The government imposed internal travel restrictions in 2006 on all foreign nationals, requiring permits to travel beyond Asmara.

Key International Actors

An international peacekeeping force, the United Nations Mission in Ethiopia and Eritrea (UNMEE) maintains troops and observers in a 25-kilometer-wide buffer line between the two countries. The force and the zone are based on the agreement suspending the conflict. In late 2005 the Eritrean government placed severe restrictions on UNMEE's patrols and grounded helicopter surveillance flights, despite the UN Security Council's strong objections. In 2006 the government periodically arrested UNMEE local staff, releasing some after a short period but keeping others jailed. It declared five UNMEE personnel persona non grata, accusing them of aiding Eritrean nationals to escape to Ethiopia. Faced with Eritrean belligerency and Ethiopian obstinacy, the Security Council in 2006 reduced the UNMEE force by about a third, to 2,300.

Because of Eritrea's woeful human rights record, it receives little other than humanitarian assistance. In 2005-06, the government cut the number of free food aid recipients from 1.3 million to 70,000 to promote self-reliance through a "food-for-work" program. In August 2006 the European Commission, which had appropriated €6 million for assistance through UN agencies, stated that it would protest the selling of food aid without consultation and might ask Eritrea to repay €2.4 million for the cost of the food.

The United States withholds non-humanitarian assistance in part because Eritrea has refused to release or bring to trial US Embassy local employees arrested in 2001 and 2005. USAID operations ended in 2005 when the government demanded that the local USAID office close. In 2006 the United States maintained the partial denial of arms export licenses first imposed in 2005 because of the government's religious persecution. It also imposed travel restrictions on Eritrean diplomats and consular officials in retaliation for restrictions placed on US officials in Asmara.

In 2006 the Eritrean government expelled six Italian aid NGOs and confiscated their equipment and supplies; it also told Mercy Corps, Concern Worldwide, and the Agency for Co-operation and Research in Development (ACORD) to leave. Other aid NGOs, including two Italian ones, have been allowed to continue operations.

China's president promised economic assistance when President Isayas traveled to Beijing early in 2006, but no major initiatives have been announced at this writing.

ETHIOPIA

The Ethiopian government continued the heavy-handed suppression and punishment of any form of political dissent as reintroduced following the 2005 elections. While most international attention focused on events in Addis Ababa, security forces and civil officials continued campaigns of repression and brutality in many parts of the country. International donors protested human rights abuses but took no meaningful action.

Ethiopia has refused to accept in full the binding arbitration decision about the border with Eritrea (over which the two countries went to war in 1998-2000), despite its obligations under the armistice agreement of 2002 and numerous United Nations Security Council resolutions. The stalemate with Eritrea persisted in 2006, but Ethiopia was forced to shift focus to its longer and more porous border with Somalia. The Islamic Courts movement that is consolidating power in the south of Somalia has declared holy war against Ethiopia because of Ethiopia's incursions into Somali territory to provide support for the ineffective, UN-recognized Somali Transitional Federal Government. This change of power in southern Somalia allowed increased infiltration by fighters of a Somali irredentist group, the Ogaden National Liberation Front (ONLF), into Somali state in Ethiopia's southeast, armed with sophisticated weapons and equipment largely supplied by Eritrea.

Post-Election Political Repression

In June and November 2005 at least 10,000 people were arrested in Addis Ababa during protests against the results of the May elections. Most were detained for more than a month without judicial hearing and then released, but hundreds were transferred to a prison camp close to Addis Ababa. In March 2006 almost 400 of these prisoners were released; it is unclear how many others remain detained.

Following the November 2005 events the government arrested 76 opposition politicians, journalists, and civil society activists, including the newly elected mayor of Addis Ababa, Berhanu Nega, and newly elected parliamentarians. It accused them of treason and genocide, as well as intentionally using violence or unlawful means to change the "constitutional order," obstructing government operations, organizing armed violence, and impairing "the defensive power of the State." The treason and genocide charges are non-bailable, capital offenses, allowing the government to keep the defendants jailed for long periods before judicial verdict. The government brought similar charges against 55 other defendants, 35 in absentia, including five Voice of America reporters in the United States; the charges against the VOA reporters were later dismissed. In March 2006 the government arrested 32 others, including elected members of the Addis Ababa city council and a newspaper publisher, and accused them of the same crimes.

The treason trial began in May 2006, but recessed for two months in August and September, and presentation of the prosecution case was still in its early stages at this writing. Except for three civil society activists, the defendants refused to defend themselves, declaring the trial a sham.

Suppression of Free Expression and Attacks on Civil Society

Following the 2005 elections the government sharply reversed a liberalizing trend and subjected independent newspapers and their editors, publishers, and reporters to renewed harassment, intimidation, and criminal charges solely because of their reporting and editorials. In addition to the 18 journalists facing treason and genocide charges, journalists were convicted under the pre-1991 military government press law, which makes alleged defamation and the printing of "false" information criminal offenses.

Beginning in September 2006, security forces detained individuals caught with copies of a political manifesto by imprisoned Mayor Berhanu published in Uganda after the manuscript was smuggled out of prison. Also arrested were people found to have copies of an anonymous civil disobedience "calendar" containing pictures of the "treason" defendants and calls to non-violent action, such as boycotts of government-controlled businesses, to win their release. The government blocked access to internet blogs critical of its policies.

The government has long tried unsuccessfully to outlaw the Ethiopian Teachers Association, the largest independent membership organization in the country.

ETA's president was one of those charged with "treason" (but avoided imprisonment by being outside the country); the chair of ETA's Addis Ababa branch was also named as a defendant and is jailed. In September the government arrested two ETA officers after ETA had complained to the International Labour Organization of unlawful interference with its ability to represent its members.

Continuing Abuses in the Countryside

Authorities in Oromia state continued to use exaggerated concerns about armed insurgency and terrorism to justify the torture, imprisonment, and sustained harassment of their critics, including school children. In late 2005 and in 2006 federal and regional police in Oromia engaged in mass arrests, often in nighttime raids. Those arrested were informally accused of being supporters of the Oromo Liberation Front (OLF), a clandestine armed rebel group, but detainees were also accused of being supporters of the Oromo National Congress (ONC), a registered opposition political party that won seats in the 2005 elections. Most of those arrested were released after having been held for some weeks and forced to sign statements disavowing the ONC as a condition for release.

Local officials used precinct (*kebele*) "social courts" run by government-party appointees without legal training to detain farmers who voiced support for recognized opposition parties. Local and regional officials also subjected the rural population to intense levels of surveillance. Farmers who were deemed politically unreliable were denied fertilizer and other agricultural aids over which the government exercises monopoly control; they were also subject to imprisonment for debt or eviction from their farms (the government owns all land). In Amhara state, *kebele* officials played key roles in identifying known or presumed supporters of opposition parties and led federal police to these persons' homes at night, where the police beat and sometimes arrested them.

Abuses by the Armed Forces

The government has taken no meaningful action to address widespread atrocities committed by Ethiopian military forces in Gambella state, bordering Sudan. A government-sponsored commission of inquiry set up to investigate December 2003 violence in Gambella resulted in a whitewash. Although the scale of abuses in Gambella moderated in 2005-06, extrajudicial killings, rapes, beatings, and arbitrary arrests by armed forces personnel still occurred.

Reports of extrajudicial executions and torture also emerged from Somali state, but access to the region has been restricted by the military and by the ONLF insurgency, making these reports impossible to confirm.

Performance of the Judiciary

In high-profile cases, courts show little independence or concern for defendants' procedural rights. The two-month recess in the treason trial in August-September 2006, coupled with frequent shorter adjournments, ensured the defendants' prolonged detention. The trial judges put off addressing defense objections to evidence and ignored claims of serious mistreatment by prison authorities.

Although criminal courts in Ethiopia have some independence with respect to less prominent cases, the judiciary often acts only after unreasonably long delays, sometimes because of the courts' workloads, more often because of excessive judicial deference to bad faith prosecution requests for time to search for evidence of a crime.

Leaders of the traditional Oromo self-help organization Mecha Tulama, arrested in 2004 and accused of supporting the OLF and of organizing a grenade attack at Addis Ababa University, remained incarcerated as of late 2006, their trial yet to begin. Other Oromo detainees have been held for eight years without judicial resolution. Fourteen years after the overthrow of the former military government (the Derg), more than a thousand of its former officials still remain jailed awaiting trial.

Human Rights Defenders

Ethiopia has only one nationwide human rights organization, the Ethiopian Human Rights Council (EHRCO). Government officials routinely accuse the organization of working to advance an anti-government political agenda and its staff is subjected to harassment and intimidation. One investigator was charged in absentia in the treason trial. While EHRCO was not forced to close, it was far less active in 2006.

The Oromo-focused Human Rights League, having been allowed to register in 2005 shortly before the elections after years of litigation, remains inactive.

Key International Actors

International criticism of government repression, while robust, resulted in no significant actions. Ethiopia is considered an essential partner of the United States and its allies in their "war on terror," all the more so after the Islamic Courts' consolidation of power in Somalia. The United States expressed dismay about post-election repression, but Ethiopia remained the US's biggest sub-Saharan-Africa aid beneficiary. In December 2005 the World Bank and the United Kingdom announced they would withhold direct budgetary support, but compensated in 2006 with even larger sums to local governments for health, water, rural development, and education programs. Those local governments are effectively controlled by the central government.

Two European Union diplomats were expelled from Ethiopia on October 20, 2006, after being caught attempting to cross into Kenya with two Ethiopian nationals. One of those detained with the EU diplomats was human rights lawyer Yalemzewd Bekele, who was working for the European Commission in Ethiopia. Bekele was arrested but subsequently released without charge.

For information on the international peacekeeping force, the United Nations Mission in Ethiopia and Eritrea (UNMEE), see the chapter on Eritrea.

GUINEA

In 2006 Guinea traversed a time of uncertainty tied to economic turmoil and impending political transition. Guinea's economy is very poor, with inflation currently running at 40 percent, placing basic foodstuffs and other essential commodities out of the reach of many Guineans. Guinea's president, Lansana Conté, age 72, is rumored to be gravely ill and made two trips to Switzerland for medical care. Guinea's military is thought to be deeply divided along both generational and ethnic lines. Many observers believe that a military takeover is inevitable in the likely event that President Conté does not finish out his term, set to expire in 2010. In 2006 Guinea's two largest trade unions emerged as significant players in Guinea's political future by organizing two nationwide strikes that effectively paralyzed the country for several weeks.

During 2006 Guinean citizens were subjected to numerous forms of brutality, including excessive use of force on unarmed demonstrators, torture, assault, and theft by the security forces responsible for protecting them. Throughout 2006 Guinean police regularly subjected criminal suspects to torture and ill-treatment to extract confessions. Once individuals are transferred from police custody to prison to await trial, many are left to languish for years in cramped cells where they face hunger, disease, and sometimes death. In addition, Guinean security forces responded to strikes organized to protest worsening economic conditions with inappropriate and excessive use of force against unarmed demonstrators. The government has largely failed to tackle the impunity that often attaches to serious human rights abuses, particularly abuses committed by security forces.

As Guinea slides deeper and deeper into economic and political chaos, Guinean civil society, once thought to be a weak voice for political change, has increasingly demonstrated its capacity to organize on a wide scale to press for political and economic reforms. In March 2006, the majority of prominent Guinean civil society organizations and opposition parties united to organize a four-day "national consultation" in an effort to press the government for major political reforms. The event was significant in that despite Guinea's repressive history, the conference was held without incidents of government violence or harassment.

Excessive Use of Force against Unarmed Demonstrators

In 2006, as in previous years, excessive use of force against unarmed demonstrators constituted a significant impediment to the ability of Guinean citizens to exercise their rights to freedom of speech and of assembly. During 2006 Guinean security forces were responsible for at least two such incidents during which scores of unarmed demonstrators were wounded by gunshot, beaten, and arbitrarily arrested. The most serious incident occurred in June 2006 when Guinean security forces responded to a strike to protest increases in basic commodity prices with excessive and inappropriate use of force, killing at least 11 demonstrators. In the course of the crackdown, police and other security forces were involved in rape, assault, and theft, victimizing not only the protesters, but many others including women, children, and elderly men who had not participated in the protests. Though investigations are reportedly underway, no one has yet been brought to justice for these crimes. Security forces responsible for previous incidents remain similarly unaccountable.

Police Torture

Torture and ill-treatment of criminal suspects, including children, during police custody is routine. During police interrogation, individuals are frequently bound with cords, beaten, burned with cigarettes, and cut with razor blades until they agree to confess to the crime of which they are accused. Many of the torture techniques used during police interrogation date back to the brutal and repressive dictatorship under Guinea's first president, Sékou Touré (1958-1984). Impunity from prosecution remains the biggest single obstacle to ending these abuses.

Prolonged Pretrial Detention

In 2006, as in previous years, prolonged pre-trial detention was a serious human rights issue. In Guinea's largest prison in central Conakry, 70 to 80 percent of incarcerated individuals are untried. Many of these individuals, including children, have spent more than two years without trial. Some have spent more than four years in pre-trial detention. In some cases individuals have spent more time awaiting trial than the maximum sentence for the crime of which they are accused. In violation of international standards, prison officials often fail to sepa-

GUINEA

"The Perverse Side of Things"

Torture, Inadequate Detention Conditions, and Excessive
Use of Force by Guinean Security Forces

HUMAN
RIGHTS
WATCH

rate convicted and untried prisoners, as well as child and adult detainees. In late 2006 the Guinean Ministry of Justice held a conference attended by Guinean judges to discuss ways to address the problem. The Embassy of the United States of America also provided funding to a local prisoner's advocacy organization to help address the problem.

Rule of Law

The judicial system in Guinea is plagued with striking deficiencies, including lack of independence of the judicial branch from the executive, inadequate resources, corrupt practices, inadequate training for magistrates and other judicial authorities, and insufficient numbers of attorneys, especially those specializing in criminal law. As a result of corruption, individuals are regularly denied access to justice due to their inability to pay bribes to judges, magistrates, and other officials working in the judicial and penal sectors.

Inadequate Detention Conditions

Detention conditions throughout Guinea are completely inadequate. Severe overcrowding is the most basic and most chronic problem. Guinea's largest prison has in recent years housed close to 1,500 prisoners in a facility designed for 240-300 individuals. Food and nutrition are grossly insufficient, and several deaths due to malnutrition occurred in 2006, though they have decreased from previous years. Many prison guards serve on a "volunteer" basis with no pay from the government, and consequently resort to extorting money from prisoners, or selling them drugs, to make money.

Key International Actors

Guinea has a proud tradition of defiance of the international community, dating back to its independence from France in 1958, which has historically resulted in a resistance to outside influences. In recent years, possibly owing to the continuing economic crisis, the government has appeared increasingly open to reforms relating to good governance and human rights. However, the willingness of Guinea's multilateral and bilateral donors to use this opening to seek improvements in the human rights situation in Guinea has been mixed. After a brutal crackdown on demonstrators in June 2006, the African Union Commission Chairperson, the Presidency of the European Union (EU), and the United Nations Secretary-General all issued statements expressing concern at the violence and deaths involved. The United States, however, failed to issue such a public statement. In 2004, the EU invoked Article 96 of the Cotonou Agreement to suspend development assistance to Guinea due to human rights concerns. In the course of subsequent consultations with the EU, the Government of Guinea undertook to implement electoral reforms and allow for private ownership of television and radio stations, among other steps. Though Guinea's success in implementing these reforms has varied, in 2006 the first licenses for privately owned radio stations were granted and the first stations began transmitting. Partly in response to these and other reforms, the European Commissioner for Development and Humanitarian Aid in October 2006 signaled that the EU could soon unblock development assistance. Development assistance from major bilateral donors such as the United States has not been similarly conditioned.

A more consistent approach on the part of international actors to helping Guinea tackle its human rights problems, including impunity, and, in particular, focused efforts by key bilateral donors such as France and the United States, would help to curb the most egregious abuses. Increasing competition for Guinea's vast natural resources, including bauxite, gold, diamonds, iron, and, in future years, oil, may present one obstacle to such an approach in the years to come.

LIBERIA

Since general elections in 2005 and the January 2006 inauguration of President Ellen Johnson-Sirleaf, Liberia has made tangible progress in transitioning from a near-failed state to a democratic state governed by the rule of law. The elections followed a 2003 peace agreement and the deployment of 15,000 United Nations Mission in Liberia (UNMIL) peacekeepers. From 1989 to 2003 Liberia had been engulfed in two armed conflicts characterized by egregious human rights violations.

As 2006 ended, solid grounds for optimism existed including a stated and demonstrated commitment on the part of government to fight corruption; progress in the retraining and restructuring of the police and army; increased control of the country's natural resources; the return of some 40,000 civilians who had fled during the war; the ability of free media and civil society to function after years of persecution; and the coming into operation of a Truth and Reconciliation Commission empowered to recommend prosecution for the worst offenders. However, the human rights situation remained precarious as a result of rising criminal acts, and civil disturbances by former combatants, met by inadequate policing; deficiencies within the judicial system; financial shortfalls for programs to train demobilized combatants; and continued regional instability, most notably in neighboring Côte d'Ivoire.

Ongoing Insecurity and Abuses in Law Enforcement

Despite the deployment of UN peacekeepers and some 1,000 civilian police, violent crime increased including hijacking, armed robbery, and murder. This was indicative of weaknesses in the Liberian National Police, including very poor logistic and transport facilities and low deployment outside the capital. UN police increased patrols in high crime areas but, in a worrying development, the justice minister called on Liberians to form vigilante groups. Numerous individuals accused of common crimes were beaten to death by mobs.

Several violent demonstrations took place by demobilized personnel from the Armed Forces of Liberia, Anti-Terrorist Unit, and Special Security Service, demanding severance benefits.

The newly trained Liberian police continued to engage in unprofessional and sometimes criminal behavior including extortion, excessive use of force, and sexual harassment. Concerns remain regarding the vetting of past human rights abusers in a 2004-05 screening and selection exercise administered by UNMIL. Problems with the process included lack of clear criteria for the elimination of potential human rights abusers, failure to allocate adequate human resources to conduct thorough and systematic background checks on applicants, and inadequate involvement of Liberian human rights groups and the general population.

Performance of the Judiciary

The judiciary remains dysfunctional, making justice not accessible to the vast majority of Liberians. Some improvements to the judicial infrastructure were evident including the renovation and reconstruction of several court houses and detention facilities. However, the system has few prosecutors and public defenders, few resources, and suffers from absenteeism by judges and other staff. Reports of unprofessional and corrupt practices by judicial staff were frequent, including releasing suspects charged with criminal offenses on payment of a bribe, or soliciting money to stop cases from proceeding to a higher court. The circuit courts of five counties did not operate at all. Magistrate and local tribal courts often try, sentence, fine, and imprison people for criminal and civil matters that are outside their jurisdiction. More than 90 percent of the prison population is being held in prolonged pre-trial detention.

Prisons and detention centers operate far below international standards, with overcrowded cells and lack of food and water for detainees.

Harmful Traditional Practices

Numerous serious abuses resulting from harmful traditional practices also occurred in 2006. These included the killing of alleged witches; killing of people for their refusal to be inducted into a secret society; and deaths and maimings associated with traditional justice practices. One such practice by local authorities requires alleged offenders to drink the poisonous sap of the local "sassy-wood" tree in order to prove their guilt or innocence. These local practices were often characterized by a lack of due process standards, extortion, elicitation of statements under torture, physical and sexual assault, and extrajudicial killings.

Women's and Children's Rights

The Rape Amendment Act, which stipulates heavier penalties for the most serious cases, came into force in January 2006. However, a general reluctance to prosecute rape cases persists, and rape and other forms of sexual assault and exploitation remain very serious problems for Liberian women and girls, including young girls.

From January through November UNMIL investigated 28 cases of sexual exploitation and abuse by UNMIL personnel against Liberia civilians, including 10 cases involving minors. At this writing none of the investigations had been concluded.

Poor labor conditions on rubber plantations including the use of child labor were reported. Substandard conditions in Liberian orphanages led the Ministry of Health and Social Welfare to announce the intended closure of 69 facilities in March 2006. Unfortunately, this was not properly implemented by government authorities and resulted in few actual closures.

Corruption

Corruption involving public monies has long been endemic, and is widely recognized as having contributed to the country's political instability and to robbing the population of funds needed to provide vital services such as education, water, and healthcare. Throughout 2006 the Liberian government and the international community took concrete steps to reduce corruption and improve economic governance. President Johnson-Sirleaf dismissed numerous senior government officials for corrupt practices and ordered an evaluation of all government contracts. In August the House of Representatives ratified the UN Convention against Corruption and the African Union Convention on Preventing and Combating Corruption. The Governance Reform Commission elaborated a code of conduct calling for public servants to declare their income, assets, and liabilities. Also in 2006 the Governance and Economic Management Assistance Program (GEMAP), a three-year anti-corruption plan drafted and imposed by key donors the previous year as a condition for development aid, came into operation. It empowers foreign financial experts to co-sign all financial matters within the National Bank of Liberia, the Finance Ministry, and several revenue generating agencies.

Accountability and the Truth and Reconciliation Commission

In February 2006 the Truth and Reconciliation Commission (TRC) was inaugurated. In October, after months of preparation and training, some 190 statement-takers began to obtain testimonies for use in formal hearings to begin in early 2007. The TRC is mandated to investigate gross human rights violations and economic crimes that occurred between January 1979 and October 14, 2003, and can recommend amnesty in cases not involving serious violations of international humanitarian law, and prosecution for the most serious cases. The TRC requested some US$10 million, but deficits in donor pledges and funds remained.

Civil society made increased calls for a mechanism to hold accountable perpetrators of war crimes and crimes against humanity in Liberia's wars. The surrender of former Liberian President Charles Taylor to the Special Court for Sierra Leone in March 2006 appeared to foster these calls. Debate occurred on whether accountability should take place during or after the completion of the TRC's work; whether TRC commissioners would act on their power to recommend individuals for prosecution; and whether the Liberian judicial system would be able and willing to try these crimes.

Liberian Army

The United States has taken the lead in recruiting and training a new Liberian army of some 2,000 soldiers. During 2006 the first 560 recruits began training after being selected from a pool of more than 7,000. The restructuring exercise is running months behind schedule, with the first fully trained battalion expected to be operational in 2008. However, the US contractor DynCorp's detailed plan to screen recruits for past human rights abuse appears to have been successfully implemented.

Disarmament of Former Combatants

More than 101,000 individuals were disarmed and demobilized in 2003-05. The disarmament exercise was criticized for not having strict admittance criteria and for including individuals who were not real combatants. The excessive numbers of individuals taking part in the disarmament exercise contributed to the shortfall of funds from international donors to support education and skills training pro-grams. At this writing some 30,000 ex-combatants have yet to enter reintegration programs. The dearth of training and education programs was believed to have contributed to the rise in violent crime and the recruitment of Liberian ex-combat-ants, including children, by the Ivorian government and rebel forces.

Key International Actors

Throughout 2006 Liberia's international partners' top priority was to establish mechanisms to fight corruption and ensure proper management of Liberia's natu-ral resources. Other rule of law issues, including the imperative to rebuild Liberia's judicial system and the pursuit of justice for past atrocities, received less attention and funding.

After considerable pressure from the European Union and the United States, and a courageous request from President Johnson-Sirleaf, the Nigerian government surrendered former president Charles Taylor to Liberia. He was then transferred to the Special Court for Sierra Leone, which had indicted him for war crimes and crimes against humanity connected to his support for rebels in Sierra Leone. The move was viewed as a positive step for stability in West Africa.

As Liberia's leading bilateral donor, the United States committed $270 million in 2006 to support democratization and reconstruction efforts, bringing its total aid funding to some $1.16 billion for fiscal years 2004-06. Since establishing peace, Liberia's government has received support from the European Commission including almost €100 million for peace support operations and post-conflict rehabilitation and institution building. China's role in Liberia's development and reconstruction is also expanding.

Following Liberia's progress in regaining control over the exploitation of timber, the UN Security Council in June 2006 lifted a UN ban on timber exports. It left in place a similar ban on diamond exports until the Kimberly Certificate of Origin regime is functioning. The UN Security Council also relaxed a 2001 ban on the sale of arms to Liberia.

NIGERIA

Since the end of military rule in 1999 Nigeria has enjoyed the longest stretch of uninterrupted civilian government in its history as a nation. While this period has seen some improvements in respect for civil and political rights, government actors including the police, military, and elected officials continued to commit serious and persistent abuses against Nigerian citizens. The lack of political will to improve the country's poor human rights situation and ensure accountability for abuses not only threatens to undermine the fragile gains made since the end of military rule but also poses daunting challenges to holding credible and violence-free elections in 2007.

As in previous years, grisly episodes of intercommunal violence were a regular occurrence in 2006. The government has done nothing to put a halt to one key factor that feeds some of this violence: unconstitutional policies that subject millions of Nigerians to discrimination and disadvantage because they are not deemed ethnic "indigenes" of the communities they live in. The police and military have not only failed to prevent intercommunal violence but have been implicated in countless acts of criminal violence themselves.

Processes meant to bring accountability continued to be crippled by corruption, inefficiency, political influence, and an underlying culture of impunity; those responsible for Nigeria's worst abuses have evaded meaningful sanction. Meanwhile thousands of prisoners accused of common crimes remained in punitively lengthy pre-trial detention, in some cases for more than a decade. However, in 2006 the authorities announced plans to free inmates who have been in prison for longer than the sentences they would face if convicted. Despite limited advances made in the federal government's "war on corruption," graft remains rampant, particularly at the state and local levels, and is largely responsible for the government's failure to meet its responsibility to provide for basic social and economic rights.

Intercommunal Violence

Since 1999 more than 10,000 Nigerians have died in violent clashes along intercommunal lines, and 2006 saw dozens of such incidents erupt around the coun-

NIGERIA

"They Do Not Own This Place"

Government Discrimination Against
"Non-Indigenes" in Nigeria

HUMAN
RIGHTS
WATCH

try. In February more than 100 people were killed and thousands displaced in a wave of interconnected religious riots that began in the northeastern city of Maiduguri and spread to Bauchi and Anambra states. The underlying causes of Nigeria's chronic intercommunal strife—including ethnic and religious divisions and competition for scarce economic opportunities—often overlap with and exacerbate one another.

In some cases, unscrupulous political leaders have manipulated intercommunal tensions or have actively sponsored violence to advance their political positions. In August 2006, for example, clashes by rival political gangs in the Rivers state town of Bodo left more than 15 people dead and terrorized the community. The state's commissioner for finance and a leading member of the state legislature were briefly arrested in connection with that incident. There is widespread concern that the run-up to nationwide polls slated for April 2007 will be marred by similar incidents, which were a defining feature of elections held in 2003 and 2004.

Abuses by Security Forces

Nigeria's police and other security forces continued to be implicated in widespread acts of torture, ill-treatment, extrajudicial killing, arbitrary arrest, and property destruction. For example, in August 2006 the bodies of 12 criminal suspects who had been in police custody were found dumped beside a road in the town of Umuahia in Abia state. Later that month, Nigerian army personnel burned to the ground a poor community on the outskirts of Port Harcourt in reprisal for the murder of an army sergeant earlier that day.

Impunity from prosecution remains the biggest single obstacle to ending abuses such as these. President Olusegun Obasanjo's public acknowledgement in August 2005 that Nigerian police officers have committed murder and torture did not translate during 2006 into any significant effort to hold members of the security forces accountable for past or ongoing crimes, in which their involvement is alleged.

Child Labor and Child Trafficking

Child labor, such as exploitation of children as domestics and as laborers in quarries, as well as child trafficking within Nigeria and across borders, remained serious problems during 2006. In the last several years, hundreds of trafficked children from Nigeria as well as from Benin, Cameroon, Togo and other African countries have been rescued by Nigerian authorities. In July 2006 a multilateral accord against the trafficking of women and children was signed in Abuja by 26 West and Central African countries.

Violence and Poverty in the Niger Delta

The Niger Delta region is awash with arms, many of which are in the hands of criminal gangs and militant groups that claim to be fighting for greater local control of the region's oil wealth. Government security operations aimed at flushing out the militants resulted in numerous arbitrary arrests and other abuses.

Much of the insecurity that plagues the Delta is directly related to disastrous failures of governance at all levels. Despite massive budget increases due to rising oil prices, government at the federal, state, and local level has made little effort to combat the poverty and environmental degradation that lie at the heart of political discontent in the region. Far from seeking to defuse violence where it occurs, many regional political figures have been directly implicated in sponsoring it. The impunity attached to such violence is starkly illustrated by the case of the chairman of Etche local government in Rivers state, who has faced no formal sanction since allegedly shooting three of his constituents during a protest in 2006, killing one young man and seriously wounding another.

Human Rights Concerns in the Context of Sharia

Since 2000 Sharia (Islamic law) has been extended to give Sharia courts jurisdiction over criminal cases in 12 of Nigeria's 36 states. Sharia has provisions for sentences that amount to cruel, inhuman and degrading treatment, including death sentences, amputations and floggings. No executions or amputations have taken place since early 2002 and capital sentences have generally been thrown out on appeal, but Sharia courts continue to hand down death sentences.

Many trials in Sharia courts fail to conform to international standards and do not respect due process even as defined by Sharia legislation: defendants rarely have access to a lawyer, are not informed about their rights, and judges are often poorly trained. The manner in which Sharia is applied discriminates against women, particularly in adultery cases where standards of evidence differ based on the sex of the accused.

Freedom of Expression and Attacks on Civil Society

Nigerian civil society and the country's independent press are generally free to criticize the federal government and its policies, and a vibrant public debate exists around such issues. However, in 2006 security forces harassed and detained activists and journalists on several occasions for discussing issues of particular sensitivity. In July police in Abuja broke up a meeting of civil society groups convened to discuss the human rights record of the Obasanjo administration. As in other such cases, the police made use of the repressive Public Order Act, a widely denounced relic of military rule. In June two journalists were detained and charged with sedition in connection with a news report questioning the cost and age of a recently acquired presidential jet.

Many local media outlets enjoy considerably less freedom than their more prominent national counterparts. State-level newspapers and independent radio stations in many areas reported numerous incidents of harassment in 2006. Newspaper editors and journalists in Rivers state, for example, reported that staff have been repeatedly harassed by security forces and threatened with criminal prosecution in response to news items deemed overly critical of state government policies and actions.

In June the head of the federal government's National Human Rights Commission was summarily sacked in reprisal for his public criticism of various government actions, a move that threatens to destroy the legitimacy and value of the institution by muzzling it.

Key International Actors

President Obasanjo has enjoyed a generally positive image in the eyes of foreign governments. Nigeria has enhanced its regional and international significance through the leading role played by Obasanjo in various diplomatic initiatives including efforts to broker peace in Darfur. This, combined with the country's economic significance as a major oil producer, perpetuates an unwillingness on the part of key governments— notably the United Kingdom and the United States— and intergovernmental organizations such as the African Union and the Commonwealth to exert meaningful pressure on Nigeria over its human rights record.

Multinational oil companies operating in the Niger Delta have become drawn into the region's conflicts in a way that has made the companies central parties to them. There are real constraints on the companies' ability to extricate themselves from this situation, but they have often failed to meet their basic responsibilities towards the communities around them. Companies have generally not responded effectively to human rights abuses committed by security forces assigned to protect their operations. They have also failed to curb environmentally harmful practices such as gas flaring, or to eliminate the occurrence of oil spills caused by aging and poorly maintained infrastructure.

RWANDA

As in previous years, Rwandan authorities in 2006 tightly controlled the country's political space. Some local elections were marred by accusations of fraud or other unfair practices. Although many citizens enjoyed relative security, hundreds of others were illegally detained and some of them physically abused by police or members of the Local Defense Forces. Rwanda drew some positive comment by a peer review team of the New Economic Partnership for Africa (NEPAD) but was criticized for restricting political space and not recognizing diversity.

Gacaca courts, meant to combine customary conflict resolution mechanisms with criminal justice for the 1994 genocide, began operating throughout Rwanda in 2006, but with some courts failing to observe procedural rules. In conventional courts several noteworthy cases, one involving former President Pasteur Bizimungu, failed to meet international fair trial standards. In another case, a priest was sentenced to 12 years in prison for minimizing the genocide.

Gacaca Jurisdictions

In July 2006 gacaca jurisdictions, previously engaged in gathering information about the genocide, began trials nationwide. Establishment of appeals courts lagged behind, limiting the possibility of recourse for those who felt wrongly judged. Among the estimated 700,000 persons accused, more than 47,000 hold local administrative posts and 45,000 are themselves gacaca judges. Officials aim to have completed all trials by 2007, and some courts spend only a few hours hearing each case. Some 50,000 persons confessed their crimes in hopes of receiving reduced sentences, but hundreds of them saw their confessions rejected as untruthful or incomplete and were refused any reduction in sentences, the maximum being 30 years. Prison populations seemed likely to increase rather than decrease, as had been intended when the gacaca jurisdictions were established.

The jurisdictions supposedly draw legitimacy from popular participation, but many Rwandans do not trust them and either boycott the sessions or attend under duress. Courts jailed dozens of witnesses and defendants for refusing to speak completely or truthfully, in some cases without following due process to determine their actual guilt. In some cases judges used their power to settle personal or political scores: for example, a panel of judges jailed journalist Jean-Leonard Rugambage for 11 months on apparently false charges after he published an article on corruption in gacaca jurisdictions. In this case, as in some others where judges acted inappropriately, gacaca officials intervened and held that arrest procedures had been illegal. Because gacaca courts do not hear accusations of crimes committed by soldiers of the Rwandan Patriotic Front (RPF), now the dominant political force in Rwanda, the system appears to deliver one-sided justice.

In 2005 nearly 20,000 Rwandans fled to Burundi and still many others fled in 2006, many because they feared action by gacaca jurisdictions. In one exceptional case, a Tutsi man said he fled because a local administrator pressed him to make a false genocide accusation. Very few received asylum in Burundi, and all except some 5,000 had returned to Rwanda by October 2006.

Confronting Divisionism and Genocidal Ideology

In a continuing campaign against "divisionism" and "genocidal ideology," authorities compiled a list of hundreds of persons suspected of such ideas. Banned by the constitution, "divisionism" is vaguely and broadly defined in a 2001 law. A priest was sentenced to 12 years' imprisonment in September 2006 for minimizing the genocide. In a sermon he had suggested it was wrong to call persons who participated in genocide "dogs." During the trial, the prosecutor allegedly said that those convicted of genocide were not human and should properly be called "dogs."

Performance of the Judiciary and Fair Trial Concerns

From 2002 to 2004 Rwandan courts came to a virtual standstill as reforms meant to increase their efficiency were implemented. In the first months of 2006 judicial activity was again stalled because extensive administrative reforms, implemented January 1, meant that territorial divisions no longer corresponded to jurisdictions. When the courts resumed work in 2006 more than 12,000 penal cases were pending, with some 70,000 of the most serious cases of genocide also scheduled to be tried in the conventional courts.

In January 2006 the Supreme Court heard the appeal of former President Pasteur Bizimungu, former minister Charles Ntakirutinka, and six co-accused convicted in a 2004 trial. After two years in detention, Bizimungu and Ntakirutinka had been tried for creating a criminal association, spreading rumors to incite rebellion, and plotting to overthrow the government; the six co-accused were charged with creating a criminal association. The conduct and outcome of the trial had raised issues of fairness: one prosecution witness told the court that he had been beaten by police and detained for two years to force him to testify, and one of the co-accused was also threatened in an effort to get him to testify falsely against the others; the court refused to allow the defendants and their counsel to fully cross-examine witnesses; and the prosecution relied largely on the testimony of a single witness who repeatedly contradicted himself and was contested by seven defense witnesses. In 2004 the court had sentenced Bizimungu to 15 years in prison, Ntakirutinka to 10 years, and the others to five years each. In its January 2006 decision the Supreme Court reversed the conviction of the six co-accused but maintained the convictions and sentences of Bizimungu and Ntakirutinka.

In another case based largely on the testimony of a single witness, former Head of External Security Col. Patrick Karegeya was convicted of desertion and insubordination, stripped of his rank, and sentenced to 20 months in military prison. Karegeya had been detained without charge for five months in 2005.

In 2006 a US District Court rejected confessions of three Rwandans accused of murdering US citizens at Bwindi, Uganda, in 1999. The judge held that the confessions had been coerced by Rwandan police and intelligence agents through "unconscionable conditions and abuse" while they held the accused at Kami military camp. The US Justice Department appeared unlikely to pursue the case, leaving in question the fate of the three who had been drugged and brought to the US in 2003 by US officials in an exercise of extraterritoriality.

Freedom of Expression and Pressure on Civil Society

After harsh criticism of the press by high officials, including President Paul Kagame, in the early months of 2006 several journalists were followed by unidentified men, threatened by phone, or detained for official questioning. One journalist was beaten by armed men who told him to warn a colleague that they wanted no further interference with their work. As during the previous year, some journalists chose to leave the country rather than work in such conditions.

Most human rights organizations and some journalists practiced self-censorship, fearing reprisals by officials. When the League for the Defense of Human Rights in the Great Lakes (LDGL) documented electoral irregularities, it was castigated by the chairman of the National Electoral Commission, who said that the LDGL must have wanted "violence, delays, and confusion" in the voting process. Intelligence agents appeared to follow closely the activities of human rights organizations, and RPF leaders pressured one organization to elect persons it favored to leadership posts.

Local-Level Democracy

In February-March 2006 Rwandans voted for local authorities. In contests at the lowest administrative levels, voters lined up behind their chosen candidates. Contests for officials at the next higher level used secret ballots, but observers reported numerous irregularities, including stuffing of ballot boxes and intimidation of candidates. Disputes over the results led to confrontations between voters and election officials in some areas. In a number of contests, only one candidate stood for election.

In June unidentified assailants assaulted a district mayor who had been in conflict with senior figures of the RPF. He was later forced to resign and fled the country.

Illegal Detentions, Torture, and Ill-Treatment

Police and members of Local Defense Forces illegally detained and abused hundreds of persons, many of them street children and members of other vulnerable groups in Kigali, the capital, during the first months of 2006. Kept in dilapidated warehouse buildings at an unofficial detention center, hundreds of detainees suffered from lack of food, water, and medical care. Children were abused by adult detainees and women reported rape by security personnel. After Human Rights Watch published a report on the center, authorities closed it, forcing most detainees to leave in the middle of the night.

Evictions and Curbs on Land Use

As part of the "modernization" of Kigali, houses built without authorization in the poor sectors of the city were demolished. Though officials claimed that 15 days' notice was provided prior to demolition, many residents said this was untrue.

As Rwanda moves to implement wide-ranging land reform adopted in 2005, officials of two districts ordered residents to cut down their banana plantations and replace them with ornamental trees or more productive crops. Following public outcry in one district, officials said that residents would not be forced but only "persuaded" to comply.

Key International Actors

In 2006 many international donors continued to provide generous financial and political support to Rwanda. In one rare case of criticism on a human rights issue, the European Commission expressed concern over the illegal detention of street children.

The peer review mechanism of the New Partnership for African Development (NEPAD) gave Rwanda a generally favorable report but criticized its apparent "desire to obliterate distinctive identities," including that of the minority Batwa, and the "'rehearsed' participation in public affairs as determined by political authorities." Concerned about limits on political space, the team recommended recognizing "the need for political parties and civil society to operate freely." After praising gacaca as a potentially useful innovation, the team raised concerns about the extent of its legitimacy among Rwandans. The team also asked why the percentage of Rwandans living in poverty had increased despite five years of efforts supposedly meant to improve their status. President Kagame responded by criticizing the team's methodology and defending the practices in question.

SIERRA LEONE

Since the end of Sierra Leone's brutal armed conflict in 2002, few improvements have been made in the dynamics that contributed to the emergence of the conflict in 1991—rampant corruption, gross public financial mismanagement, inadequate distribution of the country's natural resources, and weak rule of law. The government's failure to address crushing poverty despite massive international aid, and alarmingly high unemployment rates among youth, render Sierra Leone vulnerable to future instability.

Persistent and serious deficiencies in the functioning of the police and judiciary continue to undermine improvements in implementing the rule of law. However, through the efforts of the United Nations-mandated Special Court for Sierra Leone, significant progress continues to be made in achieving accountability for war crimes. Meanwhile, the government made slow progress in implementing key recommendations made by Sierra Leone's Truth and Reconciliation Commission and in instituting the National Human Rights Commission, established by Parliament in 2004. In 2006 Parliament passed several laws aimed at improving the human rights of women, including laws on inheritance and property rights.

Following the complete withdrawal of UN peacekeepers in December 2005 and in recognition of Sierra Leone's continued institutional weaknesses, the UN Security Council in August 2005 approved the establishment of a peacebuilding mission— the UN Integrated Office for Sierra Leone (UNIOSL). The priorities of UNIOSL include fighting corruption, establishing the rule of law, and supporting the planned July 2007 general elections.

During 2006 there were numerous allegations of violations of civil and political rights in anticipation of the 2007 elections. These included the politically motivated arrest of opposition figures and the use of police to prevent opposition meetings. Donors and civil society complained that state institutions and aid money were being used to advance the political aims of the ruling party.

Accountability for Past Abuses

Throughout 2006 the Special Court for Sierra Leone, established in 2002 to bring justice for victims of atrocities committed during the war, continued to make progress. At this writing three trials involving nine individuals were in process. After mounting international pressure, former Liberian President Charles Taylor was surrendered to the Special Court on March 29 from Nigeria, where he had remained since August 2003. Taylor is charged with war crimes and crimes against humanity for his role in supporting the rebel Revolutionary United Front (RUF). Due to security concerns, the Special Court president requested that Taylor's trial be relocated to The Hague, and he was transferred there in June 2006. His trial is expected to begin in 2007.

Despite contributions by governments and a UN grant, the court continues to lack funds to complete its work and carry out "post-completion" activities such as long-term protection for witnesses. The court's financial needs are intensified by new costs associated with Taylor's trial.

Truth and Reconciliation Commission

Civil society and UNIOSIL made considerable efforts to educate rural populations about the findings of the 2005 report of the Truth and Reconciliation Commission. The report noted that decades of corrupt rule by Sierra Leone's political elite had largely created the conditions that led to the armed conflict. The recommendations include abolishing the death penalty, repealing laws that criminalize seditious libel, increasing the transparency of the mining industry, improving good governance, and establishing a reparations fund for war victims. The government has made very little effort to implement most recommendations and has rejected others, including abolition of the death penalty.

Efforts to Establish the Rule of Law

Striking defects within the judicial system that severely undermine the rights of victims and the accused remained evident throughout 2006. These defects include extortion and bribe-taking by court officials; insufficient numbers of judges, magistrates and prosecuting attorneys; very little representation for the accused; absenteeism by court personnel; inadequate remuneration for judiciary personnel; and extended periods of pre-trial detention. Mismanagement and corruption within Sierra Leone's detention facilities resulted in sub-standard conditions, including overcrowding and lack of proper nutrition and health care, as well as numerous deaths in custody.

In April 2006, some six years after their arrest in connection with a war-related incident, 10 former RUF members were convicted and sentenced for conspiracy to commit murder. The detention and trial of scores of other former RUF combatants arrested in conjunction with the same incident was from 2000-2006 characterized by gross judicial abuses including the procurement of statements under duress, detention without charges, and lack of counsel for up to five years from the date of arrest.

At this writing, 10 men were on death row following a December 2004 conviction for treason in connection with a 2003 coup attempt; their case is under appeal. An additional three men, including former RUF spokesman Omrie Golley, were arrested in January 2006 on treason charges. The grounds for arrest appear to be politically motivated and unsubstantiated, and the trial has been beset with numerous due process violations including the alleged fabrication of evidence and lack of an arrest warrant.

The system of local courts controlled by traditional leaders and applying customary law, which is often discriminatory particularly against women, is the only legal system accessible to an estimated 70 percent of the population. Local court officials frequently abuse their powers by illegally detaining persons and charging high fines for minor offenses, as well as by adjudicating criminal cases beyond their jurisdiction.

The presence in each district of a resident magistrate, funded by the United Nations Development Programme (UNDP), helped relieve judicial backlog, as did the ongoing United Kingdom-funded Justice Sector Development Program (JSDP), which aims to update laws and procedures, refurbish court facilities and reduce the number of prisoners on remand.

Corruption

Corruption in the public and private sectors in Sierra Leone remains widespread and continues to rob the population of funds needed to provide vital services such as education, water, and healthcare. In 2000, the Anti-Corruption Commission (ACC) was established to investigate charges of corruption. However, the power to refer cases for prosecution rests with the president-appointed attorney general and in practice, only cases involving lower level officials are referred for prosecution. As in previous years, 2006 saw few convictions for corruption-related offenses, and there were none involving high-level government officials. The ACC lost further legitimacy when President Ahmed Tejan Kabbah in late 2005 appointed a close relative as ACC commissioner.

Police and Army Conduct

The Sierra Leone police and army have been a longstanding source of considerable instability, corruption, and human rights violations, and have enjoyed near-complete immunity from prosecution. Despite a Commonwealth-run training program from 1998 to 2005 and current efforts by the JSDP and UNIOSIL, throughout 2006 the police exhibited unprofessional and often illegal conduct. This included widespread extortion from civilians (such as the placing of unauthorized checkpoints to obtain money from passing vehicles), rape of female detainees in remand facilities, and requiring victims of crimes to pay the police to file reports or conduct investigations. While numerous police officers were dismissed for purported criminal acts during 2006, there was little effort to hold them accountable for these crimes.

Efforts by the UK-led International Military Advisory and Training Team (IMATT), which since 1999 has worked to reform the Republic of Sierra Leone Armed Forces (RSLAF), have led to considerable improvements in professionalism and accountability within the army. In 2006 there were a few reports of abuses, extortion, and indiscipline by the army, and the RSLAF leadership demonstrated some commitment to penalize and sanction soldiers for offenses committed.

Trafficking in Persons

Trafficking of persons, particularly women and children, remained a problem in 2006. Numerous children are trafficked from the provinces to work in diamond mines, as commercial sex workers, and in street labor, both within Sierra Leone and to neighboring countries. There was also growing recognition of the problem of adoption fraud in which indigent parents are duped into terminating their parental rights.

Key International Actors

In spite of providing billions of dollars in assistance to Sierra Leone since the end of the armed conflict, international donors have been largely reluctant to publicly denounce ongoing problems of corruption and bad governance, which both undermine Sierra Leone's recovery and make it vulnerable to future instability. While key donors have made considerable effort to reform expenditure accounting mechanisms, they have been reluctant to refer cases to the Anti-Corruption Commission and press for that body's proper functioning.

The UK has for the last several years been the top bilateral donor, providing some GBP 40 million (US$76 million) in 2006 as direct budget support and program assistance aimed at strengthening the justice, security, and governance sectors. The United Nation's concern about a potential relapse into violence is not only illustrated by the presence of UNIOSL, but also by Sierra Leone's inclusion on the agenda of the new UN Peacebuilding Commission, created in December 2005 by UN Resolution 60/180. The commission, which is a UN effort to bridge the gap between peacekeeping and the consolidation of peace, selected Sierra Leone and Burundi as its countries of focus at its inaugural meeting in June 2006.

SOUTH AFRICA

After 12 years of democracy, South Africa is still struggling to implement the progressive human rights protections guaranteed in the country's constitution. Particular areas of concern relate to the rights of migrants, refugees and asylum seekers, sexual violence against women and children, access to primary education in rural areas, and the government's response to one of the world's most serious HIV/AIDS epidemics.

Refugees, Asylum Seekers, and Migrants

During 2006, the number of people applying for asylum in South Africa noticeably increased. According to the United Nations High Commissioner for Refugees, from January to March alone, 18,800 applications were filed (28,000 were filed in all of 2005), and more than 100,000 applications are currently pending. While the greatest number of refugees and asylum seekers are from the Democratic Republic of Congo, the number of Zimbabwean asylum seekers has grown significantly: Zimbabweans were the largest group to file in early 2006 with 38 percent of applicants.

The Department of Home Affairs is making slow progress in tackling a backlog of applications; in the first quarter of 2006, it approved only 112 applications and rejected 1,144, and these were all pre-2006 applications. At present there are only 30,000 recognized refugees in South Africa.

In this context, implementation of the Refugees Act by government officials remains a serious concern. Persistent administrative obstacles and delays in the processing of claims for asylum put asylum seekers at constant risk of unlawful arrest and possible deportation. The government's inconsistent application of a court decision giving asylum seekers the right to work and study, corrupt practices and deficient procedures for unaccompanied minors seeking asylum continue to render protections for asylum seekers inadequate.

The number of migrants being deported from South Africa has also steadily increased. For example, in 2005, the number of Zimbabweans deported rose to

SOUTH AFRICA

Unprotected Migrants

Zimbabweans in South Africa's Limpopo Province

HUMAN
RIGHTS
WATCH

almost 100,000 (up from 74,765 in 2004) out of more than 170,000 total
tions; this number continued to climb in 2006.

Migrants entering South Africa from Zimbabwe, documented or undocum
are vulnerable to human rights abuses and are inadequately protected. Th
tions of immigration and employment laws by police and immigration offi
including routine breaches of the lawful procedures for arrest, detention, a
deportation of undocumented foreigners established in the Immigration A
deficiencies in these laws, result in the infringement of migrants' rights un
South Africa's Constitution. These rights include the right to personal freed
and security, and to conditions of detention that are consistent with human
ty and privacy. The South African government's failure to protect the constit
al rights of migrants also frequently violates the government's obligations ur
the International Covenant on Civil and Political Rights (ICCPR). The Constitut
also protects the rights of at least documented migrants to fair labor practice

In addition, commercial farm owners often do not provide foreign workers with
basic protections they are entitled to under South Africa's labor laws. Farm ov
ers employing foreign migrants openly flout the minimum wage and make unla
ful deductions from workers' wages. Though migrant workers are legally entitle
to workers' compensation, there are obstacles to receiving compensation settle
ments, such as providing South African identification and possessing a bank
account, which foreign migrant workers often lack. In addition, the basic conditions of employment for farm workers create disincentives for employers to provide housing for workers, and the government has no housing policy for farm
workers.

Violence against Women and Children

Between April 2005 and March 2006, 54,926 rapes and attempted rapes and
9,805 indecent assaults were reported to the South African Police Services
(SAPS). While the national statistics for reported rapes are slightly lower than for
2005, some provinces experienced dramatic hikes. In Eastern Cape, for example,
reported rapes increased by 21 percent and there was an 11.7 percent increase in
indecent assaults. However, SAPS itself has observed that sexual violence is
largely underreported throughout South Africa, suggesting that the numbers of

reported rapes in the last year underestimates the extent of the problem. Of those cases that are reported, the South Africa Law Commission found that only five percent of adult rape cases and nine percent of cases involving children end in conviction.

The South Africa Parliament has been considering amendments to existing criminal law on sexual offences for several years, and introduced the Sexual Offenses Bill in 2003. The bill was intended to reform criminal law on sexual offenses to ensure that it conform with Constitutional principles and to improve access to justice and the efficiency of the justice system for survivors of sexual violence.

In the original draft, the bill obliged the state to provide and bear the costs of medical care, treatment, and counseling for sexual violence survivors who may have sustained physical injuries or psychological harm or been exposed to sexually transmitted infections as a result of a sexual offense. This would include, but not be limited to, HIV post-exposure prophylaxis (PEP), the short course of anti-retroviral (ARV) drugs that can reduce the risk of HIV after rape. The current version of the bill excised this provision, limiting available services to PEP. Moreover, access to PEP is dependent on the victim laying criminal charges or reporting the incident at a "designated health establishment." These requirements may prevent rape survivors from receiving PEP within the required 72 hours and can impede the ability of medical and police officials to obtain medical evidence that may be crucial for successful prosecution of a case.

Other important changes to the bill include the removal of several protective measures for vulnerable witnesses (including children) and the reinsertion of the element of consent in defining rape.

At this writing, while the Sexual Offences Bill was approved for submission to parliament on November 10, it was not voted on. The delay appears to be related to discussions over government provision of PEP to victims of sexual assault, which parliament's legal advisers have suggested should be in a separate bill. Adoption is likely to be delayed for several months.

Violence—including sexual violence—and crime in schools is an ongoing problem. South Africa's 27,000 schools, serving approximately 12 million children are ill-prepared to respond to these abuses and few have policies and procedures in place to address them. In September 2006 public hearings on "School Based Violence" were held under the auspices of South Africa's Human Rights Commission. Testimonies revealed that the situation is much more serious than initially thought, with witnesses referring to the prevalence of students with weapons, pupils inflicting violence on other pupils, as well as the rape of teachers. While violence is being perpetrated by pupils, teachers, and principals, girl pupils are the main victims of sexual assault.

Access to Education in Rural Areas

While South Africa's education system has experienced considerable reform since 1994, much-needed improvements are still required, particularly in access to primary education in rural areas.

According to the Department of Education, 300,000 children still do not attend school across the country; the reasons vary from a lack of services for children with special needs to a child's inability to pay school fees. Rural education is confronted by even more problems, such as the generally poor condition of schools on commercial farms; the high level of illiteracy; lack of parental participation in school governing bodies; poor transportation; and the non-attendance and shortage of teachers.

In 2006 the government made a commitment to implement a no-fee school policy for primary education in South Africa's poorer areas to address the problem of pupils too poor to pay the required school fees. As of September 2006, the provinces of KwaZulu-Natal and Gauteng had started to identify schools that will be declared no-fee schools; the other South African provinces are still compiling their lists of no-fee schools.

HIV/AIDS

An estimated 5.5 million people—more than 11 percent of the population—are living with HIV/AIDS in South Africa; this is one of the largest national totals of people living with HIV/AIDS in the world. The prevalence is highest among women aged 15 and up; UNAIDS estimates there are some 3,100,000 South African women living with HIV/AIDS.

The government response to the epidemic has been weak. For example, South Africa's efforts to introduce ARVs have been impeded by international pressure to protect multinational pharmaceutical companies' patents on ARV drugs, as well as by misguided political leadership on the national level. This includes misleading statements about the safety and efficacy of ARVs by the Health Minister and other high level government officials. A new AIDS strategy to strengthen the government's response to HIV/AIDS is expected to be announced in December 2006.

Civil society continues to play a critical role in forcing South Africa to address its HIV/AIDS epidemic. In 2006, for example, following actions taken by the AIDS Law Project, the Durban High Court issued an order compelling the Durban prison to provide ARV treatment, a decree upheld despite a government appeal. In September the government produced a plan to provide treatment to the prisoners.

International Role

South Africa continues to play a key international and regional role within the African Union. It continues to provide troops in peace support operations in Darfur through the African Union Mission in Sudan and as part of the UN Mission in the Democratic Republic of Congo. South Africa also supports post-conflict reconstruction in Burundi and Ethiopia and Eritrea, and mediation efforts in Cote d'Ivoire.

International disunity and controversy persisted regarding the strategy to address the deteriorating human rights situation in Zimbabwe. South Africa, Zimbabwe's neighbor and a leader within the African Union and the Southern African Development Council, continued to insist upon a strategy of quiet diplomacy despite enduring insistence by many countries in the West that it had not yielded visible improvements to date.

SUDAN

Sudan's human rights record remained abysmal in 2006. A May 2006 peace accord aimed at ending the three-year conflict in Darfur exacerbated divisions among the rebel movements in Darfur when it was signed by the Sudanese government and only one rebel faction in Darfur. Dissent over the mediation process and terms of the peace accord generated further conflict and serious abuses of civilians, including forced displacement, rape, killings, and increasing attacks on humanitarian aid workers. The establishment in 2005 of a national tribunal to respond to the crimes in Darfur had no effect on the continuing impunity of militia leaders and government officials responsible for crimes against humanity.

Despite the introduction of a new interim national constitution and some progress implementing the January 2005 Comprehensive Peace Agreement (CPA) between the central government in Khartoum and southern-based rebels, many of the national reforms specified in the CPA, including the establishment of a National Human Rights Commission, are lagging well behind schedule. The ceasefire was largely respected in southern Sudan and the new Government of South Sudan (GoSS) made some progress setting up the top level of regional institutions and administration, including a Human Rights Commission for the south.

At the end of 2006, emergency laws remain in place in Darfur, but have been lifted throughout the rest of Sudan. Patterns of arbitrary arrest and detention, torture, and other abuses by Sudanese military and security forces remain widespread in Darfur and other areas of the country. Freedom of expression continues to be restricted, and there was a sharp rise in arbitrary arrests, harassment, preprint censorship, and bureaucratic restrictions of Sudanese and international media in late 2006.

The Conflict in Darfur

Darfur's conflict escalated and became more complex in 2006, partly due to the splintering of alliances within the main rebel movement, the Sudan Liberation Army (SLA); the government's continuing policy of supporting local militia groups; the proliferation of armed groups along the Chad-Sudan border; and localized violence among communities in different areas of Darfur.

SUDAN

Entrenching Impunity

Government Responsibility for International
Crimes in Darfur

HUMAN
RIGHTS
WATCH

All of the warring parties violated the 2004 ceasefire agreement, subsequent security protocols, and a UN arms embargo imposed on Darfur under UN Security Council resolution 1591 in March 2005. Sudanese government forces and allied "Janjaweed militias" were responsible for serious abuses of civilians, including killings, torture and regular incidents of rape and sexual assault of women and girls. Some rebel factions were also responsible for serious crimes against civilians in Darfur. At least 200,000 people were displaced by violent attacks in Darfur in 2006, some for the second or third time.

After more than a year of negotiations, the Sudanese government and one faction of the SLA led by Mini Minawi signed an African Union-mediated Darfur Peace Agreement (DPA) in May 2006. Several other rebel factions—including the Justice and Equality Movement (JEM) and the SLA faction led by Abdul Wahid Mohamed Nour—refused to sign the agreement, citing deficiencies in the security and compensation arrangements. The controversy over the deal further weakened the credibility of the 7,000-member African Union mission in Darfur, which was criticized by many internally displaced civilians and even came under attack in several of the internally displaced persons camps.

The May peace agreement provoked increased fighting among the rebel factions and between the Sudanese government and non-signatory rebel groups. Tens of thousands of civilians were displaced by the increased fighting in 2006 and joined the almost two million displaced people already residing in camps around Darfur. Chadian civilians in eastern Chad also came under increasing attack from Sudanese government-backed militias based in Darfur.

Inter-factional fighting between two of the larger SLA factions (SLA-Minawi and the SLA faction lead by Abdul Wahid Mohammed Nour) increased in the lead up to and following the signing of the Darfur Peace Agreement, apparently due to efforts by both groups to expand or retain control over territory. Fighting between the two SLA factions affected villages around Korma town in April and around the Tawila area in July, both locations in north Darfur. Both groups were responsible for incidents of killings, torture and rape of civilians perceived to be supporters of the other faction, and several thousand civilians were displaced by the clashes.

Attacks by Sudanese government forces also increased in 2006, and the government reneged on earlier commitments to end offensive military flights over Darfur. The Sudanese air force repeatedly used its Antonov aircraft and helicopter gunships to re-supply the army and militia forces and indiscriminately bombed civilians during joint air-ground attacks. The Sudanese government made no effort to disarm the "Janjaweed," and instead continued to incorporate many of these pro-government militiamen into paramilitary groups, such as the Border Intelligence Brigade. Government officials also continued to support local tribal militias against rebel groups and civilians in strategic areas of Darfur, such as in Gereida and Muhajariya, south Darfur.

Beginning in August 2006 the Sudanese government launched a new offensive, partly in response to attacks on government targets from a new coalition of non-signatory factions called the National Redemption Front. Sudanese government forces indiscriminately bombed villages in rural North Darfur with Antonov aircraft, causing civilian deaths, injuries and the displacement of hundreds of civilians. Militia attacks in Jebel Mun, west Darfur, at the end of October resulted in the death of at least 60 civilians, half of them children.

Rape and sexual violence continue to be pervasive throughout Darfur, with attacks on women and girls taking place both in the context of hostilities between the warring parties as well as when internally displaced women and girls travel outside camp settings to collect firewood and other items. In just one example in August, aid workers reported that more than 200 women and girls were sexually assaulted over a five week period in Kalma, the largest displaced persons camp in south Darfur.

Humanitarian aid workers came under increasing attack by armed groups from all sides in the months following the May peace deal, with 12 humanitarian staff killed between May and August 2006. The insecurity caused many international organizations to restrict their movements, particularly along the dangerous roads, jeopardizing the supply of relief to almost half a million of the more than four million people partially or wholly dependent on aid for their survival.

The ruling National Congress Party made no substantive effort to investigate or prosecute those individuals responsible for the most serious crimes in Darfur, despite establishing a national tribunal in mid-2005 allegedly for that purpose. The tribunal tried a handful of cases, none of them linked to the massive crimes that took place in 2003 and 2004, and there were no meaningful investigations into the responsibility of any individuals with command responsibility. Meanwhile senior Sudanese officials continued to state publicly that there would be no Sudanese cooperation with the International Criminal Court, which is investigating crimes in Darfur following the March 2005 referral by the UN Security Council.

International efforts to improve civilian protection in Darfur focused on simultaneously bolstering the weak African Union force on the ground in Darfur and preparing for an eventual transition to a UN force. However, the Sudanese government consistently refused to consent to the deployment of UN troops in Darfur, despite an August UN Security Resolution authorizing such a force and providing it with a Chapter VII mandate to protect civilians.

Mixed Progress in South Sudan

The January 2005 Comprehensive Peace Agreement created high expectations among the millions of Sudanese who suffered the effects of the 21-year civil war. Many southern Sudanese expressed disappointment in the slow progress implementing the CPA in 2006. Although the UN estimated that some 12,000 refugees returned to the region, the majority of the four million people displaced by the war did not, with many citing fears of continuing insecurity and lack of services as the key obstacles.

Although weakened by the death of its chairman, John Garang, in August 2005, the Sudan People's Liberation Movement avoided a leadership struggle with the appointment of Garang's deputy, Salva Kiir, to head the new regional Government of South Sudan. Setting up a new administration, developing the infrastructure-poor south and disarming or integrating the many southern militia groups into the southern army were among the formidable challenges faced by the new southern government. SPLA efforts to forcibly disarm the White Army—a group of armed Nuer civilians in Upper Nile—without a comprehensive disarmament program targeting the many armed groups in the region, backfired in early 2006, provoking serious inter-communal attacks and hundreds of deaths, many of them civilians.

Although there was sporadic violence in different areas of the south, the north-south ceasefire agreement largely held and both the Sudanese Armed Forces and the Sudan People's Liberation Army made progress redeploying their forces under the terms of the CPA. However, the status of Abyei, a resource-rich area claimed by north and south, remained unresolved, one of several key areas of friction jeopardizing the cohesion of the Government of National Unity and the implementation of the CPA.

Press Freedom and Human Rights Defenders

Journalists and human rights defenders continued to suffer harassment, arrest and detention without charge, and other forms of intimidation, mainly from Sudanese security forces in Darfur and Khartoum. At least 15 international and Sudanese journalists were arrested and detained in 2006, and many more faced harassment, beatings, and arbitrary bureaucratic restrictions, particularly vis-à-vis efforts to travel to and report on the situation in Darfur and other sensitive issues.

Despite the guarantees of freedom of expression and press freedom provided in Article 39 of the Interim National Constitution (approved in 2005), press censorship and restrictions on Sudanese media increased in September and October, with security officials resuming pre-print inspections of editions and, in some cases, banning editions altogether.

Human rights activists continue to face harassment or mistreatment in Sudan. Individuals or organizations raising concerns about the humanitarian or human rights situation in Darfur did so in an atmosphere of increasing intimidation, with Sudanese officials making threatening accusations in the pro-government press. Security forces stormed a meeting of Sudanese and international human rights activists during the January 2006 African Union Summit in Khartoum, detaining the group for hours and confiscating personal belongings. Staff working for the Sudanese Organization against Torture and other non-governmental organizations were repeatedly arbitrarily detained and questioned by government security agencies in Darfur.

Key International Actors

Sudanese relations with Chad deteriorated substantially in 2006. The Chadian government cut diplomatic relations following a failed April 2004 Chadian rebel attempt to topple the Déby regime from bases in Darfur. Relations were restored in August and both governments committed to cease supporting insurgent groups under a Libyan-mediated agreement. However at year's end both governments continue to support rebel movements against their neighbor.

Despite the rise in violence within Darfur and fears of regional instability in Chad and neighboring Central African Republic, the international community's position on Darfur was marked by division, both regionally and within the UN Security Council (UNSC).

Waning international confidence in the under-resourced African Union (AU) mission's ability to protect civilians led to international efforts to bolster the AU force with UN troops. In August 2006 the UN Security Council authorized a new UN force for Darfur of more than 20,000 troops and police under resolution 1706. The UNSC provided the force with a mandate under Chapter VII of the UN Charter to protect civilians (in addition to the existing 10,000 UN peacekeepers in southern Sudan), but conditioned the deployment on consent of the Sudanese government, which the ruling party refused to give. The stalemate resulted in a three-month extension of the African Union mission, through December 31, 2006, and a proposal to expand the force with approximately 4,000 troops, but these steps are unlikely to end the abuses or restore stability in Darfur.

The Arab League and individual member states voiced little or no criticism of the Sudanese government's massive abuses in Darfur, while key African nations varied in their response. Both the African Union and Arab League held their regional summits in Khartoum in January and March respectively, but although it lobbied for the honor, Sudan was temporarily refused the chair of the African Union in 2006 due to its record in Darfur.

Although the UN imposed individual targeted sanctions on four individuals in April, none of the individuals were high-level Sudanese officials. The International Criminal Court (ICC) continued to investigate the crimes in Darfur, largely from outside the region although ICC officials visited Khartoum several times in 2006.

UGANDA

In 2006 Uganda missed a key opportunity to reverse its deteriorating human rights record when its first multiparty presidential and parliamentary elections in 26 years were marred by intimidation of the opposition and widespread voting irregularities. Torture by security forces of detained suspected rebels and dissidents continued. One such detainee, Abdu Semugenyi, was reported electrocuted to death on May 4, 2006 in a "safe house" maintained by the Joint Anti-Terrorist Task Force. Hopes were raised, however, for an end to the 20-year conflict in northern Uganda between the rebel Lord's Resistance Army (LRA) and the Ugandan government. A cessation of hostilities agreement is in effect while peace talks mediated by the regional government of southern Sudan continue.

The War in Northern Uganda

Prior to the start of peace talks in mid-July, LRA attacks on civilians in northern Uganda, a hallmark of the conflict, continued, although at lower levels than reported in prior years. Widespread insecurity also resulted from alleged LRA activity across the Sudanese border in Equatoria. In March LRA rebels were allegedly responsible for raids on UN Mission in the Sudan (UNMIS) installations and non-governmental organizations in Yambio, Sudan, while LRA rebels in Garamba National Park in the Democratic Republic of Congo (DRC) were suspected of killing eight Guatemalan peacekeepers on January 23 in an attack on the UN Mission in DRC (MONUC).

Peace talks in Juba initiated in 2006 by the regional government of southern Sudan, and mediated by southern Sudan's Vice-President, Dr. Riek Machar, appear to represent a realistic opportunity for an end to the conflict. Under the terms of a cessation of hostilities agreement reached by the parties on August 26, and amended on November 1, 2006, following violations of the agreement by both sides, LRA rebels are to assemble at two sites in southern Sudan. Other governments have pledged financial assistance for the talks through a UN-established fund.

Issues of accountability for serious human rights abuses committed during the conflict remain the subject of debate after the LRA called for the International

Criminal Court (ICC) arrest warrants against LRA leaders charged with crimes against humanity and war crimes to be dropped. The government of Uganda, reversing course after having invited the ICC to investigate the LRA, proposed to seek the withdrawal of the arrest warrants and the substitution of traditional justice mechanisms in the event of a successful peace agreement. Government of Uganda representatives have, in fact, no authority to unilaterally rescind the arrest warrants and have thus far not sought their withdrawal through an admissibility challenge.

Some traditional, religious, and civil society leaders in northern Uganda and some in the international humanitarian community have urged the prioritization of peace over prosecutions. Others, like the Victims' Rights Working Group, the affiliated organizations of which include nongovernmental organizations from Uganda, have supported the view that prosecutions must not be sacrificed and that there must be cooperation with the ICC to arrest persons against whom warrants have been issued.

Human Rights Watch has taken the view that any outcome must include both peace and justice and that justice must involve fair and credible prosecutions of perpetrators of the most serious crimes, including prosecution before the ICC of the four surviving LRA leaders against whom arrest warrants have been issued. Fair and credible prosecutions for the most serious crimes are crucial to promote not only accountability, but also a durable peace. Broader accountability efforts for lesser offenses could be promoted through national and local initiatives that might include trials, a truth telling exercise, and, where appropriate, use of traditional mechanisms.

The prospect of peace also raised expectations of a return home for the 1.7 million persons confined to displaced persons camps. Camp residents continue to endure hunger and overcrowding, and remain vulnerable to abuses by the undisciplined Uganda Peoples' Defence Forces (UPDF), local militias, and LRA rebels. Improved security conditions in 2006, however, have made possible the movement of some displaced persons to smaller "settlement sites," which have better access to farmland but often lack health and education services.

Disarmament in Karamoja

Allegations of human rights abuses including torture and rape by UPDF soldiers surfaced in connection with "cordon and search" disarmament campaigns conducted in the Karamoja region. A leaked report of the government's commission of inquiry was quoted in the national press as acknowledging that some abuses had taken place. After clashes between the UPDF and a Karamojong community led to the deaths of at least 22 soldiers and an unknown number of civilians in Kotido district in October and November, the UN expressed grave concern about the escalation in violence and reports of abuses committed on all sides.

Political Freedoms

On February 23, 2006, President Museveni—in power since 1986—won re-election and his ruling National Resistance Movement Organisation (NRM-O) a majority of seats in Uganda's first multiparty presidential and parliamentary elections in 26 years.

Prosecutions were brought or threatened against opposition leaders, including front-runner presidential challenger Dr. Kizza Besigye of the Forum for Democratic Change (FDC), in a clear attempt to undermine his presidential campaign. The Electoral Offences Squad, formed by the Uganda Police Force, had received reports of election-related intimidation and assault in at least 22 districts by the end of January 2006. While some allegations were made against opposition supporters, the majority were pressed against the ruling NRM-O and state officials. The NRM-O's inheritance of personnel and facilities from the "Movement" national political system secured privileged access to state resources. There were also reports of illegal military involvement in the election campaigns on behalf of NRM-O candidates.

Election-day violence was minimal, but both local and EU observers noted major irregularities across the country, including election officers turning away hundreds of thousands registered voters who allegedly did not appear on the voter register. Voting results reported by the Ugandan Electoral Commission reveal a divided country, with voters in the north and most of the east choosing opposition candidates, while Museveni's support came from the south and west.

Freedom of Expression

Local journalists faced intimidation and prosecution in the months preceding the elections. In November 2005, the Ministry of Information issued a directive to media outlets forbidding them from running stories on the trial of presidential challenger Besigye. Acts of intimidation against radio stations, including arrests of station personnel, were reported. After accusations from the opposition FDC that the president and top military officials were persecuting Besigye on ethnic grounds appeared in the privately owned Weekly Observer, its editor, James Tumusiime, and reporter, Semujju Ibrahim Nganda, were charged on December 13, 2005, with "promoting sectarianism." Petitions challenging the "promoting sectarianism" provision of Uganda's penal code are pending before the Constitutional Court.

Torture by Security Forces

Ugandan security and military forces continue to use "safe houses," unauthorized secret detention centers, and, increasingly, civilian police facilities to detain and torture suspected rebels and dissidents. In April 2006, Abdu Semugenyi, after being accused of being associated with the rebel group Allied Democratic Forces, was detained in a "safe house" maintained by the Joint Anti-Terrorist Task Force in an upscale neighborhood of Kampala. Other individuals detained in the "safe house," some of whom were also tortured, witnessed Semugenyi's torture and one reported that Semugenyi was electrocuted to death on May 4, 2006. Although the authorities first denied holding Semugenyi, they later claimed in press reports that he was killed while trying to escape. His body has not been recovered by his family.

HIV/AIDS Treatment and Prevention

Although HIV prevalence has greatly decreased since the early 1990s, the number of new HIV infections has recently increased from 70,000 in 2003 to about 130,000 in 2005. A shift toward U.S.-funded "abstinence-only" HIV prevention programs has continued in 2006, undermining the country's fight against HIV/AIDS by questioning the effectiveness of condoms and removing comprehensive HIV/AIDS information from school curricula.

Corruption is an on-going concern. The temporary suspension of more than US$200 million in grants by the Global Fund in 2005, and a subsequent inquiry into fiscal mismanagement led to the dismissal of three health ministers but no criminal charges have been filed. In September 2006, anti-retroviral medicine worth between $400,000 and $500,000 was destroyed because it had expired at the national medical stores in Entebbe.

Lesbian, Gay, Bisexual, and Transgender Rights

Publication of identifying information of 45 alleged homosexuals in the tabloid paper "Red Pepper" in August 2006 raised concerns of an escalation in the government's long-standing campaign of harassment of lesbian, gay, bisexual, and transgender Ugandans. Homophobic allegations by the same tabloid in 2002 that two women had married led to their arrest and detention.

Key International Actors

In January 2006 the UK government's development ministry announced the withdrawal of US$26 million of direct funding to the government because of concerns over a lack of democratic and economic reforms. The United Kingdom, the Netherlands, Norway, Sweden, and Ireland also previously reduced aid in 2005. The EU Election Observation Mission to Uganda, which deployed 200 monitors during the February 2006 elections, concluded that "the elections fell short of full compliance with international principles for genuine democratic elections, in particular because a level playing field was not in place."

The situation in northern Uganda received mention in resolutions of the UN Security Council for the first time. By resolutions in January and March 2006 the Security Council requested that the UN Secretary-General make recommendations as to how UN agencies and missions could better address the LRA problem. The Secretary-General's recommendations, issued in June 2006, included continued collaboration between donor governments and the government of Uganda to finalize the national peace, recovery, and development plan for northern Uganda; support for the appointment of a special envoy; and cooperation between the security forces of the governments of the region with limited assistance from UNMIS and MONUC.

Representatives of the UN, Ugandan and core donor group governments also met in March 2006 to discuss the conflict and humanitarian situation in northern Uganda. One output was the establishment of a Joint Monitoring Committee (JMC) composed of Ugandan government ministries, donor governments, international institutions, and representatives of national and international civil society to oversee an emergency humanitarian plan for northern Uganda.

ZIMBABWE

Human rights violations in Zimbabwe continued unabated in 2006. President Robert Mugabe's government maintained its assault on the media, the political opposition, civil society activists, and human rights defenders. Police and state agents continue to arbitrarily arrest and detain peaceful activists, and the latter half of the year saw a marked increase in reports of torture and ill-treatment of government critics while in detention.

More than a year after the government's program of mass evictions and demoli-tions—Operation Murambatsvina—tens of thousands of people continue to suffer the catastrophic consequences. Despite numerous public statements from the government that it would initiate a reconstruction program to address the home-lessness created by the evictions, few of the people displaced by the evictions have received housing and many remain in need of food, water, and other forms of assistance. In addition, the government has repeatedly hindered efforts by the United Nations to provide emergency shelter and has subjected many of the vic-tims to repeated forced evictions.

The humanitarian situation of the evictees and the HIV/AIDS situation are among problems that are being exacerbated by acute food shortages in the country. Food security is likely to remain precarious for many vulnerable groups.

Freedom of Assembly

Peaceful protests in Zimbabwe are often violently disrupted by the police. At vari-ous times in 2006 hundreds of peaceful demonstrators including student activists, trade unionists, and human rights activists were arrested. On several occasions, protestors were forced to lie down and were brutally beaten by police with batons before their arrest. On September 25, for example, police violently disrupted a peaceful march by some 500 activists from the National Constitutional Assembly in Harare. Riot police armed with batons stopped the march, asked the activists to sit down and proceeded to beat them one at a time with batons before ordering them to leave. During the beatings a number of peo-ple panicked, leading to a stampede that injured about 24 people, seven serious-ly.

The government has used repressive legislation to systematically deny activists their right to peacefully assemble and associate. For example, most of the activists arrested in 2006 were charged with violating the Public Order and Security Act (POSA), which gives police wide powers regulating public gatherings, and is also loosely interpreted by police. Tellingly, in many of the cases the charges were later dropped and those arrested released without charge.

Freedom of Expression and Information

The government launched a new assault on the country's remaining independent press through a wave of criminal prosecutions and arrests. On January 24, 2006, the authorities brought charges of operating a broadcasting service without a license against six trustees and three employees of the privately owned radio station Voice of the People. The charges were subsequently dismissed by the High Court. In the same month, the government-appointed Media and Information Commission (MIC) threatened to cancel the license of the Financial Gazette, a privately-owned newspaper, if it did not retract a story that questioned the commission's independence. On January 29 the MIC refused to renew the accreditation of 15 journalists working for the Zimbabwe Independent, another privately-owned newspaper, until the paper retracted a similar story.

Despite condemnation from civil society, in July the government introduced in Parliament the Interception of Communications Bill, which seeks to give extraordinary powers to Zimbabwe's Central Intelligence Organization, the Commissioner of Police, and the Zimbabwe Revenue Authority to intercept citizens' phone calls and emails without credible safeguards. The bill is currently under review by the parliamentary Legal Committee. The Suppression of Foreign and International Terrorism Bill, gazetted in March but withdrawn after the parliamentary Legal Committee found some provisions to be unconstitutional (and pending resubmission with revisions at this writing), has raised fears similar to those arising from the Interception of Communications Bill about its potential use in silencing government critics.

ZIMBABWE

"You Will Be Thoroughly Beaten"

The Brutal Suppression of Dissent in Zimbabwe

HUMAN RIGHTS WATCH

Torture and Ill-Treatment in Detention

Torture and ill-treatment in Zimbabwe's police cells is rife. The government has taken no clear action to halt the rising incidence of torture and ill-treatment of opposition supporters and civil society activists while in the custody of the police or intelligence services.

In a shocking example of police torture and ill treatment, 15 members of the Zimbabwe Congress of Trade Unions were arrested and brutally assaulted by police at Matapi police station following peaceful protests on September 13 against poor working conditions. The unionists reported that a group of five police officers beat them with fists and batons, kicked them, banged their heads against the wall, and verbally abused and threatened them. They were initially denied medical treatment and access to their lawyers for 24 hours but were later taken to a hospital where some were found to have serious injuries such as fractured limbs. The High Court in Harare ordered an immediate investigation, but at this writing it was unclear whether the police would comply. After the incident President Mugabe expressed approval for the actions of the police, stating that those who protested in the street deserved to be "thoroughly beaten."

The authorities have also targeted student activists and in some cases subjected them to police torture and ill-treatment while in custody. In May 2006 the authorities reacted to a spate of student protests against unpopular government polices with mass arrests and violence. For example, on May 29 police arrested student leader Promise Mkwanazi and detained him at a police station in the northeastern town of Bindura for five days without charge. Each night a group of three or four policemen stripped Mkwanazi naked, shackled him with his hands between his legs so he could not move, and beat him severely with batons; they also threatened to kill him. They accused him of belonging to the opposition and of trying to overthrow the government.

Human Rights Defenders

The authorities intensified their attacks on human rights defenders and lawyers in an attempt to silence their condemnation of the government's poor human rights record. Government officials routinely accuse human rights groups of being sup-

ZIMBABWE

No Bright Future

Government Failures, Human Rights Abuses and
Squandered Progress in the Fight against AIDS in Zimbabwe

HUMAN
RIGHTS
WATCH

porters of the opposition and of receiving funds from western donors whom the government accuses of trying to destabilize the country. Human rights defenders and lawyers are constantly subjected to harassment, arbitrary arrests, and attacks by the police, intelligence agents and government officials. In May two human rights lawyers from the organization Zimbabwe Lawyers for Human Rights were threatened by supporters of the ruling ZANU-PF party and state agents when they attempted to represent students arrested by the police for protesting the high cost of student fees.

Hundreds of members of the women's organization Women of Zimbabwe Arise were arrested throughout the country in 2006 during peaceful protests against the worsening social, economic, and human rights situation. Scores of the organization's members were subjected to ill-treatment while in custody.

HIV/AIDS

Although the HIV/AIDS prevalence rate has dropped, the HIV/AIDS epidemic in Zimbabwe remains critical. The government's abusive practices such as Operation Murambatsvina as well as inadequate health and social welfare policies have contributed to the denial of access to healthcare for hundreds of thousands of Zimbabweans living with HIV/AIDS: some 350,000 of the 1.6 million people carrying the virus are in immediate need of life-saving antiretroviral drugs and another 600,000 are in need of care and support. Such policies and practices risk undermining the progress that the government has achieved thus far in addressing the HIV/AIDS crisis.

Key International Actors

President Mugabe has persistently responded with defiance and at times contempt to attempts to address Zimbabwe's interrelated political, human rights, and humanitarian crises by international partners such as South Africa and other Southern African Development Community (SADC) countries. There is little consensus internationally about the way forward in dealing with the crises. The South African government remains firmly entrenched in its position of quiet diplomacy, while European Union member states and the United States have maintained targeted sanctions against government officials but have done little else.

Recent attempts to solve the political crisis in Zimbabwe by UN Secretary-General Kofi Annan and SADC member countries have largely failed. A planned visit by Annan in January 2006 to investigate the situation in the aftermath of the evictions did not take place. Instead, at the July summit of the African Union Annan was forced to step aside and allow former Tanzanian President Benjamin Mkapa to deal with the crisis, at Mugabe's insistence. Little clarity exists about what form Mkapa's efforts will take.

Zimbabwe's humanitarian crisis has been worsened by the reluctance of western donors to provide direct humanitarian assistance to the government of Zimbabwe. More worryingly, donors have failed to heed calls for further funding of UN humanitarian assistance programs. For example, in October 2006 the World Food Programme declared that it was cutting food aid to Zimbabwe by two-thirds because funding for food assistance to Zimbabwe was running out.

MEXICO

The Second Assault

Obstructing Access to Legal Abortion after Rape in Mexico

HUMAN RIGHTS WATCH

HUMAN
RIGHTS
WATCH

WORLD REPORT
2007

AMERICAS

ARGENTINA

Argentina has taken important steps to bring to justice former military and police personnel accused of having committed grave human rights violations during the country's "dirty war." In 2006 two police officers were convicted for "disappearances," the first such convictions since the Supreme Court struck down the "Full Stop" and "Due Obedience" laws in 2005.

Inmates are held in deplorable conditions in Argentina's overcrowded prisons. Inmate violence and brutality by guards are a continuing problem.

Confronting Past Abuses

Since President Néstor Kirchner took office in 2003, Argentina has taken historic steps to prosecute military and police personnel responsible for "disappearances," killings, and torture during its last military dictatorship (1976-1983). President Kirchner has forcefully encouraged these prosecutions, reinforcing what began as a legal challenge to impunity in the courts. Several important cases were reopened in 2003 after Congress annulled the 1986 "Full Stop" law, which forced a halt to the prosecution of all such cases, and the 1987 "Due Obedience" law, which granted automatic immunity in such cases to all members of the military except those in positions of command. In June 2005, the Supreme Court declared the laws unconstitutional, and in 2006 the first trials in nearly 20 years were held for "disappearances" and torture.

In August 2006, a federal court in Buenos Aires sentenced former police official Julio Héctor Simón to 25 years in prison for the illegal arrest and torture of José Poblete Roa and Gertrudis Hlaczik de Poblete, a Chilean/Argentine couple who "disappeared" after being detained in November 1978 and held at the "Olympus," a secret detention center run by the federal police. The following month a court in La Plata sentenced another former police official, Miguel Osvaldo Etchecolatz, to life imprisonment for illegal arrest, torture, and homicide in connection with six "disappearances." Etchecolatz had been convicted in 1986 on numerous counts of illegal arrest and sentenced to 23 years in prison, but he was released the following year when his sentence was nullified by the "Due Obedience" law.

Since 2005 several federal judges have struck down presidential pardons decreed by President Menem in 1989 and 1990 in favor of former officials convicted or facing trial for human rights violations. In September 2006, the Cassation Court upheld a ruling that the pardon of General Santiago Omar Riveros, a former military commander in Buenos Aires, was unconstitutional. The Supreme Court has not yet ruled on the constitutionality of the pardons.

Witness Protection

The security of witnesses in human rights trials became a serious concern in 2006, with the mysterious disappearance in September 2006 of a torture victim who had testified in the Etchecolatz case. Jorge Julio López, a 77-year-old construction worker, vanished from his home in La Plata the day before he was due to attend one of the final days of the trial. Another torture witness, Nilda Eloy, had previously reported receiving death threats by telephone, accompanied by noises that sounded like a torture session. Judges and prosecutors involved in human rights cases also received threats, adding to fears that López may have been kidnapped by individuals who had served in the police during the dictatorship and aimed to sabotage the trials. The government mounted a major police operation to find López, but by mid-October his whereabouts and the reason for his disappearance were still unknown.

Prison Conditions

Overcrowding, abuses by prison guards, and inmate violence continue to be serious problems in Argentine prisons. In 2006 there was a slight reduction in overcrowding in Buenos Aires province. The number of detainees held in police lockups—which for years have absorbed the overflow from the prison system—also decreased.

Nevertheless, according to a report by the Justice Ministry of Buenos Aires province, cited in the newspaper *Clarín* in August 2006, almost 4,000 prisoners were still being held in police facilities as of then.

In a landmark ruling in May 2005, the Supreme Court declared that all prisons in the country must abide by the United Nations Standard Minimum Rules for the

Treatment of Prisoners. One of the causes of overcrowding is the high percentage of criminal suspects sent to prison to await trial (only two out of every 10 prisoners in Buenos Aires prisons have been sentenced). Following the recommendations of the court, in March 2006 the province of Buenos Aires reformed its criminal procedure code, restricting the circumstances under which judges could order suspects remanded to custody, and obliging judges to consider alternatives to preventive detention.

Although there were fewer fatal incidents in 2006 than in 2005, prisoners continue to die as a result of preventable inmate violence. In December 2005 a prison inspector from the Public Defender's office of San Martin, in Buenos Aires province, denounced prison guards for selling home-made knives, known as *facas*, to inmates in Campana prison. The following month, 35-year-old Alejandro Leiva Duarte was stabbed to death with one of these weapons in Magdalena prison.

Judicial Independence

After years in which the independence and quality of Argentina's top judges were constantly put in question, President Kirchner has taken important steps to increase the transparency of appointments to the Supreme Court by requiring that executive branch nominations are debated in public hearings, and that civil society groups can have the opportunity to express their views.

At the same time, however, President Kirchner signed legislation in 2006 that threatens the independence of the judiciary by restructuring the Council of the Judiciary, the body responsible for selecting judges for appointment by the executive branch. The new law increases the power of the governing party at the expense of minority parties (which have been eliminated from the council) and of judges, lawyers, and academics (whose numbers have been reduced), thereby decisively altering the balance between political and professional opinion on the council envisaged by the constitution. In October, lawyers across the nation elected their two representatives to the new council, but thousands abstained. At this writing, the Supreme Court was due to rule on a constitutional challenge to the new law brought by the Buenos Aires Bar Association.

According to the Chief Justice, President Kirchner's long delay in replacing two justices on the Supreme Court made it difficult for the court to reach decisions. At this writing, the court had only seven members, as opposed to the nine stipulated by law, but all decisions still had to be based on a majority of five votes. Several civil society groups also expressed concern that without the new appointments this high voting requirement was holding up rulings on issues of public concern.

Freedom of Expression

After being under debate for several years, bills to strengthen press freedom and access to information have failed to clear Congress. A bill to make defamation of public officials punishable only by civil damages and not criminal penalties, which was presented in compliance with a friendly agreement brokered in 1999 by the Inter-American Commission on Human Rights, has not advanced. Additionally, a bill giving Argentine citizens the right to information held by public bodies made no progress for a second consecutive year. The lower house approved the bill in May 2003, but the Senate voted for a much-weakened version that had been approved by a committee chaired by the president's wife, Cristina Fernández de Kirchner. In November 2005 the bill was dropped altogether from the parliamentary agenda.

Some provincial governments discriminate in the distribution of official advertising by rewarding local media that provide favorable coverage and punishing those with a critical editorial line. In 2003 the newspaper *Rio Negro* filed a writ with the Supreme Court alleging that the provincial government of Neuquen had drastically reduced its advertisements in reprisal for the newspaper's coverage of a bribery scandal that indirectly implicated the governor. In September 2006 the attorney general issued an opinion on the appeal. Although he stated that the Neuquen government had not violated the Constitution, he urged the legislature to issue laws at the national and provincial levels to regulate the distribution of official advertising, limiting the wide discretion currently enjoyed by government authorities. At this writing, the *Rio Negro* case was still awaiting final decision by the Supreme Court.

Access to Legal Abortion

Women in Argentina face arbitrary and discriminatory restrictions on their reproductive decisions and access to contraceptives and abortion, while sexual violence goes unpunished at times. Abortion is legal for mentally disabled rape victims, but women face obstacles even when their rights are protected by law. In
one notorious case in 2006, a mentally disabled woman who had been raped and
impregnated by her uncle had to go to court and pass a series of legal hurdles
before she could obtain a legal abortion that the hospital doctors initially had
been willing to perform.

Human Rights Defenders

In a welcome new trend, Argentina's Supreme Court has allowed civil society
organizations to present *amicus curiae* briefs on issues of public interest. The
case involving restructuring of the Council of the Judiciary and the *Rio Negro* case
are among those for which the court has authorized the presentation of *amicus
curiae*.

Key International Actors

The Inter-American Court of Human Rights continued to monitor the performance
of the government in implementing provisional measures ordered by the court to
protect the lives and physical security of prisoners held in the province of
Mendoza. In March 2006 the court renewed the measures, noting that the situation in prisons in Mendoza had not tangibly improved.

In proceedings before the Inter-American Commission on Human Rights in 2005,
the Argentine government formally accepted partial responsibility for failing to
prevent the 1994 bombing of the Jewish Argentine Mutual Association (AMIA),
and for subsequently failing to properly investigate the crime, in which 85 people
died. In October 2006 an Argentine special prosecutor accused Iran of planning
the attack, and Hezbollah of carrying it out. The following month, a federal judge
issued an international warrant for the arrest of former Iranian president Ali Akbar
Hashemi-Rafsanjani and eight other former Iranian officials.

BRAZIL

Significant human rights violations continue in Brazil. Police are often abusive and corrupt, prison conditions are abysmal, and rural violence and land conflicts are ongoing. Human rights defenders suffer threats and attacks. This year was marked by violent clashes between police and criminal groups, and by a series of rebellions in Brazilian prisons.

While the Brazilian government has made efforts to redress human rights abuses, it has rarely held accountable those responsible for the violations.

Police Violence

Police violence—including excessive use of force, extrajudicial executions, torture and other forms of ill-treatment—persists as one of Brazil's most intractable human rights problems.

According to official figures, police killed 328 people in the state of Sao Paulo during the first six months of 2006, an 84 percent increase from the same period in 2005. Many of these killings occurred in May, after members of the First Command of the Capital (Primeiro Comando da Capital, PCC), a criminal gang, launched a series of coordinated attacks against police officers, prison guards, city buses, banks, and public buildings. Police responded to these attacks aggressively and, in some instances, with excessive force. The resulting clashes between police and gang members caused the death of more than 100 civilians and some 40 security agents in the state of Sao Paulo, according to official estimates. A preliminary investigation by an independent committee found strong evidence that many of the killings documented during this period were extrajudicial executions.

Police violence was also common in the state of Rio de Janeiro, where police killed 520 people in the first half of 2006, according to official data describing the situations as "resistance followed by death." Sixteen police officers were killed during the same period of time.

Torture

Torture remains a serious problem in Brazil. There have been credible reports of police and prison guards torturing people in their custody as a form of punishment, intimidation, and extortion. Police have also used torture as a means of obtaining information or coercing confessions from criminal suspects.

In June 2006, Brazil's Special Human Rights Secretariat created a National Committee for the Prevention and Control of Torture. The committee, comprised of public authorities and civil society representatives, is charged with proposing and monitoring mechanisms aimed at curbing the use of torture in the country, as well as conducting inspection visits to detention centers. Several states have committed themselves to implementing an Integrated Action Plan for the Prevention and Control of Torture that was developed by a commission of experts convened by the federal government.

Brazil also recognized the competence of the United Nations Committee against Torture to receive and evaluate complaints of torture filed by individuals within Brazil, pursuant to Article 22 of the UN Convention against Torture.

Prison Conditions

The inhumane conditions, violence, corruption, and overcrowding that have historically characterized Brazilian prisons remain one of the country's main human rights problems. According to the Ministry of Justice, Brazilian prisons held 371,482 inmates in June 2006, exceeding the system's capacity by more than 150,000 inmates.

Prison authorities in Sao Paulo responded to a riot that destroyed detention facilities in the Araraquara Prison in June 2006 by cramming some 1,500 detainees into a single open-air yard with an estimated capacity for 160 people and reportedly forcing them to remain there for three weeks, without adequate clothing or blankets, and exposed to the elements. Although some of the inmates reportedly suffered from diseases such as tuberculosis, HIV, and diabetes, they were denied access to medical assistance.

Similarly, in the Mirandopolis Prison, also located in Sao Paulo, 1,200 inmates were reportedly kept in an area designed to hold no more than 450 for two months after a rebellion destroyed the detention facilities.

Violence continues to be commonplace in prisons throughout the country. In Espirito Santo, two inmates were killed, one of them decapitated, during a riot at the Viana Penitentiary, a maximum security facility located in the municipality of Vila Velha. In Rondonia, more than 200 people were held hostage for 24 hours at Urso Branco Prison during uprisings in June and July 2006. The Inter-American Court of Human Rights has ordered Brazil to adopt measures to guarantee the safety of inmates in Urso Branco on four occasions since 2002, but Brazil has failed to do so. Many uprisings throughout the country could be avoided if Brazil were to improve prison conditions.

Although children and adolescents are granted special protection under Brazilian and international law, they are also subjected to serious abuses by the juvenile detention system in Brazil. Young inmates are subject to violence by other youths or prison guards. In May 2006, an inmate was knifed to death in Unit 12 of the Fundacao Estadual do Bem-Estar do Menor (FEBEM), the juvenile detention center in Sao Paulo. Human rights groups reported at least 28 deaths of adolescents during the past three years, all of which occurred while they were in custody at state-run juvenile detention centers in Sao Paulo. Inhuman conditions and violence are also pervasive in juvenile detention centers in Rio de Janeiro, where the judiciary and other institutions have failed to provide effective oversight.

Rural Violence and Land Conflict

Indigenous people, landless peasants, and human rights defenders face threats, violent attacks, and killings as a result of land disputes in rural areas. According to the Pastoral Land Commission, 38 people were killed, 166 were wounded, and 261 were arrested in rural conflicts throughout the country in 2005. In August 2006, two leaders of the Movement of Landless Rural Workers (MST) were killed in the municipality of Moreno, in Pernambuco.

Forced Labor

Brazil has made progress in curbing the use of forced labor. Since 1995, some 21,000 workers have been freed by mobile inspection teams comprised of labor inspectors, prosecutors, and the federal police.

Yet forced labor still thrives in some rural areas. Estimates indicate that between 25,000 and 40,000 people are subject to forced labor in Brazil. The International Labor Organization reported in 2006 that impunity is one of the main obstacles to ending the practice in Brazil. A bill proposing the expropriation of land where forced labor is used has lagged in the Brazilian Congress since 2001.

Impunity

Human rights violations in Brazil are rarely prosecuted. In an effort to remedy this problem, the Brazilian government passed a constitutional amendment in 2004 that makes human rights crimes federal offenses. The amendment allows certain human rights violations to be transferred from the state to the federal justice system for investigation and trial. Yet, to date, there have been no such transfers, and thus in practice, this amendment has had little real impact.

In 2006, the Sao Paulo State Supreme Court overturned the conviction of Colonel Ubiratan Guimarães, who was responsible for the 1992 operation to put down a rebellion in the Carandiru Prison which resulted in the death of 111 prisoners. Colonel Guimarães was sentenced in 2001 to 632 years in prison for his role in the operation. However, the Sao Paulo Supreme Court annulled the decision on the grounds that Guimarães had been acting strictly in line with his duties. No other officer has been tried in relation to this case so far.

In a positive step, a jury in Rio de Janeiro convicted military police officer Carlos Jorge Carvalho in August 2006 to 543 years in prison for his involvement in the Baixada Fluminense massacre, in which 29 people were summarily killed on March 31, 2005. Four other police officers charged in relation to the massacre are still awaiting trial. In October 2006 a police officer initially accused of involvement in the massacre was murdered after contributing to the investigations.

In another important decision, 14 prison officials and guards were convicted in October 2006 of torturing 35 inmates at the juvenile detention facility in Raposo Tavares, Sao Paulo, in 2000. Two high-ranking officials were sentenced to 87 years in prison, the highest punishment ever meted out in the country for torture.

Human Rights Defenders

Human rights defenders continue to face threats and intimidation in Brazil. After Conceicao Paganele, a prominent juvenile rights advocate, denounced the use of torture in a juvenile detention center in Sao Paulo in January 2005, the state's juvenile detention agency filed a complaint against her with the police, alleging that she had incited rebellions in the center and facilitated the escape of several inmates. As a result, the police opened a criminal investigation against her.

Key International Actors

The Inter-American Court of Human Rights ruled against Brazil for the first time on August 17, 2006. The court held that Brazil was responsible for the death of Damião Ximenes Lopes, a young psychiatric patient who was subjected to ill-treatment and died while in the custody of a mental health clinic in the state of Ceara, on October 4, 1999. The court ordered Brazil to pay reparations to Lopes' family, as well as to guarantee that the case is properly investigated and that those responsible for his death are held accountable.

In May 2006 Brazil was elected one of the 47 members of the recently created Human Rights Council of the United Nations, and it will hold its seat for two years.

CHILE

Chile continues to prosecute former military personnel accused of committing grave human rights violations during the dictatorship of General Augusto Pinochet. Since she took office in March 2006, President Michelle Bachelet has said she will push legislation to prevent an amnesty law from obstructing prosecutions for past abuses, and to allow Chile to join the International Criminal Court.

Chile has also made significant advances in protecting the rights of detainees and ensuring due process in criminal trials. Conditions in Chile's seriously overcrowded prisons remain a serious concern, however, and Chile's over-extended system of military justice still allows civilians to be prosecuted by military courts.

Prosecutions for Past Human Rights Violations

As of October 2006, courts had convicted 109 individuals for crimes including "disappearances," extrajudicial executions, and torture under military rule. Thirty-five former generals of the army, police, and air force have been convicted or are facing trial. Paradoxically, these advances have been achieved even though successive governments have allowed an amnesty law exempting military personnel from punishment for crimes committed between 1973 and 1978 to stand. In cases of enforced disappearance the Supreme Court has generally held the law to be inapplicable, considering them to be kidnappings that are ongoing until the victim's death can be proven. For example, in May and June 2006, the Supreme Court reversed decisions of the Santiago Appeals Court which had granted amnesty to the alleged kidnappers of Jacqueline Binfa and Diana Aron in 1974.

Several judges, however, consider the amnesty applicable to killings that took place during the period covered by the law. In March, for example, Judge Víctor Montiglio amnestied three military officers accused of "disappearances" in Arica in 1973, after concluding that the victims had been killed. Other appellate judges disagree and have ruled that international human rights law invalidates the amnesty in all cases of grave human rights abuse. At this writing, the Supreme Court had yet to issue a ruling on this crucial issue.

In October 2006, however, President Bachelet announced that she would present a bill to prevent the amnesty law from being applied in cases of grave human rights abuse. Her announcement came in response to a ruling of the Inter-American Court of Human Rights that the law was incompatible with the American Convention on Human Rights, and therefore without legal effect.

Court cases against former dictator Augusto Pinochet continue to accumulate. In October 2006, Pinochet was charged for the torture and disappearance of more than 50 people who were held after the military coup at the Villa Grimaldi, a notorious Santiago detention center. He is still being prosecuted for an elaborate scheme in 1975 to cover up the abduction and murder of 119 Chilean leftists, known as Operation Colombo. Pinochet also faces charges of tax evasion and forgery following the discovery of secret bank accounts in the United States in which he had stashed away millions of dollars.

Identifying the remains of victims of the dictatorship continues to be a major problem. Mistaken identifications have caused the victims' relatives uncertainty and anguish for many years. In April 2006, the director of the Medical Legal Service (Servicio Medico Legal, SML), the forensic service affiliated with the Justice Ministry, admitted that the SML had wrongly identified the remains of at least 48 victims of extrajudicial executions whose bodies had been exhumed in 1991 from unmarked graves in the Santiago General Cemetery. In August 2006, a panel of international experts arrived in Santiago to revise and correct the SML's procedures and findings.

Army Abuses Committed after the Return to Democracy

Court investigations into human rights abuses by the army committed after the return to democracy in 1990 have advanced. Such abuses include killings to prevent former agents from testifying in human rights and arms trafficking cases. In April 2006, three Uruguayan army officers were extradited to Chile to face charges of involvement—with two former directors of Chilean army intelligence—in a conspiracy to hide in Uruguay a former Chilean agent who had developed chemical weapons believed to have been used in political assassinations. The agent, Eugenio Berríos, was found on a Uruguayan beach in 1995 with a bullet through his head. In addition, five army officers, including two generals, are facing trial for covering up the murder in 1992 of Gerardo Huber, a Chilean army colonel who was a key witness in an investigation into illegal arms sales to Croatia.

Torture Commission

The government has continued to confront the military-era legacy of torture, even though it has not supported prosecutions for this systematic abuse. The main political parties agreed in 2006 that torture victims who were unable to give their testimonies to the Commission on Political Imprisonment and Torture, which reported in November 2004, should be given an opportunity to do so. On the negative side, in June 2006, the Supreme Court unanimously upheld former President Ricardo Lagos's order that all testimonies be kept secret for 50 years.

Prison Conditions

Chile's prison population increases by 8 percent a year and its prisons are severely overcrowded. In 2006 approximately 39,000 prisoners were being housed in facilities designed to accommodate 24,000. Much of the increase is due to the greater efficiency of the courts following the introduction of a new nationwide prosecutorial system. It has been aggravated by delays in the construction of new prisons contracted out to private companies.

A report published by the Diego Portales University Law Faculty in June 2006 highlighted serious problems of overcrowding, lack of adequate medical attention, violent deaths, torture and ill-treatment, and corruption by prison guards. The Southern Santiago Center for Preventive Detention, with a maximum capacity of 3,170, contained 5,617 inmates at the time of the report's publication. According to a report sent to the Minister of Justice by a Supreme Court official, prisoners were kept locked up in overcrowded cells, mostly without sanitation or ventilation and poorly lit, for 15 hours at a time.

Prison overcrowding and an inadequate prison service contribute to violent deaths in prison fights. Thirty-three prisoners were reported in September 2006 to have died during the year in fights, many of them stabbed to death with homemade knives.

Terrorism Prosecutions of Mapuche

The Bachelet government has tried to end the use of Chile's anti-terrorism law to prosecute members of Chile's largest indigenous group, the Mapuche, for crimes against property committed during land protests. In April, the government announced that it would cease invoking the law in such cases. However, Congress has refused to allow parole for Mapuche prisoners already convicted under the law, three of whom, together with a sympathizer, staged an unsuccessful 70-day hunger strike in May to obtain their release. A bill proposed by the government to remove from the anti-terrorism law crimes against property in which there are no victims, also failed to garner support.

Police Abuses and Military Justice

Police brutality and excessive use of force against the Mapuche are problems in parts of southern Chile where there are continuing conflicts over land. Investigations into these incidents are usually conducted by military prosecutors. Any charges of violence against the police, or of violent abuses by the police, are heard by military courts that are staffed by officers on active service and therefore provide no guarantees of independence and impartiality.

A government-sponsored commission exists to draw up proposals to restrict the scope of military courts and to bring them into line with due process standards, but no bill has yet been presented to Congress.

International Criminal Court Ratification

Chile is the only nation in Latin America that has signed but not yet ratified the Rome Statute for the International Criminal Court. The reform has been stalled since April 2002, when the Constitutional Court, ruling on a petition by a group of opposition senators, declared the ratification bill unconstitutional. In August 2006, senators postponed the debate once again, asking the government to clarify the potential effects on Chile's defense acquisitions should the United States apply sanctions under the American Service-Members' Protection Act (ASPA), which prohibits US aid to countries that ratify the Rome Statute without promising not to refer United States citizens for prosecution by the court.

Key International Actors

The Inter-American Court of Human Rights has issued several landmark rulings on Chilean cases. In November 2005, it ruled against Chile in the Palamara case, involving a former civilian navy employee whose treatise on military intelligence was censored by the navy, and who was convicted by a naval court in 1995 for disrespect. The court found that Chile's military tribunals had excessively wide jurisdiction, including over civilians, and failed to comply with international standards of competence, independence, and impartiality. It ordered Chile to reform its military courts, to ensure that they meet these standards, and to end their jurisdiction over civilians.

In September 2006, the court ruled against Chile for failing to provide a nongovernmental environmental group with access to information about a logging project in the south of Chile. It ordered the government to take measures to ensure the right of access to public information.

COLOMBIA

Colombia remains mired in a decades-long internal armed conflict, which continues to result in widespread abuses by irregular armed groups, including both guerrillas and paramilitaries, as well as by the Colombian armed forces.

Civilians suffer the brunt of the conflict, as every year thousands become displaced by the violence, losing their homes and livelihoods. Forced disappearances, extrajudicial executions, targeted assassinations, threats, and kidnappings remain commonplace. The vast majority of abuses remain unaddressed.

Both paramilitary groups and guerrillas continue to be well-financed through resources from the drug business. Paramilitaries have also become increasingly involved in large-scale corruption schemes, infiltrating national governmental institutions, controlling local politicians, and diverting funds from state agencies.

Demobilization of Paramilitary Groups

The Colombian government claimed in 2006 that it had successfully completed the demobilization of more than 30,000 supposed paramilitaries, but serious questions remain as to the effectiveness of the demobilization process in dismantling paramilitaries' complex criminal and financial structures, and ensuring truth, justice, and reparation.

Paramilitary commanders have not taken significant steps to give up their massive illegally acquired wealth, return stolen land, or show that they have ceased their lucrative criminal activities. Disturbing indicators of their persistent influence in 2006 included: reports of paramilitary infiltration of the Intelligence Service; increasing threats against academics, union leaders, human rights defenders, and journalists; and the formation of new paramilitary groups, as reported by the Organization of American States' (OAS) Mission to Support the Peace Process.

In May 2006, the Colombian Constitutional Court ruled on the constitutionality of the government's controversial "Justice and Peace Law," which offers dramatically reduced sentences to paramilitaries responsible for atrocities and other serious crimes. The court approved the reduced sentences, but through interpretation, made several important improvements to the law, ruling that paramilitaries would have to confess and pay reparations out of their legal and illegal assets, and that if they lied or committed new crimes, they could risk losing their reduced sentences. It also held that prosecutors would have to fully investigate all confessed crimes.

In September, the government issued a decree that partially implemented the court ruling, but that also conferred upon the paramilitary leadership even greater benefits by allowing them to avoid prison altogether by serving their reduced sentences on farms or at home instead.

A number of commanders turned themselves in for voluntary confinement in a retreat house in the state of Antioquia, but many others remain at large.

New paramilitary abuses, including killings and forced disappearances, continued to be reported throughout the year. In October, the Attorney General's office revealed that a confiscated computer owned by an associate of the paramilitary leader known as "Jorge 40" had turned up evidence of over 500 assassinations committed in just one Colombian state between 2003 and 2005. The computer also pointed to continuing plans by the paramilitaries' Northern Block to expand their political power and territorial control.

Talks with Guerrillas

Throughout 2006, the Colombian government engaged in preliminary talks with the National Liberation Army (ELN) guerrillas, to set the terms for eventual peace negotiations. President Uribe announced that he would seek to obtain resources to support the ELN during peace talks and replace the revenue this group would otherwise obtain from kidnappings and extortion.

Meanwhile, the largest guerrilla group in Colombia, the Revolutionary Armed Forces of Colombia (FARC), expressed interest in discussing an exchange of its hostages for imprisoned guerrilla members. Talks on this issue were cancelled after a bombing in October 2006 for which the government charged the FARC was responsible.

The government persisted in its decision to offer demobilization benefits to FARC members who had already been convicted and were in prison for gross violations of international humanitarian law, such as kidnappings and killings.

Both the FARC and ELN continued to engage in abuses against civilians, which in 2006 included kidnappings, killings, and indiscriminate bombings. Guerrilla groups are responsible for most reported cases of the use of anti-personnel land-mines, which result in hundreds of civilian injuries and deaths every year. Guerrillas are also responsible for most recruitment of child soldiers in Colombia. At least 80 percent of the children under arms in Colombia belong to the FARC or ELN. At least one of every four irregular combatants in Colombia is under 18 years of age. Of these, several thousand are under the age of 15, the minimum recruitment age permitted under the Geneva Conventions.

Impunity and Military-Paramilitary Links

Colombia's long-running failure to effectively investigate, prosecute, and punish human rights abuses has created an environment in which abusers correctly assume that they will never be held accountable for their crimes.

The problem is particularly acute in cases of military abuses, including cases involving credible allegations of military-paramilitary links. Low-ranking officers are sometimes held accountable in these cases, but rarely is a commanding officer prosecuted.

Early in 2006, scores of allegations were made public that units of the army had executed civilians and dressed the corpses as guerrillas so that they could record them as killed in combat. In another case, 21 military recruits were allegedly tortured by their supervisors during training, subjected to beatings, burning, and sexual abuse.

In May 2006, an army unit shot and killed 10 elite anti-narcotics police officers who had been trained by the US Drug Enforcement Administration. Prosecutors labeled the killings intentional, not accidental. Investigation of the case, however, was initially hampered by the fact that the civilian judge charged with the case refused to review it. As of this writing, prosecutions were ongoing.

In one encouraging development, prosecutors announced that they had obtained new evidence in a case involving the "disappearances" of 10 people in the 1985 retaking by security forces of Colombia's Palace of Justice (which housed the Supreme Court), after its invasion by the M-19 guerrilla group.

Internal Displacement

With a cumulative total of more than 3.7 million displaced persons, Colombia continues to have the world's largest internal displacement crisis after Sudan, and incidents of forced displacement rose from 2003 to 2005, according to the non-governmental Consultancy for Human Rights and the Displaced (Consultoria para los Derechos Humanos y el Desplazamiento, CODHES). While government data for these years are lower, they reflect the same trend. (At this writing, data for 2006 were not available.)

Those who are internally displaced are generally worse off than the poorest members of their host communities, with two-thirds living in inadequate housing with no access to basic sanitation, according to studies by the International Committee of the Red Cross, the Catholic Church, and the University of the Andes. Only one in five displaced persons receives medical care, and some 300,000 displaced children do not have access to education, the Geneva-based Internal Displacement Monitoring Centre reported in June 2006.

The Colombian government quietly has backed away from its earlier policy, roundly criticized by local and international observers, which had promoted return to home communities as its principal response to displacement. But the central government refuses in some instances to extend recognition to groups thought to be taking a "political stance" against the government. As a practical matter, the denial of recognition means that most displaced individuals return to their home communities even though the security situation does not enable a safe and dignified return.

In response to a 2004 Constitutional Court finding that the government's system for assisting displaced persons was unconstitutional, the Colombian government substantially increased its budget for protection and humanitarian assistance for displaced persons, committing more than US$2 billion dollars for the five-year period ending in 2010.

A major assistance program funded by the US Agency for International Development and managed by the International Organization for Migration and the Pan-American Development Foundation had a slow start in 2006.

Access to Legal Abortion

In May 2006 Colombia's constitutional court declared that the country's blanket criminalization of abortion violated women's constitutional rights, a landmark decision for the region. The court declared that neither women nor doctors can be penalized for procuring or providing abortions where one of three conditions is met: 1) the pregnancy constitutes a grave danger to the pregnant woman's life or health; 2) the fetus has serious genetic malformations; and 3) the pregnancy is the result of rape or incest.

Human Rights Monitors and Other Vulnerable Groups

Human rights monitors, as well as labor leaders, journalists, and other vulnerable groups continue to be the subjects of frequent threats, harassment, and attacks for their legitimate work. Investigations of these cases rarely result in prosecutions or convictions.

President Uribe once again made statements attacking the media for its coverage of public issues, singling out individual journalists and papers, and accusing them of being dishonest, malicious, and harmful to democratic institutions.

The Ministry of Interior has a protection program, established with US funding, to offer protection to threatened persons. Nonetheless, a number of individuals have complained about feeling intimidated by the armed escorts—who have often been agents of the intelligence service—assigned to them.

Key International Actors

The United States remains the most influential foreign actor in Colombia. In 2006 it provided close to US$800 million to the Colombian government, mostly in military aid. Twenty-five percent of US security assistance is formally subject to human rights conditions, but the conditions have not been consistently enforced. In 2006 the United States also started providing financial support for the paramilitary demobilization process, certifying Colombia's compliance with related conditions in US law.

The OAS Mission to Support the Peace Process in Colombia, which is charged with verifying the demobilization process, began offering more critical analyses in 2006 after having endorsed the process uncritically in the past. Nonetheless, the mission's effectiveness continues to be limited by its failure to scrutinize judicial proceedings against the paramilitaries and monitor the progress of Colombian authorities in dismantling their complex financial and criminal networks.

Several European governments, including those of Sweden and the Netherlands, continue to provide substantial funding to the OAS Mission.

The Office of the UN High Commissioner for Human Rights is active in Colombia, with a presence in Bogota, Medellin, and Cali. Despite the office's high quality and professional work, the Colombian government repeatedly criticized it in 2006. After protracted negotiations lasting much of the year, the Colombian government extended the office's mandate by one additional year. However, government officials, including Vice President Francisco Santos, stated that they planned to continue negotiating "adjustments" to the scope of the office's mandate.

Cuba

Cuba remains the one country in Latin America that represses nearly all forms of political dissent. President Fidel Castro, during his 47 years in power, has shown no willingness to consider even minor reforms. Instead, the Cuban government continues to enforce political conformity using criminal prosecutions, long- and short-term detentions, mob harassment, police warnings, surveillance, house arrests, travel restrictions, and politically-motivated dismissals from employment. The end result is that Cubans are systematically denied basic rights to free expression, association, assembly, privacy, movement, and due process of law.

Castro's decision in early August to temporarily cede power as a result of medical problems to his brother, Raúl Castro, has prompted intense speculation about the possibility of reform in Cuba. As of this writing, it was unclear whether the older Castro would be able to return to power and what his political absence might signal for the island's future.

Legal and Institutional Failings

Cuba's legal and institutional structures are at the root of rights violations. Although in theory the different branches of government have separate and defined areas of authority, in practice the executive retains clear control over all levers of power. The courts, which lack independence, undermine the right to fair trial by severely restricting the right to a defense.

Cuba's Criminal Code provides the legal basis for repression of dissent. Laws criminalizing enemy propaganda, the spreading of "unauthorized news," and insult to patriotic symbols are used to restrict freedom of speech under the guise of protecting state security. The government also imprisons or orders the surveillance of individuals who have committed no illegal act, relying upon provisions that penalize "dangerousness" (*estado peligroso*) and allow for "official warning" (*advertencia oficial*).

Political Imprisonment

In early July 2006 the Cuban Commission for Human Rights and National Reconciliation, a respected local human rights group, issued a list of 316 prisoners who it said were incarcerated for political reasons. The list included the names of 12 peaceful dissidents who had been arrested and detained in the first half of 2006, of whom five were being held on charges of "dangerousness." Of 75 political dissidents, independent journalists, and human rights advocates who were summarily tried in April 2003, 60 remain imprisoned. Serving sentences that average nearly 20 years, the incarcerated dissidents endure poor conditions and punitive treatment in prison.

Travel Restrictions and Family Separations

The Cuban government forbids the country's citizens from leaving or returning to Cuba without first obtaining official permission, which is often denied. Unauthorized travel can result in criminal prosecution. In May 2006 Oswaldo Payá, the well-known Cuban human rights advocate, was awarded an honorary doctor of laws by Columbia University in New York City in recognition of his work. However, he was denied an exit visa by the Cuban authorities and therefore could not receive the degree in person.

The government also frequently bars citizens engaged in authorized travel from taking their children with them overseas, essentially holding the children hostage to guarantee the parents' return. Given the widespread fear of forced family separation, these travel restrictions provide the Cuban government with a powerful tool for punishing defectors and silencing critics.

Freedom of Expression and Assembly

The Cuban government maintains a media monopoly on the island, ensuring that freedom of expression is virtually non-existent. Although a small number of independent journalists manage to write articles for foreign websites or publish underground newsletters, the risks associated with these activities are considerable. According to Reporters Without Borders, there are currently 23 journalists serving prison terms in Cuba, most of them charged with threatening "the national independence and economy of Cuba." This makes the country second only to China for the number of journalists in prison.

Access to information via the internet is also highly restricted in Cuba. In late August 2006 the dissident and independent journalist Guillermo Fariñas ended a seven-month hunger strike in opposition to the regime's internet policy. He began the strike after the Cuban authorities shut down his e-mail access, which he had been using to send dispatches abroad describing attacks on dissidents and other human rights abuses.

Freedom of assembly is severely restricted in Cuba, and political dissidents are generally prohibited from meeting in large groups. This was evident in mid-September 2006 during the 14th summit of the Non-Aligned Movement in Havana, when the Cuban government issued a ban on all gatherings that might damage "the image" of the city.

Prison Conditions

Prisoners are generally kept in poor and abusive conditions, often in overcrowded cells. They typically lose weight during incarceration, and some receive inade-quate medical care. Some also endure physical and sexual abuse, typically by other inmates and with the acquiescence of guards.

Political prisoners who denounce poor conditions of imprisonment or who other-wise fail to observe prison rules are frequently punished with long periods spent in punitive isolation cells, restrictions on visits, or denial of medical treatment. Some political prisoners have carried out long hunger strikes to protest abusive conditions and mistreatment by guards.

Death Penalty

Under Cuban law the death penalty exists for a broad range of crimes. It is diffi-cult to ascertain the frequency with which this penalty is employed because Cuba does not release information regarding its use. However, as far as is known, no executions have been carried out since April 2003.

Human Rights Defenders

Refusing to recognize human rights monitoring as a legitimate activity, the government denies legal status to local human rights groups. Individuals who belong to these groups face systematic harassment, with the government putting up obstacles to impede them from documenting human rights conditions. In addition, international human rights groups such as Human Rights Watch and Amnesty International are barred from sending fact-finding missions to Cuba. In fact, Cuba remains one of the few countries in the world to deny the International Committee of the Red Cross access to its prisons.

Key International Actors

Cuba's election to the new United Nations Human Rights Council in June 2006 was contrary to the Council's requirement that its members "uphold the highest standards of human rights promotion and protection." Although the new body was designed to replace the discredited Human Rights Commission, whose membership often included notorious human rights violators, the election of Cuba and other countries with poor human rights records confirmed that the Council has not yet risen above this disturbing practice. Equally troubling was the Cuban government's characterization of the mandate of the High Commissioner of Human Rights as "spurious" and its assertion that it would not cooperate with her office.

The US economic embargo on Cuba, in effect for more than four decades, continues to impose indiscriminate hardship on the Cuban people and to block travel to the island. An exception to the embargo that allows food sales to Cuba on a cash-only basis, however, has led to substantial trade between the two countries.

In an effort to deprive the Cuban government of funding, the United States government enacted new restrictions on family-related travel to Cuba in June 2004. Under these rules, individuals are allowed to visit relatives in Cuba only once every three years, and only if the relatives fit the US government's narrow definition of family—a definition that excludes aunts, uncles, cousins, and other next-of-kin who are often integral members of Cuban families. Justified as a means of promoting freedom in Cuba, the new travel policies undermine the freedom of movement of hundreds of thousands of Cubans and Cuban Americans, and inflict profound harm on Cuban families.

Countries within the European Union continue to disagree with respect to the best approach to take toward Cuba. In January 2005 the EU decided to temporarily suspend the diplomatic sanctions that it had adopted in the wake of the Cuban government's 2003 crackdown against dissidents. In June 2006 the EU decided to maintain the sanctions freeze for an additional year, although it also issued a statement lamenting the "further deterioration of the human rights situation in Cuba" and "several dozen acts of violent harassment and intimidation" over the past year. The Czech Republic was the member country most strongly in favor of a tougher stance towards Cuba.

GUATEMALA

Twenty years after the return of civilian rule, Guatemala has made little progress toward securing the protection of human rights and the rule of law, essential features of a functioning democracy. Impunity remains the rule when it comes to human rights abuses. Ongoing acts of political violence and intimidation threaten to reverse the little progress that has been made toward promoting accountability in recent years.

Impunity

Guatemala continues to suffer the effects of an internal armed conflict that ended in 1996. A truth commission sponsored by the United Nations estimated that as many as 200,000 people were killed during the 36-year war and attributed the vast majority of the killings to government forces.

As Human Rights Watch has noted in the past, Guatemalans seeking accountability for these abuses face daunting obstacles. The prosecutors and investigators who handle these cases receive grossly inadequate training and resources. The courts routinely fail to resolve judicial appeals and motions in an expeditious manner, allowing defense attorneys to engage in dilatory legal maneuvering. The army and other state institutions fail to cooperate fully with investigations into abuses committed by current or former members. The police do not provide adequate protection to judges, prosecutors, and witnesses involved in politically sensitive cases.

Of the 626 massacres documented by the truth commission, only two cases have been successfully prosecuted in the Guatemalan courts. In 1999, a Guatemalan court sentenced three former civil defense patrol members to prison for the murders of two of the 177 civilians massacred in Rio Negro in 1982. In addition, in October 2005, the Supreme Court of Justice upheld the 2004 sentencing of a lieutenant and 13 soldiers to 40 years in prison for the 1995 Xaman massacre in which 11 civilians were killed.

By contrast, the prosecution of former military officers allegedly responsible for the 1982 Dos Erres massacre, in which at least 162 people died, has been held up for years by dilatory defense motions. Furthermore, the trial of six other civil defense patrol members, alleged to be complicit in the Rio Negro massacres, has been delayed since October 2004 because of defendants' appeals.

The few other convictions obtained in human rights cases have come at considerable cost. In the case of Myrna Mack, an anthropologist who was assassinated in 1990, it took more than a decade to obtain the conviction of an army colonel, Valencia Osorio, for his role in orchestrating the killing. During that time, a police investigator who gathered incriminating evidence was murdered, and two other investigators—as well as three witnesses—received threats and fled the country. Osorio, meanwhile, escaped police custody and has not served his sentence.

The July 2005 discovery of approximately 70 to 80 million documents of the disbanded National Police, including files on Guatemalans who were murdered and "disappeared" during the armed conflict, could play a key role in the prosecution of those who committed human rights violations during the conflict. Unfortunately, there is no legal framework in place to ensure adequate long-term management of the archive, nor to regulate public access to its files.

Impunity remains a chronic problem with common crimes as well. The Guatemalan Human Rights Ombudsman's Office estimates, for example, that arrests are only made in 3 percent of the cases involving murders of women and girls. The prosecution of those who commit violence against women is impeded by discriminatory legislation that prevents punishment for some violent crimes against women, and impunity is further fueled by deeply ingrained gender discrimination within the government agencies responsible for the investigation and prosecution of these crimes.

Frustration with the lack of justice in Guatemala has undoubtedly contributed to acts of vigilantism in the last several years. Public lynching is a common problem, with 25 lynching cases reported in 2004 and 32 in 2005. The majority of lynching victims were suspected of having committed a crime, but there has also been lynching in the past few years which was motivated by other factors, such as disputes over land or water.

Several steps have been taken by the Guatemalan government in 2006 to combat impunity, improve the justice system, and guarantee the rights of prisoners. In

October 2006, Guatemalan President Oscar Berger approved a prison reform law (Ley del Regimen del Sistema Penitenciario), passed by Congress the previous month, which includes provisions setting up rehabilitation programs and schools within prisons.

Attacks and Threats by "Clandestine Groups"

Over the past five years, there has been an alarming number of attacks and threats against Guatemalans seeking justice for past abuses. The targets have included human rights advocates, justice officials, forensic experts, and plaintiffs and witnesses involved in human rights cases. They have also included journalists, labor activists, and others who have denounced abuses by the authorities. Guatemalan human rights organizations state that 161 such acts of violence or intimidation were reported between January and August 2006.

On April 2, 2006, Meregilda Súchite was murdered, apparently in connection with her work as a community leader and member of a women's human rights group, which is supported by the Center for Legal Action in Human Rights (Centro para la Accion Legal en Derechos Humanos, CALDH). Members of the Guatemalan Foundation for Forensic Anthropology (Fundacion de Antropologia Forense de Guatemala, FAFG) continued to receive death threats in 2006, in connection with their work exhuming bodies buried in clandestine cemeteries throughout the country.

There is widespread consensus among local and international observers that the people responsible for these acts of violence and intimidation are affiliated with private, secretive, and illegally armed networks or organizations, commonly referred to in Guatemala as "clandestine groups." These groups appear to have links to both government officials and organized crime—which give them access to considerable political and economic resources. The Guatemalan justice system, which has little ability even to contain common crime, has so far proven no match for this powerful and dangerous threat to the rule of law.

Excessive Use of Force

While political violence is no longer carried out as a matter of official state policy, members of the national police still sometimes employ excessive force against suspected criminals and others. The perpetrators are often poorly trained police officers. Between January and June 2005, there were 257 complaints made to the Guatemalan Human Rights Ombudsman's Office for abuse of authority by police or prison guards and 18 complaints filed for extrajudicial killings by police or prison guards. For example, a transgender woman was murdered and another was critically wounded on December 17, 2005, when they were gunned down on a street in Guatemala City. Eyewitnesses reported that the gunmen were uniformed police officers.

Key International Actors

The UN High Commissioner for Human Rights opened an office in Guatemala in 2005 to provide observation and technical assistance on human rights practices. In February 2006, the office issued a report on human rights in Guatemala, expressing its concern over the current situation and urging the government to take a number of steps in order to combat violence and impunity, such as ratifying the Optional Protocol to the Convention against Torture and Other Cruel, Inhuman or Degrading Treatment or Punishment.

Efforts continue to secure the implementation of the 2004 agreement between Guatemala and the UN to establish a special commission to investigate and promote the prosecution of "clandestine groups." The Commission for the Investigation of Illegal Groups and Clandestine Security Organizations (Comision de Investigacion de Cuerpos Ilegales y Aparatos Clandestinos y de Seguridad, CICIACS) grew out of a proposal developed by the Guatemalan government and local human rights groups, in consultation with members of the international community. In 2004, Guatemala's Constitutional Court held that several of the agreement's provisions were unconstitutional. In May 2006, the Guatemalan government presented to the UN a revised version of the agreement. At this writing, the Guatemalan government and the UN are still negotiating the contents of the CICIACS agreement.

In a landmark ruling, Spain's Constitutional Court held on September 26, 2005 that, in accordance with the principal of "universal jurisdiction," cases of alleged genocide committed during Guatemala's internal armed conflict could be prosecuted in the Spanish courts, even if no Spanish citizens were involved. On June 24, 2006, Spanish Judge Santiago Pedraz, a Spanish prosecutor, and two private prosecutors went to Guatemala to take testimony from the defendants. However, no testimony was given because the defendants filed numerous appeals, and the Guatemalan Constitutional Court suspended the proceedings indefinitely. On July 7, 2006, Judge Pedraz issued international arrest warrants for eight Guatemalan defendants and issued an order to freeze the defendants' assets, both in Spain and internationally. In November, a Guatemalan court authorized the arrest of four of the defendants. At this writing, Spain had not yet sought extradition of the suspects from Guatemala.

The Inter-American human rights system continues to provide an important venue for human rights advocates seeking to press Guatemala to accept responsibility for past abuses.

HAITI

Haiti made important progress in restoring democratic rule in 2006, successfully holding national elections without any of the major security disturbances that had prevented people from voting in past elections. The new government of President René Préval faces entrenched lawlessness and chronic human rights problems, including pervasive police violence and inhumane prison conditions.

Elections

Parliamentary and presidential elections were held in February 2006, after having been postponed four times due to security concerns and logistical difficulties. These were Haiti's first elections since Jean-Bertrand Aristide was ousted from the presidency in 2004. An electoral monitoring mission sent by the Organization of American States considered the elections a success. Yet when initial results showed that Préval had not won enough votes to avoid a run-off election, rumors of fraud triggered street protests and riots, which only ended after a political compromise was reached and Préval was officially declared president-elect.

Violence, Lawlessness, and Instability

Violent crime remains rampant in Haiti. Kidnappings for ransom of businessmen, students, journalists, aid workers, and foreigners are commonplace. Criminal gangs effectively control certain neighborhoods of the capital, most notably Cite Soleil, and gang violence often results in civilian deaths. In July 2006, for example, 22 people, including children, were killed in Grand Ravine, a poor neighborhood in Port-au-Prince.

The gangs have also clashed with the joint United Nations and Haitian security forces. Three peacekeepers from the Brazilian battalion of the Haiti Stabilization Mission (MINUSTAH) were shot and wounded in Cite Soleil in July 2006.

Police Abuses

Police lawlessness continues to be a major contributor to overall insecurity. The Haitian National Police (HNP) are largely ineffective in preventing and investigating crime. Moreover, they are themselves responsible for arbitrary arrests, torture, beatings, and the excessive and indiscriminate use of force. They also face credible allegations of having committed extrajudicial executions and of involvement in drug trafficking and other criminal activity. Untrained and unprofessional, the police suffer from severe shortages of personnel and equipment. Police perpetrate abuses with almost total impunity. Human Rights Watch knows of no members of the HNP who have faced criminal prosecution for their abusive conduct.

Justice, Accountability, and Prison Conditions

Haiti's highly dysfunctional justice system is plagued by corruption, politicization, and a lack of personnel, training, and resources. In the provinces, judges complain there are no police to execute warrants and no prisons in which to keep detainees. Few crimes are investigated. Where prisons exist, conditions are dire, with prisoners held in dirty and overcrowded cells often lacking sanitary facilities.

Arbitrary and long-term pretrial detention of suspects is commonplace. In several prominent cases, people who had been imprisoned without proper trial were released in 2006. For example, activist and folksinger Annette Auguste (known as So Ann), as well as her co-defendants, Georges Honoré, Yvon Antoine (Zap Zap), and Paul Raymond, were released in August 2006 after more than 27 months in jail without formal charges. Similarly, former Prime Minister Yvon Neptune was released in July 2006 after spending 25 months in prison, and his former interior minister, Jocelerme Privert, was released in June of the same year after serving 26 months in prison. Both men were incarcerated without trial on allegations of participation in the killing of 50 Aristide opponents in La Scierie, Saint-Marc in February 2004.

Accountability for past abuses remains out of reach. While the release of Neptune and Privert may have been warranted given the state's failure to properly try them, the La Scierie case was never fully investigated and the atrocities that the two men allegedly committed remain unpunished. While Haiti took an important step in 2005 by arresting 15 police officers for their alleged participation in a Martissant soccer stadium massacre in August 2005, many of these men, including two senior officers, were released from prison in 2006 by the judge handling the case.

Persecution of Human Rights Defenders

Haitian human rights activists and journalists remain targets of acts of violence and intimidation. Bruner Esterne, the coordinator of the Grand Ravine Community Human Rights Council (CHRC-GR), was killed by unknown individuals on September 21, 2006, as he was returning from a meeting concerning the July massacre in Grand Ravine. Esterne had also witnessed the soccer stadium massacre in August 2005, which had allegedly been carried out by the same criminal gang that is believed to have been responsible for the Grand Ravine killing. Following Esterne's death, Evel Fanfan, a human rights lawyer who had worked closely with Esterne, received death threats.

Key International Actors

The UN stabilization mission in Haiti has been heavily involved in efforts to support and train the local police force to carry out its security functions. The UN Security Council voted unanimously in August 2006 to extend MINUSTAH until February 15, 2007. In mid-July 2006, the force, which was created by a Security Council resolution in April 2004, included approximately 6,200 troops and 1,687 police. The new resolution supported an increase in personnel and called on MINUSTAH to "reorient its disarmament, demobilization and reintegration efforts" in Haiti and to focus on a community violence-reduction program.

The United States is Haiti's largest donor and in 2006 made a new pledge of almost US$210 million, to be allocated over a one-year period to aid in Haiti's economic recovery.

Canada, Haiti's second-largest donor, continues in its efforts "to restore security and stability" in the county. One hundred Canadian civilian police officers are currently part of MINUSTAH and Canada has pledged more than $500 million to the country which will be distributed over a five-year period.

In 2006, the European Union remained committed to the presence of UN forces in Haiti and in June the European Commission's President, José Manuel Barroso, announced that the Commission's aid to Haiti would "rise to €233 million (US$293 million) for the 2008-13 period, from the €168 million set aside to cover 2002-7."

In October 2006, a federal court judge in New York ordered Emmanuel "Toto" Constant, the former leader of Haiti's notorious death squad known as the FRAPH who currently resides in New York City, to pay $19 million in damages to three women who survived rape and torture committed by paramilitary forces under his command from 1991 to 1993.

UN High Commissioner for Human Rights Louise Arbour met with government and civil society representatives during a visit to Haiti in October 2006.

MEXICO

Among Mexico's most serious human rights problems are those affecting its criminal justice system. Persons under arrest or imprisonment face torture and ill-treatment, and law enforcement officials often neglect to investigate and prosecute those responsible for human rights violations.

The presidency of Vicente Fox ended in 2006 with the ambitious human rights agenda that he had brought to office left largely unfulfilled. While the Fox administration succeeded in promoting greater transparency in government, including greater receptivity to international scrutiny of Mexico's human rights practices, the administration made little progress in curbing longstanding abusive practices. When Fox stepped down, the Special Prosecutor's Office that he created in 2001 to address past atrocities had yet to win a single conviction and his comprehensive 2004 proposal to reform the justice system had not been passed by Mexico's Congress.

Police Brutality, Torture, and Pretrial Detention

Mexican police forces routinely employ excessive force when carrying out crowd-control operations. In April 2006, for example, during a police intervention to disperse a miner's strike in Lazaro Cardenas, police forces killed two workers and injured dozens. In May, while dispersing demonstrators in San Salvador de Atenco, police officers killed two people, including one teenager, and arbitrarily detained, beat, and kicked demonstrators. Police also sexually harassed women while they were being transported to a penitentiary.

Torture remains a widespread problem within the Mexican criminal justice system. One perpetuating factor of the practice is the acceptance by some judges of evidence obtained through torture and other mistreatment. Another is the failure to investigate and prosecute most cases of torture.

Over 40 percent of prisoners in Mexico have never been convicted of a crime. Rather, they are held in pretrial detention, often waiting years for trial. The excessive use of pretrial detention contributes to overcrowding in prisons. Prison inmates are also subject to abuses, including extortion by guards and the imposition of solitary confinement for indefinite periods of time. Foreign migrants are especially vulnerable to such abuses.

The justice reform proposal presented by President Fox in 2004 included measures aimed at addressing these chronic abuses. Only a few reforms were adopted and at this writing Congress has yet to vote on most measures addressing the critical problems of torture and pretrial detention.

In a positive development, Congress passed a constitutional reform in December 2005 that forces all jurisdictions to make their juvenile justice systems compatible with human rights norms.

Impunity

The criminal justice system routinely fails to provide justice to victims of violent crime and human rights abuses. The causes of this failure are varied and include corruption, inadequate training and resources, and a lack of political will.

The failure for over a decade to resolve the murders of hundreds of young women and girls in Ciudad Juarez, in Chihuahua state, offers a paradigmatic example of impunity in Mexico. Several individuals facing charges for some of the Juarez killings recanted confessions that they claim were coerced through torture. In one of these cases, David Meza, who in 2003 had confessed under torture that he had murdered his cousin, recanted and was acquitted in June 2006. His cousin's murder has not yet been solved. A shift in policy by the state prosecutor's office in 2004 has led to better investigations of these cases, however.

A major shortcoming of the Mexican justice system is that it leaves the task of investigating and prosecuting army abuses to military authorities. The military justice system is ill-equipped for such tasks. It lacks the independence necessary to carry out reliable investigations and its operations suffer from a general absence of transparency. The ability of military prosecutors to investigate army abuses is further undermined by a fear of the army, which is widespread in many rural communities and which inhibits civilian victims and witnesses from providing information to military authorities.

MEXICO

Lost in Transition

Bold Ambitions, Limited Results for Human Rights Under Fox

HUMAN
RIGHTS
WATCH

The Special Prosecutor's Office

The Special Prosecutor's Office that President Fox established in 2001 to address past abuses has produced limited results. Its initial advances—such as the November 2003 landmark decision from the Mexican Supreme Court holding that statutes of limitations do not apply to old "disappearance" cases as long as the victims' bodies have not been found—have been counterbalanced by significant failures.

The special prosecutor has made only limited progress in uncovering the fate of hundreds of people who were "disappeared" in the 1970s. His most ambitious move—the indictment of former president Luis Echeverria for genocide—was thrown out by the courts. The few cases in which the special prosecutor managed to indict those responsible for forced disappearances were dismissed by courts after Congress modified the federal criminal code in June 2006. There have thus far been no convictions related to the crimes committed during Mexico's "dirty war."

The Special Prosecutor's Office produced a draft report on past abuses which shows there is extensive documentation in government archives implicating former officials and military officers in the "dirty war" crimes. However, far more information could have been collected if a more thorough investigation had been carried out. The draft was leaked to the press in February 2006, but the report still has not been officially published at this writing.

Domestic Violence and Sexual Abuse

Mexican laws do not adequately protect women and girls against domestic violence and sexual abuse. Some laws on violence against women run directly counter to international standards, including provisions of Mexican law that define sanctions for some sexual offenses with reference to the "chastity" of the victim and provisions penalizing domestic violence only when the victim has been battered repeatedly. Legal protections that do exist are often not enforced vigorously. As a result, victims are often reluctant to report crimes and such underreporting in turn undercuts pressure for necessary legal reforms. The net effect is that sexual and domestic violence against women and girls continues to be rampant and shrouded in impunity.

Girls and women who report rape or violence to the authorities are generally met with suspicion, apathy, and disrespect. For pregnant rape victims who want to terminate their imposed pregnancy—as they are legally entitled to do in Mexico— this reaction is even more pronounced. They are ignored or actively silenced in disregard of their human dignity and their rights to nondiscrimination, due process, and equality under the law.

In 2006, both the United Nations Committee on Economic, Social and Cultural Rights and the United Nations Committee on the Elimination of Discrimination against Women reiterated previous calls on Mexico to prevent and punish violence against women, and to provide adequate access to safe abortion services for rape victims.

Freedom of Expression

Journalists—particularly those who have investigated drug trafficking or have been critical of state governments—have occasionally faced harassment and attacks. In February 2006, unidentified individuals attacked the newspaper *El Mañana* in Nuevo Laredo, damaging the installations and wounding a journalist. A photographer was gunned down in Michoacan in March 2006, and a journalist was killed in Chihuahua in August 2006. In February 2006, the federal government created a special prosecutor's office to investigate crimes committed against journalists.

Mexican defamation laws continue to be excessively restrictive and tend to undermine freedom of expression. Besides monetary penalties, journalists are subject to criminal prosecution for alleged defamation of public officials. In December 2005, Lydia Cacho was arrested because she had supposedly failed to answer a court summons in a defamation case against her. Cacho is being criminally prosecuted for the publication of a book that describes a child prostitution ring that, according to her, operated with the complicity of local police and politicians. In March 2006, Isabel Arvide was convicted for defamation in relation to an article published in 2001 on the involvement of state government officials in a drug cartel in Chihuahua. She received a one-year prison sentence (which the judge suspended) and was ordered to pay a fine of approximately US$18,000.

Access to Information

A 2002 federal law on transparency and access to information increased avenues for public scrutiny of the federal government. However, there is still considerable risk that secrecy will reassert itself in the future: the federal agency in charge of applying the law to the executive has not been granted autonomy from the executive branch, remains vulnerable to political interference, and has encountered resistance from several key government agencies. The progress made in promoting transparency within the executive branch has not been matched in other branches of government nor in the autonomous state institutions.

Labor Rights

Legitimate labor-organizing activity continues to be obstructed by collective bargaining agreements negotiated between management and pro-management unions. These agreements often fail to provide worker benefits beyond the minimums mandated by Mexican legislation. Workers who seek to form independent unions risk losing their jobs, as inadequate laws and poor enforcement generally fail to protect them from retaliatory dismissals.

Right to Education

A chronic concern in Mexico is the government's failure to ensure that tens of thousands of rural children receive primary education during the months that their families migrate across state lines to work in agricultural camps. A large number of parents decide to take their children to work with them in the fields rather than attend school during these months. This decision is largely due to economic conditions, as well as to the government's failure to enforce child labor laws. Although there is a federal program to provide primary schooling in the agricultural camps, the classes are generally offered in the evening, when children are too exhausted from their work to study.

Key International Actors

As part of a Technical Cooperation Agreement signed by President Fox, the United Nations High Commissioner for Human Rights maintains an in-country office that, in December 2003, produced a comprehensive report which documented ongoing human rights problems and provided detailed recommendations for addressing them. Based on this report, the administration initiated a national human rights program. In December 2005, the administration established a committee with representatives from the government and civil society to monitor implementation of the program.

Along with the United States and Canada, Mexico is party to the North American Free Trade Agreement and its labor side accord. This accord commits the three countries to enforcing their laws protecting workers' rights, and creates a complaints mechanism whereby, in principle, each has the authority to hold the others accountable for any failures to do so. However, because the complaint process is convoluted and enforcement mechanisms are weak, the accord has had little impact on labor rights violations in Mexico.

Mexico has maintained its leading role in promoting human rights at the international level. In June 2006 Mexico became the first country to preside over the newly formed United Nations Human Rights Council.

PERU

Justice for past abuses continues to be a leading human rights concern in Peru. While authorities have made some progress in holding accountable those responsible for abuses committed during its 20 year armed conflict (1980-2000), most perpetrators continue to evade justice. Investigations of massacres and "disappearances" by government forces have been held up by lack of military cooperation and insufficient funding.

Cases of torture and police brutality continue to occur. Victims and witnesses in torture cases are vulnerable to intimidation and reprisals. Journalists reporting on corruption in Peru's provincial cities face harassment and physical attacks, apparently instigated by local authorities.

Confronting the Past

In 2003 the Truth and Reconciliation Commission reported that left-wing insurgents and government forces committed grave abuses during the 1980s and 1990s. Peru has made significant progress in prosecuting former members of insurgent groups for their past crimes. After annulling in 2003 the sentences of more than 700 prisoners convicted without due process for crimes under Peru's antiterrorism law, the state has conducted new trials that have resulted in the conviction of more than 450 people for killings, attacks with explosives, and other violent crimes. In October 2006, the National Criminal Court sentenced Abimael Guzmán, leader of the Shining Path, an armed group notorious for atrocities, and his partner Elena Iparraguirre, to life in prison. The court held them responsible for a 1983 massacre of 69 peasants at Lucanamarca and numerous killings and car-bombings. Nine other Shining Path leaders received lesser prison sentences.

Peru has also made some progress in bringing to justice those responsible for abuses committed by state agents during the rule of Alberto Fujimori (1990-2000). More than 50 alleged members of the Colina Group, a specialized squad of military and intelligence officers which was created in 1991 to "eliminate" suspected terrorists, are on trial in Lima. An ad-hoc solicitor's office, created by Fujimori himself before he abandoned the country and backed at the outset by former President Toledo, has played a vital role in these investigations.

Altogether, more than 1,780 individuals implicated in abuses and corruption during this period are facing charges.

Based on evidence collected by the ad-hoc solicitor, numerous charges have been brought against Fujimori himself since he left office and took up residence in Japan in 2000. In November 2005 Fujimori left Japan and arrived unexpectedly in Santiago, Chile, evidently intending to return to politics in Peru. As of October 2006 a Chilean Supreme Court justice was still considering the Peruvian government's request for him to be extradited to Peru. More than sufficient grounds exist to justify Fujimori's extradition for the killing of 25 people in two separate incidents in 1991 and 1992 attributed to the Colina Group (the Barrios Altos and La Cantuta cases). Additionally, abundant evidence has been presented to support other charges of corruption and abuse of authority. In May 2006 a Supreme Court panel granted Fujimori pre-trial release, but barred him from leaving the country. The Criminal Chamber of the Chilean Supreme Court is expected to make a final decision on the extradition request in 2007.

Compared with the record of the ad-hoc solicitor's office, advances in the prosecution of former military and police personnel for human rights violations committed during the first decade of the conflict have been far more modest. As of July 2006 judges had filed charges in at least 37 cases and at least 188 others were still under preliminary examination by prosecutors, but there were only a handful of convictions, only one of them involving a commanding officer. In March 2006 a Lima court sentenced a police colonel to 16 years of imprisonment and three junior officers to 15 years for the "disappearance" in October 1990 of student Ernesto Castillo Paez—the first ever sentence in Peru for a forced disappearance.

Peru's new president, Alan García Pérez, who took office in July 2006, served an earlier term during the second half of the 1980s, at the height of the country's political violence. During his first presidency killings and "disappearances" were widespread and went almost completely unpunished. President García's responsibility for a 1986 massacre at El Fronton, a maximum security jail—for which the Truth Commission considered him politically responsible—has been scrutinized by prosecutors, although no criminal charges have been brought against him. Investigations currently pending in the courts include this case and two army massacres that occurred during García's first term in office, in which scores of soldiers face charges. In September 2006 the government passed a decree committing the state to cover the legal fees of police and military defendants in human rights cases.

Up until now, lack of cooperation by the armed forces has hampered faster progress of these investigations. The Ministry of Defense has consistently failed to provide information needed by prosecutors and judges to identify men who served in rural counterinsurgency bases during the conflict and who are potentially key witnesses. It has also failed to identify servicemen known only by their aliases, while denying that official records of this information exist.

The probe currently underway into the alleged responsibility of former presidential candidate Ollanta Humala for the torture and "disappearance" of civilians while he was stationed in the Madre Mia counterinsurgency base in 1992 exemplifies this lack of military cooperation. In August 2006 a Lima court charged Humala with the "disappearance" and killing of two people and the wounding of a third and banned him from leaving the country. The prosecutor was unable to obtain from the former minister of defense a list of the men stationed at the base at the time, and the investigating judge had to repeat the request. Its outcome was not known at this writing.

The failure of successive governments to provide enough resources for these investigations has made it difficult for prosecutors to process cases swiftly. The special prosecutor in Ayacucho, who is responsible for investigating around 200 cases, has insufficient staff and equipment. In other districts prosecutors have to deal with complex human rights cases along with their regular workload, all without additional assistance.

Torture and Police Brutality

Torture and police brutality continue to be a problem. The Human Rights Commission (Comision de Derechos Humanos, COMISEDH), a human rights NGO that has monitored the issue over many years, documented 11 such complaints in the first six months of 2006.

Witness Protection

Victims pursuing complaints of torture in the courts, as well as their relatives, are sometimes attacked and intimidated. In April 2006 for example, Juan Fidel Zamudio Bocángel, a victim of a police beating whose case was being tried, was reportedly confronted in the street by men who tried to force him into a station wagon. He fought them off, but one pulled a gun and shot him in the back as he was running away. Although he survived, the bullet perforated his lung.

Attacks on Journalists

Journalists who publicize abuses by local government officials are vulnerable to intimidation, assault, and even murder by individuals acting in support of, or hired by, municipal authorities.

During 2005 and 2006 courts made some progress in solving past killings of journalists. In December 2005 a court in Ancash sentenced the mayor of Yungay, Amaro León León, and two accomplices to 17 years in prison for the 2004 murder of radio journalist Antonio de la Torre Echeandía after he had broadcast accusations against local government officials. However, the defendants appealed and in July 2006 the First Transitory Criminal Bench of the Supreme Court absolved and released León and the other two defendants. According to local human rights groups, the Supreme Court panel disregarded a large body of evidence incriminating the three.

Human Rights Defenders

Peru's human rights organizations are frequently criticized and accused of bias in their legal work on behalf of victims. In September 2006 Vice-President Luis Giampetri, whose alleged role in the El Fronton prison massacre has also been investigated by prosecutors, convened a meeting of the congressional intelligence committee (which he chairs) to scrutinize the work of the Legal Defense Institute (Instituto de Defensa Legal, IDL). Lawyers from IDL, a well-respected human rights organization which specializes in justice issues, represent relatives of one of the El Fronton victims. Giampetri claimed that IDL was interfering in trials affecting the military and affecting the morale of the armed forces.

In November 2006, Peru's congress approved the first draft of a bill that would allow the government to "supervise" the activities of Peruvian NGOs that receive foreign funding. The bill, which posed a major threat to the independence of the country's human rights NGOs, was on the brink of final approval but was returned for further debate after strong protests from civil society groups.

Key International Actors

In April 2006, the Inter-American Court of Human Rights ordered Peru to "identify, judge and punish" those responsible for the torture and death of Bernabé Baldeón García, a peasant who died after torture by an army patrol in 1990.

In July 2006 the United Nations Committee against Torture issued its concluding observations on Peru's periodic report on the implementation of the UN Convention against Torture. The Committee noted that complaints of torture continue to be received. It expressed concern that victims or witnesses seeking redress in court are sometimes threatened and intimidated and urged Peru to set up an appropriate mechanism to protect them.

VENEZUELA

After repeatedly winning elections and referendums, and surviving a coup d'etat in 2002, President Chávez and his supporters have sought to consolidate power by undermining the independence of the judiciary and the press, institutions that are essential for promoting the protection of human rights.

Independence of the Judiciary

The Venezuelan National Assembly dealt a severe blow to judicial independence in December 2004 by packing the country's Supreme Court with twelve new justices. A majority of the ruling coalition, dominated by President Chávez's party, named the justices to fill new seats created by a law passed earlier that year that expanded the court from 20 to 32 members. At that time, 80 percent of lower-court judges had provisional appointments and could be summarily dismissed by the Supreme Court's Judicial Commission.

During 2005 and 2006 the court granted tenure to hundreds of the provisional judges. By October 2006 only about 20 percent of the country's judges had provisional appointments, according to a Supreme Court spokesman. However, the judges who gained tenure during this period were not required to win public competitions as prescribed in the Constitution.

The judges on the First and Second Administrative Courts, which have jurisdiction over challenges to administrative actions by the government, continue to be provisional appointees. In September 2005 the judicial commission fired all six judges of both courts and their six substitutes, and once more replaced them with temporary appointees. The official reason given was that they failed to pass performance tests. The lack of guarantees to ensure that these key judges may make decisions free of government pressure remains a problem.

The 2004 court-packing law also gave the majority party in the National Assembly the power to remove judges from the Supreme Court without the two-thirds majority vote required under the constitution. In May 2006 Justice Luis Velázquez Alvaray, who had been a leading proponent of the law as a congressman in 2004, was himself suspended from the Supreme Court for allegedly mismanaging the construction of a court complex. After his appointment to the Court, Velázquez had chaired the Judicial Commission charged with appointing and dismissing lower court judges. He claimed that he had been targeted for impeachment because he resisted the efforts of the Chávez administration to control the selection of judges. In June the National Assembly impeached Velázquez with a two-thirds majority vote after he failed to appear at a hearing on the charges.

Freedom of Expression

Laws passed since late 2004 have created onerous restrictions on the media that pose a serious threat to freedom of expression. The Law of Social Responsibility in Radio and Television establishes detailed regulations for the content of television and radio programs. For example, stations deemed to "condone or incite" public disturbances or publish messages "contrary to the security of the nation" are subject to heavy fines, and can be ordered to suspend broadcasting for seventy-two hours. Upon a second offense, they may be stripped of their broadcasting licenses for up to five years. Key terms in the law, such as those quoted above, are left ill-defined, inviting politically motivated application. The National Commission of Telecommunications (CONATEL) may issue "precautionary measures" prohibiting the transmission of outlawed content.

The radio and television law has not led to a clampdown on the audiovisual media. At moments of political tension, however, CONATEL officials warn media directors about punishments they face for coverage that infringes the law. For instance, in April 2006 the president of Globovision, Venezuela's 24-hour cable news channel, received a letter from the director of CONATEL warning him that the station could be suspended for seventy-two hours if it resorted to "sensationalist techniques" (*tecnicas amarillistas*) in reporting on street protests about rising levels of criminal violence.

In one instance, a court banned reporting about a controversial criminal investigation. In January 2006 the attorney general obtained an injunction to prevent the media from discussing the credibility of a key prosecution witness who had testified about the car bomb assassination of Danilo Anderson, the prosecutor who had been leading the probe into the aborted 2002 coup against President Chávez. The witness's testimony implicated two opposition figures in the crime.

The newspaper *El Nacional* had published evidence that the witness, who claimed to be a psychiatrist, was an impostor. The ban on any further stories about the witness remained in force until August, during which time CONATEL closely monitored media coverage of the case.

In March 2005 amendments to the Criminal Code came into force which extended the scope of Venezuela's *desacato* (disrespect) laws, and increased penalties for *desacato*, criminal defamation, and libel. In February 2006 television journalist and well-known Chávez critic, José Ovidio Rodríguez Cuesta (known in Venezuela as Napoleón Bravo), was prosecuted under the *desacato* provision of the criminal code for insulting the Supreme Court. Bravo had publicly criticized the alleged inefficiency of the court and suggested that it should be replaced by a brothel. A judge rejected the charges, but a Caracas appeals court overruled the judge and the case remained open at this writing.

Police Killings

Thousands of extrajudicial executions by police officers have been reported over the past several years, although the problem long predates the current administration. In August 2006, 24 soldiers and policemen were sentenced to up to 30 years in prison for the murder of three university students in June 2005. The agents had opened fire on the students' car and then summarily executed two of the occupants when the car stopped. Such rapid prosecutions for police and army abuses are exceptional, however. In April 2006 Attorney General Isaías Rodríguez reported that 6,110 officials were implicated in alleged killings between 2000 and 2005, yet only 760 had been charged, and only 113 convicted.

Political Violence in Rural Areas

Land reform measures introduced by the Chávez administration have brought a wave of violence against peasant leaders and beneficiaries of the reform. According to a report by the national human rights ombudsman in May 2006, 54 peasants were killed and 21 were wounded between 1999 and 2006 because of their activities in defense of land claims, particularly after the Land and Agricultural Development Act entered into force in 2001. According to the ombudsman, contract killers hired by landowners appear to have been responsible for most of the killings. The nongovernmental human rights organization PROVEA (Program of Education and Action on Human Rights) reached similar conclusions, although it found that military and police units were also responsible for some abuses against peasants.

Kidnappings and contract killings are common in the states of Zulia, Tachira, and Apure, where there are frequent cross-border incursions by Colombian guerrillas and paramilitaries. Impunity for these crimes has been the rule. According to the ombudsman's report, 72 percent of the investigations conducted by prosecutors have not progressed beyond the preliminary stage. However, in October 2006 the attorney general announced that 56 individuals had been charged for killing peasants.

Prison Conditions

Conditions in Venezuela's prisons are notoriously abusive. Overcrowding is chronic and armed gangs maintain effective control within the prison walls. Prison riots and inmate violence claim hundreds of lives every year. Venezuelan Prison Watch (*Observatorio Venezolano de Prisiones*), a Caracas-based group, reported that 194 prisoners were killed and 407 were wounded in violent incidents over the first six months of 2006.

Human Rights Defenders

In June 2006 the National Assembly began considering legislation on a "Law of International Cooperation," which seeks to regulate the activities of both national and international NGOs in Venezuela. If enacted, the law would require all such organizations to register in order to be able to receive funds from abroad. The bill allows the president to determine by decree the requirements for registration, raising concern that if the restrictions are onerous they could seriously obstruct non-governmental activities in the country. As of October 2006, the bill remained under review with a legislative committee.

Key International Actors

Venezuela abstained in the United Nations General Assembly vote on the creation of the Human Rights Council (HRC) in March 2006. At the time of the vote, the Venezuelan ambassador to the United Nations offered "reservations" on 10 of the 14 operative paragraphs of the resolution setting up the council. The ambassador asserted that Venezuela would not be bound by resolution language establishing the Council's most basic functions, such as "promoting universal respect for the protection of all human rights and fundamental freedoms for all" and "address[ing] situations of violations of human rights, including gross and systematic violations, and mak[ing] recommendations thereon." Venezuela subsequently sought a seat on the Human Rights Council but failed to obtain the necessary votes.

Venezuela has stalled in setting a date for a mission by the Inter-American Commission on Human Rights, which has not visited the country since 2002. In 2006, the Inter-American Court of Human Rights issued provisional measures to protect the lives and physical integrity of prisoners held at Yare and La Pica prisons, where scores of prisoners have died as a result of violence in recent years.

Too High a Price

The Human Rights Cost of the Indonesian Military's
Economic Activities

**HUMAN
RIGHTS
WATCH**

WORLD REPORT

2007

ASIA

AFGHANISTAN

By late 2006 Afghanistan was on the precipice of again becoming a haven for human rights abusers, criminals, and militant extremists, many of whom in the past have severely abused Afghans, particularly women and girls, and threatened the stability of the country, the region, and the world.

Resurgent Taliban forces, tribal militias, and rearmed warlords exploited the power vacuum in many parts of the country. These groups increasingly used bombings and assassinations, including attacks on "soft targets" such as schools, teachers, and religious figures, to terrorize ordinary citizens and demonstrate the central government's inability to protect them. Much of the violence and insecurity was driven and financed by another record-setting year for poppy production, which exceeded 2005's crop by 60 percent and generated nearly half of the country's income and 92 percent of the world's supply of heroin.

As NATO forces in the United Nations-mandated International Security Assistance Force finally extended their reach across the entire country, the insurgency they confronted in southern and southeastern Afghanistan escalated into open warfare. In other parts of the country, Afghans were routinely subject to abuses and oppression by regional warlords and militias, most of them ostensibly allied with the government. Throughout the country, including Kabul, Afghans were disappointed and frustrated by insufficient and poorly coordinated international security and financial assistance. They also suffered from the poor governance and corruption of the government of President Hamid Karzai, which often lacked the will or the capacity to protect the rights of ordinary Afghans.

Despite an increase in the country's average per capita income (much of it fueled by the narcotics trade), economic growth remained mostly limited to urban areas, in particular Kabul. Human rights abuses, poverty, and insecurity increased markedly with distance away from city centers. The armed clashes and insecurity seriously hampered, and even reversed, economic development in many parts of Afghanistan, which remains one of the poorest countries in the world. Reconstruction was particularly hurt in the south, adding fuel to local resentments.

AFGHANISTAN

Lessons in Terror

Attacks on Education in Afghanistan

HUMAN
RIGHTS
WATCH

Violence and Insecurity

At this writing, more than 1,000 civilians have been killed in 2006 as a result of violence related to the insurgency, most of them in southern Afghanistan. Overall more than 3,000 Afghans have died in the violence in 2006, twice as many as in 2005 and more than in any other year since the 2001 fall of the Taliban. The United Nations estimated that the violence displaced 15,000 families—about 80,000 people—in southern Afghanistan.

In a new development, Taliban and other anti-government forces carried out more than 80 suicide bombings, mostly killing civilians. In a sharp rise from 2005, anti-government forces carried out hundreds of attacks against teachers, students, and schools; these attacks constituted war crimes because of their civilian targets. In entire districts, attacks have closed all schools and driven out teachers and NGOs providing education. More than 200,000 students who were in school in 2005 were consequently deprived of an education in 2006.

More than 170 foreign troops died in the fighting in 2006. While NATO and US-led coalition forces tried to minimize harm to civilians, there were serious concerns about NATO's ability to distinguish between combatants and civilians due to extensive reliance on aerial bombardment to compensate for insufficient numbers of ground troops.

In southern Afghanistan, tribal chiefs like senator Sher Mohammad Akhundzada, who was removed as governor of Helmand due to allegations of corruption and involvement in the drug trade, have been allowed to operate abusive militias with the blessing of President Karzai. Across the country, warlords with records of war crimes and other serious abuses during Afghanistan's civil war in the 1990s, such as parliamentarians Abdul Rabb al Rasul Sayyaf and Burhanuddin Rabbani, Gen. Abdul Rashid Dostum, and Vice President Karim Khalili, continue to hold and misuse positions of power.

Government Failures

President Karzai's government did not credibly attempt to quell rampant corruption or rein in abuses by militias and warlords. Too often, the government bowed to demands for political repression justified by the insecurity, though such moves alienated ordinary Afghans and weakened the government's legitimacy. In June the National Directorate of Security (NDS, the state intelligence agency) distributed to Afghan journalists a list of restrictions intended to curtail their reporting on the deteriorating security situation. The NDS increasingly resorted to intimidation and strong-arm tactics to gather information and silence government critics.

In May Karzai seriously undermined the crucial process of reforming Afghanistan's police by appointing several known human rights abusers and warlords such as Baseer Salangi and Ghulam Mustafa as regional police chiefs, although they had failed to meet human rights standards for senior police appointments. Kabul police under the command of Amanullah Guzar in July used excessive force to quell demonstrations in Paghman against illegal land grabs by Abdul Rabb al Rasul Sayyaf, a member of parliament with a notorious record of human rights abuses.

Women and Girls

Afghan women and girls continue to suffer extremely low social, economic, and political status. They rank among the world's worst off by most indicators, such as life expectancy (46 years), maternal mortality (1,600 deaths per 100,000 births), and literacy (12.6 percent of females 15 and older). Women and girls confront barriers to working outside the home and restrictions on their mobility; for example many still cannot travel without an accompanying male relative and a burqa.
While the number of girls in school increased quickly after the fall of the Taliban in 2001, only 35 percent of school-age girls were in school in 2006. The violence directed at schools hit girls' schools particularly hard.

Women active in civil or political affairs braved violence and intimidation, such as death threats often conveyed through "night letters." Safia Amajan, a prominent educator, women's rights activist, and government official was assassinated in Kandahar in September. Malalai Joya, a member of parliament from Herat, was physically attacked in parliament and threatened with death when she criticized members of parliament notorious for past and current human rights abuses.

Violence against women remains endemic, with few avenues for redress. The Afghan Independent Human Rights Commission registered 704 cases of violence against women, including 89 cases of forced marriages and 50 cases of self-immolation, in 2006—significant increases over 2005. The AIHRC believes these numbers seriously under-represent the true scale of the violence due to factors such as social stigma and poor response from the justice system. More than one-third of all marriages were forced, according to the Ministry of Women's Affairs, and more than half of girls were married before the age of 16, the legal age for marriage.

The government took several steps that weakened the already weak government commitment to women, in part because of pressure from ultra-conservative political supporters, and in part to counter anti-Western propaganda by opposition groups. In June, Karzai sent the Afghan parliament a proposal for reestablishing the Department for the Promotion of Virtue and the Prevention of Vice, which under the Taliban had established a record of arbitrary abuses, notably for beating and harassing women and girls for traveling without male guardians and for even slight infractions of stringent dress requirements. At this writing the National Assembly had not debated the proposal. In November, parliament began debating the possibility of closing the Ministry of Women's Affairs, which, although weak in terms of implementing programs, served as an important symbol of support for Afghanistan's women.

Delivering Justice

Karzai failed to adequately implement the Transitional Justice Action Plan, a five-year process to gather information about Afghanistan's legacy of warfare and violence and to consider methods of achieving accountability. His cabinet approved the plan in December 2005, but it has languished pending the required presidential announcement.

The Taliban and other anti-government forces used the government's failure to confront warlords in the government to gain public support and discredit Karzai's administration and its international backers. The Taliban have reintroduced their brutal brand of justice in southern Afghanistan, taking advantage of the failure of the international community to provide promised assistance in reestablishing Afghanistan's judiciary.

Assadullah Sarwari, who headed Afghanistan's brutal intelligence agency during the communist government of the late 1970s, was sentenced to death in March 2006 after a trial that violated basic due process standards. At this writing the sentence had not been carried out.

The Afghan judiciary in September released the chief suspect in the 2004 murder of five staff members of Medecins sans Frontieres. The suspect had been acquitted in January 2006 for lack of evidence but had remained in custody pending a prosecution appeal. He was released because the judiciary said it had lost his file and he had already been detained for the maximum time allowed by Afghan law.

Key International Actors

International military and economic aid to Afghanistan since the fall of the Taliban was, and remains, a fraction of that disbursed in other recent post-conflict situations. On January 31–February 1, 2006, high-level delegations from more than 60 countries attended a conference in London to establish a framework for Afghanistan's development. This framework, known as the Afghanistan Compact, replaced the Bonn Agreement that had guided Afghanistan's political process after US forces ousted the Taliban. The London conference netted Afghanistan pledges totaling about US$11 billion over the next five years, significantly less than the $28 billion viewed as necessary by the World Bank and the Afghan government.

Similarly, international security assistance to Afghanistan (a total of 40,000 troops under NATO and US command) was far less than deemed adequate by military experts. While the US reversed its plan to draw down its forces, other NATO countries have been reluctant to meet the coalition's request for greater manpower and logistical support.

Anti-government forces and drug traffickers traveled widely and sought refuge in the border areas between Pakistan and Afghanistan, raising suspicions of Pakistani government negligence or complicity.

BANGLADESH

Political and security conditions continued to deteriorate in Bangladesh in 2006. The country's already poor human rights record worsened, as security forces continued to commit numerous abuses, including extrajudicial killings, excessive use of force, and custodial torture. The Rapid Action Battalion (RAB, an elite "anti-crime" and "anti-terror" unit) and the police were responsible for hundreds of extrajudicial killings in 2006. A culture of impunity—reinforced by legislation which largely shields the security forces from legal challenge and by government praise for many of the unlawful killings—leads to abuses going largely uninvestigated and unpunished.

Security forces used mass arrests as a means to suppress demonstrations. Workers in the export garment industry were subjected to violence and job dismissal in response to demands for wage increases and safe work conditions. Violence by religious extremists increased, and fundamentalist political groups gained influence in government.

With elections approaching in early 2007, tensions increased between the two main political parties, the Bangladesh Nationalist Party (BNP) and the Awami League (AL). There were fears of widespread violence in the pre-election period as the parties argued over the election modalities, including serious disputes over the impartiality of the caretaker government and the Election Commission.

The BNP-led government did little to protect or promote human rights. A bill to create a Human Rights Commission promised by the government was never tabled in parliament. Several other bills that could have promoted human rights—such as bills on freedom of information, nationality, or domestic violence—were shelved.

Political Tensions and Violence in the Run-Up to Elections

Article 58 of the constitution stipulates that parliamentary elections be conducted by an independent election commission during the three-month tenure of a neutral, non-party caretaker government. At the close of the parliament's five-year term in October 2006 and the resignation of the four-party alliance government led by the BNP, the Awami League and its 14-party alliance renewed their long-standing demands. The demands include the appointment of neutral persons to the caretaker government; reform and restructuring of the election commission; and withdrawal of officials seen as partial to the outgoing government. President Iajuddin Ahmed, contrary to precedent, appointed himself as chief caretaker advisor and selected 10 advisers to assist him.

Political violence between supporters of different political parties in October led to 28 deaths and many injuries. During the year, violence between political parties had accounted for the deaths of 30 activists.

Extrajudicial Killings

2006 saw an increase in extrajudicial killings by RAB and the police, although these were regularly euphemistically dubbed "crossfire" killings. Many killings were of criminal suspects, but some had a political taint. RAB and other security agencies also perpetrated torture during custody and interrogation, and the public display of tortured and executed victims appeared to be a RAB tactic to instill fear among criminals and the population. Instead of holding RAB accountable the government heaped praise on it. Despite substantial evidence, no RAB member has been criminally convicted for extrajudicial killings.

Death in custody is common. In 2006, 51 prisoners, of whom 32 were standing trial, were reported to have died from various causes, including violence by guards and fellow prisoners, and delays in medical treatment.

Rise of Extremist Militancy

Since 1999, 19 bomb and grenade explosions by religious extremists belonging to militant organizations such as Jama'tul Mujahideen Bangladesh (JMB), Harqatul Jehad, and Ahle Hadith have left 181 people dead and over 1,700 injured. It was only after synchronized bombings in 63 districts in August 2005 raised national and international concern that the government started investigating and prosecuting suspects. Between December 2005 and October 2006 over 300 alleged militants were arrested (including the six leaders of the JMB), 241 cases were filed, and 29 people were sentenced to life in prison or capital punishment. Four organizations were banned. It was alleged, however, that madrasas used for training were not investigated and donations from foreign Muslim organizations did not cease.

After a suicide bomber killed two judges in 2005 the judiciary has operated in a climate of fear and uncertainty. This has been exacerbated by political interference and pressure at the national and local levels. On November 12, 2006, judges' associations in the lower courts asked for additional protections from the government.

Freedom of Expression, Assembly, and Association

Opposition demonstrations for the appointment of a neutral chief advisor to the caretaker government and restructuring of the Election Commission were brutally suppressed. On September 6, 2006, police used force to disperse an Awami League (AL) rally, and several leaders including Saber Hussain Chowdhury and Asaduzaman Noor were beaten with rifle butts and batons. The government resorted to imposing Section 144—which bans assembly of more than four persons—on 93 occasions in six districts, followed by preemptive mass arrests of over 28,000 persons to prevent demonstrations by political parties. Most of those arrested were ordinary citizens such as transport workers and day laborers.

Women activists participating in political rallies or demonstrations faced assaults and sexual harassment by police. At an AL rally on March 12, 2006, several young women were assaulted and arrested during a political strike, among them Shaheen Sultana Santa, who was pregnant at that time, but a magistrate dismissed Santa's assault complaint against the Dhaka Metropolitan Police as unfounded after a police investigation. In November six women professionals were assaulted and arrested by police when they joined a march to submit a memorandum to the chief election commissioner.

Journalists, particularly in the southwest of the country, were targets of violence by business syndicates and politicians. In 2006 three journalists were killed, allegedly for their reports on corrupt syndicates or religious militants. Seventy-two reporters were assaulted by gangs allegedly belonging to the ruling party alliance, fundamentalist groups, or powerful businessmen. Criminal or defamation cases were filed against 63 journalists. In Kushtia a BNP member of parliament assaulted and threatened a journalist for reporting his illegal activities. Reporters and photojournalists have also been the target of police assault during political demonstrations.

Minorities

Land-grabs from religious and ethnic minorities have become a common phenomenon. Hindus have complained that the repeal of the Vested Property Act in 2001 has not helped in the recovery of properties appropriated by powerful individuals.

Discrimination against religious minorities is manifest in their low participation in political and other decision-making institutions and their poor access to bank loans and other opportunities. They have also been subjected to violence because of their beliefs. Although Hindus appeared to be freer to perform puja festivals in towns in 2006, village gangs aligned with the BNP were known to attack temples and demolish deities. The Buddhist *Ras Mela* festival had to be canceled in a few villages because of intimidation.

The Ahmaddiyas, a small Muslim sect, have been threatened with expulsion, violence, and occupation of their mosques by religious zealots under the banner of the Khatme Nabuwat Movement. The government has not revoked its ban on Ahmaddiya literature, nor has it prosecuted persons who attacked Ahmaddiya mosques, but in 2006 under international pressure the police were able to prevent large-scale violence.

Workers' Rights

Contrary to expectations, following the expiry of the Multi-Fibre Arrangement, Bangladesh's garment exports to the United States and the European Union increased substantially. But over two million workers who contributed to exports from 4,000 factories did not see improvements in their labor conditions. Unsafe working environments remained common. Following the collapse of a garment factory in 2004 and fire in another factory in Chittagong in 2005, workers became more vocal in their demands for a minimum wage, maternity leave, overtime pay,

and safe working conditions. In May-June 2006 strikers in several knitwear factories in Gazipur and Savar were attacked by gangs allegedly hired by management
and police. A tripartite Minimum Wage Board recommended an increase in the
minimum wage that fell far short of workers' expectations.

Bangladeshi workers migrating to Persian Gulf states continue to confront a wide
range of abuses, including non-payment of their full wages, having their passports withheld, and suffering hazardous working conditions. Many are made
especially vulnerable to labor exploitation as a result of exorbitant debt payments
to labor recruiters.

Corruption

In 2006 Bangladesh ranked the third lowest in the Transparency International
index of corruption. The Anti-Corruption Commission appointed in 2005 has been
inoperative.

Corruption in the energy sector leads to scarcity of electricity and water for many
people, provoking protests by affected villagers who complain that power distribution favors Dhaka's luxury malls over irrigation. Police shot five persons,
including a 10-year-old boy, in a demonstration in Kansat, while protesters in
Sonir Akhra were assaulted by gangs led by a BNP member of parliament.

In August 2006 police shot and killed five people demonstrating against plans by
the Asian Energy Company for opencast coal mining and the consequent eviction
of several hundred indigenous families from Phulbaria.

Key International Actors

There was a lack of urgency in the efforts by outside actors that belied the risks of
military intervention or increased militancy facing Bangladesh if elections did not
proceed credibly. The European Union troika, on a visit to Bangladesh in February
2006, expressed concerns about free and fair elections, abuses in counterterrorism efforts, poor governance, and a lack of respect for human rights. It asked for
strengthening of the Anti-Corruption Commission and for the establishment of a

Human Rights Commission. The United States expressed concern with the rising scale of political violence and offered its support for a fair and free election.

Bangladesh was elected to the United Nations Human Rights Council in March, even though it has failed to submit its initial reports to the UN Committees on Civil and Political Rights, on Torture, and on Economic, Social and Cultural Rights. Reservations to articles 2 and 16.1(c) of the Convention on the Elimination of All Forms of Discrimination against Women (CEDAW) have not been withdrawn, and parliament did not amend citizenship laws to enable women to pass their nationality to their partner and children as recommended by the CEDAW Committee.

BURMA

Burma's international isolation deepened during 2006 as the authoritarian military government, the State Peace and Development Council (SPDC), continued to restrict basic rights and freedoms and waged brutal counterinsurgency operations against ethnic minorities. The democratic movement inside the country remained suppressed, and Daw Aung San Suu Kyi and other political activists continued to be detained or imprisoned. International efforts to foster change in Burma were thwarted by the SPDC and sympathetic neighboring governments.

These regressions were epitomized by the SPDC's move in November 2005 to a new "administrative capitol" called Nay Pyi Taw, 300 kilometers north of Rangoon and deep in the interior. The regime relocated key ministries and thousands of public servants to the purpose-built city during 2006, and notified foreign embassies that they could begin voluntary relocation during 2007. No official reason was given for the surprise move, although the main factors appear to include concerns over possible civilian protests in Rangoon, foreign criticism of the SPDC, a fear of a foreign military intervention, and the need to locate the SPDC more centrally to direct its military campaigns against ethnic insurgencies along the eastern border. Forced labor was used in building the capitol, and many public servants were given no choice over moving there.

Lack of Progress on Democracy and Human Rights

There was no progress in 2006 on national reconciliation or the 2003 "road map" for a transition to democracy. In May, National League for Democracy (NLD) leader Daw Aung San Suu Kyi's detention was extended by another year despite continuing international calls for her release. This marks her eleventh year under house arrest, where she is held in solitary confinement and denied most visitors, newspapers, telephone, or correspondence.

On September 27 three members of the "88 Students Generation," Min Ko Naing, Ko Ko Gyi, and Htay Kywe, were arrested in Rangoon for issuing a statement in support of an impending United Nations Security Council debate on Burma. As of this writing they remain imprisoned. More than 1,200 people are imprisoned for their political beliefs and activities. Most political party offices, including the

NLD's, remain closed or under strict surveillance, and political party activities are generally curtailed.

The protracted National Convention to write a new constitution was suspended again in January, and resumed on October 10 at Nyaunghnapin camp in Hnawby township near Rangoon. The SPDC claimed that 75 percent of the work on the constitution had been completed. This process has involved many legal political parties and ethnic militias with which the government has signed a ceasefire, but many more have been excluded. All of the discussions have been conducted within strict guidelines that deter debate or dissent.

Continued Violence against Ethnic Groups

In the conflict areas, human rights violations such as forced labor for Burmese army units, rape of women and girls, and summary executions continue. Army predation on the civilian population for money, land, and food is widespread.

A large-scale military offensive in northern Karen state during 2006 displaced an estimated 27,000 civilians, and destroyed some 232 villages and their crops and food stocks. Scores of civilians were killed and thousands taken as forced porters to support the operation. Prisoners were used as forced porters, and many of them were summarily executed during operations. Ceasefire talks with factions of the Karen National Union (KNU) broke down in October.

In Shan state, leaders of the Shan Nationalities League for Democracy (SNLD) continued to be incarcerated following their arrest in 2005, with one member dying in prison from ill-treatment in 2006. A faction of the Shan State Army-South (SSA-S) surrendered to the SPDC in June, but soon broke the agreement and many of its members returned to the SSA-S. The SPDC has pressured ethnic ceasefire militias, including the Wa and Pa-O armies, into attacking the SSA-S. The SPDC uses other ethnic militias as auxiliary forces to suppress the rural population. Many of these militias are thought to be financing themselves through trade in illegal drugs.

The SPDC continues to forcibly recruit children into its armed forces.

Humanitarian Concerns, Internal Displacement, and Refugees

Internal displacement in minority ethnic areas continues to be a serious concern, with over 500,000 civilians deemed to be internally displaced in eastern Burma, and thousands more whose numbers cannot be reliably ascertained, in parts of the country where effective monitoring is impossible. The SPDC restricts the activities of foreign aid agencies generally, and blocks humanitarian aid to areas of ongoing conflict. Untreated cases of malaria, tuberculosis, HIV/AIDS and other illnesses have reached serious levels.

In February 2006 the SPDC issued new guidelines setting out the rules for travel, partnerships and project implementation of all international agencies, including the UN. Significant variation between the English and Burmese texts of the guidelines raised fears that there would be disagreements in interpretation between agencies and SPDC authorities. As a result of these restrictions, some aid agencies withdrew from Burma, most notably Medecins Sans Frontieres.

Following the 2005 withdrawal of the multi-sectoral Global Fund to Fight HIV/AIDS, Tuberculosis and Malaria, the Three Disease Fund, which provides funding for treatment, pledged US$100 million over the next five years for health projects. Independent of the SPDC and of the mainly European and Australian donors, this Fund is run by the UN Office for Project Services, and is scheduled to begin work in late 2006.

The Thai army continues to restrict refugees coming into Thailand, although more than 2,000 Karen civilians fleeing the fighting in northern Karen state were permitted into established camps. A small Shan refugee camp was ordered to move back into Burma in April 2006 by Thai authorities, although this order was soon rescinded and the refugees were permitted to stay, but newer Shan refugees are not allowed in. In total there are some 156,000 refugees from Burma in Thailand. In August the UN High Commissioner for Refugees and a senior US State Department official visited a refugee camp in Thailand and pledged more assistance for refugee resettlement to third countries. In a positive development, the US government in May and August issued waivers for many ethnic Karen refugees on the material support condition under Homeland Security guidelines, permitting them to resettle in the United States.

Key International Actors

In May 2006 UN Under-Secretary-General for Political Affairs Ibrahim Gambari visited the new capital Nay Pyi Taw and spoke with Burmese President Than Shwe and other SPDC leaders, who assured him that national reconciliation efforts were proceeding on schedule. Gambari also visited Aung San Suu Kyi (the visit was two days before her detention was again extended). The UN special rapporteur on human rights in Burma, Paulo Sérgio Pinheiro, has not been permitted to visit the country since November 2003. His report to the UN General Assembly in September detailed "continuing impunity" by SPDC officials, which has resulted in "the criminalization of the exercise of fundamental freedoms by political opponents, human rights defenders and victims of human rights abuses." Razali Ismael resigned as the UN Secretary General special envoy in January 2006 because the SPDC continued to deny him permission to visit since March 2004. He has not been replaced.

In December 2005 and again in May 2006 the UN Security Council (UNSC) held briefings on conditions in Burma to determine whether the country constituted a threat to international peace. On September 29, 2006, the Security Council discussed Burma as part of its formal agenda, but opposition from China and Russia frustrated attempts to pass a resolution.

The International Labor Organization (ILO) called on the SPDC to cease prosecuting Burmese citizens who report incidents of forced labor to the ILO. Two Burmese citizens, Su Su Nway and Aye Myint, had charges against them dropped in June and July respectively, for reporting forced labor to the ILO the previous year. However, civilians continue to be prosecuted for passing information to the organization.

The Association of Southeast Asian Nations (ASEAN) voiced increasing frustration with the SPDC over its slow pace of reform and limited engagement with international actors. Scheduled visits from ASEAN officials were postponed or curtailed by the SPDC, at the same time that the government asked members of the regional group not to support UNSC action on Burma. Expressing the new approach of ASEAN, Malaysian Foreign Minister Syed Hamid Albar declared, "ASEAN has reached a stage where it is not possible to defend its member when that member is not making an attempt to cooperate." However, in August 2006 Thailand's then-Prime Minister Thaksin Shinawatra paid an unscheduled one-day visit to Burma designed to procure business contracts, including gas exploration concessions in Arakan state and a resumption of logging concessions. Over the objections of some Asian and European countries, the SPDC sent representatives to the Asia-Europe Meeting (ASEM) in Helsinki in September 2006.

China and India continued to provide political and economic support to the SPDC, and failed to fully back international calls for reform. China and Russia continued to sell the SPDC large numbers of weapons, while the United States and European Union maintained sanctions.

CAMBODIA

Cambodia's veneer of political pluralism wore even thinner in 2006. The year saw the jailing of government critics; attempts to weaken civil society, independent media, and political dissent; crackdowns on protests by villagers and peaceful public demonstrations; and the continuing pillaging of Cambodia's land and natural resources. Prime Minister Hun Sen in March demonstrated his contempt for human rights by labeling United Nations human rights monitors as "human rights tourists," and demanding that the UN secretary-general's special representative for human rights in Cambodia be dismissed after he issued a critical evaluation.

Iron Fist

Hun Sen continued to consolidate his power through strategic weakening or co-optation of his coalition partner, Funcinpec, and the opposition Sam Rainsy Party (SRP). He ordered the dismissal or forced the resignation of dozens of Funcinpec officials and parliamentarians.

Opposition leader Sam Rainsy's reconciliation with his former foe Hun Sen led to a noticeable decline in his party's traditional role as government watchdog and advocate for the poor. After striking a deal with Hun Sen, Rainsy, who had been convicted in absentia for defamation in December 2005, was pardoned and allowed to return to Cambodia in February 2006 from a year of self-imposed exile.

SRP parliamentarian Cheam Channy, who had served one year of a seven-year sentence for allegedly forming an illegal army, was also pardoned in February and released from prison. The UN Working Group on Arbitrary Detention had announced in January that it deemed Channy's imprisonment arbitrary and illegal.

The National Assembly handed more power to the ruling Cambodian People's Party (CPP). In March it approved a constitutional amendment allowing its decisions to be made by a simple majority rather than a two-thirds vote, virtually ensuring passage of all legislation proposed by the CPP. In August the Assembly approved a law that allows parliamentarians to be prosecuted for criminal defamation and to be arrested without prior lifting of their immunity. Both practices have been used against CPP opponents.

Suppression of Political Dissent and Free Expression

By early January 2006, five human rights leaders and government critics had been imprisoned after Hun Sen ordered their arrests on charges of criminal defamation, disinformation, or incitement for criticizing his Vietnam policy. While he subsequently ordered their release on bail, the charges have not been dropped. In response, some activists curtailed their activities, while others fled the country and sought political asylum abroad.

Hun Sen pledged in February to decriminalize defamation, but instead only removed the penalty of imprisonment, retaining punitive fines. Incitement and disinformation remain criminal offenses.

Authorities continued to disperse or reject most requests for peaceful public demonstrations, rallies, and marches, such as the International Labor Day rally in May. Riot police blocked roads leading to the capital to prevent thousands of workers from attending. Authorities continued to censor slogans on signs and banners at rallies that received permits.

Forced Evictions and Illegal Exploitation of Resources

The rural poor continued to lose their land to illegal concessions controlled by foreign firms, senators, and people with connections to government officials. Authorities threatened, attacked, and arrested villagers opposed to land confiscation, logging, and concessions, or prohibited them from airing grievances in public. For example, in August Koh Kong villagers protesting a land concession controlled by tycoon and CPP senator Ly Yong Phat were attacked by military police. At 20,000 hectares, the concession is twice the maximum size permitted by the Land Law. In several cases during the year, villagers were jailed on charges of destruction of property or defamation when they protested against the loss of their land.

Syndicates comprising relatives of senior officials and elite military units continued illegal logging operations with impunity in several provinces, notably Kompong Thom. A relative of the prime minister who shot at two community forestry activists in Tumring commune in 2005 after they attempted to stop his illegal logging activities has yet to be arrested or charged. In the same province the HMH company started logging a 5,000-hectare swathe in an illegal operation that is being protected by armed government soldiers.

In Phnom Penh, the government forcibly evicted thousands of families, claiming the land was owned by private companies or needed for public projects. Many of these poor urban families had lived in their settlements for more than a decade. Police used unnecessary force during evictions. In June, for example, 600 armed military police officers were dispatched to evict Sambok Chap residents. Afterwards, the 1,000 displaced families were dumped at a one-hectare relocation site 20 kilometers from Phnom Penh. It lacked houses, running water, sanitation facilities, and electricity.

Performance of the Judiciary

The courts—widely viewed as corrupt and incompetent—continue to be used to advance political agendas, silence critics, and strip people of their land. The Ministry of Justice continues to have oversight over the Supreme Council of the Magistracy's secretariat, a disciplinary body for the judiciary that is meant to be independent.

Excessive pre-trial detention continued, with accused people routinely detained for more than the six months allowed by law. In addition, hundreds of prisoners who have served their sentences remained behind bars because of a judicial practice in which prisoners must remain in prison until their appeals have been heard.

Khmer Rouge Tribunal

In July, the 30 international and Cambodian judges and prosecutors for the Khmer Rouge tribunal, which is to be established as an extraordinary chamber within the Cambodian court system, were sworn in and prosecution investigations began.

Many of the Cambodian judicial officials have poor track records in terms of judicial independence and competence. The US$56 million tribunal is expected to commence its trial phase in mid-2007, at a military base outside of Phnom Penh.

Khmer Rouge leader Chhit Chhoeun (Ta Mok), 82, died in July. He had been detained without trial since 1999, along with Kaing Khek Lev (Duch), chief of the Khmer Rouge's S-21 (Tuol Sleng) prison. Other senior Khmer Rouge leaders, including Leng Sary, Khieu Samphan, and Nuon Chea, continued to live freely in Cambodia.

Key International Actors

Donors, whose aid constitutes roughly half Cambodia's national budget, increased their annual pledge in 2006 to US$601 million, from $504 million in 2005. Cambodia's largest donors included the European Union, Japan, the United States, France, Australia, Sweden, the United Kingdom, and Germany.

Some, including the EU, Germany, UK, France, and the US, publicly condemned the arrest and harassment of civil society leaders in January, but were less vocal about other serious, ongoing abuses by the government. Such behavior sent mixed signals to the Cambodian government.

In March the US ambassador praised National Police Chief Hok Lundy's cooperation in addressing human trafficking and drug smuggling, and the FBI awarded a medal to him for his support of the US global "war on terror." Hok Lundy has long been linked to political violence. The US continued to withhold direct funding for the Khmer Rouge Tribunal, largely because of concerns about the incompetence and bias of the Cambodian judges.

China, Cambodia's largest investor, pledged US$600 million in grants and loans in April, outside of the more structured Consultative Group process. As is typical with Chinese aid, no conditions were attached to the package.

In June the World Bank announced suspension of several of its Cambodian projects because of fraud and corruption by Cambodian officials. Instead of investigating the allegations, Hun Sen claimed that if money was being siphoned off, World Bank consultants should also be held responsible.

The UN special rapporteur on adequate housing and the special representative on human rights defenders issued statements condemning forced evictions in the capital, the "humanitarian emergency" at relocation sites, and the arrest and harassment of rights defenders. During a May visit, the UN high commissioner for human rights said that the human rights situation had "deteriorated" and identified the lack of an independent judiciary as the single most important problem. "Hun Sen's government continues its repressive, undemocratic governance, nowhere near the fulfillment of its international human rights obligations," she stated.

CHINA

Human rights conditions in China deteriorated significantly in 2006. Authorities greeted rising social unrest—marked at times by violent confrontation between protesters and police—with stricter controls on the press, internet, academics, lawyers, and nongovernmental organizations (NGOs).

Several high-profile, politically-motivated prosecutions of lawyers and journalists in 2006 put an end to any hopes that President Hu Jintao would be a progressive reformer and sent an unambiguous warning to individuals and groups pressing for greater respect for the fundamental rights and freedoms of Chinese citizens. Domestic observers believe that these constraints will remain in place at least through the 2008 summer Olympics being hosted by Beijing.

Layers of Control

The Chinese government continues to use a vast police and state security apparatus to enforce multiple layers of controls on critics, protesters, and civil society activists. Such controls make actual arrests—which draw unwanted international attention—less necessary in silencing critics.

The system includes administrative and professional pressures, restrictions on domestic and foreign movements, covert or overt tapping and surveillance of phone and internet communications, visits and summons by the police, close surveillance by plainclothes agents, unofficial house-arrests, incommunicado confinement in distant police-run guest houses, and custody in police stations. Many are charged with vaguely defined crimes such as "disrupting social order," "leaking state secrets," or "inciting subversion."

Some 100 activists, lawyers, writers, academics, HIV/AIDS campaigners, and human rights defenders were subject to such treatment in 2006, indicating a new crackdown.

China's Legal System

Despite expectations of major new legislative initiatives and vigorous legal debates in academic and professional circles, legal reforms stalled in 2006.

The Criminal Procedure Law has not been amended. The scheduled adoption of a property law, which would have secured private ownership and bolstered the legal rights of common citizens, was unexpectedly shelved. Long-discussed proposals to add a judicial component to "reeducation through labor" regulations also appear to have stalled.

The government took initial steps to reform the death penalty system by requiring the review of all cases by the Supreme People's Court, which is likely to limit the approximately 10,000 executions carried out every year.

New regulations governing organ procurement enacted on August 1, 2006, failed to address the fact that judicial executions are the major source of organs used in transplant surgery in China.

Despite exponentially increasing demands for justice, dispute resolution, and vindication of constitutional rights, the court system provides minimal redress. Although the Chinese Communist Party (CCP) leadership acknowledges that many social protests have been fueled by abuses by local officials, institutionalized political interference in the judiciary allows local power holders to deny justice from plaintiffs and vulnerable groups. The lack of judicial remedies further exacerbates social unrest. The Ministry of Public Security reported August 9, 2006 that there were 39,000 cases of "public order disruptions" in the first half of the year, quadruple what it was a decade ago. Thirteen Chinese villagers arrested after such an incident in Dongzhou, Guangdong Province, where security officers shot at least three protesters, were sentenced on May 24, 2006, to prison terms raging up to four years.

In March 2006, in an effort to curb legal activism around issues such as land seizures, forced evictions, and environmental and labor grievances, the government imposed new restrictions on lawyers representing protesters. As of April, new "Guiding Opinions on Lawyers" require lawyers and law firms to report to and seek instructions from local judicial authorities—often themselves party to the disputes—in all cases involving 10 plaintiffs or more.

Coerced confessions, legal procedures weighted in favor of the state, closed trials, and administrative sentencing continue to undermine defendants' rights.

Restrictions on Freedom of Expression

The "Great Firewall of China" restricts not only access to the internet, with its 123 million users in China, but also to newspapers, magazines, books, television and radio broadcasts, and film. During 2006, the Chinese government and Communist party officials moved aggressively to plug the wall's holes and to punish transgressors. Premier Wen Jiabao justified the renewed crackdown, stating that "internet censorship is necessary to safeguard national, social and collective interests."

Journalists, bloggers, webmasters, writers, and editors, who send news out of China or who merely debate politically sensitive ideas among themselves, face punishments ranging from sudden unemployment to long prison terms. Censors use sophisticated filters, blocking, and internet police to limit incoming information.

During the first half of 2006, Chinese officials shut down more than 700 online forums and ordered eight search engines to filter "subversive and sensitive content" based on 10,000 key words. In July, a website called Century China and its eight online forums, popular among Chinese intellectuals, was shut down for illegally providing news. In September, two chief editors of *Wang Yi* (NetEase), a top internet portal, were fired for allowing an unauthorized opinion poll. Blogs from prominent commentators and activists continued to be regularly shut down.

By their own admission, global corporations such as Google, Microsoft, Yahoo!, and Skype continue to assist in the Chinese government's system of arbitrary and opaque political censorship in an effort to ingratiate their companies with Chinese regulators. Yahoo! released the identity of private users to Chinese authorities, contributing to four critics' lengthy prison sentences. Microsoft and Google censor searches for what they think the government considers sensitive terms.

虎搜索！

一搜就知！　　　雅虎搜索

w.yahoo.com.cn

CHINA

"Race to the Bottom"

Corporate Complicity in Chinese Internet Censorship

HUMAN
RIGHTS
WATCH

Although a Chinese government Information Office official said "no one in China had been arrested simply because he or she said something on the internet," subversion charges in 2006 led to 10, 12, four and two-year sentences respectively for internet writers Ren Ziyuan, Li Jianqiang, Guo Qizhen, and Li Yuanlong.

The CCP and government authorities grew less tolerant of newspapers' exposés of official corruption, rural protests, suspect land deals, and legal misconduct. In January 2006, on orders from party officials, *China Youth Daily* temporarily closed *Freezing Point* (*Bingdian*), its weekly supplement, ostensibly for running an article asserting that Chinese textbooks rewrote history. Despite some unusually outspoken protests, the first ever by former senior party officials, *Bingdian* could not reopen until editor-in-chief Li Datong and his deputy were "reassigned."

China has also impeded circulation of several kinds of news events. A proposed new "Law on the Handling of Sudden Incidents" would require that journalists obtain permission before reporting news of disasters such as floods, public health emergencies, mining accidents, and public order disturbances. In September 2006, new measures mandated that foreign news agencies not sell stories directly to Chinese outlets but submit them first to Xinhua, the official Chinese news agency, for clearance and subsequent distribution.

Foreign journalists are not exempt from harassment, detention, and occasional violence. In August, the Foreign Correspondent Club of China (FCCC) reported "widespread detentions" and some instances of physical assaults of foreign reporters. Chinese nationals working for foreign newspapers are especially vulnerable. In September, Zhao Yan, a researcher for the *New York Times*, was sentenced to three years on fraud charges following a trial marred by due process violations.

Human Rights Defenders

As human rights defenders in China have become more adroit at documenting abuses, Chinese authorities, who have never tolerated independent monitoring, have retaliated with harassment, unlawful detention, banishment from Beijing, and long prison sentences, often on trumped-up charges.

Authorities have particularly targeted a small, loosely-organized network of lawyers, legal academics, rights activists, and journalists, known as the weiquan movement, which aims to pursue social justice and constitutional rights through litigation. The movement focuses on housing rights, family planning abuses, land seizures, workers' rights, and police abuse, among other issues.

Defenders who attempt to track abuses against other activists are particularly vulnerable. Since mid-July 2006, Hu Jia has been held under house arrest and repeatedly taken by the police for interrogation.

Chen Guangcheng, a blind legal activist who exposed abuses connected to family planning was sentenced in August to more than four years in prison on charges of obstructing traffic. In apparent response to considerable international attention, the appellate court in November ordered a retrial, though Chen remains in jail.

After many months of house arrest, police harassment, and threats, Gao Zhisheng, a prominent human rights lawyer, was arrested in October 2006 on state security charges of "inciting subversion." At this writing, Beijing police continued to deny Gao's lawyer permission to visit him.

Legal activist Yang Maodong (also known as Guo Feixiong), who was assisting Guangdong villagers resist land seizures, was formally arrested in September 2006 on charges of "illegal business activities."

In June 2006, a local court sentenced Huang Weizhong, elected by villagers in Fujian to protest land acquisition procedures, to three years in prison.

Labor Rights

The Chinese government continues to prevent workers from forming independent trade unions, arguing that the party-controlled All-China Federation of Trade Unions (ACFTU) sufficiently ensures their rights. As a result, increasing numbers have taken to the streets and to the courts, seeking redress for lost wages and pensions, forced and uncompensated overtime, unlawful wage deductions, employers' violations of minimum wage regulations, and unhealthy and dangerous working conditions.

In what has been viewed as a victory for workers, Wal-Mart accepted unionization within its stores in China in 2006 after the ACFTU, rather than following traditional top-down organizing, began store-by-store grassroots organizing. However, the ACFTU's insistence on a "trade union with Chinese characteristics" and its commitment to work with management in setting up local ACFTU braches have cast doubt on its commitment to advocate for workers on rights such as freedom of association and collective bargaining.

Religious Belief and Expression

China does not recognize freedom of religion outside of the state-controlled system in which all congregations, mosques, temples, churches, and monasteries must register.

Registration entails government vetting and ongoing monitoring of religious personnel, seminary applicants, and publications; scrutiny of financial records and membership rolls; and veto power over group activities. Failure to register renders a religious organization illegal and subject to closure, fines, and criminal sanctions. Despite the restrictions, the number of religious practitioners continues to grow.

Policies have been reflected in round-ups of Protestants—possibly as many as 1,958 in a one-year period ending in June 2006—for attending training sessions and Bible study meetings in unregistered venues. Most are released quickly, some after paying fines. Some leaders are held on trumped up charges, such as "illegal business practices."

The Catholic underground church community and the official Chinese Catholic church continue to disagree over the ordination of bishops. In May, over the objections of the Vatican, the official church installed four new bishops.

The government also curtails religious freedom by designating some groups as cults, such as the Falungong. Leaders and those caught publishing and distributing Falungong literature face severe repression.

Xinjiang and the "War on Terror"

In 2006, China intensified its efforts to use the "war on terrorism" to justify its policies to eradicate the "three evil forces"—terrorism, separatism, and religious extremism—allegedly prevalent among Uighurs, a Turkic-speaking Muslim population in China's Xinjiang Uighur Autonomous Region.

Under current policies local imams are required to vet the text of weekly Friday sermons with religious bureaus. "Strike Hard" campaigns subject Uighurs who express "separatist" tendencies to quick, secret, and summary trials, sometimes accompanied by mass sentencing rallies. Imposition of the death penalty is common.

In 2006, China continued to pressure neighboring countries to arrest and deport politically active Uighurs. In June 2006, Uzbekistan extradited to China Huseyin Celil, a Uighur and a Canadian citizen. At this writing, Celil was being held in Xinjiang with no access to Canadian consular services. In May 2006, Kazakhstan acceded to China's demand that it extradite two Uighurs. In October, China sentenced Ismail Semed to death for "separatism" following his deportation from Pakistan. China also pressed hard, though unsuccessfully, to get Albania to repatriate five Uighurs who, until 2006, had been held by the US at Guantanamo Bay.

Chinese officials have labeled Rebiya Kadeer—a Nobel Prize nominee—a terrorist, and in retaliation for her championing of Uighur rights following her exile to the US in March 2005, have beaten and arrested members of her family in Xinjiang. In October 2006 two of her sons, Kahar Abdureyim, 42, and Alim Abdureyim, 31, were put on trial on tax charges.

Tibet

Chinese authorities view the Dalai Lama, in exile in India since 1959, as the linchpin of the effort to separate Tibet from China and view Tibetan Buddhist belief as supportive of his efforts.

Suspected "separatists," many of whom come from monasteries and nunneries, are routinely imprisoned. In January 2006, Gendun, a Tibetan monk, received a four-year prison sentence for opinions expressed in his lectures on Tibetan history and culture. In June 2006, five Tibetans, including two nuns, were detained for publishing and distributing independence leaflets. In July, Namkha Gyaltsen, a monk, received an eight-year sentence for his independence activities. In August, armed police detained Khenpo Jinpa, an abbot. In September, Lobsang Palden, another monk, was charged with "initiating separatist activities."

On September 30, Chinese People's Armed Police shot at a group of approximately 40 Tibetan refugees attempting to cross the border into Nepal, killing a 17-year-old nun, Kelsang Namtso, and possibly others. The rest of the group fled, though witnesses reported seeing Chinese soldiers marching approximately 10 children back to a nearby camp. The official press agency *Xinhua* claimed that the soldiers were "forced to defend themselves," but film footage showed soldiers calmly taking aim and shooting from afar at a column of people making their way through heavy snow.

In spite of plans for economic development of Tibetan regions, the opening of the Qinghai-Lhasa railroad in July 2006 exacerbated concerns among Tibetans that they would be unable to compete economically with an anticipated influx of Han migrants.

HIV/AIDS

Central government officials have announced new steps to reverse the country's HIV/AIDS crisis, but serious challenges remain. HIV/AIDS is expected to cost China's economy nearly US$40 billion over the next five years.

Local officials and security forces continue to obstruct efforts by activists and grassroots organizations to contribute to prevention and education efforts and to organize care-giving. Although there are hundreds of nongovernmental HIV/AIDS organizations in China, only a few are recognized by the government. In 2006, security officers in several provinces detained and beat activists lobbying for improved compensation for AIDS sufferers who contracted the disease through blood transfusions.

In October 2006, local authorities in Xinjiang shut down the Snow Lotus HIV/AIDS Education Institute, an HIV/AIDS advocacy group with funding from the Global Fund for HIV/AIDS, Tuberculosis and Malaria. The group was closed after it exposed the exclusion of 19 junior high school students from their school because they were suffering from Hepatitis B.

Forced Evictions and the 2008 Beijing Olympics

Forced evictions have increased as Beijing clears entire neighborhoods to make room for Olympic sites and to beautify the city. An official with the Beijing Municipal Administration of State Land, Resources and Housing has indicated that some 300,000 people are scheduled for relocation to accommodate beautification projects alone.

With courts offering little protection, residents have banded together to protest collusion between developers and local officials who forcibly evict them from their homes or sell off the land they have been farming. Residents rarely win, in part because land is not individually owned.

In mid-September, Beijing municipal authorities shut down over 50 unregistered schools for children of migrant workers, leaving tens of thousands of children without access to education. This followed a discussion by the authorities about ways to expel one-million migrant laborers from Beijing.

Hong Kong

When Hong Kong became a Special Autonomous Region within the People's Republic of China in 1997 under the principle of "one country, two systems," it was promised a "high degree of autonomy." But Beijing has vetoed moves toward universal suffrage and ruled out direct elections for Hong Kong's legislature in 2007 and for its chief executive in 2008.

In August 2006, pro-Beijing lawmakers adopted a sweeping surveillance bill allowing extensive wiretapping—including of lawyers and journalists. The government has refused to specify when it will reintroduce anti-subversion laws shelved three years ago after the largest demonstration in Hong Kong since 1989.

In August, Albert Ho, a senior legislator from the Democratic Party, was physically assaulted in broad daylight, apparently in connection with his professional activities as a lawyer. The chief executive publicly condemned the incident.

Key International Actors

In 2006 China was elected to the newly-formed UN Human Rights Council. Its candidacy statement asserted that "the Chinese government respects the universality of human rights and supports the UN in playing an important role in the protection and promotion of human rights." However, Chinese diplomatic efforts have focused on doing away with independent UN investigations, on the grounds that "the internal affairs" of a state should not be subject to investigation. China continues to work closely with the "like minded" group of countries, which includes Iran and Zimbabwe, to roll back important human rights protections.

In August, the UN Committee on the Elimination of Discrimination against Women (CEDAW) faulted China for not having incorporated a legal definition for gender discrimination and for failing to act on the Committee's previous recommendations.

China continues to maintain relations with and provide aid to a wide variety of countries, including Sudan and Burma. In 2006, China became the largest investor in Sudan's oil sector but did not use its leverage to publicly press the government to end egregious human rights violations in Darfur or accept a UN force there, and blocked the imposition of targeted sanctions. China provided military assistance to Burma's military junta, which continues to violently suppress civilians.

The Chinese government still refuses to cooperate with the UN special rapporteur on North Korea, and continues to assert that North Koreans are economic immigrants, not refugees. In the wake of Pyongyang's October nuclear test, China took the highly unusual step of curtailing some of its fuel shipments to North Korea, indicating deep unease with Pyongyang's behavior.

Although the European Union and others continued to pursue human rights dialogues with China in 2006, the sessions produced no concrete results and no further movement toward ratification by China of the International Covenant on Political and Civil Rights (ICCPR).

President Hu Jintao visited the United States in April 2006. Meetings with President Bush and other senior officials focused on business and shared security interests, addressing human rights issues in a largely ritualistic manner with no meaningful pressure for reform. The same pattern held when Premier Wen Jiabao attended the EU-China summit in Helsinki in September, then traveled to Germany and the UK for meetings with Chancellor Angela Merkel and Prime Minster Tony Blair. Despite China's intense lobbying, the EU refused to lift its arms embargo on China, imposed after the crackdown on the pro-democracy movement in June 1989.

INDIA

India, widely hailed as the world's largest democracy, has a vibrant press and civil society, but also suffers from a number of chronic human rights problems. A critical issue is impunity: officials and members of the security services who abuse their power are rarely if ever brought to justice for torture, arbitrary detentions and extrajudicial killings in places like Jammu and Kashmir, the insurgency-affected states in the North East, and in areas where there is an extremist Maoist movement by groups known as Naxalites. Legally sanctioned impunity, such as in the Armed Forces Special Powers Act and the Criminal Procedure Code, also plays a role in India's failure to effectively stem caste or inter-communal conflict.

Armed groups have been responsible for attacks as well. A series of explosions on Mumbai's rush hour commuter trains in July 2006 that killed 183 and severely injured hundreds were attributed by the Indian government to Islamic groups. Both the Naxalites and the insurgent groups in the North East have been blamed for many attacks on civilian targets

Other leading human rights concerns in India include the failure to implement policies that protect the rights of children, religious minorities, those living with HIV/AIDS or those belonging to vulnerable communities such as tribal groups, Dalits and other 'backward' castes.

Rights of Dalits and Indigenous Tribal Groups

Local authorities regularly fail to implement laws set up to end discrimination against and protect Dalits and members of tribal groups. The laws even provide administrative measures for enforcement including Special Courts and the appointment of Special Public Prosecutors. These courts have enormous powers, including the power to remove potential offenders from some areas, and to confiscate property. Public officials who do not perform their duties can be punished with a jail term extending up to a year. But these powers are rarely used.

Abuses against Dalits include harassment, mutilations and killings by members of other castes. For instance, in January 2006 Bant Singh, a Dalit man who had led a campaign to protect the rights of agricultural workers, was so brutally assaulted by members of the feudal upper caste that his limbs had to be amputated.

Indigenous peoples, known as Scheduled Tribes or Adivasis, have suffered from high rates of displacement due to economic and infrastructure development programs. The proposed Scheduled Tribes (Recognition of Forest Rights) Bill, which is designed to protect the rights of those who had been occupying forest land, is still to be enacted.

Naxalites

Prime Minister Manmohan Singh described the Naxalite movement, which has spread to 13 states, as the single biggest threat to internal security. Initially, Naxalites found widespread support among the poor, particularly tribal groups and Dalits, who feel left out by India's modernization process and surging economic growth. But increasingly these same groups have suffered at the hand of the Naxalites because of illegal taxes, demands for food and shelter that put them at risk of retaliation by security forces, abduction and killing of "class enemies" and others opponents, and the hampering of the delivery of development aid to the isolated countryside, which adversely affects the lives of the people that the Naxalites claim to represent.

As the government clamps down on the Naxalite groups, these already vulnerable communities have been caught between two sets of guns. National and state governments have overreacted with force and legal measures. In Chattisgarh state, which witnessed the most Maoist violence in 2006, the state government adopted a vague and overly broad law that allows for detention of up to three years for "unlawful activities." The term is so loosely defined in the law that it threatens fundamental freedoms set out by the Indian constitution and international human rights law, and could severely restrict the peaceful activities of individuals and civil society organizations.

Impunity of Security Forces

In a report "Everybody Lives in Fear," released on the human rights situation in Jammu and Kashmir, Human Rights Watch noted that Indian security forces, including the military, paramilitary forces, and the police, routinely abuse human rights with impunity. The Indian federal government rarely prosecutes army and paramilitary troops in a credible and transparent manner. The result has been an increase in serious violations by security forces throughout the country.

Laws such as the Public Safety Act (Jammu and Kashmir), the Disturbed Areas Act, the Armed Forces (Special Powers) Act have spawned abuses in various parts of the country. Section 197 of the Criminal Code of Procedure provides security forces virtual immunity for crimes committed in the course of duty.

A report of the committee headed by Justice B.P. Jeevan Reddy to review the Armed Forces (Special Powers) Act has recommended that this law be repealed because it is "too sketchy, too bald and quite inadequate in several particulars." The government has yet to act upon this recommendation.

Kashmir Conflict

The Kashmir insurgency, which began in 1989, has displaced tens of thousands of people, claimed over 50,000 lives. Human rights abuses and impunity have been a cause and fuel for the conflict.

Accountability remains a serious problem. Despite Prime Minister's Manmohan Singh's claim that there would be 'zero tolerance' for human rights violations, troops continued to be responsible for arbitrary detention, torture and extrajudicial executions. Militants have been responsible for indiscriminate bombings and grenade attacks, targeted killings, torture, and attacks upon religious and ethnic minorities. Abuses are continuing, despite talks between India, Pakistan and some separatist groups and the election of a state government in Jammu and Kashmir in 2002 with an avowed human rights agenda.

Indian security forces claim they are fighting to protect Kashmiris from militants and Islamic extremists, while militants claim they are fighting for Kashmiri independence and to defend Muslim Kashmiris from a murderous Indian army. In reality, both sides have committed widespread and numerous human rights abuses and violations of international humanitarian law (the laws of war), creating among the civilian population a pervasive climate of fear, distrust, and sadness. Years of impunity for serious abuses have led to a vicious cycle of continuing violence. The

INDIA

"Everyone Lives in Fear"

Patterns of Impunity in Jammu and Kashmir

HUMAN
RIGHTS
WATCH

Indian government has effectively given its forces free rein, while Pakistan and armed militant groups have never taken any action against militants who carry out atrocities.

Legacy of Communal Violence

The Indian government has failed to contain violent religious extremism and to prosecute most of those who instigate or participate in religious violence. Such failures only reinforce communal resentments. Investigations into attacks by armed groups, particularly after the Mumbai bomb explosions, invariably lead to widespread interrogation, detention and torture of Muslims by police, causing further alienation.

There has still been no accountability for the deaths of more than 2,000 Muslims in the western state of Gujarat during communal violence that erupted after a train carrying Hindu pilgrims in 2002 caught fire, killing 59 passengers. There continue to be delays in the investigation and prosecution of these cases. For instance, in April 2006, 52 accused in a riot case in Panchmahal district were acquitted for lack of sufficient evidence, once again leading to accusations of a failure of proper police investigation.

Meanwhile, in a number of cities in Gujarat, communal hate has led to internal displacement along religious lines, while Muslim businesses have been boycotted by Hindus. The National Commission of Minorities said in October that 5,703 riot-affected Muslim families were yet to be properly compensated and rehabilitated, with chairman Hamid Ansari describing this as an "abdication of Constitutional responsibility on the part of the state government with reference to victims of the 2002 riots who are living in barely human conditions."

In February 2005, a Commission headed by Justice G.T. Nanavati to probe the 1984 anti-Sikh riot submitted its report to the government. Although some senior Congress leaders blamed for their part in organizing the anti-Sikh pogrom resigned their posts in the government, those responsible for planning and instigating the riots are yet to be prosecuted.

Christians have come under attack as Hindu fundamentalist groups continue their campaign to force them to convert to Hinduism. At the same time, several states governed by the right-wing Bharatiya Janata Party has banned, forced, or coerced conversions in an effort to end the influence of the church and missionaries in rural, underdeveloped areas.

Failure to Implement Children's Rights

Despite a scheme launched two years ago to provide universal education, millions of children in India still have no access to education and work long hours in the worst forms of child labor. India accounts for a significant proportion of the world's out-of-school children. This is because many Indian children work, cannot afford school fees, do not have access to education, or belong to deprived communities such as Dalit or other marginalized castes, tribal groups or minority religions, particularly Islam. In October 2006, the government proscribed the employment of children as domestic servants or in tea stalls and restaurants; while this is a good step, previous experience has shown that without proper implementation and adequate rehabilitation of child workers, such laws are of very limited utility. The government has also announced plans to establish a national commission for children that activists hope will prove effective in protecting their rights.

Rights of Those Living with HIV/AIDS

The government estimates that in 2005, 5.7 million people in India were living with HIV/AIDS. People living with AIDS, as well as those whose marginalized status puts them at highest risk—sex workers, injection drug users, and men who have sex with men—face widespread stigmatization and discrimination, including denial of employment, access to education and healthcare. A promised law that would ban discrimination against people living with HIV has not been enacted, sodomy laws have not been repealed, and the government has not taken appropriate steps to address abuses against children affected by AIDS. Although numbers of people on anti-retroviral treatment went up to 40,000 as of September 2006, India still fell far short of the 100,000 people a government minister had promised to put on treatment in 2002.

Key International Actors

Viewed increasingly as a strong economic and trade partner, the international community is generally unwilling to challenge India to address its human rights concerns. Ties between the United States and India have strengthened through increasing trade, joint military exercises and Washington's efforts to provide India with assistance to develop its nuclear energy program. This has left the United States, the most influential external actor, much less willing to confront India on rights issues.

India receives significant aid from multilateral donors such as the World Bank and the Asian Development Bank, but accepts bilateral assistance from only a few countries. Increasingly, India is providing aid to some smaller countries.

India has not used its increasing influence with smaller neighbors like Burma and Maldives, achieved through significant amounts of financial and military aid, to call publicly for better compliance with human rights standards. India is supplying military hardware to Burma in return for the military junta's cooperation in flushing out separatist groups that cross the border for sanctuary. After the Indian government announced its intention of supplying two British-built maritime surveillance aircraft to Burma, the UK declared it would be unable to provide spare parts and maintenance support.

In 2006 India played a significant part in encouraging Nepal's King Gyanendra to end his illegal rule and restore democracy. In Sri Lanka, India has been engaged in discussions with the government to put an end to the recent violence and restore a 2002 ceasefire between government troops and the Liberation Tigers of Tamil Eelam.

INDONESIA

In February 2006 Indonesia acceded to the International Covenant on Civil and Political Rights (ICCPR) and International Covenant on Economic, Social, and Cultural Rights (ICESCR). But those new commitments were not accompanied by any immediate improvement in human rights practices.

Continuing areas of concern in Indonesia include impunity for past human rights violations, the slow pace of military reform, conditions in Papua, imposition of the death penalty, and infringements on freedom of expression and religious freedom.

Impunity

Indonesia has made little progress in addressing the human rights crimes of the Soeharto era. No charges have been brought against the former president for human rights violations committed during his more than three decades of power, or for the violence instigated by pro-Soeharto forces in a failed attempt to stave off his 1998 fall from power. Although corruption charges were brought against Soeharto, the Jakarta High Court in August 2006 approved a decision by the Attorney General's Office to drop the case due to Soeharto's poor health.

Despite significant international pressure and interest, trials of senior Indonesian officers at an ad hoc human rights court in Jakarta have failed to give a credible judicial accounting for atrocities committed in East Timor in 1999. In March 2006 the Supreme Court rejected the appeal of Eurico Guterres, the only person convicted at the ad hoc court in Jakarta. He started serving his 10-year prison sentence in May.

In July 2006 the UN secretary-general reported on justice and reconciliation for Timor Leste, calling the Jakarta ad hoc court "manifestly deficient" in delivering justice for the victims of human rights violations in East Timor in 1999. The secretary-general recommended a series of measures aimed at apprehending and trying alleged perpetrators.

Military Reform

Military reform efforts have largely stalled. At this writing, there was no government plan to review the country's defense structure, which is currently based on a territorial defense model that independent experts have declared outmoded and ill-suited for a maritime state and that civil society groups have challenged on human rights grounds. Some government officials also continue to actively resist measures to bring soldiers before civilian courts to answer for non-military crimes.

The Indonesian military continues to raise money outside the government budget through a sprawling network of legal and illegal businesses, by providing paid services, and through acts of corruption such as mark-ups in military purchases. This self-financing undermines civilian control, contributes to abuses of power by the armed forces, and impedes reform. Authorities have made little progress in implementing a 2004 law (Law 34/2004) that addresses several of these issues.

Aceh

Human rights violations in Indonesia's northwest Aceh province have decreased significantly since an August 2005 ceasefire and peace agreement between the government and rebels of the Free Aceh Movement (Gerakan Aceh Merdeka, or GAM). On July 11, 2006, Indonesia's national parliament passed the Law on Aceh Governance, which implemented the peace agreement. Although the law establishes a human rights court for the province, the court has only prospective jurisdiction and cannot address any of the myriad past human rights crimes that accompanied three decades of armed conflict in the province. The law establishes a truth and reconciliation commission to examine events of the past.

Papua and West Irian Jaya

Five members of Indonesia's security forces were attacked and, when defenseless, killed in clashes between student activists and police in Papua, Indonesia's easternmost province, in March 2006. Dozens of people were arrested in police sweeps after the riots, some of whom were subsequently convicted in trials that failed to meet international standards for fairness.

In January 2006 twelve men were arrested in Papua for the 2002 killing of two Americans and one Indonesian in Tembagapura, Papua. In November seven defendants were found guilty, and Antonius Wamang was sentenced to life imprisonment for premeditated murder. The other six defendants were charged with involvement in the ambush and sentenced to between 18 months and seven years in prison.

Death Penalty

In September 2006 the government executed three men in Central Sulawesi for inciting violence and premeditated murders in the province in 2000. These were the first executions since May 2005. At least 90 other people remain under sentence of death in Indonesia.

Freedom of Expression and Press

Broadly-worded laws limiting freedom of expression are still used by authorities to target outspoken critics. In October 2006 an Indonesian student was convicted of insulting President Susilo Bambang Yudhoyono during a protest and sentenced to three months and 23 days in prison by the South Jakarta district court.

Journalists and editors who publish controversial material face intimidation. A prominent case in 2006 concerned *Playboy Indonesia*, the first edition of which went on sale in early April without any nude photos. The new magazine was greeted by protests and violent attacks on its Jakarta editorial offices. In a welcome decision in September 2006 judges at the South Jakarta Court dismissed blasphemy charges against an editor of the online edition of *Rakyat Merdeka* for republishing the offensive Danish cartoons of the Prophet Muhammad.

Freedom of Religion

Instances of religious intolerance appeared to be on the rise in 2006 with attacks on Ahmadiyah places of worship and Christian churches.

Joint Decree No. 1/2006 on the establishment of places of worship, issued by the Religious Affairs Ministry and the Home Ministry in March 2006, requires a 90-

member minimum congregation prior to the issuance of permits for a place of worship. The decree provoked a string of protests from minority religious groups, and prompted the forcible and sometimes violent closure of several Christian churches across Indonesia by vigilante groups.

In June 2006 the Central Jakarta District Court convicted Lia Aminuddin, the leader of a minority religious sect, the Kingdom of Eden, for blasphemy against Islam and sentenced her to two years imprisonment.

Forced Evictions

Disputes over land and forced evictions continue to be a frequent source of conflict. Security forces often demolish homes and destroy personal property without notice, due process, or compensation, and residents often are ill-treated. Women, children, and rural migrants typically suffer particularly severe long-term consequences, including impairment of their ability to earn a livelihood or to attend school.

Indonesian Migrant Workers

More than one million Indonesians work abroad, sending home remittances critical to the country's economy. Women comprise over 75 percent of legal migrant workers, mostly migrating as domestic workers to the Middle East and other parts of Asia.

Migrant domestic workers commonly become heavily indebted to pay unregulated, exorbitant recruitment agency fees. Many are confined in locked, overcrowded training centers for months prior to migration, and receive inadequate or incorrect information about the terms of their employment. In the worst cases, such conditions contribute to making the migrants vulnerable to even more egregious abuses abroad, including forced labor, debt bondage, and human trafficking.

In May 2006 Indonesia signed an agreement with Malaysia on migrant domestic workers. The long-delayed agreement does not protect the right of migrants to keep their passports, guarantee standard labor protections, or include bilateral measures to prevent and respond to cases of abuse.

INDONESIA

Condemned Communities

Forced Evictions in Jakarta

HUMAN
RIGHTS
WATCH

Child Domestic Workers in Indonesia

More than 688,000 children, mainly girls, are estimated to work as domestic workers in Indonesia. Typically recruited between the ages of 12 and 15, and often on false promises of decent wages and working conditions, girls may work 14 to 18 hours a day, seven days a week, and earn far less than the prevailing minimum wage. In the worst cases, child domestics are paid no salary at all and are physically and sexually abused.

At this writing, draft legislation was pending that would mandate an eight hour work day, a weekly day of rest, an annual holiday, and a minimum wage for domestic workers. The draft contained no provisions for sanctions against employers or recruiting agencies for violations.

Human Rights Defenders

The September 2004 murder of Munir Said Thalib, one of Indonesia's most outspoken and respected human rights defenders, remains unsolved. President Yudhoyono established an independent fact-finding team to investigate Munir's killing and the team identified Pollycarpus Budihari Priyanto, a Garuda Airlines pilot linked to high-ranking intelligence officials, as a leading suspect in the case. Although Pollycarpus was convicted of premeditated murder and sentenced to 14 years in prison in 2005, the Supreme Court threw out the murder verdict in October 2006, deeming the evidence insufficient. Pollycarpus continues to be imprisoned on subsidiary charges. At this writing, it was unclear whether new charges would be filed against Pollycarpus, and there was little evidence that police or prosecutors were seriously pursuing higher ranking intelligence officials widely believed to have played a role in the killing.

Lt. Gen. (ret.) Hendropriyono, the head of Indonesia's State Intelligence Body at the time of the murder, who had refused to comply with a summons from the fact-finding team, subsequently filed criminal defamation charges against two members of the team, respected human rights defenders Usman Hamid (the head of Kontras) and Rachland Nashidik (the head of Imparsial). The charges were still pending at this writing.

In Papua, human rights defenders still suffer threats and intimidation from security forces when monitoring and investigating human rights abuses. Defense lawyers in the March 2006 Abepura case received anonymous death threats.

Key International Actors

In November 2005 the US Congress voted to maintain some restrictions on US military assistance to Indonesia pending progress in accountability for human rights violations and increased civilian control over the military. These restrictions were lifted several weeks later when US Secretary of State Rice exercised her power to waive them in the name of pressing US national security interests. The US has made it clear that cooperation in counterterrorism operations is more critical than human rights to normalization of the relationship.

In March 2006 Prime Minister Tony Blair became the first UK leader visit to Indonesia since 1985. During the visit Blair announced that Britain would normalize defense ties and renew military cooperation with Indonesia.

Indonesia cemented its relationship with Australia in November 2006 with the signing of a new security treaty between the two countries. This came after a difficult year. Diplomatic tensions had mounted in March 2006 after Australia granted temporary asylum to 42 asylum seekers from Indonesia's Papua province, who had arrived in January claiming political persecution. Tensions then mounted again after Australia sounded strong disapproval over the June 14, 2006, early release of Abu Bakar Bashir, believed by many to be the spiritual head of the terrorist organization Jemaah Islamiyah and the mastermind of the 2002 Bali bombs in which 88 Australians were killed.

In April 2006 World Bank President Paul Wolfowitz visited Indonesia and pledged support for the Aceh peace process but urged more measures to combat corruption.

In May 2006 Indonesia was elected to be a member of the new UN Human Rights Council.

MALAYSIA

When he took office three years ago, there were great hopes that Prime Minister Abdullah Badawi would make a break with the poor human rights record of his predecessor, Mahathir Mohamad. Badawi raised hopes when he promised good governance and human rights improvement. While there has been a reduction of pressure on human rights groups and lawyers, there has been virtually no institutional reform.

The Badawi administration has failed to dismantle the legal framework that allows security officials to detain persons indefinitely without charge or trial. Recommendations by the government-appointed Royal Commission to Enhance the Royal Malaysia Police to amend and repeal such laws and to set up an independent commission to oversee the Royal Malaysia Police have yet to be implemented. Abuses against refugees and migrants continue to be reported and public discussions on inter-faith issues and religious freedom are restricted.

Detention without Trial

At this writing more than 90 persons were being detained without charge or trial for alleged threats to national security under the 1960 Internal Security Act (ISA). Since 2001 the ISA has been used against suspected Islamist militants, primarily alleged members of the Islamist group Jemmah Islamiyah (JI), and against individuals suspected of involvement in counterfeiting and document forgery. Many of the alleged JI detainees have been held for four years. In 2006, without explanation, the government extended the detention of 25 detainees for another two years. In May the government announced the arrests of 11 persons affiliated with the Islamist group Darul Islam.

Under the Emergency Ordinance (Public Order and Prevention of Crime), enacted in 1969 as a temporary measure to respond to race riots, the government has detained 700 persons indefinitely without charge or trial in Simpang Renggam detention center in Johor state for alleged involvement in criminal activities. Government officials publicly acknowledge that the Emergency Ordinance is used against criminal suspects because the police do not have sufficient evidence to charge them. Detainees are barred by law from challenging the merits of their detention. Some have been detained for eight years. While detainees may raise procedural challenges and on this basis occasionally are ordered released by courts, the government often re-arrests them on the same charges. In June 2006 police re-arrested 11 detainees as they were leaving the Simpang Renggam detention center after a court-ordered release.

Another tactic police use to extend the arbitrary detention of suspects is through what are known as "road shows": when a pretrial 15-day detention order is due to expire, police seek another order in a different district. Police are known to have used this tactic to hold individuals for as many as 143 days.

In 2006 Prime Minister Badawi joined the near universal call to close the US detention center in Guantánamo Bay, Cuba, and also urged that the two Malaysian detainees transferred from CIA secret facilities to Guantánamo be given a fair trial. But the prime minister failed to afford similar rights to detainees held under the ISA or the Emergency Ordinance.

Migrant Workers, Refugees, and Asylum Seekers

Malaysian authorities continued to enforce the punitive Immigration Act. Anyone found guilty of being in the country without the appropriate legal documentation faces a mandatory sentence of up to five years imprisonment and up to six strokes of the cane. The amendment also imposes mandatory caning on those convicted of harboring five or more undocumented individuals. Malaysian authorities have continued to round up and deport undocumented migrant workers. The lack of effective screening procedures means that refugees, trafficking victims, abused migrant workers, and other vulnerable groups are at risk of detention and prosecution under the immigration laws.

A volunteer civilian armed corps, the Rela, has been authorized by the government to question and arrest undocumented migrants. The bodies of five migrants were recovered in February in Selayang allegedly as a result of a Rela raid. Later that month more than 60 Indian migrant workers were clubbed by Rela and taken to a detention camp. The workers were waiting outside the Indian High Commission to draw attention to the unpaid wages owed them by Malaysian employers.

In May 2006, Malaysia signed a Memorandum of Understanding (MOU) with Indonesia regarding recruitment and treatment of approximately 300,000 migrant domestic workers. These workers confront a wide range of abuses, including forced confinement in the workplace, excessively long work hours, lack of rest days, unpaid wages, and physical and sexual abuse. The new MOU does little to address exploitative working conditions, and domestic workers continue to be excluded from key provisions of Malaysia's Employment Act of 1955, which would entitle them to one rest day per week and an eight-hour work day. Their work permits are tied to their employers, making it difficult to report abuse for fear of repatriation. Some positive reforms were still being considered by the government at this writing, including a requirement that domestic workers be paid at least once a month.

Despite hosting a large number of refugees and asylum seekers Malaysia is not a signatory to the 1951 Refugee Convention and does not have in place proper procedures to register, document, and protect such people. According to the United Nations High Commissioner for Refugees, as of May 2006 there were more than 46,000 refugees and asylum seekers in Malaysia, including 20,000 Achenese from Indonesia, and 11,000 Rohingyas and 11,000 Chins from Myanmar. In July 2005 the minister of home affairs announced plans to allow refugees and asylum seekers to join the work force, but more than a year later there was no evidence the policy was being implemented. Without work permits refugees remain vulnerable to exploitation by employers and the police.

At this writing, the government was drafting new anti-trafficking legislation.

Freedom of Religion

Islam is the official religion of Malaysia, and ethnic Malays by definition must be Muslim. Faiths of other ethnic groups are protected under article 11 of the constitution which guarantees freedom of religion. For Muslims, marriage, property, and divorce are governed by Sharia courts. Muslims who wish to renounce Islam must seek permission from Sharia courts, although rarely granted, and can be subject to sanctions involving years of rehabilitation.

Lina Joy, who converted to Christianity from Islam, at this writing was awaiting a decision from the Federal Court—the highest court in Malaysia—on whether her conversion should be considered a right under the constitution instead of a religious matter for Sharia courts. Joy's application to have her religious status on her identification card changed had been rejected by the National Registration Department on grounds she was an ethnic Malay, a decision she challenged in the courts.

Human Rights Defenders

Fora organized around the country by non-governmental organizations to discuss religious freedom were disrupted on several occasions in 2006 by a coalition of Muslim groups calling themselves the Anti-Interfaith Commission. In May a mob forcibly stopped a forum in Penang. Two Islamic Party of Malaysia (PAS) leaders and a Muslim religious scholar were charged with illegal assembly for allegedly participating in a demonstration against the forum in Penang. A subsequent forum in Johor Bahru was also stopped on the advice of the police due to a demonstration by Islamic groups outside the venue. Instead of taking action against the groups, on July 26 Prime Minister Badawi ordered such public discussions on inter-faith issues to be stopped.

Human rights lawyer Malik Imtiaz Sarwar, who is outspoken on religious freedom and inter-faith issues and wrote a brief in support of Lina Joy's case before the Federal Court, received an anonymous death threat in August 2006. The threat entitled "Wanted Dead" was circulated with Sarwar's picture and text condemning him for his support of Lina Joy.

Key International Actors

Since September 11, 2001, international criticism of Malaysia's human rights records has decreased. The United States, once a strong critic of Malaysia's preventive detention laws, is now less critical. Malaysia is the United States tenth largest trading partner and negotiations are underway on a free trade agreement between the two nations. The US and the United Kingdom have strong relations with Malaysia on security issues, cooperating on training and counterterrorism operations and conducting joint exercises.

Malaysia plays a significant role in regional and global issues. It currently chairs the Association of Southeast Asian Nations and the Organization of the Islamic Conference and is facilitating negotiations between the Philippine government and the Moro Islamic Liberation Front.

NEPAL

The human rights situation improved markedly after April 2006, when 19 days of widespread public demonstrations dubbed the Jana Andolan, or people's movement, ended King Gyanendra's year-long usurpation of all authority and created conditions conducive to a ceasefire in the brutal civil war between government forces and the Communist Party of Nepal—Maoists (CPN-M).

With both parties declaring a ceasefire by the beginning of May, civilian casualties directly caused by the conflict dramatically declined, as did human rights abuses such as extrajudicial execution, arbitrary detention, and torture. The removal of restrictions imposed by King Gyanendra after seizing power on February 1, 2005, also significantly improved the ability of Nepalese to exercise freedom of speech and association.

On November 21, 2006, the government and the Maoists signed a comprehensive agreement to govern a peace process, to establish a constituent assembly to redraft the country's constitution (including the continued existence of a monarchy), and to establish an interim government. This agreement explicitly referred to the parties' respect for human rights and included the creation of several high level commissions to address more than a thousand cases of "disappearances" as well as accelerate the process of returning tens of thousands of displaced people to their homes.

Notwithstanding the hope and jubilation following the Jana Andolan and the resulting peace process, many Nepalese continue to voice concerns about the country's human rights and political situation. Human rights activists complained that the peace agreement did not create any effective monitoring or implementation mechanisms to address violations by both sides. The issue was particularly relevant because both warring parties, and particularly the Maoists, regularly violated the letter and spirit of the ceasefire code of conduct they had signed on May 26, 2006. Despite changes in leadership, the Nepali Army failed to cooperate with investigations about the fate of hundreds of "disappeared" Nepalese and the government failed to properly investigate or prosecute a single case of extrajudicial execution, "disappearances", and torture.

Close to the Precipice

As 2006 began, Nepal seemed poised on the edge of disaster. On January 2 the Maoists ended a unilateral, three-month ceasefire because the government had not reciprocated. Intensifying fighting between government security forces and the Maoists quickly engulfed nearly every one of the country's 75 districts. Civilian casualties, which had decreased during the ceasefire, quickly soared once fighting resumed. Maoists increasingly carried out attacks on urban areas and sought shelter among civilians. Security forces used jury-rigged helicopters to drop mortar shells on Maoist positions, in several instances in civilian areas.

The government tried to establish a facade of normalcy and legitimacy by proceeding with local and parliamentary elections in February despite intense opposition at home and abroad. Nearly all the country's political parties boycotted the elections. Maoist forces attacked several candidates and forced many to withdraw their candidacy. Not surprisingly, the results were widely viewed as illegitimate and were severely criticized as flawed and unrepresentative by most Nepalese as well as the United States, the European Union, and Japan.

The Jana Andolan

Following the failed elections, on April 4 a broad-based opposition movement instigated street-protests by hundreds of thousands of Nepalese throughout the country. The protesters sought an end to King Gyanendra's authoritarian rule and demanded an end to the civil war. The royal government attempted to quell the protests with excessive force and brutality, killing 18 people and injuring some 4,000 people, many of them children.

After 19 days of increasingly large protests that paralyzed the country's economic and political life, the Jana Andolan succeeded in forcing King Gyanendra to reinstate the House of Representatives on April 24, 2006. (Many Nepalese called the movement the Jana Andolan II, a reference to the people's movement that ushered in constitutional monarchy and multi-party rule in 1990.) An alliance of seven opposition parties assumed authority and immediately implemented a ceasefire agreement with the Maoists. The newly reinstated parliament removed King Gyanendra as commander-in-chief and stripped him of all but ceremonial authority. The seven-party alliance and the Maoists committed to establishing a constituent assembly to revise the country's constitution.

After the Jana Andolan: Hope and Fear

The end of King Gyanendra's dictatorial rule and the cessation of hostilities immediately decreased human rights abuses. Violations of the laws of war diminished significantly and casualties caused by armed clashes nearly disappeared. The government released hundreds of detainees held under the draconian Public Security Act (PSA) and Terrorist and Disruptive Activities (Control and Punishment) Ordinance; the only exception was the preventive detention of several senior members of the deposed royal government under the PSA. Strict limitations on freedom of speech and association were removed. Maoist cadres began operating openly, including in Kathmandu, and committed to allowing other political parties to operate in areas under their control.

Ongoing human rights violations by both sides nevertheless contributed to concerns that those in power would again trample the human rights of ordinary Nepalese. The new government and the Maoists agreed to a Ceasefire Code of Conduct that includes several references to international human rights standards and the laws of war. However, the code of conduct lacks specific language about implementation or penalties for infractions. A National Monitoring Committee began monitoring the Code of Conduct in August, but at this writing it had not established its credibility and independence.

Both sides failed to institute accountability for past violations by their troops. The Maoists freed some of those responsible for a 2005 bombing attack in Chitwan, which killed 35 civilians and injured dozens of others, after sentences of two to three months of "corrective punishment." The UN's Office of the High Commissioner for Human Rights (OHCHR) monitoring mission complained of ongoing failure by the renamed Nepali Army (formerly the Royal Nepali Army) to honor its commitment to provide access to documents related to disciplinary procedures and courts martial. In one of the most egregious instances, the army has actively obstructed attempts to investigate the death of Maina Sunuwar, a 15-year-old girl who was killed shortly after she was taken into custody by the army in 2004. Although the Ceasefire Code of Conduct commits both parties to publicize the whereabouts of citizens who have been "disappeared," some 800 people remain unaccounted for at this writing.

Maoist forces did not release any of the thousands of children under age 18 believed to be serving in their ranks, and Nepali rights groups reported ongoing recruitment campaigns throughout the country. Their commitment to the contrary notwithstanding, the Maoists continued to intimidate and restrict the activity of political activists from competing political parties, including more than a dozen cases in which political activists were allegedly killed by Maoist cadres throughout Nepal. Nepali human rights groups as well as monitors from the OHCHR in Nepal documented dozens of abductions of individuals by the Maoists, including at least 16 members of other political parties. Farmers and businesses increasingly complain about being forced to "donate" to the Maoists. The Maoist leadership issued a directive on September 5 to its cadres to halt beatings, abductions, killings, and extortion. At this writing, however, Nepali human rights groups continue to register ongoing violations by Maoist cadres.

On July 25, 2006, parliament asked the government to sign and ratify the Rome Statute of the International Criminal Court, but at this writing the government had not acted. The government also failed to satisfy the proper accession procedures for the Additional Protocol to the Convention on the Rights of the Child, which establishes 18 as the minimum age for combatants.

The parties' agreement to draft a new, more representative constitution provoked complaints by already marginalized groups that they were being left out of the process. The initial committee in charge of guiding the constituent assembly was composed only of men, but was broadened after protests to include women as well as those from so-called untouchable castes, or Dalits. But other groups continue to be sidelined, for instance Nepal's beleaguered population of lesbian, gay, bisexual and transgender people.

Humanitarian Concerns, Internal Displacement, and Refugees

Nepal ranks near the bottom of nearly all indexes of human well-being and development. Aggravating the problems of Nepal's already impoverished population, the decade of conflict seriously hampered aid distribution, health care and education. Economic disruptions caused by fighting and frequent blockades and checkpoints have curtailed food production and distribution, resulting in high rates of malnutrition and associated childhood maladies. Conditions are particularly bad for people displaced by the fighting and attendant economic problems, believed to number in the tens of thousands. After the ceasefire and the commitments made by the Maoists some displaced Nepalese returned to their homes, but thousands of others remained displaced, not returning because of a fear of reprisals or ongoing repression by Maoist forces. Unexploded ordinance and mines, mostly left behind by the Maoists, continue to injure civilians, particularly children.

Nepal continued to host more than 100,000 refugees from Bhutan. There was some hope for a resolution of the 15-year impasse in 2006 as the US offered to accept up to 60,000 refugees.

Thousands of Tibetans braved a perilous crossing over glaciers and mountain passes to escape the Chinese government's increasing pressure in their homeland, or to seek to visit the exiled Dalai Lama. The status of Tibetans in Nepal remains precarious as the Tibetan Welfare Office—which had provided assistance to refugees and served as the political representative of the Dalai Lama—remains closed since shortly before the King's usurpation of power in 2005.

Key International Actors

The human rights monitoring team established by the UN Office of the High Commissioner for Human Rights in Nepal, the largest of its kind in the world, materially improved respect for human rights and provided Nepal's brave but beleaguered civil society with the ability to operate effectively. The new Nepali government and the Maoists requested assistance from the UN to establish a peace process, convene a constituent assembly, and monitor eventual disarmament and management of the parties' arms.

Concerted international pressure made a difference in promoting greater respect for human rights by both government forces and by the Maoists, both of which curtailed some of their worst behavior in order to maintain international support. Another area where international action clearly benefited Nepali civilians was the restriction on lethal military assistance by some of the country's biggest suppliers—including India, the United States, and the United Kingdom—which limited the access of both parties, and particularly the government, to more lethal weapons and ammunition that could have resulted in far higher numbers of civilian deaths and injuries. In particular, the US's human rights conditions for military aid helped push the military to improve its treatment of detainees and respect for the laws of war.

Major donors to Nepal, such as the United States and United Kingdom, generally supported the ceasefire and the process of revising the country's political structure, though their suspicion of Maoists at times elicited criticism from Nepalese involved in the peace process. China and India also supported the process, each anxious to maintain its influence on events while ensuring that violence did not create problems that would spill over the borders.

NORTH KOREA

In October 2006 the Democratic People's Republic of Korea (North Korea) announced that it had conducted its first nuclear weapons test. The move led to a prompt United Nations Security Council resolution condemning the test and calling for sanctions against North Korea by member states. The nuclear detonation followed the test firing in July of seven ballistic missiles, which also led to a condemnatory Security Council resolution.

North Korea's humanitarian crisis continued to deepen. Following the suspension of its activities in December 2005, the World Food Programme (WFP) was allowed to resume operations in May 2006, but in a much reduced capacity with far fewer staff. Massive floods that hit North Korea in the summer further exacerbated the nation's chronic food shortage, while South Korea, North Korea's largest food donor of recent years, suspended its food aid in response to the missile firing in July.

North Korea showed no visible sign of improvement in its dire human rights conditions. In November 2005 the UN General Assembly adopted a resolution expressing serious concern for "systematic, widespread and grave violations of human rights" in North Korea, following multiple resolutions by the UN Commission on Human Rights. North Korea allowed neither the freedom of information, association, movement, and religion, nor organized political opposition, labor activism, or independent civil society. Arbitrary arrests, torture, lack of due process and fair trials, and executions remain of grave concern. Collective punishment of entire families for "political crimes" remains the norm. North Korea continues to block access by international human rights organizations.

Right to Food

A series of recent policy changes in North Korea jeopardized access to food for the most vulnerable segments of the population. In late 2005 North Korea banned the buying and selling of grain by individuals at farmers' markets, and announced it was reviving the Public Distribution System, under which only the state can distribute grain. About a million people died of starvation and many more suffered severe malnutrition under similar policies in the 1990s. The 2006

NORTH KOREA

A Matter of Survival

The North Korean Government's Control of Food
and the Risk of Hunger

**HUMAN
RIGHTS
WATCH**

floods worsened food shortages. The WFP reports that North Korea currently faces a deficit of some 800,000 tons of food. The food shortages are especially worrisome for the most vulnerable populations, including young children, pregnant or nursing women, and the elderly, as North Korea has a long history of first feeding the elite class, including high-ranking military, intelligence, police, and other law-enforcement officials. Smaller rations, often less than the minimum needed to keep a person healthy, are then distributed to the general population.

Criminal Proceedings

Those who are accused of having committed a crime in North Korea seem to suffer the most severe abuses. Legal counsel for the suspect is rarely available at any point in the process, and many suspects are tortured or mistreated during interrogation. Almost all prisoners are subject to forced labor and face cruel, inhuman, and degrading treatment; many die in prison because of mistreatment, malnutrition, or lack of medical care. Under North Korea's penal code, premeditated murder and so-called anti-state crimes such as treason, sedition, and acts of terrorism are punishable by death. However, numerous testimonies by North Korean refugees attest to executions of people charged with lesser crimes as well, such as stealing food or other state property. Eyewitnesses say such executions are often carried out publicly, and in the presence of children.

North Korean Escapees

Tens of thousands of North Koreans are believed to live in hiding in China, having fled to avoid hunger and political repression. People who return from China often face abuse and detention under North Korean law, which makes leaving North Korea without state permission an act of treason punishable by heavy penalties. China routinely harasses aid workers providing assistance to North Koreans. A relatively small number of North Koreans have taken a long and dangerous journey to other countries of the region, including Cambodia, Laos, Mongolia, Thailand, and Vietnam, to ultimately reach South Korea, and recently, the United States. Hundreds of others remain in detention centers in these transit countries.

At this writing, the US government has granted refugee status to 10 North Koreans, the first group to benefit from the North Korea Human Rights Act of

2004. Separately, US immigration courts granted political asylum to four North Koreans who had previously settled in South Korea and obtained South Korean citizenship before applying for asylum in the United States, citing the same Act. Jay Lefkowitz, US special envoy for human rights in North Korea, has hinted in several press interviews that the US would admit more North Korean refugees. According to a Radio Free Asia report from February 2006, seven EU member states—Belgium, Denmark, Germany, Netherlands, Norway, Sweden, and the United Kingdom—have granted refugee status to almost 300 North Koreans since the late 1990s.

Humanitarian groups report that the trafficking of North Korean women and girls persists, especially in the area of the border with China. Many are abducted or duped into marriage, prostitution, or outright sexual slavery, while some voluntarily enter such situations to survive or to earn money.

Abductees

According to the Korea Institute for National Unification, based in South Korea, a total of 3,790 South Koreans were kidnapped and taken to North Korea between 1953 and 1995, of whom 485 remain in detention. Some of the abductees have been used in propaganda broadcasts to South Korea, while others have been used to train North Korean spies. Unlike its admissions regarding 13 Japanese abductees (five of whom were allowed to return home in 2002, the others being said to have died), North Korea has rejected repeated requests from families of the South Korean abductees to confirm their existence, to return them, or, in the cases of the dead, to return their remains.

Kaesong Industrial Complex

North Korea opened the Kaesong Industrial Complex (KIC) in June 2004. Two years later, over 8,000 North Korean workers are employed by 13 South Korean companies, producing watches, shoes, clothes, kitchenware, plastic containers, electrical cords, and car parts, among other items. The KIC's labor conditions came under public scrutiny as South Korea has tried to include items produced there in a Free Trade Agreement under negotiation with the United States. South Korean companies, under pressure from Pyongyang, are violating the existing KIC Labor

Law by paying workers' wages to the North Korean government instead of directly to the workers. The KIC Labor Law falls far short of international labor protection standards on the freedom of association, the right to collective bargaining, prohibitions on sex discrimination and harassment, and harmful child labor.

Key International Actors

North Korea's announcement on October 9, 2006, of its first nuclear weapons test provoked grave concern and protest internationally. The UN Security Council resolution adopted in response condemned the test, called for sanctions including a ban on exporting material for weapons of mass destruction and ballistic missiles to North Korea, and authorized inspection of cargo entering or leaving the country to prevent illegal trafficking in unconventional weapons or ballistic missiles. In early November, North Korea agreed to return to the long-stalled six-party talks on its nuclear weapons program (involving also China, Japan, Russia, South Korea, and the United States), which it had been boycotting since November 2005 in reaction to US financial sanctions against it for its alleged complicity in counterfeiting US dollars and money laundering. At this writing the talks have yet to resume.

North Korea's test firing of seven ballistic missiles on July 5, 2006, also led to a UN Security Council resolution, and South Korea bilaterally protested the missile launch in a high-level inter-Korea meeting. When North Korea refused to discuss the issue, Seoul suspended shipment of its promised food aid, and North Korea in turn stopped reunions of Korean families separated by the border for over half a century.

South Korea continues to recognize all North Koreans arriving in South Korea as southern citizens (about 9,000 North Koreans have resettled in South Korea mostly over the last decade), and provides them with generous resettlement subsidies. South Korea's then-Foreign Minister Ban Ki-moon (at the time a candidate for, and since confirmed as UN secretary-general), raised North Korean human rights issues during his keynote speech at the inaugural session of the UN Human Rights Council in June 2006, signaling a possible change of Seoul's policy of maintaining silence on North Korea's human rights conditions. Previously, South

Korea has been either absent or abstained from voting on UN resolutions condemning North Korea's human rights conditions.

The European Union played a more active role in calling for international attention to North Korea's human rights conditions. It sponsored the UN General Assembly resolution in 2005, and its Parliament passed a separate resolution in June 2006 asking North Korea to respect international human rights treaties.

North Korea has not responded to repeated requests in the past three years by Vitit Muntarbhorn, the UN special rapporteur on North Korea, to engage in dialogue.

Pakistan

In office since a 1999 coup d'etat, President Pervez Musharraf's military-backed government did little in 2006 to address a rapidly deteriorating human rights situation. Ongoing concerns include arbitrary detention, lack of due process, and the mistreatment, torture, and "disappearance" of terrorism suspects and political opponents; harassment and intimidation of the media; and legal discrimination against and mistreatment of women and religious minorities.

Significant developments with human rights implications in 2006 included the passage of the Women's Protection Bill amending the discriminatory Hudood Ordinances, a marked increase in hostilities between the government and armed militants in the mineral rich south-western province of Balochistan, a controversial peace deal between the government and Taliban supporters in Waziristan, and reconstruction efforts in post-earthquake Pakistan-administered Kashmir, which were marred by allegations of corruption.

Gender-Based Violence and Legal Discrimination

In a significant though partial step towards ending legal discrimination against women, Pakistan's National Assembly passed the Women's Protection Bill on November 15 with the support of the opposition Pakistan Peoples Party. The passage of the bill removed some of the most dangerous provisions of the Hudood Ordinances. Judges have now been given authority to try rape cases under criminal rather than Islamic law. One important consequence of the change is that a woman claiming rape need no longer produce four witnesses, a requirement which had made successful prosecution almost impossible and put the rape victim at risk of being charged with adultery. The amendments also include dropping the death penalty and flogging for persons convicted of having consensual non-marital sex.

However, the Women's Protection Bill fails to comply with many of Pakistan's obligations under the Convention on the Elimination of Discrimination against Women, which calls on states to modify or abolish laws that discriminate against women. Discriminatory provisions of the Hudood Ordinances that criminalize non-marital sex—which remains punishable by a five-year prison sentence and a fine—remain in place and the law fails to recognize marital rape.

As in previous years, violence against women and girls, including domestic violence, rape, "honor killings," acid attacks, and trafficking, remained serious problems in Pakistan. Survivors of violence encounter unresponsiveness and hostility at each level of the criminal justice system, from police who fail to register or investigate cases of gender-based violence to judges with little training or commitment to women's equal rights. According to Pakistan's Interior Ministry, there have been more than 4,100 honor killings since 2001. However, provisions of Pakistani law that allow the next of kin to "forgive" the murderer in exchange for monetary compensation remain in force, and continue to be used by offenders to escape punishment in cases of honor killings.

Religious Freedom

Discrimination and persecution on grounds of religion continued in 2006, and an increasing number of blasphemy cases were registered. As in previous years, the Ahmadi religious community was a particularly frequent target. Ahmadis have been legally declared non-Muslims under Pakistani law and they can be charged under the blasphemy law for simply calling themselves Muslims. Scores were arrested in 2006. In June, three Ahmadis were badly beaten by a mob, while 10 houses, a mosque, and shops and other property belonging to Ahmadis were set on fire in a village near the town of Daska in Punjab province.

Other religious minorities, including Christians and Hindus, also continue to face legal discrimination, though the government appears to have instructed the police to avoid registering blasphemy cases against them.

"War on Terror"

Counterterrorism operations in Pakistan continue to be accompanied by serious violations of human rights. Suspects held on terrorism charges frequently are detained without charge or tried without proper judicial process. Human Rights Watch has documented scores of illegal detentions, instances of torture, and "disappearances" in Pakistan's major cities. Counterterrorism laws also continue to be misused to perpetuate vendettas and as an instrument of political coercion.

Pakistani authorities have presented figures suggesting that more than 1,000 terrorism suspects have been arrested in the five years since 2001. The Pakistani government has processed only a fraction of the cases through the legal system. Hundreds of suspects have been handed over to the United States, often for sizeable bounties; many have ended up at Guantanamo. Among the "high-value" terrorism suspects whom Pakistan is believed to have handed over to the United States is Syrian-Spanish citizen Mustafa Setmariam Nasar, who was reportedly arrested in late October or early November 2005 in Quetta, Pakistan.

It is impossible to ascertain numbers of people "disappeared" in counterterrorism operations because of the secrecy surrounding such operations and the likelihood that the families of some of the "disappeared" do not publicize their cases for fear of retaliation. Notable "disappearance" cases in 2006 include Haji Yasin, an Afghan national who was abducted in Peshawar on June 22, and Imran Munir, who was summoned by Pakistan's Inter-Services Intelligence (ISI) in late July 2006 and failed to return. The families of some 41 other "disappeared" persons publicly alleged in 2006 that their loved ones were being illegally detained.

Until a September peace agreement between the government and tribal leaders and militants closely allied with the Taliban, the Pakistan Army engaged in aggressive counterterrorism operations in Pakistan's Federally Administered Tribal Areas along the Afghan border, with efforts particularly focused on the Waziristan region. Authorities restricted access to the region, but there were steady reports of extrajudicial executions, house demolitions, arbitrary detentions, and harassment of journalists.

Serious questions remain about the security of both Afghan people living across the border and residents of Waziristan after the signing of the peace deal. Armed groups in Pakistan's tribal areas have engaged in vigilantism and violent attacks, including murder and public beheadings, and the government has done little to apprehend, let alone prosecute Taliban and militant leaders guilty of committing serious human rights abuses across the border in Afghanistan and, increasingly, in Pakistan.

PAKISTAN

"With Friends Like These..."

Human Rights Violations in Azad Kashmir

HUMAN
RIGHTS
WATCH

On October 30, the government's aerial bombing in Bajaur Agency of the tribal areas killed 82 people, including several children. The Pakistan government claimed all the dead were militants and rejected requests for an independent investigation. On November 8, in a retaliatory attack, 42 soldiers at a military training camp were killed by a suicide bomber in the town of Dargai in the North West Frontier Province.

Repression of Political Opponents

The government continues to use the National Accountability Bureau and a host of anti-corruption and sedition laws to keep in jail or threaten political opponents, particularly members of former Prime Minister Benazir Bhutto's Pakistan Peoples Party and the Pakistan Muslim League (Nawaz). As elections approach in 2007, such persecution is expected to increase. Makhdoom Javed Hashmi, of the Alliance for the Restoration of Democracy, who received a 23-year sentence for sedition in April 2004, a charge brought against him for reading an anti-Musharraf letter to journalists, remained in jail at this writing.

Political unrest in the southwestern province of Balochistan took a serious turn for the worse in 2006. Though the dispute in Balochistan is essentially political, centered on issues of provincial autonomy and exploitation of mineral resources, the Pakistani military and Baloch tribal militants have increasingly sought a military solution to their disagreements.

The Balochistan Liberation Army, a guerilla outfit comprising tribal militants, has not limited its attacks to Pakistani military targets, but has also attacked economic infrastructure and civilians using rockets and landmines. Meanwhile, hundreds of Baloch political activists have been arbitrarily detained, scores have been disappeared, and torture by security forces of political opponents has become routine. Military operations in the province have frequently been accompanied by allegations of the excessive use of force, particularly in periodic attacks on Dera Bugti, the stronghold of tribal chieftain Nawab Akbar Bugti. The August 26, 2006, killing of Bugti in a controversial military operation plunged Balochistan into further unrest and was followed by a new round of arbitrary arrests and "disappearances."

Freedom of Expression

Though media freedoms have increased in recent years, particularly for the English-language press, free expression and dissemination of information were persistently undermined in 2006 by the murder, torture, kidnapping, illegal detention, and coercion of reporters working for local, regional, national, and international media.

In Waziristan, journalist Hayatullah Khan was found dead six months after he was abducted in December 2005. Powerful circumstantial evidence suggested the involvement of Pakistan's Inter-Services Intelligence agency. In the southern province of Sindh, journalist Mehruddin Mari went missing on June 27. Mari, a correspondent for the Sindhi-language newspaper *The Daily Kawish,* was taken by police, according to journalists who witnessed his detention. On June 22, Mukesh Rupeta and Sanjay Kumer were finally produced in court and charged after being held illegally by the Pakistani intelligence services for more than three months. The two were tortured while detained for filming a Pakistani air force base. Saeed Sarbazi, a newspaper reporter, was released on September 23 after being beaten and interrogated for three days by intelligence agents on suspicion of supporting Baloch militants. On September 17, two journalists from Pakistan's ATV and a correspondent of the Dubai-based satellite news channel ARY One World were badly beaten and injured by police in Lahore as they covered a religious gathering. The above list is far from exhaustive. In addition, many print and television journalists were verbally threatened by intelligence personnel, government officials, and non-state actors.

Tight controls on freedom of expression have also been a hallmark of government policy in Azad Kashmir. Pakistan has prevented the creation of independent media in the territory through bureaucratic restrictions and coercion. Publications and literature favoring independence are banned. While militant organizations promoting the incorporation of Indian-administered Jammu and Kashmir state into Pakistan have had free rein to propagate their views, groups promoting an independent Kashmir find their speech sharply, sometimes violently, curtailed.

Key International Actors

President Musharraf remains heavily dependent on the Bush administration for political support, while Pakistan remains equally dependent on the United States for economic and military aid. The United States has notably failed to press strongly for human rights improvements in the country, muting its criticism in recent years in exchange for Pakistan's support in the US-led "war on terror."

International donors have poured billions of dollars of urgently needed relief and reconstruction aid into Pakistan-administered Azad Kashmir since the October 2005 earthquake. Before the earthquake struck, Azad Kashmir was one of the most closed territories in the world. Corruption allegations in late 2006 against senior government officials highlighted serious ongoing weaknesses in governmental accountability in the region. Donors have not used their leverage to insist on improvements in human rights practices and the rule of law.

Pakistan's record of ratifying principal international human rights treaties remains poor. It has signed only five international conventions which notably do not include either the International Covenant on Civil and Political Rights or the International Covenant on Economic, Social and Cultural Rights. Pakistan played a negative role as a member of the new UN Human Rights Council and fought doggedly within the council to shield OIC states from criticism.

PAPUA NEW GUINEA

In 2006 hope persisted that the Papua New Guinean government's stability would contribute to reform of the government and the violent police force. But despite new resources for police and advances in the juvenile justice system, turmoil in police leadership, entrenched corruption, and weak independent accountability mechanisms remain.

Police Violence

Human Rights Watch investigations in 2006 revealed that police continue to routinely use violence, including sexual violence and torture, against individuals in custody. Children are frequent targets.

Police are rarely held accountable, either internally or in a court of law. As of August 2006 the public prosecutor's office had not received the cases of two officers charged in the October 2005 shootings of unarmed schoolboys in Enga province in which at least one boy was killed and 21 injured. Then-Minister of Police Bire Kimisopa sent an investigatory team that arrested the two officers, following armed resistance from local police.

Despite extensive evidence available to authorities, no police officers have been charged or prosecuted for beatings and gang raping women and girls arrested in a raid on the Three-Mile Guest House in March 2004.

Human and financial resource allocations for police increased in 2006. Several hundred new police officers were recruited. However, implementation of the government's 2004 review of police, which proposed sweeping changes in discipline and structure, was limited to housing and salary increases.

Juvenile Justice and Detention of Children

The government progressed in developing the juvenile justice system in 2006, although actual changes in police treatment of children remain elusive.

PAPUA NEW GUINEA

Still Making Their Own Rules

Ongoing Impunity for Police Beatings, Rape, and Torture
in Papua New Guinea

HUMAN
RIGHTS
WATCH

Reception centers for processing children began operating in the Port Moresby and Lae police stations, and police established a small unit to divert children from the formal justice system and monitor their treatment by police. Juvenile magistrates agreed to screen children for police violence and to visit places of juvenile detention but had not done so as of August 2006.

Police routinely detain children with adults in police lockups, where they are denied medical care and placed at risk of rape and other forms of violence. Although Human Rights Watch found instances of children being separated from adults in 2006, separation remains the exception, not the rule.

In prisons and other juvenile institutions, children awaiting trial are mixed with those already convicted. Many facilities lack blankets, beds, mosquito nets, clothes, or any education or rehabilitation programs—acute problems, given that children may face months or even years in detention awaiting trial. At least one national court judge inspected prisons and police lockups in 2006 and ordered repairs.

On January 15, 2006, corrections officers at Buimo prison in Lae beat and sexually abused boys by forcing them to have anal sex with each other in the institution's reception center. Although corrections officials told Human Rights Watch that officers were punished, they confirmed that the officers continued to work at the prison.

Violence and Discrimination against Women and Girls

Violence against women and girls—including domestic violence, gang rape, and torture and murder for alleged sorcery—are pervasive. Police often ignore complaints and ask victims for money or sex. Girls' and women's low status also is reflected in discrimination in education, health care, and employment; heavy household workloads; and polygyny. The parliament of Papua New Guinea has only one woman member.

HIV/AIDS

With as many as 140,000 people living with HIV/AIDS, Papua New Guinea has the highest prevalence in the South Pacific. Access to antiretroviral therapy is limited, and few have the tools to protect themselves from infection. Violence and discrimination against women and girls likely is fueling the growing epidemic. People living with HIV/AIDS often face violence and discrimination in their communities.

Ill-treatment by police heightens HIV risk. Police target street vendors as well as female sex workers, men, and boys suspected of homosexual conduct for beatings and rape. Police also extort money from such individuals, using the threat of arresting them for illegal activities. Police are also known to abuse people simply for carrying condoms, in the most egregious instances forcing men and women to eat condoms; such actions deter condom use and undermine protection efforts. However, nongovernmental organizations (NGOs) reported some improvements on the part of a few individual officers in 2006.

Human Rights Monitoring Mechanisms

The Ombudsman Commission, which primarily monitors government corruption, has a human rights unit, but the latter had only one staff member in 2006. The unit's active cases are against police or corrections officials. Following the commission's referral of several ministers and parliamentarians to the public prosecutor for investigation in early 2006, parliament established a committee to review the office's mandate, raising concerns that the commission's oversight power would be weakened.

Prohibitive costs and procedural difficulties make it all but impossible for many citizens to pursue civil claims against police officers suspected of abuse. Where victims are able to bring successful claims, the penalties imposed fail to deter police violence because the costs are born by the state, not the police force or individual officers.

Revived proposals to establish a National Human Rights Commission again stalled without reaching parliament in 2006.

Human Rights Defenders

NGOs and women's rights activists play an essential role in obtaining services for victims of violence, but some continue to be threatened for their work. Some HIV/AIDS educators again faced police harassment in 2006.

Environmental groups faced threats after they published new reports on the powerful logging and mining industries in 2006. The reports charged that companies paid police who arbitrarily beat, detained, and intimidated landowners.

Key International Actors

Australia continues to be the largest foreign donor. Following the collapse in 2005 of an agreement to deploy Australian Federal Police alongside Papua New Guinea's police, Australia's engagement with the Papua New Guinea police remained under negotiation at this writing.

UNICEF has taken the lead on juvenile justice, with AusAID funding several recent reforms.

Other donors include the Asian Development Bank, the European Union, Germany, Japan, New Zealand, and the World Bank.

In 2006 the UN special rapporteur on torture requested an invitation to visit Papua New Guinea. In late 2005, the special rapporteur on extrajudicial, summary, or arbitrary executions wrote to the government regarding the police shootings of schoolboys in Enga province. At this writing, the government had not responded to either communication.

This summary does not address human rights developments in Bougainville.

THE PHILIPPINES

2006 was not a good year for human rights in the Philippines. Extrajudicial killings and "disappearances" appear to be on the rise. Armed insurgents and militant Islamist groups continue to kill civilians, politicians, and members of the security forces around the country.

Political tensions persist. On February 24, 2006, President Arroyo declared a week-long state of emergency after claiming to have uncovered a coup plot by members of the military, the political opposition, and communist rebels. Public assembly was temporarily banned, and scores of soldiers and leftists were detained or threatened with arrest, including five members of congress.

In June 2006 President Arroyo gave the army a two-year deadline to eradicate the New People's Army (NPA), the armed wing of the Communist Party of the Philippines (CPP), which has been engaged in an armed rebellion against the government since the 1960s.

In August 2006, groups opposed to Arroyo brought impeachment charges against her for allegedly tampering with the results of the 2004 presidential elections. The impeachment effort failed in congress, where a majority of representatives continue to support the president.

In a positive development, President Arroyo and the Philippines congress approved legislation that abolished the death penalty in June 2006. A ceasefire with the Moro Islamic Liberation Front (MILF) remained in force throughout 2006.

Extrajudicial Killings and "Disappearances"

Human rights defenders, community activists, politically active journalists, outspoken clergy, and members of left-wing political parties were killed or "disappeared" throughout 2006. Although different political parties and civil society groups produce differing estimates of the number of victims, research conducted by Human Rights Watch confirms that scores of individuals were killed in 2006 and that military personnel played a role in many of the killings.

Suspected victims of politically motivated killings range from the young to the old. Two such examples are 20-year-old Cris Hugo, a student leader with the League of Filipino Students in the Bicol region of southern Luzon, who was gunned down on March 19, 2006; and Bishop Alberto Ramento of the Philippines Independent Church, who was stabbed to death on October 3, 2006, at age 69. Some attacks clearly target members of legal left-wing political parties, such as the grenade thrown at the office of the Anakpawis political party in Kidapawan City, Cotabato, on May 7, 2006, which severely injured Roderick Abalde, a coordinator for Anakpawis, and Jobanie Tacadao, a spokesperson for the left-wing Bayan Muna party. But many other victims appear to be low-level community activists—Pastor Isaias Sta. Rosa, shot behind his house on August 3, 2006, for instance—or to have left active political life many years ago—such as Danilo Escudero, who was gunned down in front of his six-year-old daughter on July 20, 2006. Escudero's main political activities appear to have been during the 1970s.

To date no individual has been convicted of any of the hundreds of political killings which local human rights groups and journalists report have been committed since 2001. Leftist groups accuse the security forces of carrying out the executions as part of their counter-insurgency campaign. The military has not acknowledged any role in the killings, let alone taken steps to investigate or prosecute any perpetrators in the ranks.

In August 2006 President Arroyo created a special police taskforce, Task Force Usig, which she charged with solving 10 cases within 10 weeks. During its 10-week mandate the Task Force claims that 21 cases were solved by filing cases in court against identified suspects, all of them members of the CPP and NPA. Twelve suspects involved in these incidents are said by the Task Force to be under police custody. Arroyo also established a special commission, under former Supreme Court Justice José Melo, to examine the killings. Opposition and human rights groups criticized the Melo Commission for having little power to carry out investigations and for being made up purely of government-picked commissioners.

The ongoing killings and the government's failure to bring even a single perpetrator to justice has contributed to deep public distrust in government and widespread fear in areas where killings have occurred, particularly among witnesses and victims' families. The latter groups often are afraid to cooperate with police for fear of reprisals.

Vigilante killings of individuals suspected of involvement in criminal activities also appear to continue in some provincial cities, with little or no condemnation or prosecution by local officials.

Abuses by Armed Groups

Filipino civilians continue to be purposefully targeted by militant groups such as Abu Sayyaf that the government denounces as terrorist organizations. Various bomb blasts on the southern islands of Mindanao and Jolo killed at least 21 people and injured at least 80, and caused serious economic damage to local communities. The Philippines government has arrested numerous suspects in these and earlier bombings, but has prosecuted almost none of them.

The NPA and CPP continue to enact "revolutionary justice" against civilians in areas under their control, including the killing of individuals they consider to be criminals, despotic landlords, or business owners.

Many in the MILF grew increasingly frustrated with the peace process in 2006, and some MILF hardliners reportedly have questioned the wisdom of continuing negotiations. The current MILF leadership, widely viewed as moderate, may be put increasingly under fire if it cannot deliver results in 2007. Some commanders in MILF have become increasingly independent and are now referred to as "lost commands" which are no longer under the authority of MILF leadership.

The Philippines military launched new operations on the island of Jolo in late July and early August 2006, after it was reported that several senior members of Jemaah Islamiyah had taken refuge with the Abu Sayyaf forces there. Observers believe that senior Jemaah Islamiyah operatives linked to the 2002 bombing in Bali, Indonesia and the August 2003 bombing in Jakarta may be in hiding in the southern Philippines.

Military Abuses

Civilians living in militarized zones or areas targeted for counter-insurgency operations are susceptible to harassment, physical assaults, arbitrary arrest, and even torture by the military. Individuals considered to have assisted or to sympathize with the NPA are at particular risk. Harassment by local security forces of human rights groups and activists affiliated with leftist causes, also continues to be of concern.

Migrant Workers

Remittances sent by Filipinos working overseas form a vital part of the nation's economy, contributing around 18 percent of the country's GNP. Many Filipinos, however, find work abroad through unlicensed agents or while on tourist visas, making them more vulnerable to abusive employers in many countries where they work. While not all such workers face problems, few receiving countries closely regulate domestic work and problems such as physical and sexual abuse, forced confinement, non-payment of wages, denial of food and health care, and excessive working hours with no rest days are all too common.

The Philippines, which has ratified the International Convention on the Protection of Migrant Workers, has done more than many sending countries to protect migrant workers, including through pre-departure awareness programs, services provided by diplomatic missions in receiving countries, and the oversight provided by the Philippines Overseas Employment Administration. The government could do more to improve existing services at embassies abroad, particularly by ensuring adequate staffing levels and access to trauma counseling. It could also improve programs to help integrate returning workers back to the Philippines, and do more to promote regional minimum standards through cooperation with other sending countries.

Key International Actors

The United States remains the closest ally of the Philippines, and military relations are strong. The two countries conduct regular combined military trainings funded by the US government.

A report on the political killings in the Philippines released by Amnesty International in August, 2006, helped focus international attention and pressure on the Philippines government. Numerous foreign civil society and human right groups also conducted research and advocacy missions to the Philippines to investigate the political killings, often focusing on specific classes of victims, such as judges, lawyers, or women.

During an international tour in September, 2006, including Finland, Belgium, and the United Kingdom, President Arroyo faced considerable pressure from European leaders and the European Commission to curtail the killings. Arroyo invited observers from Finland, Spain, and Belgium to investigate the killings.

The Philippines was elected as a member of the new United Nations Human Rights Council in May 2006.

SOUTH KOREA

The Republic of Korea (South Korea) has come under increased pressure to change its policy of passively keeping silent on North Korea's human rights record as its own former foreign minister, Ban Ki-moon, called for South Korea to take on a more proactive role in improving the latter's human rights condition. Ban will take office as the new United Nations secretary-general in January 2007.

Meanwhile, some of South Korea's important human rights concerns, including the National Security Law, imprisonment of conscientious objectors to military service, and the death penalty, remain unresolved, despite a series of recommendations by the National Human Rights Commission calling for relevant laws to be abolished or amended. Human rights activists have also complained about the widespread mistreatment of migrant workers, and about South Korea's reluctance to recognize non-Korean refugees and asylum seekers.

Security Legislation

South Korea continues to arrest people accused of pro-North Korea activities under the National Security Law. Human rights activists remain particularly concerned about the provision that bans "praising or supporting" North Korea, a vaguely worded phrase that has been often used by past governments to arrest dissidents for peacefully expressing their views. In September 2004 the National Human Rights Commission recommended abolition of the law to the National Assembly chairman and the minister of justice, citing human rights violations caused by the law itself, and its arbitrary application. In September 2006 Hwang Kwang-min, a 26-year-old man, was sentenced to a suspended two-year prison term for charges including producing and distributing pro-North Korea materials.

Conscientious Objectors

South Korea requires all healthy adult men to perform 26 months of military service. Those who refuse to serve in the military on moral or religious grounds face up to three-years' imprisonment. According to a local rights organization, World Without War, about 900 people, most of them Jehovah's Witnesses, remained in prison for refusing to serve in the military as of August 2006. A coalition of South Korean human rights organizations has been urging the government to adopt alternative state service for conscientious objectors, a call echoed in a National Human Rights Commission recommendation to the National Assembly chairman and the minister of defense in December 2005.

Death Penalty

South Korea declared an unofficial moratorium on executions in December 1997 when Kim Dae-Jung, a long-term democracy activist once sentenced to death himself, was elected president. Under the current government of President Roh Mu-hyun the moratorium remains in place. In April 2005 the National Human Rights Commission submitted a recommendation to the National Assembly chairman calling for the abolition of the death penalty, but there was no movement on this in 2006. It is believed that between 40 and 50 inmates are on death row.

Sex Workers

Prostitution is illegal in South Korea, though numerous brothels operate in major cities and around US military bases. Sex workers often suffer from grave abuses, including arbitrary detention and verbal or physical abuse by their employers. For migrant sex workers, language and cultural barriers exacerbate their vulnerable legal status. Most of them are staying in the country illegally, which makes it difficult to report abuse or seek redress. In September 2004 South Korea enacted a law that included a provision stipulating a prison term of up to 10 years for people who force their employees to sell sex, and nullifying all debts the employees incurred in the course of such employment. The new law also paved the way for trafficking victims to pursue cases against brothel owners. However, the law does not protect those that either want to stay in the sex industry or cannot prove that they were coerced, while critics argue that police crackdowns pursuant to the law have driven many sex workers further underground, putting them in an even more vulnerable situation.

Migrant Workers' Rights

In August 2003 South Korea passed the Act Concerning the Employment Permit for Migrant Workers, which allowed firms to legally employ undocumented workers who had stayed in the country for less than four years. Those who had stayed for more than four years, however, were asked to leave the country by a mid-November 2003 deadline, with a promise that they would be allowed to return after six months provided they first obtained legal work permits. Since then, many migrant workers have obtained legal status, while some voluntarily left and tens of thousands were deported.

According to an August 2006 report by Amnesty International, there are about 360,000 migrant workers in South Korea, and about two-thirds are believed to be undocumented. Migrant workers are not allowed to form trade unions, and suffer from serious human rights violations, including discrimination, physical and verbal abuse by their employers, and limited chances of redress when their rights are violated. Sexual harassment and violence against female migrant workers and physical abuse of those in detention facilities are alarmingly widespread, Amnesty International reported.

Refugees and Asylum Seekers

South Korea recognizes North Korean refugees as South Korean citizens, under the Constitution that defines the entire Korean Peninsula as the territory of the Republic of Korea. South Korea has admitted about 9,000 North Koreans, most of whom came after North Korea's famine in the 1990s drove them to cross the border into China to find food.

For non-Korean refugees and asylum seekers, however, South Korea has been anything but generous. Since South Korea signed the UN Refugee Convention in 1992, it has granted refugee status to only 48 out of some 950 applicants. Unlike North Koreans, financial assistance for those with refugee status is almost non-existent.

Key International Actors

The relationship with North Korea remains central to South Korea's international relations. Under its nine-year-old "sunshine" policy of engaging North Korea, South Korea has transformed itself from North Korea's Cold War foe to its major humanitarian aid donor, investor, and trade partner. In line with this policy, South Korea has previously been absent or abstained from voting on resolutions condemning North Korea's human rights record at the United Nations while generally keeping silent on the issue, leading to criticism by domestic and international human rights organizations.

The government came under intense public pressure to change course after North Korea test fired ballistic missiles in July 2006 and then conducted its first nuclear weapons test in October. South Korea suspended its food aid to North Korea in response to the July launch, but objected to tough sanctions that the United States proposed after the nuclear test. Incoming UN Secretary-General Ban Ki-moon has said his top priority will be resolving the North Korean nuclear issue, but he also called on the South Korean government to assume a more proactive role in improving human rights conditions in North Korea, only days ahead of another expected vote on North Korea's human rights record at the UN General Assembly. At this writing, the vote has not taken place yet.

SRI LANKA

In 2006 the Sri Lankan government and the armed opposition Liberation Tigers of Tamil Eelam (LTTE) both undertook major military operations for the first time since agreeing to a ceasefire in 2002. The fighting resulted in a dramatic increase in serious violations of international humanitarian and human rights law and massive displacements of the largely Tamil and Muslim populations in the embattled north and east of the country.

Government forces were implicated in several massacres of civilians, indiscriminate aerial bombing and shelling, and complicity in the abduction of children for use as combatants. The LTTE was responsible for direct attacks on civilians with landmines and suicide bombings, targeted killing of political opponents, and the continued recruitment of children into their forces. Both sides conducted military operations with little regard for the safety of civilians in the conflict zone and interfered with the delivery of relief assistance by humanitarian agencies.

In the latter half of the year, government security forces and associated armed groups, as well as the LTTE, were implicated in dozens of killings and "disappearances" of Tamils in the north and east, and in Colombo. Impunity prevailed as government investigations of serious abuses produced no successful prosecutions.

Violations of International Humanitarian Law

The resumption of major military operations between the Sri Lankan government and the LTTE in April 2006 placed civilians at greater risk than at any time since the signing of the 2002 ceasefire agreement. Violations of international humanitarian law, including indiscriminate attacks and summary executions, have resulted in numerous preventable civilian deaths and injuries. The Sri Lankan armed forces have engaged in indiscriminate shelling and aerial bombing with little regard to the expected harm caused to civilians. For example, in the fighting over Mutur town in early August, indiscriminate shelling by the military resulted in the deaths of at least 49 civilians, mostly Muslims, who had sought shelter in schools. As many as 51 young women and girls died in an August 14 bombing raid in Mullaitivu district deep in LTTE-controlled territory. While the Sri Lankan military

SRI LANKA

Improving Civilian
Protection in Sri Lanka

Recommendations for the Government and the LTTE

HUMAN
RIGHTS
WATCH

claimed the young women were LTTE military recruits, available evidence indicates that they were students receiving civil defense training, and thus civilians. The military's shelling of a displaced persons camp on November 8 left at least 35 civilians dead and 100 wounded.

The Karuna group, led by a former LTTE commander who broke away from the LTTE in 2004 and whose forces have been increasingly linked to the government forces, has forcibly abducted children for use in combat operations. Since June 2006 the Karuna group has abducted several hundred boys and young men in government-controlled areas of Batticaloa, Trincomalee and Ampara districts, in which local police and military have been complicit or even actively participated.

The LTTE has directly targeted civilians with Claymore mines—a remotely targetable landmine—and suicide bombings, summarily executed persons in its custody, and conducted so-called perfidious attacks (in which combatants feign being civilians) against Sri Lankan military personnel. The LTTE's landmine attack on June 15, 2006 on a bus in Anuradhapura killed 67 civilians, including many children. In August the LTTE diverted to territory under its control some thirty thousand displaced persons fleeing Mutur and detained a dozen young men, who remain missing and are feared dead.

The LTTE imposes mandatory military and civil defense training on a large scale on the civilians in areas it controls and arms civilians to fill checkpoints and sentry posts, dangerously blurring the line between combatants and civilians. Despite widespread international criticism, the LTTE continues to recruit children to be soldiers in its forces.

Extrajudicial Killings, Abductions, and Communal Violence

Politically motivated killings and abductions drastically increased in 2006. Sri Lankan security forces are believed responsible for a number of serious incidents in 2006, including the summary execution of five Tamil students in Trincomalee on January 2, the "disappearance" of eight young men from a Hindu temple in Jaffna on May 6, the execution-style slaying of five Tamil fishermen on Mannar island on June 17, and the killing of 11 Muslims in Pottuvil on September 18. The pro-LTTE Tamil National Alliance blamed the government for the murder of parliamentarian Nadarajah Raviraj in Colombo on November 10. Father Jim Brown, a Sri Lankan Catholic priest who had reportedly been receiving threats from the military, "disappeared" on Kayts Island near Jaffna in August after last being seen at a government checkpoint. Dozens of other abductions implicating the security forces, the Karuna group and other armed groups associated with the government were reported in the second half of the year.

Since the beginning of the 2002 ceasefire, the LTTE has been implicated in more than 200 targeted killings, mostly of Tamils viewed as political opponents. Alleged LTTE cadres shot and killed eight Sinhalese men in April, including three sixteen-year-old boys, while they worked in their paddy fields outside a village in Trincomalee. An LTTE car bombing on August 8 in Colombo injured a Tamil member of parliament and killed a bodyguard and a three-year-old child. On August 12, suspected LTTE gunmen shot and killed Kethesh Loganathan, the highly respected Tamil deputy head of the government's Peace Secretariat, at his home in Colombo.

The government and the LTTE generally failed to take steps to prevent or stop serious incidents of communal violence between Tamils, Muslims, and Sinhalese. On April 12 in Trincomalee, seemingly organized Sinhalese mobs responded immediately to an apparent LTTE bombing by razing dozens of Tamil businesses and homes and killing several people; military and police personnel stood and watched for two hours before putting an end to the violence. After the body of a murdered young Sinhalese man was found in a village outside Trincomalee on April 14, Sinhalese villagers went on a rampage in a neighboring Tamil village and set fire to over forty homes and a Hindu temple. More positively, the government promptly intervened to stop anti-Tamil violence in Galle in the south after an LTTE attack on the town.

Interference with Humanitarian Assistance

Humanitarian aid often did not reach those in need in 2006. Neither the government nor the LTTE took necessary measures to ensure that humanitarian relief got to the 240,000 people who were forced to flee their homes or the hundreds of thousands who otherwise required assistance because of the fighting. Aid workers were the targets of threats, harassment, and sometimes armed attack.

Government efforts to provide aid was slow and cumbersome, and the Ministry of Defense placed new and unnecessarily onerous visa requirements on foreign staff to work in the north and east, especially in LTTE-controlled areas. Ever since the end of major fighting on the Jaffna peninsula in August, the government and the LTTE have hindered the delivery of humanitarian assistance.

Local and international non-governmental organizations faced increasing hazards in their work. Harassment, threats, and violence became a common occurrence for aid workers in the north and east, threatening the delivery of aid. Unidentified attackers threw grenades at the compounds of several humanitarian organizations during the year. The execution-style killings on August 5 of 17 Sri Lankan aid workers from the international organization Action Contre la Faim (Action Against Hunger), allegedly by government security forces, and the failure of the government to vigorously conduct an investigation had a major chilling effect on humanitarian work.

Impunity

Impunity for perpetrators of human rights abuses remained the greatest obstacle to ending the daily political killings in Sri Lanka's north and east. The government has frequently initiated investigations into alleged rights violations by government security forces, but rarely have these investigations led to prosecutions, let alone convictions. A particular impediment has been the failure of the government to institute meaningful witness protection, which would encourage witnesses to politically motivated crimes to come forward. This was evident in the case of the killing of five students in Trincomalee in January 2006, in which the one witness willing to come forward and his family have been repeatedly subject to threats and harassment by government security forces. President Mahinda Rajapakse's effective immobilization of the Sri Lankan Human Rights Commission and the Police Commission because of an ostensible constitutional dispute weakened two important arms for accountability.

In September, President Rajapakse announced the creation of a presidential commission of inquiry that would, with international observers, investigate the fifteen most serious cases of the past year, most of which have been attributed to government security forces. As of this writing, it was not clear when the commission would become operational.

Key International Actors

International expressions of concern about the situation in Sri Lanka were greater in 2006 than at any time in recent memory, but these did not translate into international action on human rights.

In March the United Nations Special Rapporteur on Extra-Judicial Executions, Philip Alston, issued a report sharply critical of both the government and the LTTE for continuing and widespread killings. He noted: "The current impasse in negotiations is no excuse for either side not taking immediate steps to end political killings and protect human rights. The dangerous escalation of the conflict in recent days is a direct consequence of killings being allowed to run unchecked." In September the UN High Commissioner for Human Rights, Louise Arbour, along with Alston, urged the creation of an international human rights monitoring mission to Sri Lanka.

Canada and the European Union joined India, the United States, the United Kingdom and Australia by adding the LTTE to their lists of terrorist organizations. When the LTTE then demanded that EU members of the Sri Lanka Monitoring Mission—Finland, Denmark, and Sweden—remove their monitors, they promptly did so, although their removal violated the ceasefire agreement.

A September 7 resolution by the European Parliament condemned violations of human rights and humanitarian norms by all parties to the conflict and supported calls for an independent international human rights monitoring mission.

On several occasions in 2006, the Co-Chairs of the Tokyo Donor Conference—Norway, the EU, the US and Japan—publicly expressed concerns about human rights abuses by all sides in Sri Lanka. On September 12 the Co-Chairs announced that they were "deeply alarmed" by the escalation of the violence that had resulted in the "abuse of human rights, the displacement of innocent citizens, a humanitarian crisis and an exodus of refugees to India." The Co-Chairs called upon both parties to "stop further violations of fundamental principles of Humanitarian Law and Human Rights." They were "particularly concerned that even major cases of human rights' abuses [were] not successfully investigated or prosecuted. As in any modern state, the culture of impunity must stop."

In October efforts by EU members on the UN Human Rights Council to adopt a resolution on human rights in Sri Lanka were opposed by states of the Organization of the Islamic Conference and several Asian governments. The US opposed efforts by the EU to include in its draft resolution a reference to an international human rights monitoring mission.

THAILAND

Human rights protections in Thailand, which had been seriously eroded by the administration of former Prime Minister Thaksin Shinawatra, took another serious blow after a military coup on September 19, 2006, ousted Thaksin from power.

The coup leaders repealed the constitution and disbanded the national assembly, the Senate, and the Constitutional Court. They also imposed martial law throughout the country, allowing authorities to ban political gatherings, censor the media, and detain people for up to seven days without charge.

Impunity for human rights violations continued in 2006. Even where there is clear evidence of official involvement, as in the "disappearance" and apparent murder of lawyer Somchai Neelpaijit, no one has been brought to justice. Similarly, no one has been held accountable for any of the approximately 2,500 extrajudicial killings that took place as part of Thaksin's "war on drugs."

Violence and the culture of impunity also continue unabated in the southern border provinces with killings and serious abuses by security forces and separatist insurgents. Reconciliation attempts proposed by the government-appointed National Reconciliation Commission in early 2006 were largely ignored by the Thaksin administration, while security forces continued to be responsible for many "disappearances" and extrajudicial killings. Militants repeatedly set off bombs in civilian areas, often targeting teachers, civil servants, and Buddhist monks. Hundreds of civilians have died in such attacks since 2004.

The September 19 Coup

On September 19, 2006, the military overthrew the Thaksin government in a bloodless coup, pledging to end political tensions, reform government, and fight corruption. Within hours the constitution was repealed and key institutions that serve as a check on the executive—including the Parliament, the Senate, and Constitutional Court—were disbanded. The coup leaders announced on October 20 that they would uphold the principles enshrined in the United Nations Charter, but fundamental rights were nevertheless restricted.

Political gatherings of more than five people were banned, with a penalty of six months of imprisonment. Existing political parties were ordered not to conduct any political activities or hold assemblies. Four senior members of the Thaksin administration as well as a parliamentarian and a pro-Thaksin activist were taken into military custody for periods ranging from one to ten days.

The media was intimidated, with armed soldiers deployed in newsrooms and direct censorship employed. Shortly after the coup, Mingkwan Saengsuwan, director-general of the Mass Communications Organization of Thailand and TV Channel 9, was briefly detained and pressured to quit his position for allowing the airing of a last ditch state of emergency declaration by Thaksin. The coup leaders called on all journalists to "cover news truthfully and constructively in order to promote unity and reconciliation in the country" and requested that the Ministry of Information and Communication Technology control or block the distri-bution of information through the internet that could affect the new regime's work. More than 300 community radios stations in Thailand's northern provinces—Thaksin's stronghold—were closed down, and 10 anti-coup websites were been taken off the internet.

On October 8 Pongthep Thetpratheep, secretary-general to the interim prime min-ister, General Surayud Chulanont, told activist groups and journalists to stop voic-ing opposition to the new cabinet line-up, saying that it could be viewed as inter-fering with the King's decision. "Lese majeste" is a serious criminal offense in Thailand, punishable by up to 15 years in prison.

Violence in the Southern Border Provinces

Insurgent violence in the southern border provinces of Pattani, Yala, and Narathiwat continued in 2006 with no end in sight. According to a study released by the Thai Journalist Association and Prince of Songkhla University, there were 5,460 violent incidents—some at the hands of insurgent groups and others by security forces—resulting in 1,730 deaths and 2,513 injuries to civilians and gov-ernment officials between January 2004 and August 2006. Failures of justice—particularly for large-scale killings of civilians in 2004 at Krue Se and Tak Bai—have helped fuel the insurgency and made it more difficult for authorities to reach out to the Malayu-Muslim population.

Thousands of Muslim men are suspected by authorities of involvement with insurgent groups. Some have been pressured to join reeducation programs or put in custody for interrogation under emergency regulations, which allow suspects to be detained for an initial 30-day period. There is no limit to the number of times such detention can be extended, creating a risk of arbitrary and indefinite detention. Most such detainees have not had access to lawyers and families during the first 48 hours.

"Blacklists" containing the names of Muslim men suspected by Thai authorities of involvement in insurgent activity have created a climate of fear amidst allegations of extrajudicial killings and "disappearances" by the police and army. For example, on June 19, 2006, Sulkifi Maeroh went to the Bajoh District Police Station in Narathiwat after learning that it had issued an arrest warrant for him. Sulkifi and his four-year-old son were shot dead on their way home. Wae-halem Kuwae-kama, a 40-year-old former deputy village chief, went missing on the evening of May 29 in Joh Airong district, Narathiwat after his name was put on a blacklist. Wae-halem was last seen being stopped and questioned at a checkpoint manned by soldiers from the Army's Special Warfare unit. In cases like this the police typically explain that the deaths or "disappearances" are due to separatist insurgents trying to prevent the individuals in question from leaking information to authorities—an explanation strikingly similar to the one offered by the Thaksin administration in 2003 for more than 2,500 unexplained killings that accompanied its anti-drug campaign.

On an almost daily basis, separatist insurgents in 2006 attacked government officials and Buddhist civilians, as well as local Muslims suspected of collaborating with Thai authorities. Insurgent violence took the form of shootings, bomb attacks, arson, beheadings, and machete attacks. Thai authorities believe the National Revolution Front-Coordinate, particularly its youth wing and guerrilla units, is behind the new wave of violence.

The use of improvised explosive devices became one of the main insurgent tactics in 2006, with statistics showing clearly the intensity and lethality of these weapons, which were often used indiscriminately. Of the 5,460 violent incidents described above, 967 were bomb attacks. On June 15 and 16 separatist insurgents launched a series of bombs attacks in 31 of 33 districts in the southern border provinces. The coordinated explosions on August 31—targeting commercial banks in Yala—and on September 16—targeting department stores and related locations in Hat Yai district of Songkhla—were further evidence of a disturbing trend toward more frequent attacks on civilian targets.

Human Rights Defenders

The 2004 "disappearance" and presumed murder of Somchai Neelpaijit—chair of Thailand's Muslim Lawyers Association and vice-chair of the Human Rights Committee of the Law Society of Thailand—remained a test case for official commitment to the recognition and protection of human rights defenders. On January 13, 2006, then Prime Minister Thaksin publicly acknowledged for the first time that government officials were involved in Somchai's abduction and killing. Still, there has been no progress in the investigation led by the Department of Special Investigation.

At this writing, the interim government of General Surayud had said nothing about how and when it would pursue justice for the 20 cases of murder of human rights defenders that took place during the Thaksin administration.

Refugee Protection

Former Prime Minister Thaksin pursued a harsh policy towards Burmese refugees. General Surayud told diplomats in October 2006 that the welfare of Burmese refugees was a top priority. The interim government also indicated to the United Nations High Commissioner for Refugees (UNHCR) that the 140,000 refugees from Burma living in Thailand may soon be issued identity cards by Thai authorities that would permit them to move freely outside their camps to work legally. This potentially significant change in Thai policy would improve the lives of refugees, many of whom have lived in camps along the long Thai-Burma border for up to 20 years, with few prospects of returning home anytime soon.

Nevertheless, at this writing, it remained unclear whether Thailand's interim government would relax its border control policy to prepare for a new influx of refugees from Burma, particularly those from the estimated 500,000 internally displaced civilians along the frontier who have escaped from the Burmese government's brutal counter-insurgency operations in Karen and Shan states.

HIV/AIDS

Government HIV prevention programs have been credited with preventing more than 200,000 HIV infections, and its antiretroviral therapy program has been hailed as a model for developing countries. More than 80,000 people (an increase from approximately 3,000 in 2002) receive antiretroviral therapy through the public health system.

Despite these advances, many people at highest risk of HIV/AIDS—including drug users, prisoners, and migrants—face significant barriers in obtaining HIV prevention, care, and treatment services.

Key International Actors

Until former Prime Minister Thaksin was ousted from power, his government remained defiant to international concerns over the erosion of human rights standards in Thailand. Thaksin's poor human rights record, however, did not make the September 19 coup a welcome development internationally.

The US State Department said it was uneasy about the military takeover and said in a statement it hopes "the Thai people will resolve their political differences in accord with democratic principles and the rule of law." Military aid and negotiations on a free trade agreement were also suspended. UN Secretary-General Kofi Annan said the coup was "not a practice to be encouraged," while UN High Commissioner for Human Rights Louise Arbour called on coup leaders to restore basic freedoms. The European Union, Australia, and New Zealand used stronger language, condemning the coup.

China was the only major power which brushed off the coup as an internal affair. Elsewhere in the region, members of the Association of Southeast Asian Nations (ASEAN) expressed concerns following the coup, saying they hoped democratic principles would soon be restored.

TIMOR-LESTE

2006 was a tumultuous year for Timor-Leste (formerly East Timor) with violence in the capital Dili leading to the intervention of an Australian led peacekeeping force and the resignation of Prime Minister Mari Alkatiri in June.

After almost five years in operation, Timor-Leste's Commission for Reception, Truth, and Reconciliation submitted its final report to parliament in November 2005. Timor-Leste's President Gusmao distanced himself from the comprehensive findings and detailed recommendations, which said that at least 102,800 Timorese people had died as a result of the Indonesian occupation and accused Indonesian authorities of crimes against humanity and war crimes. The report was largely ignored by the Timorese government and the international community.

Dili Violence

Up to 38 people were killed in fighting in Timor-Leste's capital Dili after clashes between the military and police, and between gangs of youths taking advantage of the security vacuum, erupted in April. The trigger for the violence was the government's sacking of almost 600 disaffected soldiers. The sacked soldiers (known as "petitioners") staged a five-day demonstration in the capital, which deteriorated into rioting, torching cars, and looting government buildings. Some members of the police force defected to join the petitioners and openly fought the military.

At the request of the Timorese government a joint task force, made up of forces from Australia, New Zealand, Portugal, and Malaysia, arrived in May in an effort to quell the violence. Their efforts, and those of the UN peacekeepers who succeeded them, were moderately successful but outbreaks of violence and arson continued throughout the year. The violence caused at least 150,000 people to flee their homes in and around Dili.

Timor-Leste's Prime Minister Mari Alkatiri resigned his post in June in response to mounting public criticism and to a request from President Xanana Gusmao. Former Senior Minister for Foreign Affairs and Defense Jose Ramos Horta replaced Alkatiri. At this writing Alkatiri had not answered a summons to appear before

prosecutors investigating his alleged involvement in setting up and arming a private militia. However, former Interior Minister Rogerio Lobato was formally charged in September 2006 for distributing arms to militia leader Vicente da Conceição, also known as "Rai Los," who was widely believed to be responsible for instigating much of the year's violence.

In June United Nations Secretary-General Kofi Annan appointed an Independent Special Commission of Inquiry for Timor-Leste, tasked with establishing the facts and circumstances of the April and May violence. One of the incidents under investigation was the May 25, 2006, massacre of eight unarmed police officers who were shot dead as they were being surrendered to Timor-Leste soldiers by UN personnel in Dili. Its report, released in October, identified numerous persons reasonably suspected of direct participation in criminal activity during the crisis, including the interior and defense ministers and defense force chief, and recommended they be prosecuted. The commission also concluded that the fragility of various state institutions and the weakness of the rule of law were the underlining factors that contributed to the crisis.

Justice and Reconciliation

Following the closure in May 2005 of the UN tribunal in Dili—comprising an investigator's office (the Serious Crimes Unit or SCU) and courts (the Special Panels for Serious Crimes)—there remained a significant gap in efforts to provide accountability and justice for victims of the Indonesian invasion, occupation, and withdrawal (1975-1999).

The Timorese judiciary undertook some trials for militiamen indicted by the UN tribunal but not tried by the Special Panels. The Office of the Prosecutor General also received at least fifteen inquiries from third countries concerning individuals whose names appeared on Interpol lists after they were indicted by the SCU.

Timor-Leste's Commission for Reception, Truth, and Reconciliation (Comissao de Acolhimento, Verdade e Reconciliao de Timor-Leste, CAVR) submitted its final report to parliament in November 2005, and a copy was handed to the UN Secretary General by President Gusmao in January 2006. The report, which is more than 2,000 pages long, drew on the commission's work of taking over

8,000 individual statements and listening to hundreds of victims' testimonies through public hearings. The comprehensive report concluded that "the demand for justice and accountability remains a fundamental issue in the lives of many East Timorese and a potential obstacle to building a democratic society based upon respect for the rule of law and authentic reconciliation between individuals, families, communities and nations." The CAVR investigation also found that the crimes committed in 1999, while egregious, "were far outweighed by those committed during the previous 24 years of occupation." The report contained over 200 recommendations for the Timorese government, the UN, and the international community. A post-CAVR secretariat was established to disseminate the report and perform outstanding administrative tasks.

In July 2006 the UN secretary-general issued a report on justice and reconciliation for Timor-Leste in which he recommended the resumption of the investigative functions of the SCU but not the judicial functions of the Special Panels. The report did however note that crimes against humanity, gross violations of human rights, and grave breaches of humanitarian law were committed in East Timor in 1999, and there should be no impunity regarding such acts.

Police

Prior to the riots of April 2006 police abuse was already one of Timor-Leste's most worrying human rights problems. Police officers regularly use excessive force during arrests, and beat detainees once they are in custody. Under Timor-Leste law, no charges need be filed against suspects during the initial 72 hours following arrest, and police officers reportedly often use this period as a punitive rather than procedural measure. Many detainees, moreover, are held without charges for more than 72 hours.

Police and other state institutions often fail to respond to incidents of police abuse appropriately. Most notably, cases of police officers alleged to have committed crimes such as assault rarely move from investigation to prosecution in either the criminal justice system or the internal disciplinary system. Insufficient police training on internal investigations and follow up, and the absence of a functioning external, independent oversight and accountability mechanism for the police service, mean that complaints are often dealt with inconsistently, or in some cases not at all. Where cases are taken up, victims are usually left uninformed about developments and outcomes.

Previous training by the UN and other bilateral programs has been weak, often inconsistent, and sometimes contradictory.

Freedom of Press

In May 2006 two of the country's daily newspapers, *Timor Pos* and *Suara Timor Lorosae*, stopped publishing for several days due to violence and instability in the capital. Journalists at the *Timor Pos* office were threatened by an army officer, and in June two *Timor Pos* employees were attacked by youths outside its premises in Dili.

In December 2005, Timor-Leste's former Prime Minister, Mari Alkatiri, signed an executive decree approving a new penal code for Timor-Leste. The new code contains several articles restricting press freedom, including one criminalizing defamation. Journalists now face up to three years in prison if they are found to have defamed anyone in a public authority role, with no limits on fines for this offense.

Human Rights Defenders

Timor-Leste's nongovernmental human rights defenders operated freely and played an active role in lobbying the UN and government. There were no attacks on human rights defenders in 2006.

Timor-Leste's Office of the Provedor started receiving complaints from the public in March 2006. The office has far-reaching powers to investigate and report on complaints against government officials and institutions, including human rights abuses by police, but suffers from a lack of human and other resources. As with other institutions in Dili, many of the office's staff were affected by the year's violence and unable to work, due to fear of remaining in the capital.

Key International Actors

Due to concern over the apparent fragile security, political, and humanitarian situation in Timor-Leste, the UN Security Council established a new, expanded mission there in August 2006. The United Nations Integrated Mission in Timor-Leste (UNMIT) replaced the smaller United Nations Office in Timor-Leste (UNOTIL) that had been established in May 2005. The new mission has a much bigger UN Police component and will focus on consolidating gains in institution building, and will have a key role in preparing for national parliamentary and presidential elections scheduled for 2007.

Timor-Leste remains wholly dependent on international aid and assistance. The World Bank is supporting a multi-donor strategy to implement a National Development Plan in coordination with the government. However, Timor-Leste remains in desperate need of long-term international financial assistance. It receives its largest financial contributions from Japan, Portugal, the United Kingdom, the European Union, the United States, and Australia.

VIETNAM

Vietnam's tenth Communist Party (VCP) Congress saw a significant turnover in the Politburo, as younger members replaced key aging party veterans. New faces, however, did not bring significant improvement in human rights practices.

Despite having one of Asia's highest growth rates, Vietnam's respect for fundamental human rights continues to lag behind many other countries, and the one-party state remains intolerant of criticism.

Hundreds of political and religious prisoners remain behind bars in harsh conditions. During 2006 the government released a handful of prisoners of conscience but arrested dozens more, including democracy activists, cyber-dissidents, and ethnic minority Christians.

Authorities continue to persecute members of independent churches, impose controls over the internet and the press, restrict public gatherings, and imprison people for their religious and political views. Media, political parties, religious organizations, and labor unions are not allowed to exist without official oversight, or to take actions considered contrary to Party policies.

The year saw unprecedented labor unrest, official efforts to muzzle an emerging democracy movement, and ongoing repression of Buddhists and ethnic minority Christians.

Labor

The year began with a series of wildcat strikes by thousands of workers at foreign-owned factories and those with heavy foreign investment around Ho Chi Minh City. They demanded wage increases and better working conditions. The strikes quickly spread to the central and northern provinces, but died down when the government increased the minimum wage at foreign-owned companies to US $54 a month—a 40 percent increase, and the first since 1999.

VIETNAM

Children of the Dust

Abuse of Hanoi Street Children in Detention

HUMAN
RIGHTS
WATCH

Democracy Movement

In April 2006 more than 100 people publicly signed an "Appeal for Freedom of Political Association" and a "Manifesto for Freedom and Democracy." The initiators of the movement (called the 8406 Bloc, after the date of the Manifesto) included Father Nguyen Van Ly, dissident Hoang Minh Chinh, and writer Do Nam Hai. By August, more than 2,000 people had signed the public appeals.

In October, activists announced the creation of an independent labor union as an alternative to the party-controlled labor confederation. Dissidents also launched several unsanctioned independent publications during 2006, including *Tu Do Ngon* Luan ("Freedom of Expression") and *Tu Do Dan Chu* ("Freedom and Democracy").

The government responded by detaining and interrogating many of the more prominent activists and confiscating their documents, computers, and cell phones (see below).

Free Expression and the Internet

Vietnam's Law on Publications strictly bans publications that oppose the government, divulge state secrets, or disseminate "reactionary" ideas. There are few privately-owned media outlets; most publications are published by the government, the Party, or Party-controlled organizations. In 2006 the state media, which have usually been allowed to write about corruption, covered the embezzlement of government and donor funds by transportation ministry officials.

The government blocks websites considered objectionable or politically sensitive, monitors email and online forums, and makes internet cafe owners responsible for information accessed and transferred on the internet by their customers.

A new law, Decree No. 56, "Administrative Sanctions on Information and Culture Activities," calls for steep fines for activities such as circulating "harmful" information, defaming the nation and national heroes, or revealing "party secrets, state secrets, military secrets and economic secrets."

Repression of Dissent

Activists who launch unsanctioned publications or use the internet to dissemi-nate opinions critical of the government are harassed, detained, and imprisoned. At this writing, at least two cyber-dissidents remained in prison.

Nguyen Vu Binh is serving a seven-year sentence for espionage for his internet postings, testimony submitted in writing to the US Congress on human rights, and communication with activists inside Vietnam and abroad.

Truong Quoc Huy, detained in 2005 for more than eight months after participating in internet discussions about democracy, was re-arrested in an internet cafe on August 18, 2006. He had reportedly expressed public support for the democracy movement.

In mid-April two journalists were detained at Ho Chi Minh City airport and pre-vented from attending a conference in Manila on free expression in Asian cyber-space.

On April 20 police arrested two Montagnard students and held them for 18 days in a district prison in Dak Lak, where they were beaten, interrogated, and accused of using the internet to send lists of political prisoners to advocacy groups abroad.

On June 30 police raided the home of dissident Nguyen Thanh Giang and confis-cated books and documents. On August 12 police raided the homes of five dissi-dents, including Nguyen Khac Toan, Nguyen Van Dai, and Hoang Tien, as they pre-pared to launch an independent publication. In October Do Nam Hai and two other dissidents were called for "working sessions" with the police.

US citizen Cong Thanh Do (Tran Nam), a representative of the People's Democracy Party, was arrested on August 14. Upon Do's expulsion from Vietnam on September 21, the state press said he had been arrested for disseminating anti-government information. At this writing, six Vietnamese arrested in August because of alleged links to the People's Democracy Party remained in detention. In November, four Vietnamese and three Vietnamese-Americans arrested in 2005 were sentenced to fifteen months' imprisonment, or time served, on terrorism charges, for allegedly smuggling radio equipment in to Vietnam.

Suspected democracy movement supporters Truong Quoc Huy and three others arrested in August — Nguyen Ngoc Quang, Vu Hoang Hai, and Pham Ba Hai — were charged with conducting anti-government propaganda.

Assembly

Public demonstrations are rare, especially after government crackdowns against mass protests in the Central Highlands in 2001 and 2004. Decree 38, signed by the prime minister in 2005, banned public gatherings in front of places where government, Party, and international conferences are held, and requires organizers to obtain government permission in advance.

In advance of the Party Congress in April 2006 and President Bush's visit in November, police in Hanoi rounded up street children and homeless people and sent them to compulsory "rehabilitation" centers on the outskirts of the city where some were badly beaten. Soldiers were dispatched to villages in the Central Highlands to prevent possible demonstrations during Bush's visit.

Religion

Vietnam's 2004 Ordinance on Beliefs and Religions affirms the right to freedom of religion. However, it requires that all religious groups register with the government in order to be legal, and bans any religious activity deemed to cause public disorder, harm national security, or "sow divisions."

Followers of some religions not officially recognized by the government continue to be persecuted. Security officials disperse their religious gatherings, confiscate religious literature, and summon religious leaders to police stations for interrogation.

Buddhist monks from the banned Unified Buddhist Church of Vietnam (UBCV), including its Supreme Patriarch, Thich Huyen Quang, and second-ranking leader, Thich Quang Do, remain confined to their monasteries.

Despite regulations to streamline the registration process, hundreds of Christian house church organizations that tried to register in 2006 were either rejected outright, ignored, or had their applications returned unopened. These included 500 ethnic minority churches in the Northwest Highlands. In the Central Highlands, some Montagnard churches linked to the government-approved Evangelical Church of Vietnam (ECVN) were reportedly able to register. However Montagnards belonging to unregistered Christian churches came under heavy pressure to join the ECVN or recant their beliefs, despite a 2005 decree banning such practices.

In May, fifty police officers raided the home and church of Mennonite pastor Rev. Nguyen Hong Quang and demolished repair work he had done to the Mennonite church building. Quang, a former political prisoner, was one of the signatories of the Bloc 8406 manifesto.

Even registered groups face problems. More than fifty monks and nuns from the officially-recognized Vietnam Buddhist Church (VBC) demonstrated in July 2006 to protest the unfair imprisonment and torture of eight Buddhists and the beating to death in custody of a monk. The case, which was heard on appeal at Bac Giang Provincial People's Court in June 2006, resulted in their temporary release.

Prisons and Torture

Hundreds of religious and political prisoners remain in prisons throughout Vietnam. They include more than 350 Montagnards who have been sentenced to prison terms since 2001, largely for peaceful political or religious activities, or trying to seek asylum in Cambodia.

There is compelling evidence of torture and other mistreatment of detainees. Prisoners are reportedly placed in solitary confinement in cramped, dark, unsanitary cells; and beaten, kicked, and shocked with electric batons.

Police officers routinely arrest and detain suspects without written warrants. Trials of dissidents are closed to the public, media, and detainees' families. Under Administrative Detention Decree 31/CP, individuals can be put under house arrest for alleged national security crimes for up to two years without going before a judge.

Key International Actors

Vietnam's donors, including the World Bank, Asian Development Bank, and Japan raised strong concerns when news broke in January about major embezzlement of donor funds by the transportation ministry, which resulted in the resignation and arrest of several ministry officials.

While noting political prisoner releases, the EU, Vietnam's largest donor, placed Vietnam on its list of countries of concern in its human rights report for 2006. In May, a European Parliament delegation to Vietnam called for the release of prisoners of conscience, free access for the international press to the Central Highlands, and an end to the death penalty. In September, the United Kingdom praised Vietnam's progress on poverty reduction but said it would link ongoing aid to progress on human rights, anti-corruption, good governance, and financial reform.

Relations with the United States reached an unprecedented high in 2006, with the resumption of its human rights dialogue, which had been suspended since 2002, and the visit of President George Bush in November. The US removed its designation of Vietnam as a Country of Particular Concern (CPC) for religious freedom violations, and it was expected that by the end of the year the US would grant Vietnam "Permanent Normalized Trade Relations."

BOSNIA AND HERZEGOVINA

Looking for Justice

The War Crimes Chamber in Bosnia and Herzegovina

HUMAN

RIGHTS

WATCH

WORLD REPORT
2007

EUROPE
AND CENTRAL ASIA

ARMENIA

The Armenian government has done little to address serious human rights violations. Threats to media freedom in Armenia continued in 2006, as more journalists faced harassment and attacks, and broadcast media lack pluralism and remain largely pro-government. Torture and ill-treatment remain serious problems in places of detention and the military. Human rights defenders did not report harassment in 2006, but the ombudsperson was dismissed in January apparently for criticizing the government, a move that raises questions about the government's commitment to the independence of that institution.

In November 2005 a national referendum vote approved constitutional amendments that aimed to introduce stronger checks and balances among government branches. Council of Europe legal experts approved the draft amendments, but Armenia's political opposition contested the legitimacy of the Armenian authorities and called for boycotting the referendum. Council of Europe observers expressed concern about the integrity of the vote.

Media Freedom

The president appoints all members of bodies that regulate and manage broadcast media, including the Public Television and Radio Company (PTRC). The PTRC is responsible for policies and programming on the public service television station H1. Media experts state that because of government control H1 does not have sufficient independence to provide objective and diverse news coverage.

The independent television station A1+, which lost its broadcasting license in 2002, has since lost 12 tenders for television and radio frequencies, including a March 2006 bid for an FM radio frequency. On June 19,2006, A1+, which produced a weekly newspaper *Ayb-Feh* and maintains a website, had to vacate the premises it had leased from the National Academy of Sciences for more than 10 years, after losing a court case in 2005 against notice of eviction. The government provided an alternative location that at the time of the move lacked electricity and telephone connections, forcing A1+ to suspend all work for several weeks.

Among incidents of harassment against journalists, on February 23 in the town of Vanadzor, a local minibus company owner threatened Narine Avetisian, executive director of the Lori television station, over her reports criticizing increases in minibus tariffs; he later apologized for the incident. On May 16 unknown people broke the windows of Avetisian's parked car following a program about violations during the eviction of residents from a Vanadzor neighborhood; a criminal investigation on the case was closed when the authorities determined they could not identify the perpetrators. On July 12 freelance journalist Gagik Shamshian reported being harassed by relatives and associates of Mher Hovhannisian, head of Yerevan's Nubarashen district administration, because of an article he published in the July 11 edition of the newspaper *Chorrord Ishkhanutiun* about a bank robbery for which two of Hovhannisian's relatives face charges. The attackers threatened and beat the journalist and took his tape recorder, mobile telephone, and wallet. The next day the electricity and telephone at Shamshian's apartment were cut off. Shamshian pressed criminal charges against his attackers. On August 3, in response to several appeals from local residents, the police instituted criminal proceedings against Shamshian allegedly for insult, cheating, and extortion. On September 6 unknown assailants attacked Hovhannes Galajian, editor-in-chief of the *Iravunk* newspaper, which has ties to a small opposition party. Galajian believes that the attack was in retaliation for his articles criticizing the government.

On September 8 a court sentenced Arman Babajanian, editor of the opposition newspaper *Zhamanak Yerevan*, to four years in prison for failing to serve the compulsory two years of military service. Although Babajanian admitted to forging documents in 2002 in order to evade military service, the harsh sentence is suspected to be retribution for the journalist's persistent criticism of government policies (draft evaders are usually sentenced to between two and three years in prison).

Torture and Ill-Treatment

On May 31, 2006, Armenia ratified the Optional Protocol to the Convention against Torture and other Cruel, Inhuman or Degrading Treatment or Punishment (OPCAT). In April the government established a group to monitor certain detention facilities (temporary holding cells and pre-trial detention cells), although its independence is questionable as the majority of members are police appointees. NGOs report that torture and ill-treatment in police custody, prisons, psychiatric institutions, and the military remain widespread.

On May 30 the Court of Appeal sentenced three army soldiers to life imprisonment on charges that they killed two fellow conscripts in December 2003. One of those charged, Razmik Sargsian, testified that military investigators beat him and threatened him with rape, thereby coercing him into signing a confession in which he named Musa Serobian and Arayik Zalian as accomplices. Serobian and Zalian also claim to have been abused by investigators, but neither confessed to the murders. In September the men appealed to the Court of Cassation.

In February 2006 a young army conscript reported that he had been repeatedly raped and beaten by superiors and other conscripts for nine months at a Yerevan military post. After making these accusations public, the victim stated that he was again beaten by his superiors in retaliation.

Four inmates of Nubarashen prison went on hunger strike to protest alleged assault by prison guards and their detention in inhuman conditions following an escape attempt. Human rights groups state that most prisons are overcrowded and prisoners are often denied basic rights.

Freedom of Religion

Despite military service reforms adopted in 2004 mandating that conscientious objectors be provided with alternative service opportunities, the civilian service is run by the army and imposes military regulations on participants. According to the Helsinki Citizens' Assembly Vanadzor office, many conscientious objectors prefer to go straight to jail rather than perform alternative service. As of November 2006, 43 Jehovah's Witnesses are serving prison terms for evading service, and five are awaiting trial.

Property Rights

Over the past two years, the government forced hundreds of central Yerevan residents to vacate their homes to allow for construction of a business district. Many felt that government compensation was well below the market value of their prop-erties. In April the Constitutional Court ruled that the government's assertion of eminent domain was unconstitutional. On August 11, 2006, President Robert Kocharian announced that the government will refund the income tax deducted from the compensation paid to those evicted, but also suggested that no addi-tional compensation would be paid, despite the Constitutional Court decision.

On February 15 authorities released Vahe Grigorian, a lawyer for many of the evictees, who had been held in pre-trial detention for over four months on charges of fraud and forgery. Grigorian denies the accusations and believes the charges were in retaliation for his advocacy in the eviction case. The charges against him have not been dropped.

Human Rights Defenders

Armenia's first ombudsperson, Larisa Alaverdian, was relieved of her duties by President Kocharian in January 2006. Alaverdian's relationship with Kocharian became strained after her office published reports critical of the government's human rights record. The government refused to allow Alaverdian to present her 2005 report to parliament, although the law requires that the ombudsperson do so. The new ombudsperson, Armen Harutiunian, previously a legal adviser to Kocharian, read Alaverdian's report in parliament on April 13.

Key International Actors

In a December 2005 report, an ad hoc committee formed by the Monitoring Committee of the Parliamentary Assembly of the Council of Europe to observe Armenia's November 27, 2005 referendum on constitutional reforms found that the authorities had engaged in fraud during the referendum and called into ques-tion Armenia's commitment to Council of Europe principles. In January 2006 the Monitoring Committee issued a declaration reiterating the ad hoc committee's findings and noting that implementation of the new provisions would indicate the government's commitment to respecting European standards.

On July 26, 2006, the Organization for Security and Co-operation in Europe (OSCE) representative on freedom of the media released a report on Armenia noting the limited pluralism in broadcasting and recommending amendment of the Law on Television and Radio to clarify licensing competition procedures. The report also recommended that defamation be decriminalized completely, that the criminal offense of "insulting a representative of the authorities" be repealed, and that guidelines be introduced to limit the amount of damages in civil defamation cases. On September 12 the OSCE's Yerevan office expressed concern over recent incidents of violence and intimidation against local journalists.

In August the European Union and Armenia successfully completed negotiations on the European Neighborhood Policy Action Plan, which will serve as the main instrument for bilateral relations for the next five years. The plan sets out clear steps that the Armenian government should achieve in numerous fields including rule of law, democracy, economic and business development, trade, energy, and resolution of internal conflicts.

The United States is the largest bilateral donor to Armenia. In March the US awarded Armenia US$235 million under the Millennium Challenge Account. The funds will finance the development of rural infrastructure and irrigation projects and will be disbursed in several installments, with each tranche conditional on the government's performance in key areas of economic reform and democratization. In September a US delegation visited Armenia to discuss increased military cooperation.

In its country strategy for Armenia approved in February 2006, the European Bank for Reconstruction and Development maintained its engagement with Armenia, but noted that the political will to implement commitments to democracy, pluralism, and market economics remains uncertain.

AZERBAIJAN

Dozens of government officials, opposition politicians, and others arrested in November 2005 on charges of attempting to organize a coup remain in custody awaiting trial, and a few were sentenced. Torture in police custody, conditions of detention, and politically motivated arrests remain unresolved problems. Media freedom deteriorated, with violence against and arrests of journalists, as well as numerous defamation cases orchestrated by government officials. Many international actors publicly criticized the Azerbaijani government for its poor human rights record.

Politically-Motivated Arrests

In advance of the November 2005 parliamentary elections, authorities arrested dozens of high-profile government officials, businessmen, and opposition politicians on allegations of attempting to overthrow the government. Almost all remain in pre-trial custody more than a year after their arrests. Many complain of severe health problems caused or exacerbated by their conditions of detention. Deputy Chairman of the opposition Azerbaijan Democratic Party Natiq Efendiev was sentenced in September 2006 to five years' imprisonment for illegal possession of firearms, after charges of plotting a coup were dropped. Former Economic Development Minister Farhad Aliev appealed to the European Court of Human Rights concerning his arrest, prolonged detention, and other alleged violations.

Among others arrested were three members of the youth group New Thinking, including its head, Ruslan Bashirli, and his two deputies, Ramin Tagiev and Said Nuri, on charges of accepting funds from the Armenian secret services to carry out a coup. Their trial began on March 31, 2006, and for several weeks was closed allegedly due to concerns about national security and the safety of witnesses. The trial was later made public, but there is evidence that it did not meet fair trial standards. At trial Bashirli stated that he had been beaten and offered money in an attempt to persuade him to confess. On July 12 all three were convicted of attempting violent overthrow of the government. Bashirli and Tagiev received prison sentences of seven and four years respectively, and Nuri received a five-year conditional sentence owing to his severe health problems. On September 28 the Court of Appeal reduced Tagiev's prison term by one year.

On December 20, 2005, police in Bilasuvar district arrested opposition activist and election commission member Gadir Musaev on drug charges. During the 2005 election Musaev refused to sign election result protocols that he said were falsified. He received a seven-year prison sentence.

Torture and Inhuman Treatment

Torture remains a widespread and largely unacknowledged problem in Azerbaijan.

In May 2006 the trial began of three boys from a village near Baku who were subjected to severe beatings and other forms of torture by police and investigators in March 2005. The main evidence against the boys were the coerced confessions and incriminating statements against one another for participation in a murder, which they all maintained none of them committed. The government refused to conduct a meaningful investigation into these and other allegations of abuse.

At least two people died in pre-trial custody in 2006: Namik Mamedov, on April 3, and Rasim Alishev, on July 25. It is not known whether authorities carried out effective investigations into their deaths.

Nongovernmental organizations continued to receive reports of torture, particularly in police lockups. Sentenced prisoners complained of ill-treatment in the form of beatings, inadequate food, insufficient medical care, and lack of information and purposeful activities. Dozens of prisoners serving life sentences in Gobustan prison went on hunger strikes to protest their particularly harsh conditions, and three suicides were reported in that facility.

Media Freedom

Journalists, particularly those associated with opposition publications, face violence and criminal charges. In March 2006 Fikret Huseinli, a reporter for the opposition daily *Azadlyg*, was severely beaten and slashed by unknown assailants. In May unidentified attackers beat Bahaddin Haziev, the editor-in-chief of the opposition newspaper *Bizim Yol* and deputy chairman of the opposition party People's Front of Azerbaijan, and demanded that he stop criticizing the government. In July police and other government officials harassed and threatened *Ayna-Zerkalo* and Institute for War and Peace Reporting correspondent Idrak Abbasov and confiscated his notebook and tape recorder while he was preparing a report on the destruction of houses in the Binagedi district of Baku.

On June 23, officials detained Mirza Sakit Zakhidov, a prominent reporter and satirist for *Azadlyg*, on spurious drug charges, apparently to silence him for newspaper columns and poems he wrote criticizing President Ilham Aliev and government corruption; he was sentenced in October to three years' imprisonment. At least six journalists and editors and a number of newspapers faced criminal and civil libel suits brought by government officials. At least three editors received prison sentences for charges including criminal libel and "insulting the honor and dignity" of a state official. On October 1 a court ordered the closure of three major media outlets after their editor, Einulla Fatullaev, was convicted on libel charges deriving from articles he published alleging financial links between Interior Minister Ramil Usubov and Haji Mammadov, a former top Interior Ministry official on trial for leading a criminal gang. Two editors imprisoned for libel were included in a presidential pardon issued in late October.

Haji Mammadov confessed on July 25 to having killed Elmar Huseinov, the editor of *Monitor* magazine who was murdered in 2005, though he was not a suspect. Mammadov claims that he committed the murder at the behest of Farhad Aliev, who in turn maintains that the claim is part of the politically motivated case against him.

Although Azerbaijan opened a public television station in August 2005 as recommended by the Council of Europe, media experts state that it is virtually indistinguishable from pro-government rivals and risks being shut down if too openly critical of the government. In June 2006 the government targeted the ANS television station, known to be comparatively more independent, by arresting some of its employees and initiating a tax investigation apparently in order to keep the station's managers from acting too independently.

In November, as this report went to press, a court has ordered the eviction of the Azerbaijan Popular Front Party and two newspapers affiliated with it, *Azadlyg* and

Bizim Yol, from a building they shared; also evicted from the building was the independent Turan News Agency. In addition, the National Television and Radio Council ruled not to extend the license of ANS, Azerbaijan's only remaining independent television station.

Human Rights Defenders

A campaign to discredit long-time human rights activists Rena and Murad Sadaddinov began following their trip to the United States in June 2006, during which they spoke about human rights concerns in Azerbaijan. Two individuals known for their close ties to the government publicly accused the Sadaddinovs of taking bribes to include certain names into lists of political prisoners, and falsely claimed that Council of Europe experts confirmed the accusation. The Sadaddinovs note that they have not prepared lists of political prisoners for more than three years and maintain they have never accepted bribes.

Key International Actors

On May 9, 2006, Azerbaijan was elected to the United Nations Human Rights Council, which replaced the Human Rights Commission, and pledged to cooperate closely with special procedures mechanisms, promote transparency and the participation of NGOs and civil society in UN meetings, and support universal periodic review of human rights records of both council members and non-members.

In January 2006 the Parliamentary Assembly of the Council of Europe (PACE) challenged the credentials of the Azerbaijani delegation in response to violations in the November 2005 parliamentary elections. The PACE ultimately confirmed the credentials, but set out a list of urgently needed reforms. In a March 2006 report on human rights of members of the armed forces, the PACE found hazing and material conditions for conscripts in Azerbaijan to be serious problems and found violations of the right to conscientious objection.

In April President Aliev traveled to the United States for a meeting with President George W. Bush, which focused on energy security and the fight against terrorism. On July 14, the US Embassy in Baku stated publicly that the right to equal defense before the law and the presumption of innocence were violated during the trial of the New Thinking leaders. The embassy also expressed concern over violence and pressure against journalists.

The European Union completed the European Neighborhood Policy Action Plan with Azerbaijan, which will serve as the primary framework guiding EU-Azerbaijan relations for the next five years. The plan sets out steps that the Azerbaijani government should achieve in fields including the rule of law, democracy, economic and business development, energy, and resolution of internal conflicts. On September 28, European Commission and Council of Europe officials called on the government to undertake reforms in the prison system.

The Organization for Security and Co-operation in Europe (OSCE) observed the May 13 repeat elections in 10 constituencies in which results of the November 2005 parliamentary elections had been annulled on account of fraud. The OSCE found progress in some areas, including a more inclusive representation of candidates, unimpeded campaigning, and increased domestic observation, yet also observed interference by local authorities. In July 2006 the OSCE office in Baku stated that the trial of the New Thinking leaders fell short of international standards in upholding the rule of law. The OSCE representative on freedom of the media raised concerns over the use of defamation suits to silence journalists.

BELARUS

The human rights situation in Belarus continued to deteriorate in 2006. A flawed presidential poll in March led to the re-election of President Alexander Lukashenka for a third term. The government continues to severely restrict the activities of the media, political opposition, and human rights groups.

March 19 Presidential Elections

Belarusian authorities prevented opposition parties from campaigning effectively in the run-up to the March 19 presidential elections. In its final report on the elections, the Organization for Security and Co-operation in Europe (OSCE) concluded that the elections failed to meet the organization's standards for democratic elections, citing harassment of opposition candidates and campaign workers, heavily biased media coverage, lack of transparency in ballot counting, and other problems.

Belarusian authorities attempted to portray opposition supporters as enemies of the state. President Lukashenka made public statements that were widely seen as threatening, including a promise to "tear the heads off" protesters. In February, police arrested four members of the NGO "Partnership," which was preparing to monitor the elections. Official statements in the media suggested that the four were plotting to overthrow the government and carry out terrorist attacks. On August 4, in a closed trial, a judge sentenced the accused—Mikalai Astreika, Tsimafey Dranchuk, Enira Branzinskaia, and Alexander Shalaika—to prison terms ranging from six months to two years on charges of "organizing and running an unregistered organization that infringes the rights of citizens."

On March 2 police beat and briefly detained opposition presidential candidate Alexander Kazulin. Prosecutors subsequently opened criminal investigations against him for allegedly attempting to hold an unsanctioned press conference and smashing a portrait of Lukashenka in the police station where he was held.

On March 9 courts in Minsk sentenced 10 supporters of opposition presidential candidate Alexander Milinkevich, including his deputy campaign head, to jail terms of 15 days each on charges stemming from a rally held the previous day.

Other opposition supporters also faced charges related to public gatherings; the Belarusian human rights center Viasna estimates that police arrested 236 opposition campaign workers and supporters during the campaign period, some 90 percent of whom were sentenced to 15 days' detention.

On March 19 after authorities announced that Lukashenka had won over 80 percent of the vote, thousands of opposition supporters rallied in Minsk to protest the conduct of the elections and express support for Milinkevich. The protests lasted for five days, during which police carried out sporadic mass arrests of protesters; Viasna estimates that authorities detained more than 700 in total. Courts sentenced the overwhelming majority to short periods of detention.

Authorities continued to persecute political opponents after the elections. On July 13 a Minsk court sentenced Alexander Kazulin to five-and-a-half years in prison for his role in the protests. The EU and OSCE strongly condemned the decision. In September the courts rejected Kazulin's appeal. Milinkevich was jailed for 15 days after he participated in a rally on the anniversary of the Chernobyl disaster in April. On October 26 the European Parliament announced its decision to award Milinkevich the Sakharov Prize, the EU's most important human rights award.

Media Freedom

The authorities further stifled the media. Amendments to the criminal code enacted in January 2006 created penalties for "discrediting Belarus" by "fraudulent representation" of developments in the country.

The government continued to target one of Belarus's only independent newspapers, *Narodnaia Volia*. In addition to the authorities' terminating the paper's publishing and distribution contracts in Belarus in September 2005, that same month a court froze the paper's assets as part of an ongoing libel case brought by a politician.

In April 2006 Minsk city authorities wrote to local independent newspaper *Nasha Niva* indicating that the paper's presence in the city was no longer "appropriate," and refusing to confirm its legal address. The letter was related to the conviction of the paper's editor-in-chief, Andrey Dynko, who was sentenced to 10 days in jail for using foul language after he was arrested during a post-election protest.

Earlier, authorities had removed the newspaper from the national subscription catalogue, cutting a key distribution channel.

On November 28, 2005, the Minsk prosecutor's office decided not to open a criminal investigation into the October killing of Vasil Hrodnikau, a freelance journalist who for seven years had published articles in *Narodnaia Volia* on society and politics. Hrodnikau's death followed the murder a year earlier of Veronika Cherkasova, a journalist with the newspaper *Solidarnost*. On December 28, 2005, Belarus' chief prosecutor announced that he was halting the probe into her death because of a lack of suspects.

Human Rights Defenders and Civil Society

Authorities continued to target the Belarusian Helsinki Committee (BHC). In October 2005 the EU expressed concern at a decision by Belarusian prosecutors to reopen an investigation into charges that the BHC evaded taxes on grants it received through the EU's TACIS program (Technical Assistance to the Commonwealth of Independent States). On December 20 the Supreme Economic Court of Belarus reversed its original negative finding and levied heavy fines and back taxes against the organization. On May 24, 2006, the Belarusian Ministry of Justice asked the Supreme Court to order the BHC to suspend its activities. The EU expressed concern that this would eventually force the closure of Belarus's only remaining registered human rights NGO and urged that the charges be withdrawn.

On September 15 Dmitri (Zmister) Dashkevich, leader of the youth opposition group Young Front, was detained after answering a summons to present himself at the prosecutor general's office. He was charged with running an unregistered organization. On October 30 a Minsk court began hearing Dashkevich's case in closed session. Several hundred protesters gathered outside the courthouse to protest the trial.

The Fate of the "Disappeared"

The fate and whereabouts of the four public figures who "disappeared" in Belarus in 1999 and 2000—Viktor Gonchar, Yury Zakharenko, Anatoly Krasovskii, and

Dmitry Zavadskii—continued to remain unclear. Belarusian authorities have yet to conduct a satisfactory inquiry into the incidents and have remained hostile to attempts by the victims' relatives to elicit information. In September 2006 UN Special Rapporteur on Belarus Adrian Severin called on the UN Human Rights Council to back an international investigation into the "disappearances," under the auspices of the UN high commissioner for human rights.

Key International Actors

Both the US and EU called for free and fair elections in Belarus. Following the announcement of Lukashenka's re-election, they imposed visa bans on the president and 30 key officials. On May 18 the EU voted to extend its visa ban and freeze the assets of Lukashenka and some 35 Belarusian officials. The US Treasury Department enacted similar limitations on June 19.

The EU and US took measures to support civil society in Belarus ahead of the presidential elections. In late February, an EU-funded consortium of media organizations began broadcasting independent radio and television programs in Belarusian and Russian, aimed at providing an alternative to the state-controlled media. The US Agency for International Development (USAID) focused its efforts on supporting civil society and addressing key problem areas such as HIV/AIDS and human trafficking, budgeting over half of the US$7 million country allocation for 2006 to address these issues.

Relations with Poland continued to be strained. In February the Belarusian KGB (state security service) accused the Polish embassy of hosting foreign spies plotting to disrupt the country ahead of the elections. The Polish government repeatedly expressed its support for pro-democracy forces in Belarus and hosted opposition candidate Milinkevich directly after the polls.

Belarusian authorities stopped a Czech embassy car transporting copies of a UN report on human rights problems in Belarus to the German embassy. Officers threatened to charge the Belarusian driver with "subversive" activity. The incident followed a major diplomatic row in 2005, when Belarusian authorities expelled a Czech diplomat in what appeared to be retaliation for Czech support of pro-democracy activists in the country.

The Lukashenka administration continued to refuse access to the country for UN Special Rapporteur Adrian Severin. Severin instead assessed Belarus's human rights situation from neighboring states. In the aftermath of the March elections, seven UN independent experts, including Severin, joined in expressing alarm at the "large number of violations of the rights to freedom of expression, freedom of association, fair trial, physical and mental integrity, and to liberty" in Belarus and in calling for independent and transparent investigations into all allegations of "serious human rights violations." In September Severin delivered a strongly critical report to the UN Human Rights Council, expressing his "increased concern at the steady deterioration" of the human rights situation in the country and urging the government to "put an end to the ongoing human rights violations" and to "bring those responsible to justice."

Belarusian authorities also barred the EU's special representative on human rights, Michael Matthiessen, from visiting the country.

BOSNIA AND HERZEGOVINA

The legacy of the 1992-95 war in Bosnia and Herzegovina continued to define the key human rights challenges during 2006, with war crimes accountability and the rights of former refugees and displaced persons the most pressing concerns.

While nationalist parties lost some ground in the October 2006 elections, the election of Bosnian Muslim and Serb nationalists to the country's three-person presidency threatened to continue the dangerous rhetoric of the pre-election period. The presidency's Muslim representative Haris Silajdzic called for the dissolution of the two entities that make up Bosnia (Republika Srpska and the Federation), while Milorad Dodik, the Republika Srpska prime minister and head of the party holding the Serb seat on the presidency, called for Republika Srpska's self-determination. The international community's high representative in Bosnia responded by threatening to remove Dodik from office should he call a mooted referendum on the issue.

War Crimes Accountability

During 2006 the specialized war crimes chamber within the Bosnian State Court began to hear cases referred from the International Criminal Tribunal for the former Yugoslavia (ICTY). The ICTY has transferred five cases (involving nine accused) since September 2005 as part of its completion strategy. In June 2006 the United States extradited two Bosnian Serbs accused of war crimes in Srebrenica in July 1995 for trial by the State Court.

At this writing, the Bosnian war crimes chamber was hearing 18 cases, some involving multiple suspects, including 11 Bosnian Serbs charged with genocide relating to Srebrenica. The chamber delivered judgments in four cases during 2006. In October its conviction of Nedjo Samardzic for war crimes was overturned by the appeal chamber and a retrial ordered.

The district courts in Republika Srpska continued to try war crimes cases, albeit at a slow pace. Only two of the entity's five district courts—Banja Luka and Trebinje— were hearing war crimes cases (one in each court) at this writing. In the

Federation, war crimes trials continued at a faster pace, with half of its 10 cantonal courts hearing cases during 2006.

The efforts of cantonal and district courts to prosecute war crimes continue to be hindered by lack of support from the public, under-resourcing, and witness cooperation issues: victims are generally reluctant to travel to another entity's courts to testify against the accused, and entity-level witness protection schemes need developing. But the non-availability of suspects remains the biggest impediment to accountability.

Many war crimes suspects are Bosnian Serbs and Croats now resident as citizens in Serbia and Croatia. The constitutions of these countries prohibit extradition of their citizens. Bosnia refused to sign up to a September 2006 agreement between Croatia and Serbia that would facilitate prosecutions in the country of residence, insisting that defendants be tried in the country where the crimes took place.

At this writing, the Bosnian authorities during 2006 had not apprehended any persons indicted by the ICTY. Five indictees remain at large, including Radovan Karadzic and Ratko Mladic.

In March the ICTY sentenced Bosnian Muslim Gens. Enver Hadzihasanovic and Amir Kubura to five and three-and-a-half years' imprisonment respectively for failing to prevent crimes against Croats and Serbs in central Bosnia. It sentenced Bosnian Croat Ivica Rajic to 12 years' imprisonment in May after he pleaded guilty to war crimes committed against Bosnian Muslims in Stupni Do village in October 1993. In July 2006 the ICTY sentenced Bosnian Muslim Naser Oric to two years' imprisonment for crimes against Bosnian Serbs in Srebrenica during 1992 and 1993. In September it sentenced high-ranking Bosnian Serb wartime official Momcilo Krajisnik to 27 years in prison for crimes against humanity across Bosnia, but acquitted him of genocide.

The ICTY Appeals Chamber affirmed in May the convictions and sentences of Bosnian Croat commanders Mladen Naletilic and Vinko Martinovic for crimes against Bosnian Muslims in the Mostar area. In March the Appeals Chamber confirmed the conviction of Milomir Stakic, a Bosnian Serb wartime official in Prijedor, for crimes committed there in 1992, but reduced his life sentence to 40 years' imprisonment.

In June 2006 the Russian Federation extradited Bosnian Serb ICTY indictee Dragan Zelenovic to Bosnia, which transferred him to the ICTY the same month.

Return of Refugees and Displaced Persons

The annual numbers of refugees and displaced persons returning to their homes continue to decline. The United Nations High Commissioner for Refugees (UNHCR) registered 2,946 such returns by July 31, 2006, compared to 5,059 by the same point in 2005. Around half of more than two million people displaced during the war have registered return to their pre-war homes, around 450,000 of them to areas where they now constitute an ethnic minority. But the actual numbers of returns are much smaller: a 2005 field study by the Bosnian Helsinki Committee for Human Rights indicated that fewer than half of those registered as returnees actually live in their pre-war places of residence.

The situation for those returning to areas where they now constitute a minority remains the most difficult. Cases of harassment and attack against minority returnees increased in the pre-election period. There was also evidence of public and private sector employment discrimination against minority returnees. Other obstacles included insufficient funds to reconstruct destroyed properties, and lack of access to social and medical benefits.

Citizenship and National Security

The formation in March of a state commission to examine more than 1,000 decisions to grant citizenship to foreign nationals since 1992 raised human rights concerns. Suspicions on the part of the Bosnian and foreign governments that a number of naturalized Bosnian citizens may be involved in terrorism provided the impetus for its establishment. Many of those under scrutiny are Arab and other Muslims who arrived during the war, either to fight for Bosnian Muslim forces or work in Islamic charities. Human rights groups are concerned that the commission's decisions and the lack of effective procedural safeguards may put individuals at risk of return to places where they could face torture or persecution. To date, the commission has revoked the citizenship of 92 persons, citing involvement in terrorism, and upheld decisions in 99 other cases.

In his June report on European states' involvement in "extraordinary renditions" by the CIA, Dick Marty, rapporteur of the Parliamentary Assembly of the Council of Europe, found that Bosnia had deliberately assisted in the 2002 rendition of six Algerian terrorism suspects to United States custody at Guantanamo.

Human Rights Defenders

In February 2006 the staff of the independent Research and Documentation Center were threatened through an anonymous phone call and warned to stop their analysis on war-related deaths. The center's downward revision of the number of wartime casualties has drawn criticism from Bosnian Muslims, the war's principal victims.

Key International Actors

In January 2006, Bosnia and Herzegovina began the first round of negotiations with the European Union on a Stabilization and Association agreement (SAA), a precursor to eventual membership. Despite initial signals from Brussels that the SAA talks could be concluded by the end of 2006, the limited progress on reform assessed in the European Commission's November progress report on Bosnia made agreement unlikely within that timeframe. The EU continues to give an insufficient focus to domestic war crimes prosecutions in its relations with Bosnia.

Also in January, Christian Schwarz-Schilling replaced Paddy Ashdown as the international community's (and the EU's) high representative to Bosnia and Herzegovina. He did not fulfill his promise to exercise his powers in a more limited manner than his predecessor: during the summer, Schwarz-Schilling lifted bans on individuals holding public office imposed by previous high representatives. In June he imposed amendments to the law on the transfer of cases from the ICTY to Bosnia, and to Bosnia's criminal procedure code (extending detention time limits). In September he appointed a special envoy to resolve outstanding issues in ethnically divided Mostar, as well as warning Dodik over calls for a referendum.

In June the Peace Implementation Council (PIC, which represents 55 governments and agencies), announced that the office of High Representative would be abolished by June 2007, and replaced by the office of the European Union's Special Representative (EUSR) with much more limited powers. The PIC will review and confirm its decision in early 2007.

In January 2006 EU peacekeeping force in Bosnia (EUFOR) personnel killed the wife of war crime suspect Dragomir Abazovic as they sought to arrest him in Rogatica; Abazovic and his 11-year-old son were wounded in the operation. EUFOR officials claimed that Abazovic, his wife and son fired first and that Abazovic's head wound was self-inflicted. EUFOR said it was acting on an arrest warrant from Sarajevo Cantonal Court. The case was later taken up by the State Court, which released Abazovic from custody in February without charge. EUFOR had previously been criticized for failing to apprehend any war crime suspects.

In September the United States announced the withdrawal from Bosnia of its remaining 150 NATO soldiers by the end of 2006, leaving peacekeeping entirely in the hands of the EU. In October EU defense ministers agreed at a meeting in Finland to reduce their force numbers in Bosnia and Herzegovina to about 1,500 from the current 6,000 personnel, but did not set a date for the reduction.

CROATIA

In 2006 sustained international pressure combined with a maturing democratic process led to some progress on human rights in Croatia. The key concerns continued to stem from the 1991-95 war, particularly the return and reintegration of Croatian Serb refugees and the rights of the Serb minority generally, together with accountability for war crimes.

Return and Reintegration of Serbs

With the qualified exception of housing, the Croatian authorities continue to make inadequate progress to facilitate the return of refugee Serbs or to address the obstacles to their reintegration into Croatian society.

Of the estimated 300,000 to 350,000 Croatian Serbs who left their homes during the 1991-95 war, mainly for Serbia, Montenegro, and Bosnia and Herzegovina, over 120,000 had registered their return to Croatia by August 2006. But international and local organizations estimate that only 60 to 65 percent remain permanently in Croatia, with many leaving after a short stay.

Resolving lost housing rights for returning Serbs remains a qualified success. Most Serbs have been able to repossess privately owned homes, and reconstruction assistance for wartime damage is available (although many applications for it are refused on minor procedural grounds, and there is a backlog in appeals). Owners are sometimes required to compensate temporary occupants for improvements the occupants made to the property. At the same time, a program designed to facilitate repair of post-war damage to Serb homes caused by temporary occupants is overly narrow, excluding many potential beneficiaries. Access to occupied agricultural land remains a problem in the Benkovac area.

There has been only limited progress in restoration of lost rights to occupy socially-owned property (tenancy rights) stripped from Serbs during the war. The government announced in August 2006 that it would implement a 2003 plan to provide housing to Serb former tenancy-right holders in urban areas. The proposal came in for criticism from Serb representatives and the European Union for limiting the right to purchase flats and delaying until 2011 the completion date for the

CROATIA

A Decade of Disappointment

Continuing Obstacles to the Reintegration of Serb Returnees

HUMAN
RIGHTS
WATCH

program (which could be as many as 20 years after the right was originally terminated).

In the former "Areas of Special State Concern" (mainly rural territory held by Serb rebels during the war), there was no progress on resolving lost tenancy rights for Serbs, who remain at the bottom of the list for assistance with housing—even below people moving to the area for the first time—according to the official rulebook.

Access to public sector employment for Serb returnees remains a problem, despite 2005 legislation to implement the 2002 Constitutional Law on the Rights of National Minorities, which requires proportionate Serb employment in national and local government and the courts (the rules do not apply to state enterprises, schools, and hospitals). The limited progress contrasted with the private sector, which employs Serbs in areas of return in greater numbers, despite the absence of any legislative requirement to do so, suggesting that in the public sector discrimination may be an obstacle to greater employment for Serbs in return areas.

The upsurge of violence against Serbs that began in 2005 continued in 2006, including the vicious beating of an elderly Serb man, Svetozar Djordjevic, in January; the case remained unresolved at this writing. There were signs, however, in 2006 that the government has begun to take the issue more seriously. Early in the year the Interior Ministry established focal points in three return areas to monitor the response of the police to incidents against minorities. Following an attack on a Serb returnee property in July in Biljani Donji, a village in the Zadar area (where intimidation of Serbs has been particularly pronounced), senior government officials publicly condemned the attack, including President Stjepan Mesic (who visited the area together with the deputy prime minister) and Prime Minister Ivo Sanader. The alleged perpetrators were immediately apprehended and charged by police. Nevertheless, the overall clear-up rate for such incidents remains low.

In June 2006 new offenses proscribing "hate crimes" were added to the Croatian penal code, following parliamentary approval of a proposal by Serb parliamentarians the same month. In July, the government added training on the new offenses to the existing police training programme, with support from the Organization for Security and Co-operation in Europe (OSCE).

War Crimes Accountability

With the December 2005 transfer to the Hague of Gen. Ante Gotovina, indicted for war crimes by the International Criminal Tribunal for the former Yugoslavia (ICTY), Croatia's obligations toward the court in 2006 consisted largely of ensuring the proper trial of the first case referred to it by the ICTY—that of Gens. Mirko Norac and Rahim Ademi, indicted for war crimes committed against Serbs in the Medak Pocket. The OSCE recommended that Croatia's judiciary was up to the task and said it would monitor the trial when it begins.

In September, the Croatian government sought the status of *amicus curiae* in the adjoined cases of Gotovina and Gens. Ivan Cermak and Mladen Markac at the ICTY in order to "correct historical and political inaccuracies" in the indictment against them for crimes committed against Serbs during the 1995 Croatian Army action "Operation Storm." The government's efforts were opposed by the ICTY chief prosecutor, who said that Croatia was seeking to influence the outcome of the proceedings. The court rejected the application in October, reasoning that allowing Croatia to intervene would not be in the interests of justice.

The Croatian judicial system continues to try war crimes cases based on domestic indictments. In a welcome development, the courts took up several important cases during 2006 involving war crimes against Serbs. But Serbs still form the vast majority of those prosecuted and convicted on war crimes charges in Croatian courts, a disproportion so large that it suggests that bias was a factor. Monitoring of war crimes cases by the OSCE mission demonstrates an inconsistent approach toward Croat and Serb defendants in relation to indictment, prosecution, conviction, and sentencing.

The opening in May 2006 of proceedings against Branimir Glavas was a significant development towards accountability for war time abuses against Serbs. Glavas, a prominent Croatian politician, is accused of ordering killings and beatings of Serb civilians in the town of Osijek during the war. But the case illustrates many of the problems that affect domestic war crimes prosecutions in Croatia, including the intimidation of witnesses and the publication of privileged information in the media.

Wartime deaths of Serbs still await investigation in other towns, including Paulin Dvor and Sisak. In the latter case, the families of over 100 wartime victims may never see justice, as the deaths have yet to be classified as war crimes (despite assurances from the State Prosecutor), leaving them subject to a fast-approaching 15-year statute of limitations for trying ordinary murders.

Prosecutors in Croatia and Serbia agreed to cooperate on exchange of information and evidence to facilitate the prosecution of war crimes suspects no longer present in the country where the alleged crimes took place. Both countries have constitutional bars on the extradition of citizens, and a number of suspects who fled from one to the other have since acquired citizenship, making extradition impossible.

Human Rights Defenders

Human rights groups continue to be viewed with suspicion, but remain largely free to operate. The reduction in funding from international donors increased the importance of national funding sources. The main local source of nongovernmental organizations' (NGOs) funding remained the National Foundation for the Development of Civil Society. Established by parliament in 2003, the foundation has been criticised by NGOs in previous years over problems with impartiality and transparency. The Civil Society Forum, which represents many NGOs in Croatia, noted some progress on those concerns in 2006.

Key International Actors

The European Union continued during 2006 to emphasise the fulfilment of political criteria—including the protection of minorities—as a prerequisite for Croatia's progress towards EU membership, although domestic war crimes were given insufficient priority. The December 2005 arrest of General Gotovina followed significant EU pressure.

The OSCE mission to Croatia remains the strongest international voice calling for fair treatment of Serbs in Croatia. It actively engages with the government on policy in this area, but is more inclined to dialogue than pressure. However, it does act as a catalyst for positive developments and a safeguard mechanism to make sure human rights in Croatia remain on the agenda of international partners. The mission's most recent report, published in June 2006, made concrete proposals for action in the fields of refugee return, the rights of Serbs, and war crimes accountability, but also indicated that the mission is drawing to a close, which increases the importance of continued EU focus on those issues.

European Union

Terrorism, and state responses to it, continue to pose serious challenges to human rights protections within the European Union. Restrictions on and, in some cases, mistreatment of migrants and asylum seekers are also of pressing concern in the region.

The threat of terrorism in 2006 induced several EU states to adopt laws weakening human rights protections; a number of states sought to deport foreign suspects to countries notorious for torture. Courts often acted as an effective check against abuse during 2006, together with parliaments in some cases, but courts failed to give sufficient weight to the importance of free expression in cases involving alleged incitement to terrorism.

Migration policy at EU and national levels remains largely focused on preventing migrants and asylum seekers from reaching EU territory and summarily returning those who do, rather than ensuring access to protection for those who need it. States continued in 2006 to routinely detain migrants, including in substandard conditions.

Counterterrorism Measures and Human Rights

There was increased momentum during 2006 toward accountability for the complicity of EU states in the United States government's abduction and illegal transfer of terrorism suspects to places where they risked torture, and detention of "high-value" terrorism suspects in secret facilities. A June report from the Parliamentary Assembly of the Council of Europe (PACE) described a "spider web" of illegal transfers and detentions, and named EU states among those that could be held responsible for violations of the rights of specific individuals "rendered" by the US, including Germany, Italy, Sweden, and the United Kingdom.

In July the European Parliament considered an interim report by a special committee tasked with investigating the alleged use of current and soon-to-be EU countries by the Central Intelligence Agency (CIA) for the movement and illegal detention of prisoners. The Parliament adopted a resolution on July 6 concluding that US government agents had been "directly responsible for the illegal seizure, removal, abduction and detention of terrorist suspects on the territory of [EU] Member States..." and determined that it was "implausible" that member states were not complicit in these operations. The committee continued its investigative work throughout 2006, visiting Germany in September, the UK and Romania in October, and Poland in November. A final report is expected in 2007.

EU governments continue to seek and secure "diplomatic assurances" against torture in their efforts to transfer terrorism suspects to countries where they would be at risk of ill-treatment (see sections below on the Netherlands and UK). This runs counter to the broad consensus among international human rights experts that diplomatic assurances do not provide an effective safeguard against torture and ill-treatment, as reflected in strong statements against their use during 2006 by the United Nations high commissioner for human rights and special rapporteur on torture, the Council of Europe commissioner for human rights, and the EU Network of Independent Experts on Fundamental Rights.

Some EU states moved in April to establish, through the Council of Europe's Group of Specialists on Human Rights and the Fight against Terrorism, guidelines for the "acceptable use" of diplomatic assurances, but failed. Having considered mounting evidence that diplomatic assurances do not protect against torture, the Group of Specialists declined to issue such guidelines.

Common EU Asylum and Migration Policy

Efforts to establish a common EU migration and asylum policy continue to raise concerns about standard setting that weakens or undermines the protections required by human rights and refugee law.

In December 2005 the EU's European Council adopted the Asylum Procedures Directive without any of the 100-plus amendments proposed by the European Parliament. In response, the Parliament petitioned the European Court of Justice (ECJ) in March 2006 to annul the entire directive. A key element of the legal challenge is a provision establishing an EU-wide list of "safe countries of origin," which would oblige EU states to deem asylum applications by nationals of the listed countries "manifestly unfounded." At this writing the court had yet to rule on the admissibility of the challenge.

The ECJ dismissed in June a complaint brought by the European Parliament in 2003 about the directive on the right to family reunification adopted the same year. The court ruled that provisions in the directive allowing member states to adopt stricter rules on family reunification than those laid down in the directive itself do not amount to disproportionate interference with the right to family life.

Countering irregular immigration remains at the top of the EU agenda. The EU's response to the large-scale migration by sea to Spain, Italy, and Malta during the summer of 2006 revolved around securing borders, interception, and repatriation rather than ensuring that the rights of migrants and refugees are respected.

That approach formed part of the EU's ongoing effort to "externalize" the control, processing, and hosting of migrants and asylum seekers to neighboring states outside its own borders, including through readmission agreements, by which states outside the EU agree to accept the return of migrants from third countries, who have transited their territory en route to the EU. In October 2006 the EU and Ukraine signed a readmission agreement. Implementation is delayed for two years, but human rights groups are concerned that the delay is insufficient for Ukraine to carry out reforms to safeguard the rights of migrants and asylum seekers.

In the first major initiative since its creation in 2005, the EU External Borders Agency FRONTEX was tasked with managing joint patrols off the coasts of Mauritania, Senegal, and Cape Verde. As the EU attempted to broker a similar agreement with Libya for joint patrols in the Mediterranean, and Italy reached a bilateral agreement with Libya for joint police operations at the Libyan coast, the human rights of asylum seekers and migrants received scant attention.

Human Rights Concerns in EU Member States

France

In July 2006 the French parliament adopted a new law on immigration and integration, increasing restrictions on family reunification for legal residents, and abolishing the automatic right to legal status for those living in France without papers for 10 years. It created an obligatory "integration contract" for those seeking temporary residency, and a proof of integration requirement for those seeking long-term residence.

In a report published in February, then Council of Europe Commissioner for Human Rights Alvaro Gil-Robles drew attention to overcrowding and unhygienic conditions in detention centers for immigrants, as well as in prisons. The holding center in the Palais de Justice in Paris, where Gil-Robles described conditions as "inhuman and degrading," was closed in June.

The August expulsion of Adel Tebourski, a Tunisian man convicted on terrorism charges, illustrated France's determination to rely on expulsion as a counterterrorism policy. Just prior to his completing a five-year sentence for terrorism offenses in July, Tebourski's French citizenship (acquired in 2000) was rescinded and the interior minister ordered his immediate expulsion. Tebourski was detained pending deportation, and despite a request from the UN Committee against Torture that he not be removed until the risk of him being tortured upon return to Tunisia could be properly examined, he was expelled as soon as his application for asylum was rejected and preliminary hearings determined that he did not face a torture risk.

In June the Paris Correctional Tribunal convicted 25 men in the so-called "Chechen network" trial, some for "criminal association in relation to a terrorist enterprise" and others for falsifying documents and other lesser offenses. Saïd Arif, a 40-year-old Algerian, was sentenced to nine years' imprisonment, despite the court throwing out his confession and other declarations obtained while he was detained in Syria on the grounds it was "nearly certain" they were obtained under torture. France's leading magistrate in terrorism cases Jean-Louis Bruguiere had provided a set of questions to Syrian authorities, and traveled to Syria at the time of Arif's interrogation in May 2004.

In April 2006, on the day it was expected to announce its ruling in the trial of six former Guantanamo Bay detainees on charges of criminal association with a terrorist enterprise, a Paris court postponed the verdict until May 2007 in order to examine the circumstances in which French intelligence officers had interrogated the individuals at the facility. The six French nationals spent between two-and-a-half and three years at Guantanamo before being handed over to French authorities in July 2004 and March 2005.

A counterterrorism law that came into force in January 2006 increases pre-charge detention for terrorism suspects from four to six days. Human rights groups expressed concern about the duration of pre-charge detention in view of the lack of appropriate safeguards, including limited access to a lawyer. A proposed reform of the justice system under discussion within the government during 2006 would require that all police and judicial interrogations in criminal cases be filmed as a safeguard against, among other things, prohibited ill-treatment and procedural violations. Interrogations of terrorism suspects would be excluded from this rule, however.

Germany

The German government foiled a terrorist bombing plot in July 2006, involving unexploded devices found on trains heading toward Hamm and Koblenz. Interior Minister Wolfgang Schaeuble warned in August that the security situation in Germany was "exceptionally serious" and called for stronger counterterrorism measures. Measures under consideration by the government include enhanced video surveillance in public spaces and a counterterrorism database.

Federal prosecutors opened an investigation in February into Germany's possible complicity in the abduction and rendition of Khalid el-Masri, a German citizen apprehended in Macedonia in 2003, handed over to US operatives, and subsequently held in secret detention in Afghanistan (his case is also the subject of investigations at the European Parliament and Council of Europe). El-Masri was released in Albania in May 2004, and never charged with a crime. He claimed that he had been beaten in detention and interrogated by a German official in Afghanistan.

A German parliamentary committee of inquiry was established in April to investigate the possible complicity of the German government in abuses by US agents in the context of counterterrorism, including whether the Federal Criminal Police Office questioned terror suspects being held abroad, and the cases of El-Masri and Mohammed Haider Zammar. A German citizen of Syrian descent, Zammar had been arrested in Morocco in 2001, transferred to US custody, and sent on by private plane to Damascus, where he is on trial before a security court. German intelligence and law enforcement officials interrogated Zammar in Syria in November 2002. The German chancellery issued new interrogation guidelines in October 2006, which no longer permit members of the German federal police to question terrorism suspects abroad.

Controversy surrounded the return of Murat Kurnaz, a German-born Turkish citizen, to Bremen in August 2006 after more than four years in US custody at Guantanamo Bay, because of revelations that he had been interrogated by German security officials during his detention, and claims by Kurnaz's lawyers that German authorities declined a 2002 offer from the US government to release him. In October 2006 the parliament's defense committee began an investigation of Kurnaz's claim that he was mistreated in US custody in Afghanistan, prior to Guantanamo, by members of the German army.

Italy

In the first nine months of 2006, an estimated 16,000 migrants leaving from the Libyan coast either arrived on the island of Lampedusa, off the Sicilian coast, or were brought there after having been interdicted by Italian naval or coast guard vessels. At least 60 people died in two separate boat sinkings in August, including one incident involving an Italian coast guard ship; the incident was under investigation at this writing.

Despite pressure from civil society groups and parties within the ruling coalition, the government of Romani Prodi, elected in April 2006, declined to abolish mandatory detention for irregular migrants, although the government established a commission to investigate detention conditions. The government announced in May that Italy would not expel anyone to countries that have not signed the UN Refugee Convention, including Libya, marking a shift from the previous administration, which in some cases removed people without first giving them an opportunity to seek asylum.

In July Milan's chief prosecutor formally submitted an extradition request for 26 US citizens (25 suspected CIA agents and the former commander of a US Air Force base at Aviano, Italy) in the investigation into the February 2003 abduction of Egyptian Hassan Mustafa Osama Nasr (known as Abu Omar), rendered to Egypt by the CIA via Aviano. The justice minister, who must approve the request, had not taken any action at this writing. Prosecutors also accused 12 Italians of involvement, including the director and former deputy director of SISMI, the Italian military intelligence agency, and six SISMI agents. Milan prosecutors concluded their investigation in October, portraying the abduction as an illegal operation organized by the CIA with the help of SISMI. In October the Prodi government told a parliamentary commission of inquiry that the issue of possible contact between the US and Italian governments on the case was protected by state secrecy.

Malta

In July, 51 African migrants rescued at sea by a Spanish fishing boat spent eight days in legal limbo after Malta refused to allow the ship to dock. Maltese authorities claimed they had no duty to admit the migrants because they were rescued outside the country's territorial waters. They were eventually allowed to disembark in Malta after Spain agreed to take the majority of the group, with Italy, the Netherlands, and Andorra accepting others. Malta had allowed a pregnant woman, a mother, and a two-year-old child to disembark earlier for medical treatment.

Officials from the office of the UN High Commissioner for Refugees (UNHCR) who visited these three migrants pending their onward travel stated publicly that they were "shocked" after they saw 11 men being held in a tiny, dark, unventilated room. The men were allegedly being punished for attempting to escape. Malta has a mandatory detention policy for asylum seekers and irregular migrants.

The Netherlands

Nine alleged members of the Hofstad Group, a militant Islamist network, were convicted in March of membership in a terrorist organization; five others were acquitted. The only evidence used to convict five of the nine was internet and phone communications in which they promoted a violent version of Islam and called for holy war with the West. Judge Rene Elkerbout stated, "Anyone who preaches hate and violence lays the basis for committing crimes directed at instilling fear among the people and destroying Dutch democracy." Although seen as a major breakthrough in the Netherlands' ability to secure terrorism convictions, the judgment gave rise to concerns that the five men were prosecuted for speech and association rather than participation in a criminal conspiracy. Among those convicted was Mohammad Bouyeri, already serving a life sentence for the murder of filmmaker Theo van Gogh in November 2004.

In May 2006 the Dutch House of Representatives approved new counterterrorism legislation. If also adopted by the Senate, which began debating it in September, the new law would give police special surveillance powers upon an "indication" (as opposed to the higher standard of "reasonable suspicion") that a suspect has committed a crime; increase the maximum period of detention without charge from three to 14 days; and allow multiple extensions of pre-trial detention for up to two years.

The Supreme Court, in a final decision in September, confirmed the ruling of a lower court halting the extradition to Turkey of Kurdistan Workers' Party (PKK) member Nuriye Kesbir. The lower court had determined that diplomatic assurances of humane treatment and fair trial from the Turkish authorities were not sufficient to protect Kesbir from ill-treatment upon return.

A proposal in February by Rita Verdonk, minister of alien affairs and integration, to lift a moratorium on the deportation of rejected gay and lesbian asylum seekers to Iran was withdrawn in April after strong protests from Dutch civil society and international human rights organizations, including Human Rights Watch. In October, the Dutch government announced a major policy shift, recognizing gay and lesbian Iranians as a "special group" facing persecution at home and deserving protection in the Netherlands.

Poland

President Lech Kaczy ski called for the restoration of the death penalty in Poland and throughout Europe in a July radio statement, drawing condemnation from the European Commission and PACE. In August the League of Polish Families, a minority party in the ruling coalition, launched a campaign for a referendum in Poland on the issue.

In January 2006 the European Parliament, motivated in part by rising homophobia in Poland, adopted a resolution calling on EU member states "firmly to condemn homophobic hate speech or incitement to hatred and violence." But overtly homophobic rhetoric from Polish government officials, coupled with attacks on lesbian, gay, bisexual and transgender (LGBT) activists, continued during 2006. The State Prosecutor in May ordered all prosecutors to review the financing of LGBT organizations after a parliamentarian from the League of Polish Families accused LGBT groups of associating with pedophiles and the narcotics trade. Minister of Education Roman Giertych dismissed the director of a teacher training center in June for using a Council of Europe publication that included sections on non-discrimination against sexual minorities, a move condemned by Council of Europe Secretary General Terry Davis. In April, despite the presence of police, LGBT activists were attacked in Krakow by a far-right group during a demonstration.

The "Vetting Act" signed by the president in November and aimed at identifying collaborators with security agencies of the Polish People's Republic between 1944 and 1990 gave rise to human rights concerns including inadequate privacy protections and limited procedural safeguards for appeals.

Spain

By September over 25,000 migrants had reached the Canary Islands, a five-fold increase on the total for the whole of 2005. Inadequate capacity in reception centers for migrants meant that hundreds of unaccompanied minors were placed in makeshift centers, which a European Parliament delegation described as a "real emergency" during a June 2006 visit.

The majority of migrants traveled through Senegal and Mauritania. Spain negotiated agreements with both countries for the return of their nationals. Senegal interrupted repatriations after the first group of Senegalese to be returned (99 persons in May) complained of ill-treatment by Spanish authorities; operations later resumed. At this writing, Spain was negotiating with both countries to permit the return of third country nationals who departed from their coasts, raising concerns that refugees and others at risk could be denied access to protection on Spanish soil.

After the Basque separatist group ETA declared a permanent ceasefire in March, Prime Minister José Luis Rodríguez Zapatero formally announced in June his government's intention to enter into negotiations to end nearly four decades of political violence over the status of the Basque region. Prosecutions of alleged ETA collaborators or members continued in the special terrorism court Audiencia Nacional, with several of the cases raising concerns about undue restrictions on freedom of expression and association. In February the court paved the way for the trial of seven staff members of the Basque-language newspaper *Euskaldunon Egunkaria* on terrorism charges when it rejected their appeal against indictment. The newspaper had been shut down in February 2003 and the staff members arrested on charges of collaborating with ETA. Batasuna leader Arnaldo Otegi was convicted in April of glorification of terrorism for a speech given in December 2003 in honor of an ETA leader killed in 1978.

In April 2006, a little over two years after the Madrid train bombings that claimed 191 lives and injured over 1,700 people, investigating magistrate Juan del Olmo formally charged 29 out of the 116 people under investigation. Eighteen of those charged are in custody. The trial is expected to begin in February 2007.

In July, citing "a total lack of prosecution evidence," the Supreme Court overturned the 2005 terrorism conviction of Hamed Abderrahman Ahmed, a Spanish citizen who had spent over two years at Guantanamo Bay, and ordered his immediate release. The court also noted lack of sufficient evidence in June when it overturned the separate 2005 conviction of Syrian-born Spaniard Imad Yarkas for conspiracy to commit the September 11 terrorist attacks in the United States, but upheld his conviction for membership in al Qaeda and his 12-year prison sentence. Ruling on other appeals by those convicted in the same 2005 trial of alleged members of an al Qaeda cell in Spain, the court acquitted three individuals entirely, but upheld the conviction of Al Jazeera correspondent Taysir Allouni.

The Audiencia Nacional began an investigation in June 2006 into the alleged use of Spanish airports in the illegal transfer of terrorism suspects by the CIA.

In a positive move, Spain ratified the Optional Protocol to the Convention against Torture in March 2006. Less than a month later, however, parliament rejected a proposal to eliminate provisions of the Criminal Code that allow terrorism suspects and others charged with serious crimes to be held virtually incommunicado (with extremely limited access to a lawyer, and no right to communicate with family members) for 13 days.

United Kingdom

Counterterrorism laws and measures implemented by the UK government came under judicial scrutiny in 2006, with the courts generally striking down measures that violated fundamental human rights protections. In December 2005 the UK's highest court, the House of Lords Judicial Committee, ruled in the case of *A and Others* that evidence extracted under torture can never be used in court proceedings, reversing an August 2004 majority decision by the Court of Appeal.

Claims by the UK government that it had foiled a major transatlantic airline bombing plot in August led to the arrest and detention of a number of terrorism suspects and the first test of extended detention powers under the Terrorism Act 2006, which became law in March and permits 28 days' pre-charge detention for terrorism suspects. The Act also criminalizes speech that "encourages" terrorism—including statements that "glorify" terrorism or are believed to indirectly encourage it—even where the statements do not directly incite violence. The restrictive nature of the new law poses a serious risk of infringing legitimate free expression.

The parliamentary Joint Committee on Human Rights published an assessment of the government's compliance with the Convention against Torture in May 2006, concluding that its policy of seeking diplomatic assurances against torture in "memoranda of understanding" with countries to which the UK wants to deport alleged terrorism suspects—Jordan, Libya, and Lebanon, to date—was likely to put those returned under the agreement at "substantial risk... of actually being tortured" as well as undermining the prohibition on returns to risk of torture.

The first legal challenge to a "memorandum of understanding" commenced in May in the case of Omar Othman, a Jordanian terrorism suspect also known as

Abu Qatada, whom the UK government wishes to deport to Jordan. Othman's lawyers argued before the Special Immigration Appeals Commission (SIAC) that he would be at risk of torture, unfair trial, and possible rendition to a third country if transferred to Jordan based on that country's inherently unreliable promises of fair treatment.

The SIAC dismissed the appeal of an Algerian man ("Y") against his deportation to Algeria on national security grounds in August, ruling he would not face a real risk of torture if returned because he would be covered by a new amnesty law. "Y" is a torture survivor granted refugee status in the UK. He was acquitted by a UK court in 2005 of charges related to an alleged terrorism plot. At this writing, the SIAC's decision was under appeal.

In August the Court of Appeal upheld a lower court ruling quashing "control orders" against six terrorism suspects on the grounds that they constituted a deprivation of liberty contrary to the European Convention on Human Rights (ECHR). The orders, authorized under the Terrorism Act 2005, imposed 18-hour curfews and other restrictions of movement on the six. The home secretary subsequently issued new orders with a 14-hour curfew period. The same month, the Court of Appeal reversed a lower court ruling that the judicial scrutiny and standard of proof required for the imposition of a control order violated the right to a fair hearing under the ECHR.

The Crown Prosecution Service, following the completion of its review into the death of Jean Charles de Menezes (mistakenly killed by the Metropolitan Police in London the day after foiled terrorist attacks on July 21, 2005), announced in July 2006 that it would not prosecute any individual police officer for murder, manslaughter, or any other criminal offense in connection with the shooting, but indicated it would prosecute the office of the Metropolitan Police Commissioner over the death using health and safety laws.

GEORGIA

Although the Georgian government takes pride in its stated commitment to the rule of law and human rights protection, it continues to have an uneven human rights record. Restoration of territorial integrity and the fight against organized crime remain the priorities of the government's agenda. Beginning in December 2005, the government stepped up its fight against crime and sought to break the power of organized crime bosses, including within the prison system, which resulted in more frequent use of force to subdue or punish detainees. Impunity for the actions of law enforcement officers remains a serious problem; effective investigations are rare. The executive wielded strong influence over the judiciary and took several steps to restrict freedom of expression. Some human rights groups reported government harassment.

Prison Conditions, Use of Lethal Force, and Torture and Ill-Treatment

The majority of Georgia's prisoners—some 63 percent of whom are held in pre-trial detention—live in overcrowded, poorly ventilated, filthy cells. They receive inadequate nutrition and substandard medical care, have limited access to information and family visits, and in 2006 some went for weeks or months without an opportunity to leave their cells for exercise or fresh air. In some cases the conditions of detention amount to degrading treatment.

Since December 2005 there has been a marked increase in the use of violence by law enforcement officers in prison facilities. Inmates report periods of frequent beatings and degrading treatment such as repeated strip searches. This treatment has at times constituted torture. Security forces repeatedly used force to suppress prison disturbances. On March 27, 2006, special forces used automatic gunfire in Tbilisi Prison No. 5 to suppress a disturbance, resulting in the deaths of at least seven inmates.

A number of suspects were killed by Georgian law enforcement officers during special operations and at the time of arrest, continuing a trend begun in 2005. In 2006, 17 suspects were killed; in one instance, over 50 bullet wounds were recorded on the suspect's body.

GEORGIA

Undue Punishment

Abuses against Prisoners in Georgia

HUMAN
RIGHTS
WATCH

The government has failed to confront the long-standing problem of impunity for excessive use of force by law enforcement agents. Senior officials, including President Mikheil Saakashvili and the minister of the interior have made public statements condoning the use of lethal force and praising the professionalism of law enforcement agents. In late November the prosecutor general's office reported that it was investigating the deaths of 13 people killed in the course of special operations, though at this writing it was not possible to determine the effectiveness of these investigations. For three months the General Prosecutor's Office failed to open an investigation into the actions of law enforcement officers during the March 27 special operation in Tbilisi Prison No. 5, and instead the Ministry of Justice investigated the planning of the alleged riot only. Investigations into torture and ill-treatment in the prison system are not prompt, do not meet international requirements for effectiveness, or are not opened at all.

Following a dispute with senior Ministry of Interior officials in a Tbilisi cafe on January 27, 2006, the body of 28-year-old Sandro Girgvliani, head of the United Georgian Bank's international relations department, was found on the outskirts of Tbilisi bearing beating signs. In July, four Ministry of Interior employees were convicted of causing the injuries that resulted in Girgvliani's death, and were sentenced to prison terms. However, many believe that the senior Ministry officials involved in the disagreement with Girgvliani had ordered his kidnapping and beating but escaped prosecution.

Independence of the Judiciary

Constitutional amendments in early 2004 increased the Georgian president's authority to dismiss and appoint judges. The government then began an effort to address corruption in the judiciary, but the procedures for removing allegedly corrupt judges have lacked transparency and due process. In 2005 the authorities told a number of judges that they should either resign or face disciplinary hearings; 21 of 37 Supreme Court judges resigned under this pressure. Nine refused to resign but were then made subject to disciplinary proceedings in December 2005, were found guilty, and were suspended from office. The proceedings addressed matters related to the judges' interpretation of law rather than issues of ethics or conduct subject to disciplinary evaluation. On August 10, 2006, the Disciplinary Chamber of the Supreme Court upheld the decision against the judges. These steps have had a chilling effect on new and remaining judges, who may legitimately see their positions as tenuous and their decisions as subject to executive approval.

Freedom of Expression

On June 29, five activists from the NGO Equality Institute peacefully protested the trial of two journalists by standing outside the Appeals Court in Tbilisi and making statements in support of the accused. Court guards detained the men and forced them into the court building, causing injuries to two of them. The five activists were charged with disrupting court proceedings and were immediately sentenced to 30 days' administrative arrest. Ten days after his release, one of the activists, Lasha Chkhartishvili, was again arrested following a peaceful protest, allegedly for swearing at police, and sentenced to two days' detention. Video footage of the incident did not reveal any violations by Chkhartishvili during the protest.

Eka Khoperia, an anchor of a popular political talk show on the Rustavi-2 television channel, announced during a live program on July 6 concerning the Girgvliani murder that she was resigning to protest government authorities' requests to alter that program's format.

On August 26 Rustavi-2's owner, reportedly a close friend of Defense Minister Irakli Okruashvili, fired the station's director general and replaced her with Koba Davarashvili, who previously headed an advertising company with links to the government and is reportedly a close friend of the chief of the presidential administration. In response, many of the station's journalists immediately went on strike, and on September 8 six resigned, citing their commitment to independence in reporting. In November, Rustavi 2's owner sold the station, reportedly under pressure, and Okruashvili resigned soon thereafter.

On July 29, police arrested former Security Minister and current leader of the Forward Georgia opposition movement Irakli Batiashvili on charges of failing to report a crime and assisting a coup attempt by providing "intellectual support" to Emzar Kvitsiani, the leader of an illegal militia. While it remains unclear whether Batiashvili committed a crime, the evidence against Batiashvili includes public statements he made on television, some or all of which may be legitimate and protected speech.

Human Rights Defenders

Several human rights defenders reported harassment at the beginning of 2006. In January top government officials, including the defense minister, publicly accused the current leadership of the Georgian Young Lawyers' Association (GYLA, a professional lawyers' association) of being politicized and of misusing US$12 million in funding. The officials, who are themselves GYLA members, called for the resignation of the organization's chairperson. GYLA claimed that this was in retaliation for its criticism of government policies.

On February 1 and 2, Ministry of Interior officials visited the office of the Human Rights Information and Documentation Center (HRIDC), claiming they wanted to learn about the organization's activities. They threatened several of the organization's employees. On February 7, an official from the Ministry's Counterterrorism Department requested that HRIDC director Ucha Nanuashvili go to the ministry to discuss the organization with senior officials. When Nanuashvili requested a formal summons, the official refused to provide one and threatened to bring him to the ministry by force. Nanuashvili did not go to the ministry and did not face any repercussions.

Key International Actors

On January 24, 2006, the Parliamentary Assembly of the Council of Europe (PACE) adopted a resolution on Georgia, concluding that despite some legislative reforms, Georgia had yet "to produce concrete results in most areas." The PACE specifically called on Georgia to prioritize ratifying the European Charter for Regional or Minority Languages, guaranteeing judicial independence, eliminating torture in prisons, and applying a policy of zero tolerance for impunity for torture and ill-treatment. The Council of Europe commissioner for human rights visited Georgia in July and made prison conditions one of his key areas of focus.

The United Nations Committee against Torture reviewed Georgia in May. The committee noted some progress but found many shortcomings, including the use of excessive force, torture, and other forms of ill-treatment by law enforcement officials, and the low number of convictions for those crimes; it also expressed concern about prison conditions. The committee called for investigations of all allegations of torture and ill-treatment and for implementation of policies to reduce prison overcrowding.

The European Union and Georgia signed the European Neighborhood Policy Action Plan, which will serve as the primary framework guiding EU-Georgian relations for the next five years. The plan sets out steps that the Georgian government should take in numerous fields including the rule of law, democracy, economic and business development, trade, energy, and resolution of internal conflicts.

The United States continued to offer the Georgian government strong public support. President Saakashvili visited the United States in July and September. On the occasion of these visits, US President George Bush praised the Georgian government for its commitment to democracy and economic reform, and expressed support for Georgia's NATO membership aspirations.

KAZAKHSTAN

President Nursultan Nazarbaev retained power in the December 2005 presidential elections, which international observers found did not meet international standards. In the year since the elections the government of Kazakhstan has flouted some of its fundamental human rights obligations, tightening control over independent media, interfering with the political opposition, and initiating politically motivated lawsuits against its critics.

Harassment and Obstruction of Political Opposition

The Democratic Choice of Kazakhstan Party (DVK), which had been banned in January 2005, attempted to register under a new name—Forward Kazakhstan!—but on June 6, 2006, the Supreme Court refused to register it because of "errors" found in the list of more than 62,000 members (50,000 are required) that was submitted as part of the application.

The government continues to bringing spurious criminal and administrative charges against opposition activists and supporters. On May 15, 2006, Alibek Zhumabaev, of the For A Just Kazakhstan bloc, received a five-year sentence for insulting the dignity and honor of the president and creating civil disorder. On July 24 Bolat Abilov, the head of the Naghyz Ak Zhol party, received a three-year suspended sentence for insulting a police officer, which bars him from running in the 2009 parliamentary elections. Abilov was also charged in 2005 with embezzlement and tax evasion, for which he is awaiting trial.

Although DVK leader Galymzhan Zhakianov was released from prison in January 2006 after having completed a four-year sentence for corruption and abuse of power while governor of Pavlodar region, he and Abilov were reportedly prevented from traveling internationally and their political activities were obstructed.

Altynbek Sarsenbaev, co-chairman of Naghyz Ak Zhol, and two of his aides were murdered on February 13, 2006. Ten individuals were convicted in August of the murders, but Sarsenbaev's family condemned the trial as a "farce." On the eve of the 2005 presidential elections another prominent opposition figure, Zamanbek Nurkadilov, a former ally of President Nazarbaev who had accused the government of corruption and joined the opposition two years previously, was found dead in his house in Almaty. The case remains unsolved. For a Just Kazakhstan claimed both murders were politically motivated and demanded independent investigations.

Media Freedom

In July 2006 amendments to Kazakhstan's media law were adopted that give the government unlimited power to close independent and opposition media outlets for technical and administrative violations, and creates unduly restrictive registration procedures for new media outlets and re-registration procedures for existing media companies.

Opposition newspapers and journalists are routinely charged with criminal libel for violating "the honor and dignity of the president." In March 2006 opposition newspaper *Juma Times* was sued for having insulted President Nazarbaev, and its operations were closed. In April the successor to *Juma Times*, *Aina Plus* newspaper, was suspended for three months for changing its thematic focus. In July journalist Zhasaral Kuanyshalin was sentenced to two years' imprisonment for having accused Nazarbaev of treason. The Committee on National Security also brought criminal charges against independent journalist Kazis Toguzbaev in June for insulting the honor and dignity of the president by blaming him for the murder of Altynbek Sarsenbaev. Toguzbaev is awaiting trial at this writing.

Independent journalists continue to be the target of physical attacks by unknown persons, which appear to be intended to intimidate and silence opposition media. On April 13 the editor for *Versiya* newspaper, Yaroslav Golyshkin, was severely beaten by two assailants. Golyshkin claims that the assault was related to an article he had published about the kidnapping of a financial police officer. On April 23 Kenzhegali Aitbakiev, an associate editor for the suspended *Aina Plus*, was also severely beaten outside his home by a group of unknown assailants, which Aitbakiev believes was in retaliation for his professional activities. A former chief editor of the opposition newspaper *Alternativa*, Albert Zhiger, was attacked by two people on October 2. The attackers allegedly said they had warned him before the attack. Zhiger is convinced he was attacked because of his reporting.

The government routinely censors opposition websites by blocking access to them through two major internet providers, Kaztelecom and Nursat.

HIV/AIDS

Although by global standards the prevalence of HIV/AIDS remains relatively low in Kazakhstan, the country suffers from one of the fastest-growing HIV/AIDS epidemics in the world. Between 1996 and October 2006 the number of officially registered HIV cases grew more than 50-fold (from 100 to over 5,440). Unofficially, the number was estimated in 2005 to be as high as 20,000.

The HIV/AIDS epidemic in Kazakhstan is fueled by human rights abuses against intravenous drug users and sex workers, who are not only the targets of stigmatization, police abuse, and false criminal charges, but also are routinely denied humane medical treatment. Police are reported to regularly rape, beat, and extort money from sex workers. Police brutality and harassment drive injecting drug users and sex workers underground and increase their unwillingness to access services. Those infected with HIV/AIDS also face widespread discrimination in employment, housing, and access to government services.

The government has taken many positive steps in the fight against HIV/AIDS, including launching a US$53 million program for 2006-2010 to fight the spread of HIV in Kazakhstan. However, Kazakhstan's HIV/AIDS laws have not been brought into compliance with international standards, and government policies, including mandatory HIV testing and the segregation of HIV-positive prisoners, are discriminatory and continue to reinforce prejudice. The government has also failed to ensure access to treatment programs for all HIV-infected persons, and to address police abuses against drug users and sex workers.

Refugee Crisis

A number of Uzbeks seeking refuge in Kazakhstan from persecution were forcibly returned to Uzbekistan to risk of torture and ill-treatment, in violation of international law.

In late November 2005 Kazakh authorities forcibly returned at least nine Uzbeks who had fled persecution in Uzbekistan, four of whom were registered with the office of the United Nations High Commissioner for Refugees (UNHCR). Upon their return to Uzbekistan some of the men were tried and sentenced, while others are awaiting trial at this writing on various charges related to "religious extremism." In addition, seven Uzbeks wanted on religious extremism charges for their alleged affiliation with Akramia (followers of an independent Islamic religious teacher) and in connection with the 2005 Andijan uprising are believed to have been forcibly returned from Kazakhstan in late November and early December 2005. To date, Kazakh authorities have not admitted their involvement in these returns.

Kazakh authorities detained but later released several other Uzbek refugees, one of whom they held for two months but then transferred to UNHCR, despite an Uzbek extradition request.

Key International Actors

Top United States officials, including Vice-President Richard Cheney, who visited Kazakhstan in May 2006, failed to comment publicly on the government's human rights record during their visits. The US ambassador to the Organization for Security and Co-operation in Europe (OSCE), by contrast, was outspoken in expressing concern about shortcomings in the Kazakh government's human rights record, including the excessively restrictive amendments to the law on mass media, in a statement on May 16. The ambassador in September also issued a strongly critical statement on Kazakhstan's bid for the 2009 OSCE chairmanship, making clear that the US would not support it due to the Kazakh government's poor human rights record. US government assistance to Kazakhstan during fiscal year 2005 was US$85.31 million, most of which ($55.69 million) was allocated to security, regional stability, and law enforcement programs. The US also supported social, economic, and democratic reform programs in Kazakhstan.

The European Union once again failed to give practical effect to the human rights clause underpinning its relationship with Kazakhstan. The conclusions of the EU-Kazakhstan Cooperation Council meeting, held on July 18, 2006, contained disappointingly vague language on human rights, noting simply that Kazakhstan must comply with OSCE standards on the human dimension if it is to be considered a viable candidate to chair the organization. The conclusions underlined the need for the Kazakh authorities to make progress in areas such as freedom of the media and the ability of political parties to operate freely, and emphasized "the need for Kazakhstan to follow the path of democratic reforms and full respect of individual human rights." During a visit to Kazakhstan on October 17 European Commissioner for External Relations and European Neighborhood Policy Benita Ferrero-Waldner noted that the country's bid for the OSCE chairmanship "cannot be done at the expense of the [organization's] core values," and expressed hope that "the necessary political reforms" would be implemented in 2007.

The adoption of amendments to Kazakhstan's media law in July 2006 went ahead despite warnings by the OSCE's special representative on freedom of the media in June that they would impose excessive restrictions on media freedom.

At a summit of the Shanghai Cooperation Organization—of which Kazakhstan is a member—held on June 15 in Shanghai, China, leaders of the six member states reaffirmed that the fight against terrorism, extremism, and separatism remained a top priority for the organization.

KYRGYZSTAN

Having come to power after the March 2005 "tulip revolution" on the promise of reform and a commitment to democracy, openness, and respect for fundamental human rights, the government of President Kurmanbek Bakiev largely failed to promote these principles. In the year-and-a-half since the ouster of former President Askar Akaev and his administration, citizens have grown disillusioned with the revolution and lost confidence in the new government and its promises. Under growing pressure from the opposition, parliament, and thousands of protesters, President Bakiev signed a new constitution on November 9, 2006, giving greater power to parliament.

Uneasy Path to Reforms

The Bakiev government in 2006 revealed itself to be fragile and unable to implement key components of its reform agenda. The government also failed to curb organized crime and bring members of crime syndicates to justice. Civil society groups strongly criticized the government for corruption and abuse of power.

A deeply disillusioned political opposition formed the movement "For Reforms" in the spring of 2006 that unites civil society and political activists, including members of parliament. The movement held several peaceful mass protests demanding that the government either adhere to the principles of the March 2005 revolution or resign. Activists demanded immediate constitutional reform, freedom of expression, independence of the mass media, and an effective government campaign against corruption and organized crime. On November 7, 2006, police used teargas and flash-bang grenades to disperse crowds after clashes broke out between Bakiev supporters and opposition protesters who had been in the central square of Bishkek since November 2.

On November 9 Bakiev and the opposition reached a compromise agreement on a new constitution that reduces presidential powers. Under the new constitution, the number of members of parliament will increase from 75 to 90, half of whom are to be elected from party lists and the other half from single-mandate districts. Parliament will form the government. The opposition believes that the new constitution paves the way for reforms.

Although in 2005 local rights groups reported greater freedom of the media following the change in government, in 2006 these achievements were rolled back. In September President Bakiev rejected the "Law on the State TV and Radio Corporation," adopted by parliament on June 8, that would have transformed the State TV and Radio Corporation into a public broadcasting entity.

Although Bakiev announced his support for the abolition of the death penalty in 2005, as of November 2006 no such legislation had been introduced. At least five people were sentenced to death in murder cases in 2006, although a moratorium on executions introduced under Akaev remained in force.

Civil society activists continued to report frequent incidents of police abuse, including torture.

Refugee Crisis

Hundreds of Uzbeks have sought refuge in Kyrgyzstan from religious and political persecution; the vast majority fled in the aftermath of the May 13, 2005 massacre in Andijan. Uzbek asylum seekers in Kyrgyzstan face harassment and a serious risk of forced return to Uzbekistan.

On August 9, 2006, the Kyrgyz government violated international law by forcibly returning to Uzbekistan five Uzbeks, four of whom the United Nations High Commissioner for Refugees (UNHCR) had recognized as mandate refugees and one asylum seeker. The five had fled to Kyrgyzstan following the Andijan massacre. The Uzbek government has accused them of violence during the Andijan events.

Kyrgyzstan ignored repeated calls from local and international rights organizations, the UN, the European Union, and the United States to refrain from returning the refugees. The returns violate the 1951 Refugee Convention, which forbids the return of refugees and asylum seekers to countries where they face persecution. Because the five men were likely to face torture in Uzbekistan, their return also violates the absolute prohibition on the return of persons to places where they risk torture, as articulated in the Convention against Torture and Other Cruel, Inhuman or Degrading Treatment or Punishment.

During the summer of 2006 Kyrgyz authorities carried out policing operations in the south, allegedly in cooperation with Uzbek security services, targeting so-called religious extremists or alleged terrorists. Many Uzbek asylum seekers were caught up in the sweeps, and UNHCR in a public statement on August 25 expressed its concern over "repeated incidents involving Kyrgyz police and migration personnel harassing asylum seekers during document checks, including alleged verbal abuse and threats of forcible return to Uzbekistan."

At least five registered asylum seekers "disappeared" in July and August from the city of Osh in southern Kyrgyzstan. Two were later reported to be in Uzbekistan, in the custody of the Andijan branch of the National Security Service.

Domestic Violence and Bride-Kidnapping

Despite progressive laws on violence against women, police and other authorities allow domestic violence and abduction for forced marriage to continue with impunity. Authorities encourage women to reconcile with their abusers instead of securing their safety and guaranteeing them access to justice. Bride-kidnapping, which is a violent and traumatic experience, is often portrayed by Kyrgyz officials as a harmless tradition.

Human Rights Defenders

Kyrgyz authorities were increasingly hostile toward civil society groups during 2006. On January 24 the minister of justice publicly instructed the ministry's registration department to launch an investigation into all nongovernmental organizations (NGOs) operating in Kyrgyzstan that receive foreign funding. Minister Marat Kaipov specifically called on the registration department to determine which NGOs funded from abroad might threaten Kyrgyzstan's national security. In March the ombudsman sent a letter to Prime Minister Feliks Kulov suggesting a ban on foreign NGOs working in Kyrgyzstan and on domestic NGOs receiving foreign funding. Civil society groups were deeply concerned about these initiatives and called on the Bakiev government not to implement them. To the government's credit, both initiatives were rejected.

KYRGYZSTAN

Reconciled to Violence

State Failure to Stop Domestic Abuse and Abduction
of Women in Kyrgyzstan

HUMAN
RIGHTS
WATCH

Government officials launched civil and criminal charges against several rights defenders—including Valentina Gritsenko, Makhamadjan Abdujaparov, Abdumalik Sharipov, and Azimjan Askarov of the group Justice, and Maksim Kuleshov of the group Peace, Light, Culture, apparently in retaliation for their work protesting the use of torture by Kyrgyz law enforcement agencies.

The Bakiev government also failed to protect civil society activists from assault by persons believed to be affiliated with organized crime. On April 12 Edil Baisalov, the head of the Coalition for Democracy and Civil Society and an outspoken critic of the increased power and influence of organized crime syndicates in the country, was physically assaulted, sustaining a skull fracture and concussion. Four days before the attack, Baisalov had led an estimated 2,000 people in a peaceful march that called for law and order in the country and protested the growth of organized crime and attempts by criminal groups to gain access to political power. Prime Minister Kulov decried the attack as politically motivated. At this writing no one had been charged with the attack.

The Kyrgyz Committee for Human Rights (KCHR) remained unregistered. The KCHR was stripped of its registration under the Akaev government for politically motivated reasons, when an alternate group was granted registration under the same name. It is illegal in Kyrgyzstan for two groups with the same name to be registered, so the genuine KCHR was denied re-registration.

Key International Actors

Kyrgyz-Russian cooperation continued to grow closer in 2006. In April President Bakiev paid his first official visit to Russia (also his first official visit abroad). Bakiev and Russian President Vladimir Putin agreed to enhance economic and military cooperation, including by increasing Russian investment in Kyrgyzstan and expanding the Russian airbase in Kant. Some suggested Russia's influence was behind the tighter restrictions on NGO activity that were proposed during the year.

The governments of Kyrgyzstan and Uzbekistan pursued a rapprochement after heightened tensions following the massive flows of Uzbek refugees into Kyrgyzstan in 2005, closer relations being signaled by the illegal return of Uzbek refugees and close cooperation between Kyrgyz and Uzbek security forces in southern Kyrgyzstan. Bakiev and Uzbek President Islam Karimov met several times during 2006 within the framework of various multilateral bodies. In October Bakiev paid an official visit to Tashkent, during which he and Karimov once again stressed the importance of cooperation in fighting terrorism and extremism.

At a summit of the Shanghai Cooperation Organization (SCO) held in Shanghai, China, in June, the leaders of Kyrgyzstan, Uzbekistan, Kazakhstan, Russia, China, and Tajikistan also agreed to intensify the fight against terrorism, separatism, and extremism within the framework of the SCO.

Relations between Kyrgyzstan and the US government were close but uneasy in 2006. Following lengthy and reportedly intense negotiations, on July 12 Kyrgyzstan and the US agreed terms for further US use of Manas airbase. As reported, the US intends to allocate more than US$150 million in total assistance, including compensation for use of the base, during 2007. US Assistant Secretary of State Richard Boucher traveled to Kyrgyzstan twice during 2006. Although Boucher raised a variety of issues with the Bakiev government ranging from the Manas airbase to the problem of corruption in Kyrgyzstan, he did not make full use of the opportunity to put human rights concerns high on the agenda. In July Kyrgyzstan expelled two employees of the US embassy for allegedly having "inappropriate contact" with leaders of local NGOs.

On July 18, 2006, the EU held its eighth meeting with Kyrgyzstan within the framework of its Partnership and Cooperation Agreement (PCA). With the exception of a call for the release of Uzbek refugees held in Kyrgyz custody (and later forcibly returned to Uzbekistan), the meeting conclusions were generally weak on human rights and failed to articulate specific benchmarks for progress required of the Kyrgyz government.

RUSSIA

The murder of journalist Anna Politkovskaia profoundly shocked the human rights movement in Russia and internationally and symbolized the further deterioration of the human rights situation in Russia. Meanwhile, the Kremlin has tightened its grip on human rights organizations and other independent institutions.

Grave human rights abuses persist in Chechnya, including torture, abductions, and forced disappearances, and the conflict threatens to spill over into other regions of the northern Caucasus.

International scrutiny of Russia's human rights record was grossly inadequate at a time when Russia assumed leadership of two international bodies in 2006, resulting in a lost opportunity to press Russia to improve its record. Russia took over chairmanship of the Committee of Ministers of the Council of Europe in May and held the presidency of the Group of Eight, hosting the organization's summit in St Petersburg in July.

The Northern Caucasus

Despite claims of stability and reconstruction in Chechnya, the ongoing armed conflict continues to claim civilian lives. Russia's federal forces play less of a direct role in Chechnya; pro-Kremlin Chechen forces under the command of Chechnya's prime minister, Ramzan Kadyrov, known as the "kadyrovtsy" now dominate law enforcement and security operations and commit grave human rights abuses.

Although local human rights groups reported a slight decline in the number of abductions leading to forced disappearances in 2006, these disappearances remain a key feature of the conflict, with as many as 5,000 people "disappeared" since 1999 and at least 54 so far in 2006. Reports of torture, especially in unofficial detention centers run by the "Kadyrovtsy" increased in 2006.

The Russian government failed to pursue any accountability process for human rights abuses committed during the course of the conflict in Chechnya. Unable to secure justice domestically, hundreds of victims of abuse have filed applications with the European Court of Human Rights (ECHR). The court issued landmark rulings on Chechnya, finding the Russian government guilty of violating the right to life and the prohibition of torture with respect to civilians who had died or been forcibly disappeared at the hands of Russia's federal troops. Hundreds of similar claims are pending before the court.

Civil Society

Nongovernmental organizations (NGOs), activists, and independent journalists working on human rights issues, particularly the war in Chechnya, faced increasing administrative and judicial harassment. In some cases, these individuals also endured persecution, threats, and physical attacks.

In October 2006 an unidentified gunman murdered *Novaya Gazeta* journalist Anna Politkovskaia. Known for her independent reporting, particularly about abuses committed in the war in Chechnya, Politkovskaia was a fierce critic of the Kremlin and the pro-Russian Chechen government. There seemed little doubt she was killed because of her work. Also, there was a rise in the number of death threats against prominent human rights defenders.

In November 2005 authorities in Dagestan held Osman Boliev—a human rights defender who investigated kidnapping and other abuses by police—for three months on charges of illegal weapons possession. He was tortured in custody and later acquitted and released. In July 2006 police charged him with aiding the terrorists who seized hundreds of hostages in a Moscow theater in 2002. Fearing for his safety, Boliev fled Russia.

In January President Vladimir V. Putin signed into law new regulations that impose burdensome reporting requirements on all NGOs and grant registration officials unprecedented authority to interfere with or restrict the work of NGOs. Under the law, officials may, without a court order, demand any document at any time from an NGO and order an intrusive inspection of an NGO's office. The law requires foreign NGOs to submit annual and quarterly work plans and permits government officials to ban planned projects or activities that conflict with Russia's national interests. All foreign NGOs had to re-register by mid-October; hundreds had to suspend their operations for weeks while their applications were pending.

In February a criminal court in Nizhni Novgorod handed Stanislav Dmitrievsky, the executive director of the Russian-Chechen Friendship Society, a two-year suspended sentence on charges of "inciting racial hatred" for articles he had published in the organization's newspaper. The articles featured statements from leading Chechen separatists that in reality amounted to protected speech. A civil court liquidated the organization, finding that it had failed to distance itself from Dmitrievsky; as of this writing the case was on appeal with the Supreme Court.

Several Russian human rights organizations were threatened with—but avoided—closure for problems with their charter or failing to report their activities. But the International Defense Assistance Center, a Russian group that represents people from Russia at the ECHR received a bill for back taxes and penalties on tax exempt grants for US$167,000. Under the tax code, money for educational, analytical, and research purposes is not taxable and the tax bill appears to be an attempt to shut down the NGO, which has 250 cases pending before the ECHR.

Xenophobia and Intolerance

Human rights groups reported more than a hundred racist and xenophobic attacks—an increase over last year—including at least 36 murders and 286 people beaten or wounded in the first nine months of the year. Notably, in September violent mobs in Kondopoga, in northern Russia, attacked residents from the Caucasus, causing hundreds to flee the city fearing for their lives. Some of the more serious attacks have been prosecuted, but police routinely characterize racist crimes as hooliganism, a misdemeanor charge, rather than use sentencing enhancement for hate-motivated crimes available in Russian law.

After months of rising tensions between the Russian and Georgian governments, in October 2006 Georgian authorities in Tbilisi briefly detained four Russian military officers on accusations of espionage. In retaliation, the Russian government deported hundreds of Georgians, forced Georgian-owned businesses to close, and asked teachers for lists of school children with Georgian last names so their parents could be investigated for visa or tax violations.

After a court upheld Moscow Mayor Yuri Luzkhov's ban on a gay and lesbian pride march, on May 27, 2006, several dozen gay activists and supporters attempted to hold two protest rallies in support of freedoms of assembly and expression. Hundreds of anti-gay protesters, including skinheads, nationalists, and Orthodox followers, attacked the participants, beating and kicking many, and chanted threats. The mayor's office had earlier made homophobic statements and circulated directives to restrict gay and lesbian rights.

Entrenched Problems

A gruesome case of hazing in the army, which resulted in a conscript having to have his legs and genitals amputated, once again pushed violent hazing in Russia's military into the spotlight. The Ministry of Defense took steps to address this crime, but maintained that violent hazing is not widespread in Russia's military and blamed television and "the decline of traditional values" for hazing rather than taking responsibility for the problem. Violent hazing results in the death of dozens of young soldiers every year, and serious injuries to thousands more. Many conscripts commit or attempt suicide and thousands defect from their units to escape harm.

Russia continued to increase attention and resources to combat HIV/AIDS. It proposed an ambitious plan to develop treatments and vaccines and raise awareness about the disease and made infectious diseases one of the key agenda items at the summit of G8 leaders in July. However, police abuse, harassment, and widespread discrimination against injection drug users and other groups at high risk for HIV/AIDS continued to interfere with HIV prevention, care, and treatment efforts. Access to treatment remained a major problem, with only a fraction of people living with the disease receiving anti-retroviral drugs.

Russia violated its obligations under the Convention against Torture by forcibly returning Uzbeks to Uzbekistan, where they face a risk of torture. In March 2006 the government announced it had returned 19 Uzbeks. In October it returned Rustam Muminov, an asylum seeker wanted on politically-motivated charges in Uzbekistan, in violation of Russian law and after the ECHR imposed an injunction to stop the deportation.

Key International Actors

While many global leaders expressed concern over developments in Russia, such as the NGO law and the murder of Politkovskaia, human rights issues remained on the margins of Russia's bi-lateral and multi-lateral relations, with many key interlocutors failing to press Russia to reform or call it to account for continuing problems, especially in Chechnya.

The EU held two rounds of human rights consultations with Russia. But human rights did not figure prominently in the broader EU-Russia agenda, which was dominated by energy security. The EU and its member states appeared to surrender to a false assumption that robust promotion of human rights would result in Russia cutting Europe's energy supply, without due concern to the long-term consequences of sidelining Russia's growing human rights problems. Germany played a key role in shaping EU policy emphasizing friendly relations at the expense of human rights; Germany's energy transportation projects with Russia were paramount in its bilateral relations.

The United States government issued several strong statements on human rights but similarly appeared to lack the appetite to challenge Russia forcefully on its worsening human rights record. However, President George Bush did issue a strong statement on Anna Politkovskaia's death and Secretary of State, Condoleezza Rice, met with her family.

In May 2006 Russia won a seat on the new United Nations Human Rights Council. After refusing access for many years, Russia issued an invitation to the UN special rapporteur on torture, but the rapporteur cancelled his visit just two days before it was planned to begin in October. The cancellation took place due to the Russian government's refusal to grant the conditions necessary for the visit, such as unfettered access to places of detention and private interviews with detainees, citing conflict with Russian law.

In January the Parliamentary Assembly of the Council of Europe adopted a strong report on Chechnya and expressed concern that many governments and the organization's Committee of Ministers failed to address human rights violations in Chechnya and impunity for them "in a regular, serious and intensive manner." The Assembly's bureau, however, subsequently decided not to renew the

Assembly's Chechnya monitoring and reporting mandate, silencing this critical voice.

The Council of Europe's Committee for the Prevention of Torture (CPT) conducted two visits to the North Caucasus in 2006, an indication of its serious concerns in the region. The Russian government is the only Council of Europe member state not to authorize the publication of CPT's reports.

In its new country strategy for Russia, the European Bank for Reconstruction and Development (EBRD) noted "concerns in the international community over the Russian authorities' continued weakening of the checks on executive power" and called for stronger protection for human and civic rights. The bank announced plans to hold its 2007 annual meeting in Kazan, in the Volga region.

SERBIA

The Serbian government's unwillingness to confront the past seriously as well as delays in undertaking legal and other reforms contributed to a still unsatisfactory human rights situation in 2006. The authorities' failure to locate Bosnian Serb wartime general Ratko Mladic undermined relations with the European Union and United States, and destabilized the governing coalition, in turn setting back its reform agenda.

Montenegro's referendum vote for independence in May 2006 led to the dissolution of the State Union of Serbia and Montenegro in June. With the dissolution of the State Union, the progressive Charter on Human and Minority Rights ceased to have effect. In September 2006 the Serbian National Assembly adopted a new draft constitution. The lack of public consultation during the drafting phase drew criticism from civil society representatives. The draft constitution was approved by national referendum in late October, and formally adopted by the National Assembly on November 8. Parliamentary elections are scheduled to follow on January 21, 2007. Among the constitution's more controversial elements is an assertion that Kosovo remains an integral part of Serbia, a move likely to further complicate negotiations over the province's status. The new constitution contains most but not all of the protections in the defunct Charter on Human and Minority Rights.

War Crimes Accountability

Serbia's cooperation with the International Criminal Tribunal for the former Yugoslavia (ICTY) came to a virtual standstill in 2006, after relative progress during 2005. The Serbian authorities' concept of cooperation—based on the so-called "voluntary surrender" of persons indicted by the ICTY rather than their arrest by the Serbian police—stopped delivering results. The failure to locate, arrest, and extradite Ratko Mladic remains the most glaring shortcoming. Under significant international pressure, the government of Serbia adopted an "Action Plan" in July 2006 with the aim of arresting Mladic and other ICTY indictees, but as of this writing the plan had yet to produce any concrete results.

The Serbian public continues to have an extremely negative perception of the ICTY as a biased institution that singles out Serbs, a view that the Serbian government did little to contradict during 2006. The two-year prison sentence imposed in July by the ICTY Trial Chamber on Naser Oric for wartime crimes against Serbs in the Srebrenica area of Bosnia provoked a public outcry in Serbia and criticism from President Boris Tadic and Prime Minister Vojislav Kostunica. Those in Serbia advocating cooperation with the ICTY assessed that the short sentence was unlikely to improve popular opinion of the tribunal in the country.

Slobodan Milosevic, former Serbian and Federal Republic of Yugoslavia president, on trial at the ICTY for genocide and crimes against humanity, died in March 2006 at the court's detention unit in the Netherlands.

Domestically, several important trials were ongoing in the War Crimes Chamber of the Belgrade District Court during 2006, although the overall number of cases dealt with by the chamber since its establishment in 2003 remains small. Among the ongoing trials are two that began in late 2005 and relate to crimes against Muslims in Bosnia: one involving two former Bosnian Serb officials from Zvornik accused of killing Bosnian Muslim civilians between May and July 1992, and the other involving five former members of the notorious "Scorpio" paramilitary unit accused of killing civilians in Trnovo in August 1995. Representatives of the victims claim that there is documentary evidence showing that the unit was under the control of the Serbian police.

In late April 2006 eight former policemen were charged with war crimes for killing 46 Kosovo Albanians in the town of Suva Reka, Kosovo, in March 1999. The trial, still pending at this writing but slated to take place in the War Crimes Chamber, will be the first in Serbia involving defendants in positions of authority within the police at the time of the alleged offenses.

Witness protection remains an obstacle to effective accountability for war crimes in the Serbian courts. A witness protection law adopted in September 2005 has helped partially to remedy the issue. The new Criminal Procedure Code, which came into force in early July 2006, should address some of the remaining concerns, by allowing courts to authorize the use of pseudonyms by witnesses giving evidence, changes of identity, and witness relocation (including to another country), without the need for a special agreement between the witness and the state.

Independence of the Judiciary

State interference in the administration of justice remains a concern. The ruling coalition used the requirement that judges be confirmed by the National Assembly as a means of blocking qualified candidates. A number of judges unanimously nominated for senior judicial office by the High Judicial Council, an appointments body that takes into account solely the candidates' expertise and merits, failed to win the required National Assembly majority, mostly because the parliamentarians from the ruling coalition refrained from voting, in most cases without any explanation. Since the law precludes the re-nomination of judges whose appointments are not endorsed by parliament, this refusal to vote for the judges contributed to disqualifying them from appointment. The process raised serious questions about the selection criteria applied by the National Assembly.

There were concerns about the ability of prosecutors to carry out their work free from state interference. Gordana Colic, a Belgrade municipal prosecutor, was suspended in June 2006 and again in July by the Republican Public Prosecutor, the country's most senior prosecutor, on the grounds of alleged incompetence. The second suspension followed a ruling by the High Judicial Council overturning the initial suspension. Colic blamed Justice Minister Zoran Stojkovic for her suspension, ascribing it to her refusal to prosecute his predecessor Vladan Batic. A final decision on her suspension was pending at this writing.

Mioljub Vitorovic, an assistant prosecutor in the Organized Crime Prosecutors' Office who led the investigation into the 2000 assassination of former Serbian President Ivan Stambolic, was forced to leave his post in July 2006 following unsubstantiated allegations that he had leaked information to the media.

Treatment of Minorities

Roma continued to face substandard economic and social conditions as well as frequent verbal abuse and physical assault. There were physical attacks on Roma in February 2006 in Nis, where a group of skinheads also broke the windows of

Roma homes and made verbal insults and threats; the perpetrators were convicted on misdemeanour charges in April and received fines. There were further physical attacks on Roma in the Belgrade suburbs in June; and in Srpski Kostur in May and June.

There were fewer inter-ethnic incidents in Vojvodina than in recent years.

Human Rights Defenders

Human rights organizations in Serbia continue to work against a backdrop of hostile criticism from the media and some political parties. The authorities failed in 2006 to react adequately to verbal attacks and threats against civil society. Government representatives frequently voiced negative opinions of civil society and nongovernmental organizations.

The most serious and ominous incident occurred in early September 2006. Witnesses described hearing what they believed (but could not confirm) were gunshots as Humanitarian Law Center Executive Director Natasa Kandic was leaving the TV B92 studio after participating in a discussion program. The police carried out a routine inquiry and stated the sounds had come from firecrackers.

Key International Actors

The government continues to list EU membership as a political priority, but the failure to arrest Ratko Mladic and overall lack of cooperation with the ICTY prompted the EU in May 2006 to suspend talks with the government on a Stabilization and Association Agreement. EU officials indicated that the talks would resume once Serbian authorities began cooperating fully with the ICTY and extradited Mladic. The European Commission's November progress report contained a negative assessment on both counts.

US government policy on Serbia remained unchanged. US officials made clear to the Serbian government that full political and economic support in its transition are contingent on full cooperation with the ICTY. In May 2006 US Secretary of State Condoleezza Rice declined to certify the continuation of aid to Serbia because of its failure to meet its international obligations, blocking US$7 million in assistance to the country.

In January 2006, the representative of the UN secretary-general on the human rights of internally displaced persons, Walter Kaelin, published the report of his 2005 visit to Serbia. His report emphasized that "[t]housands of [internally displaced persons] continue to live in very difficult conditions in collective centres and irregular settlements," and that they faced problems obtaining official documents. The report urged the authorities to find durable solutions for IDPs.

Serbia ratified the Optional Protocol to the UN Convention against Torture in September.

Kosovo

Negotiations over Kosovo's final status overshadowed its pressing human rights problems during 2006. Stalled talks between Kosovo's predominantly Albanian provisional government and the government of Serbia, which retains formal sovereignty over the province despite seven years of United Nations administration, make an internationally imposed settlement increasingly likely. Meanwhile, minorities live in marginal and sometimes dangerous circumstances, the return of refugees and displaced persons to their homes has all but come to a halt, and the justice system continues to fail victims.

Protection of Minorities

The overall number of reported inter-ethnic crimes fell. The physical separation of communities may be the most important factor. Minorities in Kosovo (including Albanians in areas where they constitute a minority) remain at risk of attack, harassment, and intimidation, and their freedom of movement remains limited in some areas. Despite anti-discrimination legislation, there is persistent discrimination in access to education, health, and other social services, including access for non-Serbs to "parallel" institutions (financed by Belgrade) in Serb majority areas.

Three incidents in June 2006 underscored the continuing threat: the murder of a 68-year-old ethnic Serb returnee in Klina, shot dead in his house; the shooting dead of a Serb youth on the road between Zvecan and Zitkovac; and the shooting of two Serbs during an attack on a gas station at Grabovac. In August a displaced Serb teacher from Decani was attacked on a return visit to the town.

Mitrovica remains a flashpoint: nine people (seven Serbs and two foreign nationals) were injured in August when a hand grenade was thrown at a cafe in the predominantly Serb northern part of the divided town. A 19-year-old Serb youth was stabbed in Mitrovica in March 2006. In June the NATO-led Kosovo peacekeeping force (KFOR) reopened its base in the north of the town and the UN Interim Administration Mission in Kosovo (UNMIK) deployed additional international police officers there.

The Roma, Ashkali and "Egyptian" (RAE) communities remain the most vulnerable and marginalized groups in Kosovo. They experience the highest rates of unemployment, educational exclusion, and infant mortality, and the greatest difficulty accessing public services. Lacking the political support of either Pristina or Belgrade, they are also largely excluded from the negotiations over Kosovo's future status.

There was movement toward a solution for displaced Roma families living since 1999 in an area of high lead contamination adjacent to the Trepca mine in Mitrovica. Most were moved to a new interim camp during 2006 while permanent accommodation is built, and medical treatment for lead exposure began. However, the new camp is itself close to a contaminated area, and some families have refused to move until their original homes are reconstructed.

Return of Refugees and Displaced Persons

A series of attacks on Serbs returning to Klina during 2006 drew condemnation from the United Nations High Commissioner for Refugees (UNHCR) and underscored the ongoing obstacles to sustainable return in Kosovo. The June killing in the town was followed in September by two bomb attacks on returnee homes, one of which seriously wounded four persons.

UNHCR statistics indicate that as of September, only 15,600 of the estimated 250,000 Serbs and other minorities displaced from Kosovo since 1999 are registered as having returned to their homes. The representative of the UN secretary general on the human rights of internally displaced persons Walter Kaelin noted in his January 2006 report on Serbia and Montenegro that for many displaced persons in Kosovo, security fears and concerns about livelihoods impede return.

In June 2006 UNHCR issued new protection guidelines for Kosovo, assessing that security improvements mean that Ashkali and "Egyptians" are generally not at risk, but reiterating that Serbs, Roma, and Albanians from areas where they constitute a minority remain at risk of being persecuted if returned. Forced returns to Kosovo from Western Europe continue, with more than a thousand RAE returned in the first nine months of 2006, despite the security risks for Roma and the precarious situation of RAE communities in general.

Impunity and Access to Justice

Kosovo's criminal justice system remains its weakest institution, fostering a climate of impunity and undermining long-term efforts to establish the rule of law. The shortcomings include: poor case management; passivity on the part of prosecutors and the police, reinforced by inadequate training; poor coordination between the local Kosovo Police Service (KPS) and UNMIK police; and problematic sentencing practices. All of these are compounded by inadequate oversight and coordination.

Inadequate witness protection remains a key obstacle to justice. Witness protection legislation remains in draft form. Kosovo lacks the basic means to protect vulnerable witnesses, much less the capacity to relocate those at high risk (in large part because of reluctance by many Western governments to accept such witnesses and their families for relocation).

UN Secretary-General Kofi Annan acknowledged in a September 2006 report to the Security Council on Kosovo that "insufficient progress has been made in investigating and prosecuting cases related to the violence of March 2004." According to UNMIK, by the end of August 2006 "over 240" people had been convicted by national judges for crimes relating to the March 2004 riots (approximately half of those charged), while 26 people have been convicted by courts with international judges. Those figures mask the reality that most March-related convictions by national judges were for misdemeanors, and lenient sentencing by international and local judges.

The slow progress on domestic war crimes prosecutions in Kosovo received a boost in 2006, although the total number of prosecutions remained extremely small. In August a panel of international judges in Kosovo found three former Kosovo Liberation Army (KLA) officers—including Gen. Selim Krasniqi, a regional commander in the post-war Kosovo Protection Corps—guilty of war crimes for the unlawful detention and abuse of ethnic Albanians at the Drenovac camp in 1998. All three were given seven-year prison terms, but Krasniqi and a second man were allowed to remain on bail pending an appeal. Charges were dropped against two other defendants, and a third was acquitted. The 2005 murder of a prosecution witness in the case remains unsolved.

In May 2006, German authorities arrested a former KLA member on an international arrest warrant for the same crimes. UNMIK has requested his extradition to face trial in Kosovo.

Despite some progress in determining the fate of those who went missing during and after the armed conflict in Kosovo, more than 2,200 cases remain, the majority ethnic Albanians.

Domestic and sexual violence against women, which remains common in Kosovo, is almost never prosecuted regardless of ethnicity. The reluctance of victims to come forward, especially in rural areas, provides only part of the explanation.

The UN secretary-general's September report indicated that the backlog in civil courts stands at over 45,000 cases, denying access to those wishing to confront discrimination or seeking to repossess their property. The failure of municipalities to implement court judgments compounds the problem.

Human Rights Defenders

The jurisdiction of the Ombudsperson Institution over UNMIK was revoked in February 2006 by a regulation limiting its oversight to the Provisional Institutions of Self-Government. This decision by UNMIK removed one of the few mechanisms for accountability over the international administration. In March UNMIK established a Human Rights Advisory Panel, with a mandate to examine human rights complaints against it, but the panel lacks autonomy and UNMIK is not bound to act on its findings. The UN Human Rights Committee noted in July that the panel "lacks the necessary authority and independence" from UNMIK to carry out its mandate.

Key International Actors

The office of United Nations Special Envoy for Kosovo Marti Ahtisaari, charged with facilitating the status talks, has drawn criticism from civil society organizations over insufficient consultation with non-Serb minorities and women, and a lack of transparency.

Joachim Rucker was appointed special representative of the secretary general and head of UNMIK in August. Upon taking office Rucker commented that he expects to be the last SRSG in Kosovo.

With little expectation that UNMIK's record of poor performance can be reversed, the European Union and the United States turned their attention toward planning for the future international presence in Kosovo once status is determined, with the EU expected to take the lead.

The six-nation Contact Group (France, Germany, Italy, Russia, the United Kingdom and the United States) continues to drive international policy on Kosovo. In June 2006 the group presented Kosovo authorities with a list of 13 priorities in the areas of security, rule of law, return of minorities, and reconstruction of homes and other sites damaged during the March 2004 riots.

In July 2006, NATO granted the Council of Europe Committee for the Prevention of Torture access to KFOR detention facilities in Kosovo, thereby facilitating implementation of a similar access agreement with UNMIK from 2004.

In its July 2006 review of UNMIK's report on human rights in Kosovo since 1999, the UN Human Rights Committee expressed concern about continuing impunity for war crimes and inter-ethnic crimes, and inadequate internal mechanisms for investigating allegations of misconduct or illegal activity by the KPS, UNMIK police, and KFOR.

TAJIKISTAN

Human rights conditions continued to worsen in Tajikistan in 2006. In the months preceding the November presidential election, the government cracked down on independent media and arrested political opposition members. Five political parties fielded candidates in the election, but the opposition remained weak and fractured and was unable to pose a serious threat to the re-election of the incumbent, Emomali Rahmonov. Said Abdullo Nuri, former Islamic Renaissance Party (IRP) chairman and once a prominent political figure in Tajikistan, died on August 9, leaving the IRP without solid unified leadership, and in September the party decided not to field a candidate in the presidential election. Two other major opposition parties, the Democratic Party of Tajikistan and the Social Democratic Party, also denounced the election and did not run candidates.

A crackdown on independent media continued, with applications for new and renewed broadcast licenses arbitrarily denied, and private television stations crippled by huge license and operating fees. Government concerns over foreign funding to nongovernmental organizations and the alleged increase in followers of extremist Muslim factions in Tajikistan led to two new draft laws that jeopardize freedom of association and religion.

November Presidential Elections

Despite President Rahmonov's claim that the November presidential election would be free, transparent, and democratic, the Organization for Security and Co-operation in Europe (OSCE) concluded that elections "were characterized by a marked absence of real competition." The OSCE also noted that "proxy voting and family voting remained a serious problem." Rahmonov has been in power since he was first elected president in 1994. A June 2003 referendum gave Rahmonov the possibility to stand for re-election for third and fourth terms, paving his way to rule the country up to 2020.

Political Arrests

Government pressure on the opposition continued in 2006 with several arrests and the suspicious death of a member of the IRP. In February a court sentenced former opposition member Tojiddin Abdurakhmonov to 16 years' imprisonment for alleged involvement in a criminal group, murder, possession of weapons, and possession of forged documents. He denies these charges. In May Sadullo Marupov, a member of the IRP, allegedly committed suicide by jumping from the third floor of a police station in the northern town of Isfara. To date it remains unclear why Marupov was arrested. The IRP claimed the autopsy showed he had been ill-treated before his fall. Two officers were later arrested on suspicion of involvement in his death.

IRP leader Said Abdullo Nuri was at the time of his death in August reportedly facing slander charges brought in May for having alleged official corruption at a public utility.

Incommunicado Detention of Jailed Opposition Leader

In October 2005 Democratic Party of Tajikistan leader Mahmadruzi Iskandarov was sentenced by a Dushanbe court to 23 years' imprisonment on terror-related charges. At the end of June 2006 party deputy chairman Jumaboi Niyozov accused the Tajik authorities of trying to hold Iskandarov in incommunicado detention; according to Niyozov, Iskandarov has not been allowed to see his relatives or his attorneys since his trial. Iskandarov is supposed to serve his sentence in a penal colony, but as of June was still being held in a Justice Ministry cell.

Nongovernmental Organizations

The government continued to clamp down on the activities of nongovernmental organizations (NGOs) that receive foreign funding, particularly in the wake of the 2005 Andijan uprising in neighboring Uzbekistan, and Kyrgyzstan's "tulip revolution." On December 2, 2005, the government introduced a draft law further reducing the freedom of NGOs to operate in Tajikistan. The law would impose mandatory state registration of public organizations and require all existing public organizations to re-register within three months. It would also grant the government excessive powers to monitor the activities of public organizations. At this writing, the draft law is pending in parliament.

Media Freedom

In February 2006 the Ministry of Communications announced a plan (unimplemented at this writing) to establish a single government-controlled communications center to which all existing internet and cell phone providers must be connected. On October 5 the ministry blocked access to five websites, claiming they were a threat to "information security in the Republic of Tajikistan." The five sites affected—centrasia.ru, ferghana.ru, tajikistantimes.ru, charogiruz.ru, and arianastorm.com—frequently carry articles critical of the government. Many believe this move was politically motivated. After much pressure from NGOs and the international community, the sites were unblocked on October 11.

Somonion TV, the only independent television station in the capital, Dushanbe, was effectively shut down in January because it failed to pay licensing fees 80 percent greater than stipulated by the original contract. The owner, Ikrom Mirzoev, claimed his company was being punished for having given fair access to opposition parties in the February 2005 parliamentary elections. According to the London-based Institute for War and Peace Reporting, other independent television stations have also been brought to court by the communications ministry to recover licensing fees of up to US$4,000; three TV stations in northern Tajikistan have already gone bankrupt. By contrast, state-run news agencies received a 25 percent increase in funding from the government.

On January 10 the government suspended BBC FM radio services to Tajikistan following a new law requiring international FM broadcasters to receive a license from the Ministry of Justice. The BBC was given 20 days to register, a procedure that usually takes up to six months. The Ministry of Justice denied that the BBC's suspension had been politically motivated. In June the registration problems were reportedly resolved, but when the BBC applied for a broadcasting license in August, the Tajikistan Committee for Television and Radio Broadcasting rejected the application, citing the absence of an applicable reciprocal agreement with the United Kingdom.

On September 18 Radio Liberty reporter Nosir Mamurzoda and Jamoliddin Sayfiddinov of Tajikistan's Avesta news agency were detained and taken in for questioning in the southern city of Qorghan-Teppa while reporting on students forced to work in cotton fields. Mamurzoda said they were released after a warning not to report news that "could destabilize the country."

Freedom of Religion

In March the government drafted a religions law that would seriously restrict religious freedoms, although at this writing parliament had postponed voting on the bill due to heavy criticism from religious communities. The law would make registration of all religious associations (a procedure requiring 200 signatures) mandatory. The law would impose state control over religious education, require state-approved higher education for all religious leaders, limit the number of mosques in Tajikistan, and impose state control over pilgrimages to Mecca. It would also ban teaching religion to children younger than seven, proselytism, and the leading of religious communities by foreigners.

In February 2006 the government announced that it would demolish the only remaining synagogue in Tajikistan, to make way for the Palace of the Nations, the intended residence of the Tajik president. The synagogue serves the Bukharian Jewish community in Dushanbe. Authorities demolished the ritual bathhouse, classroom, and kosher butchery, but halted further demolition after international outcry. The government has made no reparations for the damage, and it remains unclear whether it intends to resume demolition.

Key International Actors

Tajikistan and China strengthened their relationship during a visit from Chinese Premier Jen Jaibao to Dushanbe in September 2006 for an economic meeting of the Shanghai Cooperation Organization, with the signing of various bilateral cooperation agreements. In June 2006 Tajikistan and China signed a deal for the reconstruction of the Dushanbe-Chanak highway, and China provided Tajikistan with a long-term loan of $281 million for implementation of the project.

The United States offered security and development assistance to Tajikistan in an attempt to increase its presence in Central Asia. Assistant Secretary of State Richard Boucher visited Tajikistan in May, and then-Secretary of Defense Donald Rumsfeld visited in July. Both failed to highlight human rights concerns and instead emphasized the US government's interest in expanding security and economic cooperation. In March the United States and Tajikistan signed an agreement to increase border security and law enforcement cooperation.

Sergei Mironov, chairman of Russia's Federation Council (upper house of parliament), visited Dushanbe in August 2006 to attend an inter-parliamentary forum. Many viewed the visit as a sign of Russia's support for Rahmonov in the November presidential election. At the parliamentary forum, Rahmonov commented that Russia is Tajikistan's main strategic ally. Also in August, Russian President Vladimir Putin met Rahmanov.

Tajikistan remains the greatest per capita beneficiary of European Commission assistance in Central Asia. However, the commission ended its humanitarian aid program to Tajikistan in June, making a final donation of US$6.4 million. In May the European Union issued a statement during an OSCE Permanent Council meeting in Vienna welcoming President Rahmonov's commitment to holding free, transparent, and democratic elections in November, but noting with concern that consolidation of power in Tajikistan had come at the expense of transparency, democratic freedoms, and independent civil society.

TURKEY

The government of Prime Minister Recep Tayyip Erdoğan failed during 2006 to implement key reforms necessary to consolidate the human rights progress of the past years. Entrenched state forces, including the military, continued to resist reform. Illegal armed groups, as well as rogue elements of the security forces, conducted violent attacks that threaten the reform process, although clashes decreased after the Kurdistan Workers' Party (PKK) declared a ceasefire in October.

Disproportionate Use of Lethal Force

There was a sharp increase in indiscriminate and disproportionate use of lethal force by security forces in dealing with protestors, as well as during normal policing. In March youths attending the funerals of PKK militants clashed with police, throwing stones and petrol bombs. During the ensuing street battles in Diyarbakır and other cities police fired bullets, gas grenades, and stones at rioters, killing eight people, including innocent bystanders and four children under 10 years of age. In other incidents during 2006, police shot and killed 13 persons either in error or because they were deemed not to have heeded orders to stop. Instead of conducting an inquiry into the use of lethal force resulting in these deaths, in June the government amended the Anti-Terror Law, authorizing security forces "to use weapons directly and without delay."

Torture and Ill-Treatment in Police Stations

Reports of torture and ill-treatment remain much lower than in the mid-1990s. However, during the March disturbances in Diyarbakır, hundreds of people were detained and allegedly tortured, including approximately two hundred children. Almost all those detained during this time reported being beaten, stripped of their clothes, hosed with cold water, or deprived of food.

Freedom of Expression

More than 50 individuals were indicted for statements or speeches that questioned state policy on controversial topics such as religion, ethnicity, and the role of the army. The government failed to abolish laws that restrict speech.

In April an Adana court sentenced broadcaster Sabri Ejder Öziç to six months of imprisonment under article 301 of the Turkish Criminal Code for "insulting parliament" by describing a decision to allow foreign troops on Turkish territory as a "terrorist act". Öziç is at liberty pending appeal. In July the Supreme Court upheld a six-month prison sentence against Hrant Dink, editor of the newspaper Agos (Furrow), under article 301 for "insulting Turkishness" in an editorial concerning the 1915 massacres of Armenians in Anatolia. The sentence was suspended, but other speech-related charges against Dink are pending. In September British artist Michael Dickinson was imprisoned for two weeks and subsequently deported for publishing a collage showing Prime Minister Erdoğan as US President Bush's poodle.

İpek Çalışlar, biographer of Latife Uşaklıgıl, first wife of Mustafa Kemal Atatürk, founder of the Turkish republic, is on trial under the Law to Protect Atatürk. In a newspaper interview, Çalışlar had related an anecdote, supposedly shameful, that Kemal had donned his wife's hijab once in 1923 to escape an armed rival.

Minority Rights

The Supreme Council for Radio and Television finally took the important step of permitting television and radio broadcasting in Kurdish, although only for one hour a day. Other restraints on minority languages in the public arena remain. In April, for example, a Diyarbakir court closed the Kurdish Democracy Culture and Solidarity Association (Kürt-Der) for infringing the Associations' Law by conducting its internal business in Kurdish.

Human Rights Defenders

Human rights defenders are routinely placed under surveillance, often prevented from holding public events, and routinely prosecuted for various speech and assembly offences. In March Eren Keskin, president of the Istanbul Human Rights Association (HRA), was sentenced to 10 months of imprisonment, converted to a fine, for "insulting the armed forces" because she had publicized sexual assaults of women by soldiers. In October Diyarbakır Criminal Court sentenced Rıdvan Kızgın, former Bingöl HRA branch president, to three years and nine months of imprisonment for "aiding an illegal organisation" because he had prepared a report on the killing, apparently by security forces, of five villagers in Yumakli village in Bingöl in 2003. Right-wing groups disrupted activities by human rights organizations, including a press conference on internal displacement organised by the Turkish Economic and Social Studies Foundation (TESEV) in July. Also in July, Ayhan Bilgen, president of the Association for Human Rights and Solidarity with Oppressed People (Mazlum-Der) asked for police protection after receiving death threats from the Turkish Revenge Brigade (TİT), which were similar to threats that preceded a near-lethal attack on HRA president Akın Birdal in 1998.

Internal Displacement

The Turkish government has failed to facilitate the return of the estimated 378,335 internally displaced persons (IDPs) from the southeast who were forced by the army to flee their villages during the armed conflict with the PKK in the 1980s and 1990s. The government has failed to rehabilitate the basic infrastructure of most villages destroyed by the army during the conflict; many villages have no electricity, telephone access, or schools. What is more, the security situation in some regions remains poor; the 58,000 village guards—Kurds armed and paid by the government to fight the PKK—often occupy or use vacated lands, and have killed 18 people, including would-be returnees, in the past four years.

IDPs who do return to their villages cannot afford to rebuild their homes or reestablish agriculture. A 2004 compensation law, which could have provided the financial means to support IDPs who want to return to their villages, has been interpreted and applied by some provincial compensation commissions so as to pay derisory sums (often as low as US$3,000) or exclude eligible IDPs from compensation altogether.

Bombings by Military and Illegal Opposition Groups

In November 2005 grenades thrown into a bookshop in Şemdinli, Hakkari province, killed one man and wounded eight. Local people captured three gendarmes in the vicinity. Gendarmes in an armored vehicle fired on the crowd at the scene of the crime, killing another man. In June Van Criminal Court sentenced two of the gendarme officers to 39 years imprisonment for the murder and for forming a gang.

Bombings in western Turkey by the Kurdistan Freedom Falcons (TAK) killed eight and injured scores, while the right-wing TİT claimed responsibility for a bomb in Diyarbakır that killed 11 people, including seven children. The identity and status of these groups is unclear, but they pose a significant threat to Turkey's fragile reform process.

Freedom of Religion

Women who wear the headscarf for religious reasons are still denied access to higher education, the civil service, and political life. However, during 2006 the ban was applied much more broadly than only to state institutions. In late 2005, the Administrative Supreme Court upheld a ruling that Aytaç Kılınç, a teacher, could not be promoted because she wore a headscarf when she was not on school premises. Officials also barred mothers who wear the headscarf from accompanying their children to school ceremonies and swimming pools; lawyers and journalists were ejected from courtrooms and public meetings at universities because they refused to remove their headscarf.

Key International Actors

Turkey's European Union (EU) candidacy remains the most effective international factor in fostering respect for human rights in the country. EU Enlargement Commissioner, Olli Rehn, repeatedly emphasized the commission's commitment to Turkey's integration in Europe, while frankly addressing shortcomings in reform. The EU Progress Report on Turkey published in November referred to the "significant political influence" exercised by the military and suggested that military leaders should confine public statements to military and defence matters.

The report criticized continuing violations of freedom of expression and concluded that Turkey had made little progress in ensuring the rights of minorities.

In September the Council of Europe's Committee for the Prevention of Torture (CPT) reported on its December 2005 visit to Turkey. It noted "encouraging" signs in the fight against torture, but expressed concern about continued cases of abuse, which included beatings and squeezing of testicles, in some police stations. The CPT also criticized the widespread use in mental institutions of electroconvulsive therapy without anaesthetic and muscle relaxants, and recommended the introduction of a comprehensive mental health law.

During 2006 the European Court of Human Rights issued approximately 200 judgments against Turkey for torture, unfair trial, violations of free expression, extrajudicial execution, and other violations. In January, for example, the court found the Turkish government had violated the right to life of Fahriye and Mahmut Mordeniz, a married couple who "disappeared" after being taken from their Diyarbakır home by police in 1996 (Mordeniz v. Turkey).

Turkey was visited by three UN human rights monitors in 2006. The UN special rapporteur on the promotion and protection of human rights and fundamental freedoms while countering terrorism, Martin Scheinin, visited the country in February. Commenting on the situation in the southeast, he noted that Turkey's experience shows that "certain counter-terrorism measures taken by the State may have consequences that are incompatible with human rights." Scheinin also expressed concern about the overly broad definition of terrorism in Turkey's anti-terror act. In May Yakin Ertürk, the special rapporteur on violence against women, visited Turkey specifically to investigate the reported frequent incidents of suicide among women and girls in some parts of the country, and found that "the patriarchal order and the human rights violations that go along with it—for example, forced and early marriages, domestic violence, and denial of reproductive rights— are often key contributing factors to suicides of women and girls in Southeast and Eastern Turkey." At the conclusion of its visit to Turkey in October, the UN working group on arbitrary detention expressed "great concern" about the fact that the new legislative safeguards against torture and arbitrary detention introduced in 2005 did not apply to individuals held on suspicion of terrorism related crimes, creating "in practice two criminal justice systems in Turkey."

TURKMENISTAN

Turkmenistan is one of the world's most repressive and closed countries. Authorities severely suppress all forms of dissent and isolate the population from the outside world. Saparmuad Niazov is president-for-life, with a pervasive personality cult. Under international pressure the government reduced harassment of some followers of minority religions, released several people from unwarranted detention in prison and psychiatric facilities, and allowed one dissident to travel abroad, but otherwise its human rights record in 2006 was disastrous.

Persecution of Human Rights Defenders and Independent Journalists

The majority of independent nongovernmental organizations are denied registration under politically motivated pretexts. To prevent uncensored information about Turkmenistan from reaching the outside world, the government continually seeks to silence journalists and rights defenders who work informally with foreign organizations. In March 2006 two Radio Liberty correspondents, Mered Khommadov and Jamadurdy Ovezov, were detained for 10 days on false charges of "hooliganism" and were released only after being forced to sign a statement promising not to work with the radio station. Also in March, Anna Kurbanova, a correspondent of the Russian news agency ITAR-TASS, was stripped of her accreditation reportedly in retaliation for critical reporting about pension reform.

Ogulsapar Muradova, a Radio Liberty correspondent, and Amandurdy Amanklychev and Sapardurdy Khajiev, members of the Turkmenistan Helsinki Foundation (THF), a Bulgaria-based rights organization, were arrested in Ashgabad in June. President Niazov publicly accused the three of "subversive activities" and "gathering slanderous information to spread public discontent." Security services also cited Amanklychev's participation in human rights trainings in Poland and Ukraine and his work with British and French journalists who visited Turkmenistan and reported on the human rights situation there. Elena Ovezova, another THF member, and Muradova's three adult children were also detained but released without charge 12 days later.

In August Muradova, Amanklychev, and Khajiev were sentenced in a closed trial to prison terms of six to seven years on false charges of "illegal weapons possession." On September 14, Muradova's children learned that she had died in Ministry of National Security custody. They saw her body and reported to relatives abroad that it bore signs of a violent death, though Turkmen officials declared that she died of "natural causes." Security agents harassed and threatened Muradova's children following her death. The fate and whereabouts of Amanklychev and Khajiev remain unknown.

On at least two occasions authorities in border areas seized Russian-language publications intended for sale in Turkmenistan and said that they could no longer be imported.

Abuse of Psychiatry

The government continued to abuse psychiatry to suppress dissent. For example, Kakabai Tejenov was subjected to nine months of forced psychiatric hospitalization in retaliation for sending a letter abroad about rights violations in Turkmenistan; he was released in October. Gurbandurdy Durdykuliev, who was incarcerated in a special psychiatric hospital in 2004 for calling for a political demonstration, was released on April 11, 2006, after 54 members of the US Congress signed a petition calling for his release.

Persecuting "Internal Enemies"

President Niazov continued Stalin-style purges of the government, identifying new "enemies" and corrupt bureaucrats among high-ranking officials. Former Prosecutor General Kurbanbibi Atajanova, who played a leading role in prosecuting people for the November 2002 assassination attempt against Niazov, was arrested in April 2006. Editors of two government periodicals were also "purged"; one was sentenced in December 2005 to eight years' imprisonment for hiring people related to "traitors."

In July 2006 about 30 convicted high-ranking officials were transferred to a special prison in Ovadandepe created in 2003 for political prisoners. The fate of more than 60 people convicted on charges related to the 2002 assassination attempt remains unknown, but eight such individuals were amnestied in October, having "repented"; also amnestied was the former mufti of Turkmenistan, who had been sentenced in 2004 to 22 years in prison on charges of anti-government activities.

Freedom of Movement

Thousands of people, including religious minorities and perceived dissidents and their relatives, are on "blacklists" banning them from leaving the country. In May 2006 security services agents removed Shageldy Atakov, a Baptist minister previously imprisoned for his religious work, from a scheduled flight to Moscow. Authorities have prevented Svetlana Orazova—whose brother heads an exiled political opposition movement in Sweden—and her family from leaving Turkmenistan, even though they have dual Russian-Turkmen citizenship.

The government allowed writer Rakhim Esenov to travel abroad in April to receive an award, after intervention by the US embassy and the Organization for Security and Co-operation in Europe (OSCE). A criminal investigation against Esenov for publication of his novel remains open.

The government continues to use internal exile to punish "enemies." In April Khajiniaz Soiunova—whose husband is active in an exiled opposition movement—and her two daughters were forcibly expelled from Ashgabad to western Turkmenistan, where they had to find their own housing. The authorities confiscated their passports and ordered them not to leave the city of their internal exile without a special permit.

Religious Repression and Ethnic Discrimination

Several new religious groups and confessions were registered, but the state strictly limits religious freedom. The activities of unregistered religious organizations remain banned. Registered churches may lawfully hold services only in certain facilities, but many do not have such facilities and had problems renting them. On June 10, 2006, Alexander Frolov, a Russian citizen, was deported from Turkmenistan for conducting worship at home and attempting to import Christian literature. In December 2005 seven members of a registered Baptist church were detained in eastern Turkmenistan and intimidated by authorities for attempting to worship in a private home.

On November 17, 2005, Hare Krishna believer Cheper Annaniiazova was sentenced to seven years in prison for visiting Kazakhstan in 2003 without an exit visa, a harsh sentence likely intended to intimidate other Hare Krishna believers; she was released under amnesty in October 2006.

Ethnic minorities continue to face discrimination in admission to educational institutions and in the hiring process, and in some cases cannot study their mother tongues. Teachers who signed an appeal to President Niazov to re-establish education in Uzbek were questioned by police about "sowing public dissent" and some were subsequently laid off, though without explicit reference to the appeal. Following international criticism, in November 2005 the constitution was amended to allow non-ethnic Turkmen to run for president. Another amendment precludes citizens of other states from being recognized as Turkmen citizens, which may cause future problems for tens of thousands who had obtained dual Russian-Turkmen citizenship before this was banned in 2003. During his visit to Turkmenistan in March, the OSCE High Commissioner on National Minorities raised with the country's leadership the issues of minorities in education and the resettlement of minority communities in northern Turkmenistan.

Social and Economic Regression

Despite official declarations that Turkmenistan has entered a "golden era," international organizations noted continuing degradation of public welfare. New pension legislation resulted in about 100,000 people losing their pensions in early 2006, which led to rising social tensions. During the first-ever review of Turkmenistan by the UN Committee on the Rights of the Child, the government came under criticism for the reduction of compulsory education from 10 to nine years and for the fact that children attend school for an average of 30 days fewer than the international standard, due in part to child labor in cotton fields. The committee also expressed concern about the domination of the curriculum by the teachings of President Niazov's book, *Ruhnama*.

Prison Conditions

Serious concerns remain about torture and ill-treatment in custody and about prison conditions. New rules introduced in January 2006 significantly decreased the number of inmates' family visits and food packages. Poor conditions led to unrest in October in a women's prison facility in Dashaguz. The habitual government response to severe prison overcrowding is blanket amnesties, and in October Niazov declared amnesty for about 10,000 of Turkmenistan's 18,000 prison inmates. The government persisted in its refusal to grant international organizations access to prisons.

Key International Actors

An October report on Turkmenistan by the UN secretary-general concluded that "gross and systematic violations of human rights continued... notwithstanding gestures made by the Government." The report noted the government's failure to issue an invitation to UN thematic special mechanisms and repeated a recommendation that all 10 be invited to visit Turkmenistan. The Third Committee of the UN General Assembly adopted a resolution on Turkmenistan in December 2005 welcoming several government steps, but expressing "grave concern" about a number of human rights problems.

Citing human rights concerns, the European Parliament in October 2006 adopted a resolution to stop further consideration of an interim trade agreement with Turkmenistan.

The European Bank for Reconstruction and Development issued a new country strategy for Turkmenistan in September, in which it reaffirmed its suspension of any public sector investment due to the government's "continued failure to take any measures which would indicate a willingness to make progress towards multi-party democracy, pluralistic society and a market-based economy." The bank also reaffirmed private sector investment only if such investments were not effectively controlled by state entities and if government officials could not personally benefit from them.

The European Union and the United States co-sponsored the December 2005 UN General Assembly resolution on Turkmenistan. The US government successfully pressed the Turkmen government on several issues noted above, but in contrast to prior years it did not initiate a UN resolution in 2006; it also resisted using US policy tools for increased pressure for positive change. It has continued to grant Turkmenistan a waiver under the Jackson-Vanik amendment, which denies certain trade benefits to countries that severely limit the right to emigrate. Despite the US Commission on International Religious Freedom's recommendation, the US State Department again did not designate Turkmenistan a "country of particular concern" under the terms of the International Religious Freedom Act.

UKRAINE

The government was incapacitated by political crises for six months of 2006, resulting in little progress in improving Ukraine's key human rights problems and dashing the hopes many had in the Orange Revolution's promise of reform. While civil society institutions operate mostly without government interference, police abuse and violations of the rights of vulnerable groups—including migrants, asylum seekers, and people living with or at risk of HIV/AIDS—continue to mar Ukraine's human rights record.

The Organization for Security and Cooperation in Europe (OSCE) found the 2006 parliamentary elections to be free and fair. In February the new parliament adopted a vote of no-confidence in the government of Viktor Yushchenko; after much political struggle a new government was formed in August headed by Viktor Yanukovich, whom Yushchenko had defeated in the 2004 and 2005 presidential elections.

Media Freedom and Freedom of Information

Ending government interference with the media remains one of the human rights achievements of the Yushchenko presidency. But numerous, anonymous attacks and threats persisted against journalists, particularly those based in Ukraine's provinces, who investigated or exposed corruption or other government malfeasance. The US-based Committee to Protect Journalists concluded that these attacks, and police reluctance in some cases to pursue the perpetrators, were "helping to foster an atmosphere of impunity against independent journalists."

Upon entering office in 2005, Yushchenko pledged to prioritize the investigation into the unsolved kidnapping and murder of investigative journalist Georgy Gongadze in 2000. Many considered progress on this a political litmus test of the seriousness with which the new authorities were pursuing the restoration of the rule of law in Ukraine. The trial of three police officers charged with the murder began on January 9, 2006, in the Kiev Court of Appeals. The court closed parts of the trial to the public after one of the defense lawyers said that the media presence was harming the health of his client. Hearings were postponed several times and, at this writing, the trial was ongoing. Media freedom activists expressed

UKRAINE

Rhetoric and Risk

Human Rights Abuses Impeding Ukraine's
Fight against HIV/AIDS

HUMAN
RIGHTS
WATCH

frustration that the court would not admit as evidence tape recordings implicating high level government officials in Gongadze's murder.

Torture and Conditions in Detention

Reports of torture and ill-treatment by police persisted, as did unduly long periods of pretrial custody. Prison conditions in most facilities in Ukraine are appalling; the most serious problems being overcrowding and lack of adequate nutrition and medical care in prisons. There have been at least four reported cases of prisoners attempting suicide to call attention to the poor conditions in detention.

In March the European Court for Human Rights ruled in *Melnik v. Ukraine* that overcrowded, unsanitary prison conditions and poor medical care contributed to the illness of a prisoner and amounted to degrading treatment. The court also faulted Ukraine for apparently failing to provide an effective mechanism for inmates to complain about conditions in detention.

Human Rights Abuses Fueling the HIV/AIDS Epidemic

Ukraine's HIV/AIDS epidemic is the worst in Europe and one of the fastest-growing in the world. The Ukrainian government has taken a number of positive steps to fight HIV/AIDS, chiefly in the area of legislative and policy reform. But these important commitments are being undermined by widespread human rights abuses against drug users, sex workers, and people living with HIV/AIDS in the criminal justice and health systems.

Human Rights Watch's research in 2005 and 2006 found that police subject drug users and sex workers to physical and psychological pressure as a means to extort money or information from them. These abuses, together with direct police interference with the delivery of HIV prevention information and services, drive those at highest risk of HIV/AIDS away from lifesaving services that the government has pledged to provide. People living with and at high risk of HIV/AIDS also face widespread discrimination in the health care system. They are denied medical treatment, and face violations of their privacy.

The criminalization of possession of small amounts of narcotics further accelerates HIV infection rates by driving those most vulnerable to HIV infection away from prevention services. It also exposes many to health risks in prison that would put them at risk of contracting HIV or that would exacerbate an existing HIV infection. Methadone and buprenorphine, widely recognized as among the most effective means to treat opiate dependence, are critical to prevent HIV among injection drug users and to support antiretroviral treatment adherence for HIV-positive injection drug users. Ukraine began to provide buprenorphine on a limited basis in 2005. In 2006, the Ministry of Health worked with international health experts and civil society organizations to address barriers to providing methadone, but to date it is unavailable.

Migrants and Refugees

Migration and asylum issues remained high on the government's agenda, particularly in the context of its relationship with the European Union. The Ukrainian asylum system barely functions due to a highly decentralized structure spanning several government agencies and departments. Plans for a single migration system to deal with all aspects of migration and asylum have progressed, but reform has been slow, political interference in the system is common and abuses of migrants and asylum seekers' rights continue (see also chapter on EU externalization policy).

Ukrainian authorities in February deported 11 Uzbek asylum seekers without giving them the opportunity to appeal their negative asylum determinations; nine had previously registered as asylum seekers with the United Nations High Commissioner for Refugees (UNHCR) in Ukraine. The forcible return of the Uzbeks was a clear violation of Ukraine's international obligation not to transfer any person to a place where his life or freedom would be under threat or where he would be at risk of torture. The government's decision to return the men was widely condemned by the international community.

With the accession to the EU of countries along Ukraine's western border, migrants increasingly transit through Ukraine to reach EU territory. Police and border guards apprehend and detain undocumented migrants and asylum-seekers, often in appalling conditions in detention facilities on the border. A large number of migrants who manage to cross the border are sent back to Ukraine in accordance with Ukraine's bilateral readmission agreements with Poland, Hungary, and Slovakia.

In October 2006, the EU and Ukraine concluded a readmission agreement that required Ukraine to readmit any undocumented third country national who transited through Ukraine before gaining access to EU territory. Human rights and refugee protection groups advocated for an agreement that would delay such returns until Ukraine's migration and asylum systems operated in conformity with international human rights standards. The final agreement contained a two-year "grace period" delaying such returns, but human right groups expressed concern that it would take much longer for Ukraine to implement reforms to ensure the rights of migrants and asylum seekers.

Human Trafficking and Discrimination against Women

Women continue to face gender-based employment discrimination and hold disproportionately few senior positions in the government and private sector. No women serve in the Cabinet of Ministers, and only one of 27 parliamentary committees is headed by a woman. The government has a mixed record of progress in combating discrimination. In May the minister of justice ordered all draft legislation to undergo a gender analysis and formed an expert panel for this purpose. Framework legislation on gender equality adopted in 2005 remains largely ineffective because implementing legislation has not been enacted.

On November 21, 2005, the government launched a national campaign to combat violence against women as part of a wider program under the Parliamentary Assembly of the Council of Europe (PACE).

Amendments to the criminal code adopted in January criminalize human trafficking and seek to bring Ukraine in line with its international commitments. Although the authorities created a 500-person anti-trafficking department, the majority of convicted traffickers received probation instead of prison sentences which a UN expert in October attributed to corruption in law enforcement and the judiciary. The government adopted a multi-year policy to fight human trafficking and took steps to raise awareness about trafficking, assist victims, and educate law enforcement. Despite these efforts, Ukraine remained a country of transit and destination for large numbers of trafficked persons.

Key International Actors

The UN Human Rights Committee's concluding observations on Ukraine's periodic report noted several positive government steps, such as the establishment of a witness protection program, but expressed concerns in a wide range of areas, including police mistreatment of detainees, the need to intensify efforts to fight domestic violence, and the lack of transparency in the appointment of the judiciary.

The Parliamentary Assembly of the Council of Europe (PACE) agreed with other international monitors in its assessment of the March elections as free and fair. PACE also expressed concerns about the parliamentary crises and several human rights problems but it noted "significant progress" by Ukraine in protecting human rights and building democracy.

The European Court of Human Rights (ECHR) ruled on an increased number of complaints against Ukraine in 2006. The court issued 160 judgments from October 2005 to November 2006, compared to 64 in the same period the year before.

Citing this improvement in the political process, in September the European Commission proposed opening preliminary negotiations on an enhanced version of its Partnership and Cooperation Agreement with Ukraine.

In March, the US and Ukraine signed an agreement aimed at facilitating the country's eventual entry into the World Trade Organization. The US also removed trade restrictions in place against Ukraine since the Cold War. The US Agency for International Development (USAID) substantially increased the flow of aid to Ukraine in 2006, budgeting over US$190 million in assistance.

Uzbekistan

Human rights conditions in Uzbekistan deteriorated further in 2006. In the year-and-a-half since Uzbek government forces killed hundreds of unarmed protestors in the city of Andijan on May 13, 2005, no one has been held accountable for the killings. Instead, the authorities conducted closed trials and continued their campaign to silence critics of the government's version of events. Many local and international civil society groups and media outlets had to cease operation, and human rights defenders and independent journalists were imprisoned or fled the country. The government secured the extradition of refugees and asylum seekers on grounds that in numerous cases appeared to be politically motivated.

Accountability for the Andijan Massacre

The Uzbek government has adamantly rejected numerous and repeated calls for an independent international inquiry into the Andijan massacre. To this day the circumstances surrounding it have not been clarified, and those responsible for the killings have not been held accountable.

In fall 2005 the Uzbek authorities began a series of trials related to the Andijan events. Between September 2005 and July 2006 at least 303 people were convicted and sentenced to lengthy prison terms in 22 trials—including one trial of Andijan Interior Ministry employees and another involving Andijan prison staff and soldiers. Some of the people tried were convicted of terrorism, the courts finding that the defendants had been plotting to set up an Islamic caliphate in Uzbekistan. With the exception of the first trial, held in the Supreme Court between September and November 2005, all trials were closed to the public.

The government portrayed the trials as a means of clarifying what happened in Andijan, but did nothing to answer the outstanding questions about the scale of—and responsibility for—the massacre. Instead, the trials appear largely to have been staged to support the government's version of events and to provide justification for the crackdown that followed. In a January 2006 statement the European Union expressed "grave concern" about the closed nature of the trials.

HUMAN
RIGHTS
WATCH

THE ANDIJAN MASSACRE
One Year Later—Still No Justice

"No civilians were killed."
Uzbek President Islam Karimov
at a press conference on May 17, 2005

Small numbered plaques allegedly
mark anonymous graves in a cemetery
on the outskirts of Andijan,
Uzbekistan, on Tuesday, May 17, 2005.
© Misha Japaridze/Associated Press

Persecution of Human Rights Defenders and Independent Journalists

Since the Andijan massacre the Uzbek government has engaged in a fierce crackdown on human rights defenders and independent journalists. Those who seek to speak out about the Andijan events and highlight the lack of accountability for the crimes committed are the targets of harassment and other forms of retaliation.

In 2006 at least nine human rights defenders and one journalist were convicted and imprisoned on politically motivated charges: Saidjahon Zainabitdinov (seven years), Dilmurod Mukhiddinov (five years), Rasul Khudainazarov (10 years), Mutabar Tojibaeva (eight years), Jamol Kutliev (seven years), Azam Farmonov (nine years), Alisher Karamatov (nine years), Mamarajab Nazarov (three-and-a-half years), Ulugbek Khaidarov (six years), and Yadgar Turlibekov (three-and-a-half years). Khaidarov was released in November. Additionally, four members of the human rights group Ezgulik were convicted and released on parole. The government closed Ezgulik's Andijan branch in February 2006.

Some human rights defenders fled the country in fear for their personal security after being subjected to harassment, threats of arrest, and beatings. For example, Tolib Yakubov, chair of the Human Rights Society of Uzbekistan, fled after a series of threats, and Rakhmatulla Alibaev fled after he was badly beaten by an unknown person.

In August Bakhtiyor Hamraev, a defender living in Jizzakh, was attacked in his home by a group of vigilantes, presumably government proxies, during a visit by a Western diplomat. Most of the human rights defenders who continue to work in Uzbekistan are routinely followed by plainclothes men, videotaped by the authorities, and occasionally prevented from leaving their apartments (for example to stop them from monitoring a trial). The authorities often deny exit visas to human rights defenders and civil society activists to prevent them from participating in international conferences or similar events.

Dadakhon Khasanov, a well known songwriter who wrote a song sharply criticizing the government's role in the Andijan massacre, was convicted in September 2006 of "anti-state activities" and received a suspended sentence. Independent journalist Djamshid Karimov has been missing since September 12 and is believed to be held in a psychiatric hospital in Samarqand.

Pressure on Civil Society

The authorities continued to close or disrupt the work of numerous local and international nongovernmental organizations. Many local groups had to cease operations as a result. In addition, international organizations closed by the authorities in 2006 alone included Freedom House, the Eurasia Foundation, Counterpart International, ABA/CEELI, Winrock International, and Crosslink Development International.

Refugee Crisis

The government has increased pressure on other countries to return alleged "criminals" to Uzbekistan so they can face trial. The government has deemed some of the refugees who fled the Andijan massacre terrorists in order to justify their return. Several dozen people who were seeking refuge in Russia, Ukraine, Kazakhstan, and Kyrgyzstan were deported to Uzbekistan or kidnapped and taken to Uzbekistan.

In addition, the government tried to assure refugees who had been evacuated in the summer of 2005 from Kyrgyzstan and resettled in Europe and the United States that they could return home without fear of reprisals; a number of refugees did return during 2006.

Details about the whereabouts and fate of those returned to Uzbekistan are scarce, but there is every reason to be concerned about their safety and well being. The Uzbek government has steadfastly denied access by independent monitors to those who have been extradited or kidnapped and subsequently imprisoned. The state-controlled media has published statements by returned refugees saying that they are happy to be home and are under no pressure. But in the current repressive climate it is extremely difficult to determine how the government is treating these individuals.

On March 17, 2006, the government ordered the closure of the Tashkent office of the UN High Commissioner for Refugees (UNHCR), presumably in retaliation for the agency's intensive and laudable efforts to protect Uzbek refugees in Kazakhstan and elsewhere from forced return to persecution in Uzbekistan.

Religious Persecution

Uzbek authorities continued their unrelenting, multi-year campaign of unlawful arrest, torture, and imprisonment of Muslims who practice their faith outside state controls or who belong to unregistered religious organizations, branding peaceful religious believers as "religious extremists." Dozens were arrested or convicted in 2006 on charges related to religious "extremism." Human Rights Watch documented abuses in many of these cases.

Torture

In 2006 there was no fundamental change in the widespread use of torture or in policies and practices that could effectively combat torture. Authorities persist in their refusal to acknowledge the main conclusion of the UN special rapporteur on torture, that "torture or similar ill-treatment is systematic," and have not taken any meaningful steps on most of the special rapporteur's recommendations. According to recent Uzbek government assertions, habeas corpus will be implemented in January 2008.

As noted by the special rapporteur in his oral report to the UN Human Rights Council in September 2006, "the very fact that torture is still practiced systematically is the best proof that the recommendations have not been implemented." Indeed, Human Rights Watch continued to receive credible, serious allegations of torture. For example, in two separate trials monitored by Human Rights Watch in the first half of 2006, defendants testified about having been tortured in pretrial detention.

Key International Actors

Key international actors such as the United Nations, the European Union, the Organization for Security and Co-operation in Europe (OSCE), and the United

States lacked a common strategy towards Uzbekistan and failed to establish consequences for the Uzbek government's persistent violations of its international human rights obligations.

EU delegations visited Tashkent in late summer and fall in preparation for the EU's one-year review of the sanctions regime imposed on the Uzbek government over human rights concerns in October 2005. In a decision announced on November 13, 2006, EU foreign ministers agreed to renew the sanctions, though disappointingly only the arms embargo was extended for another full year, while the visa ban on a number of senior officials was renewed for only six months. The EU further decided to conduct a review of these measures in three months, based on vague criteria regarding "the actions of the Uzbek government in the area of human rights."

Among EU countries, Germany was particularly well-positioned to shape the EU's policy towards Uzbekistan, but failed to extract concrete concessions in human rights, instead appearing intent on softening the EU's stance. Germany failed to arrest the former Uzbek Interior Minister Zokir Almatov, who was allowed into Germany on humanitarian grounds for medical treatment (despite being subject to an EU travel ban) in late 2005. After Almatov left Germany, the German federal prosecutor announced on March 30, 2006, that he would not open a criminal investigation into Almatov's responsibility for crimes against humanity. A motion for reconsideration of the federal prosecutor's decision was rejected in October.

In the spring of 2006 the US Department of State concluded that human rights conditions in Uzbekistan had worsened considerably. Visiting Tashkent in August, Assistant Secretary of State Richard Boucher said that the US would not neglect fundamental rights in its future relations with Uzbekistan. Yet the US did not impose sanctions on Uzbekistan. In a welcome move, on November 13, 2006, the Department of State designated Uzbekistan a "country of particular concern" for its severe violations of religious freedom.

Russia and China intensified their friendly relations with Uzbekistan. In April 2006 the lower house of the Russian parliament ratified a military alliance treaty with Uzbekistan. On the eve of the first anniversary of Andijan, Uzbekistan's President Islam Karimov was a guest at Russian President Vladimir Putin's holiday residence, a demonstration of Russia's diplomatic support. After several years' absence Uzbekistan rejoined the Collective Security Treaty Organization in August, a decision that further signaled Uzbekistan's warming relations with Russia. In September China and Uzbekistan signed a cooperation protocol for the next two years. Uzbekistan participated in joint military exercises with Russia and China in 2006.

On June 30, 2006, the OSCE Centre in Tashkent was downgraded to OSCE Project Coordinator in Uzbekistan after several international staff members were denied accreditation.

The newly-established UN Human Rights Council discussed the human rights situation in Uzbekistan during its second session in September, but failed to mark heightened concern by moving this consideration from closed session to a public procedure. The Uzbek government failed to issue the required invitations to a number of UN special procedures with outstanding requests to visit Uzbekistan.

IRAQ

Judging Dujail

The First Trial before the Iraqi High Tribunal

H U M A N
R I G H T S
W A T C H

WORLD REPORT

2007

MIDDLE EAST
AND NORTH AFRICA

BAHRAIN

Bahrain's human rights practices improved significantly following reforms decreed by the king, Shaikh Hamad bin `Isa Al Khalifa, in 2001-02, but the government did not institutionalize in law protection of basic rights such as freedom of assembly, association, and expression. Some new laws ratified in 2006—on counterterrorism and public gatherings, for instance—contain provisions that undermine those rights.

Among the earlier reforms was the establishment of a 40-member elected National Assembly. The government scheduled elections for November 25, 2006. Some opposition political societies that boycotted the first elections, in 2002, planned to participate in the 2006 contest, but others continued to protest what they regarded as the absence of real legislative authority for the elected representatives.

Freedom of Expression

Following the 2001-02 reforms Bahrainis have enjoyed a greater measure of freedom of expression, although the Press Law (47/2002) contains measures that unduly restrict press freedoms, such as prohibitions on insulting the king and on reports that "threaten national unity." The authorities invoked the law in 2006 to ban coverage of controversial matters. The country now has two independent daily newspapers, but other dailies as well as Bahrain's radio and TV stations are state-run. Journalists exercise a considerable degree of self-censorship, particularly on issues such as corruption implicating the ruling family. The country's sole residential internet service provider, Batelco, is also government-owned; the independent Bahrain Center for Human Rights said in October that the authorities were blocking 17 websites, including its own.

In September 2006 Shaikh Hamad promulgated an amendment to the Penal Code (Act 65/2006) that provides criminal penalties for publishing the names or pictures of accused persons prior to a court verdict without permission of the public prosecutor. Human rights advocates protested that the law is intended to prevent public campaigns on behalf of persons wrongly charged with criminal offenses.

In remarks on September 2, Prime Minister Shaikh Khalifa bin Salman Al Khalifa warned that "democracy, openness and freedom of opinion should not be used as a pretext to violate the law, sow sectarian sedition, or falsify truths in international arenas, claiming internal liberties are curbed." Platforms for expressing opinions are open "to accommodate all stances and trends as long as they serve the national interests rather than personal designs," he said. He also warned against what one Bahraini newspaper termed "misusing the parliament to raise controversial issues."

Freedom of Assembly

Law 32 of 2006 requires the organizers of any public meeting or demonstration to notify the head of Public Security at least three days in advance. The law authorizes the head of Public Security to determine whether a meeting warrants police presence on the basis of "its subject... or any other circumstance." The law stipulates that every public meeting must be organized by a committee of at least three members who are responsible for "forbidding any speech or discussion infringing on public order or morals"; it leaves "public order or morals" undefined, however.

Bahraini authorities, citing Law 32/2006, have banned meetings on the grounds that the organizers failed to get authorization and on several occasions forcibly prevented or dispersed meetings. On September 15 police prevented the Movement of Liberties and Democracy (Haq) from holding a public seminar on the group's petition calling for a new constitution, on the basis that the group had not sought permission from the Ministry of the Interior. On September 22 when the group tried a second time to hold the meeting, police used rubber bullets and teargas to disperse the gathering, reportedly wounding several people.

Counterterrorism Measures

On August 12, 2006, Shaikh Hamad signed into law the "Protecting Society from Terrorist Acts" bill. The UN special rapporteur on human rights and counterterrorism had publicly urged the king to seek amendments to the bill passed by the legislature, expressing concern that it contained an excessively broad definition of terrorism and terrorist acts. Article 1 prohibits any act that would "damage national unity" or "obstruct public authorities from performing their duties." Article 6 prescribes the death penalty for acts that "disrupt the provisions of the Constitution or laws, or prevent state enterprises or public authorities from exercising their duties." The law also allows for extended periods of detention without charge or judicial review, heightening the risk of arbitrary detention and torture or inhumane treatment during detention.

Women's Rights

Women are eligible to vote and stand for office in national and municipal elections.

Bahrain has no written personal status laws. Instead, separate Sharia-based family courts exist for Sunni and Shia Muslims. These courts hear marriage, divorce, custody, and inheritance cases, with judges exercising authority to render judgments according to their own reading of Islamic jurisprudence. Judges presiding over these courts are generally conservative religious scholars with limited formal legal training. Many are unapologetically adverse to women's equality and persistently favor men in their rulings. The Women's Petition Committee continued to campaign for codifying Bahrain's family laws and reforming family courts. In November 2005 the official Supreme Council for Women launched a campaign to raise public awareness of the need for a codified personal status law. In March 2006 the government introduced draft legislation containing separate sections for Shia and Sunni Muslims. Women's rights organizations continued to call for a unified personal status law.

Human Rights Defenders

The independent Bahrain Center for Human Rights (BCHR), which the authorities ordered dissolved in September 2004 after one of its leaders publicly criticized the prime minister, remained closed. The center's activists continued to monitor human rights practices, issue reports and statements, and provide legal counsel, but do not have access to the group's former office or to its funds, which the government confiscated.

The Bahrain Human Rights Society (BHRS), set up by the government in 2002, inspected Jaw prison, a major detention facility, in December 2005, and in May 2006 issued a report critical of conditions there. The BHRS has also been active in promoting women's rights, and in particular a unified personal status code.

Decree 56/2002 confers immunity from investigation or prosecution on present and former government officials alleged to be responsible for torture and other serious human rights abuses committed prior to 2001. In April 2006 the BCHR and other groups, including the Committee of Families of Martyrs and Victims of Torture, sponsored a seminar on the need for accountability for serious human rights violations such as torture. Government-controlled media harshly criticized the meeting and its organizers, but the authorities took no steps to interfere with the event.

On June 26, the International Day in Support of Victims of Torture, the authorities objected to the planned route for a march sponsored by the Committee of Families of Martyrs and Victims of Torture and prevented the march from taking place. The Ministry of Social Affairs denied local Amnesty International members permission to stage a mock soccer match on June 26 between Guantanamo "detainees" and "guards" intended to highlight inhumane treatment at the US detention facility because the organization was not officially registered with the ministry.

Key International Actors

The United States remains a major ally of Bahrain. In 2001 President George Bush designated Bahrain a Major Non-NATO Ally. Bahrain hosts the headquarters of the US Navy's Fifth Fleet as well as "important air assets." The State Department's Fiscal Year 2007 budget justification submitted to Congress identified access to Bahrain-based military facilities and airspace as "critical" to US military operations in Iraq, Afghanistan, and the Horn of Africa as well as "any contingency operations and/or force projections in the Gulf and Southwest Asian areas." The US provided almost US$21 million in military and counterterrorism assistance to Bahrain in fiscal year 2005 and an estimated $19.3 million in 2006. The Bush administration has requested $17.3 million for fiscal year 2007. The US and Bahrain entered into a Free Trade Agreement in September 2004. US officials did not publicly raise specific human rights concerns during the year outside of the State Department's annual country report.

In May 2006 Bahrain was among the states elected to the first UN Human Rights Council, the body established to replace the Commission on Human Rights. Bahrain is not a state party to the International Covenant on Civil and Political Rights or the International Covenant on Economic, Social and Cultural Rights, but is a state party to the Convention against Torture, the Convention against All Forms of Discrimination against Women, and the Convention on the Rights of the Child. Following Bahrain's initial report to the Committee against Torture in May 2005, the committee commended Bahrain for a number of positive developments, particularly in bringing an end to systematic torture, but also expressed a number of concerns, including "the blanket amnesty extended to all alleged perpetrators of torture or other crimes by Decree No. 56 of 2002 and the lack of redress available to victims of torture." The committee also expressed concern with provisions of the then-draft counterterrorism law that would "reduce safeguards against torture."

EGYPT

Egypt displayed a heavy hand against political dissent in 2006. In April 2006, the government renewed emergency rule for an additional two years, providing a continued basis for arbitrary detention and trials before military and state security courts. Torture at the hands of security forces remains a serious problem.

After a period of relative tolerance of political opposition and dissent in early 2005, the government reversed course starting in late 2005. In November 2005 the government responded to the Muslim Brotherhood's strong showing in the first round of national elections with extensive irregularities and violence by police and ruling party vigilantes in the subsequent two rounds. It renewed its crackdown on the Muslim Brotherhood in March 2006, arresting at least 792 members of the banned organization over the following six months. The crackdown was emblematic of continuing limits on freedom of association and expression in Egypt.

Emergency Rule

The government renewed the Emergency Law (Law No. 162 of 1958) in April 2006 for an additional two years. The state of emergency has been in effect without interruption since October 1981. Although President Husni Mubarak, during the September 2005 presidential re-election campaign, said that he would allow it to expire, officials claimed the renewal was necessary because they had not yet drafted what Mubarak termed "a firm and decisive law that eliminates terrorism and uproots its threats." Egyptian human rights defenders fear that this legislation will perpetuate many objectionable features of the Emergency Law. Egyptian human rights organizations estimate that up to 10,000 people remain in prolonged detention without charge under the terms of the law.

Political Violence and Internal Security

Three explosions in the Sinai resort town of Dahab killed 23 people and wounded 80 more on April 24, 2006, the third such attack in Sinai resorts in two years. After the first attack, in which car bombers struck the resort town of Taba in

October 2004, authorities carried out mass arbitrary arrests, detaining 3,000 people for questioning; more than 100 of them remained in detention without charge at this writing. A devastating series of bombings in Sharm al-Shaikh in July 2006 was followed by another spate of mass arrests. The Egyptian Organization for Human Rights reported that as of August, 300 people had been detained in connection with the bombings.

On September 7, 2006, the Emergency Supreme State Security Court in Ismailiyya sentenced Osama al-Nakhlawi and Mohamad Hussein to death for their alleged role in the Taba bombings, based on what the defendants said were false confessions extracted under torture. A third man, who died in a gun battle with police, was sentenced in absentia. As of mid-November 2006, twelve others were on trial for their alleged roles in the bombings.

Torture

Human rights organizations continue to receive credible reports that security services and police routinely torture and mistreat detainees, particularly during interrogations. On May 25 State Security officers detained Karim al-Sha`ir and Mohamed al-Sharqawi, badly beat them both, and sexually assaulted al-Sharqawi. The authorities had detained the two for participating in protests supporting the Judges' Club (see below).

In its 2006 annual report, the Egyptian Organization for Human Rights (EOHR) reported that it documented 34 torture cases in 2005. There are no indications that the government conducted any criminal investigations of, or imposed any disciplinary measures against, State Security Investigations (SSI) officials for torture or ill-treatment of detainees in 2006. The most recent investigation into allegations of torture by SSI officers was in 1986, despite numerous credible allegations of serious abuse in SSI custody in the past twenty years.

Freedom of Assembly

Before daylight on December 30, 2005, police used excessive force to disperse approximately 2,000 Sudanese, including many refugees and asylum seekers, who had staged a sit-in protest near the offices of the UN High Commissioner for

Refugees (UNHCR) for more than three months. Twenty-seven Sudanese, more than half of them women and children, were killed, and a 14-year-old boy died a month later after he was hospitalized for injuries sustained in the melee. Most demonstrators carrying proof of their status as refugees or asylum-seekers were released within a few days, and the remainder over the following two months.

In the early hours of April 24, 2006, plainclothes police beat activists who had staged a sit-in to support senior judges facing disciplinary action after they publicly criticized election irregularities and campaigned for greater judicial independence. At subsequent demonstrations police beat dozens of protesters and detained hundreds more. At a May 11 demonstration, police also assaulted journalists, including `Amr `Abd-Allah, a staff photographer for the daily *Al-Misri al-Yom*, `Abir al-Askari, a writer for the weekly *Al-Dustur*, Yasir Suleiman, a cameraman for Al-Jazeera, and Nasri Yusef, a soundman for the network.

Freedom of Expression

On May 24 the state security prosecutor charged Wa'el al-Ibrashi and Hoda Abu Bakr, reporters for the independent weekly *Sawt al-Umma*, and `Abd al-Hakim `Abd al-Hamid, editor-in-chief of the weekly *Afaq `Arabia*, with defaming Mahmud Burham, the judge in charge of the electoral commission in the Dakhlia governorate. Their December 2005 articles included a "blacklist" of initials of judges that implied Burham was implicated in electoral fraud. The presiding judge twice postponed their trial, which was still pending at this writing.

On June 26 a local court sentenced Ibrahim `Issa, editor of the opposition weekly *Al-Dustur*, and Sahar Zaki, a journalist for the paper, to a year in prison on charges of "insulting the president" and "spreading false and tendentious rumors" after they reported on an anti-government lawsuit. At this writing the two were free, pending a ruling on their appeal.

On July 11, President Mubarak signed an amended version of Egypt's press law that left intact provisions allowing the authorities to detain journalists who criticize the president or foreign leaders, or who publish news "liable...to cause harm or damage to the national interest."

The Law on Political Rights (Law 73/1956), revised in 2005, includes criminal penalties for journalists and publishers convicted of reporting "false information" intended to affect election results.

Freedom of Association

Egypt's law governing associations, Law 84/2002, severely compromises the right to freedom of association, giving the government unwarranted control over the governance and operations of nongovernmental organizations (NGOs). The law provides criminal penalties for carrying out activities prior to an NGO's official authorization and for receiving donations without prior approval from the Ministry of Social Affairs. It also provides criminal rather than civil sanctions for certain other activities, including "engaging in political or union activities, reserved for political parties and syndicates." The broad terms in which the prohibitions are framed discourage legitimate NGO activity.

Egypt maintains strict controls over political associations as well. In July 2005, the parliament passed government-sponsored revisions to the Political Parties Law (Law 40/1956) providing that new parties be legally registered automatically unless the Political Parties Affairs Committee (PPC), headed by the chair of the ruling National Democratic Party, rejects the application. The revised law also empowers the PPC to suspend an existing party's activities if it judges this to be "in the national interest" and to refer alleged breaches of the law to the Prosecutor General.

Between March and July 2006 security services detained at least 792 members of the Muslim Brotherhood, which, though officially banned, is the country's largest opposition group, with 88 out of 454 seats in parliament. The crackdown accelerated in April and May, as members of the Muslim Brotherhood joined secular activists in street protests in support of judicial independence and fair elections.

Ill-Treatment of Street Children

The government periodically conducts arrest campaigns of homeless or truant street children who have committed no crime. In custody many face beatings, sexual abuse, and extortion by police and adult suspects, and police at times deny them access to food, bedding, and medical care. The authorities do not routinely monitor conditions of detention for children, investigate cases of arbitrary arrest or abuse in custody, or discipline those responsible. In many cases, the police detain children illegally for days before taking them to the public prosecutor on charges of being "vulnerable to delinquency."

Women's Rights

Despite recent reforms of Egypt's family and nationality laws, additional steps are needed to amend laws that discriminate against women and girls, to prosecute gender-based violence, and to grant women and girls equal citizenship rights. Discriminatory personal status laws governing marriage, divorce, custody, and inheritance have institutionalized the second-class status of women in the private realm. The penal code does not effectively deter or punish domestic violence, and police are routinely unsympathetic to the concerns of battered women and girls.

Religious Intolerance and Discrimination against Religious Minorities

Although Egypt's constitution provides for equal rights without regard to religion, discrimination against Egyptian Christians and official intolerance of Baha'is and unorthodox Muslim sects continue. Egyptians are able to convert to Islam generally without difficulty, but Muslims who convert to Christianity face difficulties in getting new identity papers and some have been arrested for allegedly forging such documents. Baha'i institutions and community activities are prohibited by law.

Key International Actors

The US remains Egypt's largest provider of foreign military and economic assistance. In 2006 it provided approximately US$1.3 billion in military aid and US$490 million in economic assistance. In June 2006, the US Congress defeated a proposed amendment that would have cut $100 million from the US aid package in response to Egypt's poor human rights record.

In 2006 The Bush administration scaled back its public pressure on the Egyptian government with respect to human rights and democracy. In a 2005 visit to Cairo, Secretary of State Condoleezza Rice spoke forcefully about the importance of political reform in Egypt. In 2006, by contrast, official US pronouncements stressed that change must come from the Egyptian people and government. And while the US government continued to express concern over human rights abuses in Egypt, no visible consequences ensued.

In April 2006 the European Parliament voted to make respect for human rights a priority in its continuing negotiations with Egypt on an EU-Egypt Action Plan under the European Neighborhood Policy. As of October 2006 negotiations were still stalled over human rights language. The deadline for reaching an agreement is January 1, 2007.

Egypt failed to respond to a July 2006 request from the UN special rapporteur on torture for an invitation to visit the country, a request that has been outstanding since 1996. In October a Canadian federal court judge ruled that Canadian authorities could not deport a suspected terrorist, Mahmud Jaballah, to Egypt because of risk of torture. In late 2005 lawyers from the US Department of Justice said that `Ala `Abd al-Maqsud Muhamad Salim—an Egyptian detained in Pakistan in 2002, transferred to Guantanamo Bay, and subsequently declared "No Longer an Enemy Combatant"—would be released and returned to Egypt. In January they filed a motion claiming that, based on new information, there were no longer "immediate plans to transfer, repatriate, or release him." Salim's Washington-based attorneys had asked that Salim be held in Guantanamo because of fears that he would face torture in Egypt. According to briefs filed by his lawyer, when Egyptian officials visited him at the Guantanamo facility, they threatened to take him somewhere where people "will never see [him] again."

IRAN

Respect for basic human rights in Iran, especially freedom of expression and assembly, deteriorated in 2006. The government routinely tortures and mistreats detained dissidents, including through prolonged solitary confinement. The Judiciary, which is accountable to Supreme Leader Ali Khamenei, is responsible for many serious human rights violations.

President Mahmoud Ahmadinejad's cabinet is dominated by former intelligence and security officials, some of whom have been implicated in serious human rights violations, such as the assassination of dissident intellectuals. Under his administration, the Ministry of Information, which essentially performs intelligence functions, has substantially increased its surveillance of dissidents, civil society activists, and journalists.

Freedom of Expression

Iranian authorities systematically suppress freedom of expression and opinion by closing newspapers and imprisoning journalists and editors. The few independent dailies that remain heavily self-censor. Many writers and intellectuals have left the country, are in prison, or have ceased to be critical. In September 2006 the Ministry of Culture and Guidance closed the reformist daily, *Shargh*, and shut down two reformist journals, *Nameh and Hafez*. In October the Ministry shut down a new reformist daily, *Roozgar*, only three days after it started publication. During the year the Ministry of Information summoned and interrogated dozens of journalists critical of the government.

In 2006 the authorities also targeted websites and internet journalists in an effort to prevent online dissemination of news and information. The government systematically blocks websites inside Iran and abroad that carry political news and analysis. In September 2006 Esmail Radkani, director-general of the government-controlled Information Technology Company, announced that his company is blocking access to 10 million "unauthorized" websites on orders from the Judiciary and other authorities.

Freedom of Assembly

The Ahmadinejad government, in a pronounced shift from the policy under former president Mohammed Khatami, has shown no tolerance for peaceful protests and gatherings. In January 2006 security forces attacked striking bus drivers in Tehran and detained hundreds. The government refused to recognize the drivers' independent union or engage in collective bargaining with them. In February government forces attacked a peaceful gathering of Sufi devotees in front of their religious building in Qum to prevent its destruction by the authorities, using tear gas and water cannons to disperse them. In March police and plainclothes agents charged a peaceful assembly of women's rights activists in Tehran and beat hundreds of women and men who had gathered to commemorate International Women's Day. In June as women's rights defenders assembled again in Tehran, security forces beat them with batons, sprayed them with pepper gas, marked the demonstrators with sprayed dye, and took 70 people into custody.

Torture and Ill-Treatment in Detention

Since President Ahmadinejad came to power, treatment of detainees has worsened in Evin prison as well as in detention centers operated clandestinely by the Judiciary, the Ministry of Information, and the Islamic Revolutionary Guard Corps. The authorities have subjected those imprisoned for peaceful expression of political views to torture and ill-treatment, including beatings, sleep depravation, and mock executions. Judges often accept coerced confessions. The authorities use prolonged solitary confinement, often in small basement cells, to coerce confessions (which are videotaped) and gain information regarding associates.

In 2006 two prisoners held for their political beliefs, Akbar Mohammadi and Valiollah Feyz Mahdavi, died in suspicious circumstances in prison. The authorities prevented their families from conducting independent autopsies. The government has taken no action to investigate the cause of the deaths.

Impunity

There is no mechanism for monitoring and investigating human rights violations perpetrated by agents of the government. The closure of independent media in Iran has helped to perpetuate an atmosphere of impunity.

In recent years public testimonies by numerous former prisoners and detainees have implicated Tehran's public prosecutor Saeed Mortazavi and his office in some of the worst cases of human rights violations. Despite extensive evidence, Mortazavi has not been held responsible for his role in illegal detentions, torture of detainees, and coercing false confessions. The case of Iranian-Canadian photojournalist Zahra Kazemi, who died in the custody of judiciary and security agents led by Mortazavi in June 2003, remains unresolved. Mustapha Pour-Mohammadi, the current interior minister, is implicated in extrajudicial massacres of thousands of political prisoners in 1988.

Human Rights Defenders

In 2006 the authorities intensified their harassment of independent human rights defenders and lawyers in an attempt to prevent them from publicizing and pursuing human rights violations. In August the Interior Ministry declared illegal the Center for Defense of Human Rights, led by Shirin Ebadi, the 2003 Nobel Peace Prize winner. Ebadi and her colleagues provide pro-bono legal counsel to hundreds of dissidents, journalists, and students facing prosecution for exercising fundamental freedoms, such as peacefully protesting or criticizing government policies. The authorities threatened Ebadi and her colleagues with arrest should they continue their activities in defense of human rights. Following international protests, the government has not carried out its threat, but Ebadi and her colleagues remain vulnerable.

In June 2006 government agents arrested Ali Akbar Mousavi Khoini, a former member of parliament and outspoken critic of the government's human rights record. The authorities held him in solitary confinement without access to his lawyers for more than four months. The Judiciary released him on October 21, only after he posted $300,000 bail. During a brief release to attend his father's funeral in September, he publicly alleged that he was being tortured and forced to "repent" for his activities.

Juvenile Death Penalty

Iran has executed at least 13 juvenile offenders in the last five years, more than any other nation. On May 11, 2006, Iran executed Majid Segound and Masoud Naghi Biranvand, both 17 years old at the time of execution. Two youths scheduled to be executed on September 20, 2006, for murders committed while under 18 had their executions suspended when the victims' families agreed to accept blood money in lieu of execution. About 30 juvenile offenders are on death row.

Minorities

Iran's ethnic and religious minorities are subject to discrimination and, in some cases, persecution. In May Iranian Azeris in the northwestern provinces of East and West Azerbaijan and Ardebil demonstrated against government restrictions on Azeri language and cultural and political activities. Security services forcibly disrupted public protests that engulfed the region. In some protests demonstrators attacked government offices. Four people died in clashes in the city of Naghadeh on May 25.

In the southwestern province of Khuzistan, unrest among Iran's Arab population intensified in 2006. Revolutionary Courts, following secret proceedings that did not meet international fair trial standards, condemned at least 16 Iranians of Arab origin to death on charges of armed activity against the state.

The government continues to deny Iran's Baha'i community permission to publicly worship or pursue religious activities. In a letter dated October 29, 2005, Supreme Leader Ayatollah Ali Khamenei instructed several government organs, including the Ministry of Information and the armed forces, "to acquire a comprehensive and complete report of all the activities of Baha'is for the purpose of identifying all the individuals of these misguided sects." In May the authorities arrested 54 Baha'i youth who were teaching English, math, and other non-religious subjects to underprivileged children in the southern city of Shiraz. None of the Baha'i youth were charged with a crime. All but three were released after a week of detention and the remaining three were released on June 14, 2006.

Key International Actors

In 2006 negotiations over Iran's nuclear program dominated the policy of the European Union towards Iran, with human rights concerns a secondary matter. The EU pledged to tie Iranian respect for human rights to progress in co-operation on other issues, but the pledge had little impact. Iran refused to resume its "human rights dialogue" with the EU that it had suspended in 2005, despite the EU's repeated calls to do so.

The United Nations General Assembly adopted a resolution in November 2005 noting serious violations and the worsening human rights situation in Iran. Under a standing invitation that Tehran issued in 2002 to the thematic mechanisms of the UN Commission on Human Rights, the special rapporteur on violence against women, Yakin Ertürk, visited Iran in February 2005. In a January 2006 report she highlighted "discriminatory provisions in both the Civil and Penal Codes, and flaws in the administration of justice," resulting in disempowerment of women. The special rapporteur on adequate housing, Miloon Kothari, visited Iran in August 2005 and issued a report in March 2006. In his March 2006 report he raised several concerns about discrimination against ethnic and religious minorities and nomadic groups, among other things.

Iran has not responded to requests by the UN special rapporteurs on extrajudicial executions and torture, made in 2004 and 2005 respectively, to visit the country.

The Bush Administration remains divided on its Iran policy, and relations between the United States and Iran remain poor. The State Department frequently invoked Iran's human rights record as a matter of concern. In February the State Department budgeted US$75 million "to support democracy promotion activities in Iran," but a vast majority of Iranian dissidents, human rights defenders, and civil society activists inside Iran publicly dissociated themselves from the initiative, making clear they do not seek any financial help form the American government. The administration did not utilize multilateral international institutions to address human rights violations in Iran, in contrast to its vigorous efforts to build international coalitions in response to Iran's alleged drive to acquire nuclear weapons and its support for Hezbollah in Lebanon and armed groups in the Occupied Palestinian Territories.

IRAQ

The human rights situation worsened significantly in 2006.The continuing armed conflict became increasingly sectarian in nature, with many commentators declaring the onset of a civil war, and Sunni and Shia armed groups targeting civilians from each other's communities. United States forces continued military operations against insurgent forces throughout the country, resulting in an unknown number of civilian deaths and injuries. In October, a Johns Hopkins-MIT mortality study estimated that 650,000 Iraqis had died as a result of the war since 2003, 600,000 of them in violent deaths; this figure was far higher than previous estimates.

The bombing on February 22 of two Shia holy sites in Samarra' catalyzed an unprecedented level of violent attacks, primarily against civilians. Despite several security plans announced by the Iraqi government and Multi-National Forces (MNF) to curb the violence and bring armed militias under control, the overall security situation continued to deteriorate. In October, Iraq's National Assembly passed legislation providing for the formation of federal regions in the country in 2008, despite strong opposition by Sunni representatives and two Shia parties. Some feared the law would fuel sectarian violence and threaten Iraq's sovereignty while depriving the central region of access to natural resources.

Further revelations emerged of Ministry of Interior and Ministry of Defense personnel systematically torturing and sometimes killing detainees in their custody. Government investigations failed to lead to the arrest and prosecution of alleged suspects, despite mounting evidence.

The Governing Authority and the Political Process

Elections were held on December 15, 2005, for a new 275-seat National Assembly. Political uncertainty continued, however, as outgoing Prime Minister Ibrahim al-Ja'fari, nominated again by the largest parliamentary bloc, failed to gain consensus. On April 23 the National Assembly elected Jalal Talabani as the country's president and nominated Nouri al-Maliki as prime minister after al-Ja'fari withdrew his candidacy.

In June, Prime Minister Maliki announced a 24-point National Reconciliation Plan addressing the political and security crises in the country. Among other things, the plan provided for mechanisms to facilitate the political process, the disbanding of armed militias and laying down security plans, tackling mass internal displacement, legislative and judicial reforms, a partial amnesty for non-terrorist offenses, and accountability mechanisms for human rights abuses. At this writing, the government had not implemented any of these provisions.

Attacks against Civilians by Armed Groups and Internal Displacement

Civilians remained the primary victims of directed or indiscriminate attacks perpetrated by Sunni and Shia armed groups. Numerous attacks appeared aimed at inflicting maximum casualties and spreading fear among the civilian population as militias targeted marketplaces, places of worship, and shops. Incidents were also rife of armed groups on both sides reportedly abducting, torturing, and killing people on the basis of their religious or sectarian affiliation. Sunni insurgent groups, including al Qaeda and Ansar al-Sunna, claimed responsibility for a number of incidents involving car bomb and suicide attacks against civilian areas, while levels of abduction by such groups remained very high. Shia armed groups, in particular the Mahdi Army and the Badr militia, were reportedly responsible for numerous abductions and killings in Baghdad and elsewhere. According to Iraqi government figures, the number of killings in Baghdad in July and August exceeded 5,000.

Relentless violent attacks caused greater displacement of civilians across Iraq, affecting Sunni and Shia communities as well as Christians and other minorities. The Iraqi government stated that 234,000 persons were displaced since February, but a study published by the Brookings Institution and the University of Bern in October estimated that the numbers were between 300,000 and 400,000. The report cited failure to register and the politicization of tracking the numbers of displaced persons as key reasons for the higher figures.

Torture by Iraqi Forces

Evidence of widespread torture and other ill-treatment of detainees in the custody of the Iraqi ministries of interior and defense continued to emerge. A joint MNF-Iraqi raid on the Ministry of Interior's al-Jadiriyya facility in Baghdad in November 2005 discovered some 170 detainees, many bearing injuries consistent with torture. At least 18 others allegedly had died in custody, and the fate of others remained unknown. Between December 2005 and May 2006, joint MNF-Iraqi teams inspected at least eight facilities run by the two ministries in and around Baghdad. The inspectors found consistent evidence of detainee abuse at most locations, including the Ministry of Interior's Site 4 facility, where in May many of the 1,845 detainees displayed recent injuries consistent with severe beatings and electric shock.

In December 2005 the government ordered an investigation into detainee abuse at the al-Jadiriyya facility. While it released tens of detainees as a result of a case review by a judicial committee, by October 2006 it had not made public the findings of the investigation. The government also failed to announce the findings of another investigation into detainee abuse at the Site 4 facility. At this writing, the government had neither arrested nor charged any of the alleged perpetrators at either facility, including 52 personnel at Site 4. No further joint inspections of detention facilities were carried out after May 31, reportedly because of governmental opposition to the program.

Illegal Detentions by Kurdish Security Forces

Security forces (*Asayish*) in the Kurdistan Federal Region continued to hold illegally hundreds of detainees, including Kurds, Arabs, and other nationals, many of them on suspicion of terrorism offenses. The majority of detainees stated during prison visits conducted by Human Rights Watch that security officials had neither referred them to an investigative judge nor charged them with cognizable offenses, often for up to three years. Many also stated that detaining officials denied them access to legal counsel and family visits, and subjected them to torture or ill-treatment under interrogation. Beginning in May, and following the unification of the administrations of the Kurdistan Democratic Party and the Patriotic Union of Kurdistan, the Kurdish authorities took positive steps to resolve some of these issues, and a partial review of case files led to several hundred detainees being released by August.

Detention by US Forces

As of October, US forces were detaining about 13,000 Iraqis on the basis of United Nations Security Council authorization, but the legal regime applicable to the detainees remained unclear. Detainees may be held indefinitely on security grounds and then released, while others were transferred after several months to Iraqi custody for prosecution. Among the detainees were journalists, including Associated Press photographer Bilal Hussein, arrested in Ramadi on April 12 and since held without charge or judicial review.

Further details of widespread detainee abuse by US military personnel emerged from new accounts by US soldiers, revealing that such abuse was an established policy of detention and interrogation processes in Iraq for much of 2003-05. Senior officers apparently rebuffed or ignored soldiers who sought to report abuse.

Accountability for Past Crimes

The first trial before the Iraqi High Tribunal (IHT), which began in October 2005, concluded in July. Eight defendants, including former president Saddam Hussein, were tried on charges of crimes against humanity in connection with the arbitrary detention and forced displacement of 800 men, women, and children from the town of Dujail in 1982, of whom 148 men and boys were executed or died in detention. In the verdict delivered on November 5, Saddam Hussein and six other defendants were convicted; Hussein and two others were sentenced to death by hanging. In a report issued in November 2006 Human Rights Watch concluded that the trial had not respected basic fair trial guarantees. A second trial opened in August, with Saddam Hussein and six other defendants facing charges including genocide, crimes against humanity, and war crimes in connection with the former government's Anfal campaign against the Kurdish population in northern Iraq, involving the systematic, deliberate murder of at least 50,000 and possibly as many as 100,000 Kurds, over six months in 1988.

NO BLOOD

NO FOUL

The High Five
Paintball Club

UNITED STATES

"No Blood, No Foul"
Soldiers' Accounts of Detainee Abuse in Iraq

HUMAN
RIGHTS
WATCH

Serious concerns remained about the capacity of the IHT to fairly and effectively try these massive crimes in accordance with international criminal law and fair trial standards. The IHT was also beset by external problems, misunderstanding and hostility in public opinion, and grave security threats to all participants. Serious administrative, procedural, and substantive legal defects characterized the Dujail trial, which was also marred by the assassination of a third defense lawyer in June, the resignation of the presiding judge, and boycotts by defense counsel. In the Anfal trial, the transfer of the presiding judge off the case in September by decision of the Council of Ministers interfered with the independence of the judiciary.

As of September 2005, US forces retained physical custody of 108 "high value detainees," most of whom were held at Camp Cropper near Baghdad International Airport. Most were awaiting trial before the IHT and had been brought before an investigative judge, but it remained unclear how many had been formally charged.

Key International Actors

In November 2005 the UN Security Council extended the mandate of the MNF-I until December 31, 2006, under resolution 1637. As of August, the United States maintained approximately 130,000 active troops in Iraq, with the United Kingdom as the key partner retaining some 7,200 troops principally in the southeastern governorates. Among the 28 countries contributing to the MNF-I forces were Australia, the Czech Republic, and Georgia.

The US government urged Iraqi officials on numerous occasions to take action in restraining armed militias operating death squads responsible for many of the abductions and killings of civilians. It pressed for decisive action in holding the leadership of such groups accountable, and for the prosecution of officials of the Ministry of Interior identified as operating detention facilities where the routine torture of inmates was discovered. US military investigative teams carried out several inspections of facilities under the authority of the ministries of interior and defense, urging Prime Minister Maliki to authorize official investigations.

In his September report to the Security Council, UN Secretary-General Kofi Annan said, "Iraq is experiencing an acute human rights and humanitarian crisis, with indiscriminate killings, targeted attacks, crime and corruption contributing to the lack of law and order." The United Nations Assistance Mission in Iraq (UNAMI) reported regularly on these abuses, describing a "vicious cycle of violence and revenge killings resulting in overall instability in the country."

Israel/Occupied Palestinian Territories (OPT)

The war between Israel and Hezbollah in Lebanon, the victory of Hamas in the Palestinian Legislative Council elections and its formation of a new government, and renewed armed conflict in Gaza dominated events in 2006.

War between Israel and Hezbollah

The war in Lebanon from July 12 until August 14 left more than 1100 Lebanese dead, a majority of them civilians, more than 4,000 people injured, and an estimated one million people displaced. Children accounted for approximately one-third of the casualties and deaths. In Israel, indiscriminate Hezbollah rockets killed 39 civilians and injured hundreds more.

In its conduct of hostilities, the Israel Defense Forces (IDF) repeatedly violated the laws of war by failing to distinguish between combatants and civilians. The IDF claims that the high proportion of civilian deaths in the war was due to Hezbollah hiding its rockets and fighters in villages and towns, but IDF attacks responsible for a majority of the civilian deaths took place at times when there was no evidence that Hezbollah fighters or weapons were even in the vicinity. While the IDF in certain cases gave advance warnings for civilians to evacuate areas likely to be attacked, such warnings do not relieve a warring party of its obligation to target only combatants. In southern Lebanon, many people remained even after warnings because of age, infirmity, responsibility for livestock and crops, inability to afford exorbitant taxi fares charged for evacuation, or fear of becoming another roadside casualty of IDF bombing. As a result, the IDF's indiscriminate bombardment had devastating consequences for civilians.

Israel's extensive use of cluster munitions also continues to be a pressing concern. The UN has estimated that Israel fired cluster munitions containing 2.6 to 4 million submunitions into Lebanon, leaving behind as many as one million hazardous duds that, at this writing, had resulted in more than 20 deaths and 100 injuries, many of them serious. According to the UN, Israel blanketed much of southern Lebanon with 90 percent of those submunitions in the last three days before the cease-fire.

For its part, Hezbollah launched thousands of rockets on cities, towns, and villages in northern Israel, using a variety of unguided surface-to-surface rockets. These rockets killed 39 Israeli civilians and injured hundreds more. Hezbollah packed some of these rockets with more than 4,000 anti-personnel steel spheres ("ball bearings") that shoot out upon impact, causing many of the civilian deaths and injuries. Hezbollah also fired Chinese-made cluster rockets, each containing 39 explosive submunitions as well as deadly steel spheres. At least 113 such cluster rockets hit Israel, causing one death and 12 injuries, according to Israeli police. The rockets also caused damage to civilian homes, businesses, the natural environment, and the economy. While Hezbollah appeared to target some of its rockets at military objectives, in some cases hitting them, many of its rockets hit civilian areas, far from any apparent military target. Such attacks—at best indiscriminate attacks on civilian areas and, at worst, deliberate attacks against civilians—violated the laws of war.

The Electoral Victory of Hamas

In January Hamas's "Change and Reform" bloc won an unanticipated victory in the second-ever Palestinian Legislative Council elections, taking 74 of 132 seats (or 56 percent). In March, Hamas formed a new government, appointing Ismail Haniyeh as prime minister.

Israel and key Western powers, which list Hamas as a terrorist organization, responded to Hamas's victory by boycotting the government, cutting diplomatic ties, and withholding the Palestinian Authority's tax revenues (in the case of Israel) and international donor funding (in the case of Western countries), which together accounted for approximately 75 percent of the Palestinian Authority's budget.

These actions caused a severe political and financial crisis in the OPT, which was continuing at this writing. From March onwards, the Palestinian Authority was unable to pay the salaries of almost all of its approximately 165,000 civil servants, salaries on which one-quarter of all Palestinians rely. Poverty and dependence on outside food aid climbed sharply. Because Israel retained effective day-to-day control over most key aspects of life in Gaza, including ingress and egress and thus the economy, it retained the responsibility of an occupying power under the Fourth Geneva Convention to ensure that the occupied population has access to food and medicine, and that basic health, security, and education needs are met.

Renewed military conflict in Gaza compounded the crisis after a Palestinian armed group kidnapped Israeli soldier Corporal Gilad Shalit on June 25. In a stated bid to free Shalit and suppress increased Qassam rocket attacks from inside northern Gaza (see "Palestinian Authority" below), Israel bombed Gaza's sole electrical power plant, which had provided 45 percent of Gaza's electricity, conducted a number of military incursions into Gaza, and engaged in a wide-scale campaign of artillery shelling into northern Gaza. At this writing, often indiscriminate and disproportionate artillery attacks in 2006 had killed 53 Palestinians, all civilians, and caused serious damage to homes, fields, and greenhouses.

As of October, the number of Palestinians killed in 2006 by Israeli security forces had reached 449, at least half of whom were not participating in hostilities at the time of their deaths, raising serious concerns for civilian protection. The Israeli army's continued failure to conduct investigations into most killings of civilians reinforced a culture of impunity in the army and robbed victims of an effective remedy.

Israeli authorities expanded already extensive, often arbitrary restrictions on freedom of movement in the West Bank and East Jerusalem. As of August 1, the UN Office for the Coordination of Humanitarian Affairs (OCHA) reported 540 physical closure obstacles, up from 376 at the same time in 2005. The closure of Gaza was more complete than at any time since the outbreak of the *intifada* in 2000, with the Rafah international border, Erez crossing, and other crossings into Israel designed for the transport of goods closed entirely or opened only irregularly, with disastrous effects on Gazan exports and imports. As of June 25, 2006, Israel prohibited Palestinian fishermen from fishing off the coast, affecting the livelihoods of 35,000 people dependent on the fishing sector, and depriving Gaza residents of fish.

In 2006 Israel stated publicly for the first time that the route of the wall it had said it is constructing to prevent Palestinian armed groups from carrying out attacks inside Israel also reflected official aspirations for a new border. Currently,

85 percent of the wall's route extends into the West Bank; if the wall were to become a permanent border, it would mean Israel's annexation of approximately 10 percent of the West Bank, including almost all major settlements there, all of which are illegal under the Fourth Geneva Convention, as well as some of the most productive Palestinian farmlands and key water resources. The International Court of Justice has condemned the construction of the wall inside the OPT. Israel also continued to expand settlements in 2006 and failed to dismantle most of the 105 "illegal outposts" (settlements not officially endorsed by the state) despite promises to do so. Settler violence against Palestinians and their property continued with virtual impunity.

Israel continued to apply a host of laws and policies that discriminate on the basis of ethnic or national origin. In June, the Israeli High Court upheld Knesset legislation that prohibits Palestinians from the OPT, who are spouses of Israeli citizens (mostly Arab-Palestinian Israelis), from joining their partners in Israel, except in certain age categories. Since 2002, Israel has frozen family reunification and forced thousands of married couples and their children to choose between living apart or living together in Israel illegally. Israel has also banned Palestinian students from the OPT seeking to study in Israeli schools and universities, and began denying visas to foreign citizens, many of Palestinian origin, who have been living, working, and raising families in the OPT for years.

Palestinian Authority

Although President Mahmoud Abbas of Fatah retained his position as president of the Palestinian Authority (PA), tensions between Fatah and Hamas increased during the year. At this writing, talks between the parties about the formation of a "national unity government" were ongoing, but the internal security situation had deteriorated drastically, with the two parties' supporters and security forces clashing in the streets, killing and wounding bystanders. In a particularly bloody 48-hour period on October 1-2, 11 people were killed and scores more were injured during clashes and demonstrations. There was also a significant rise in clashes between armed clan members.

Armed Palestinian groups continued to fire unguided homemade Qassam rockets from Gaza into civilian areas in Israel in 2006, causing several serious civilian

OCCUPIED PALESTINIAN TERRITORIES

A Question of Security

Violence against Palestinian Women and Girls

HUMAN
RIGHTS
WATCH

injuries and at this writing, two deaths. These attacks, either targeted at civilians or indiscriminate in their impact, are illegal under international humanitarian law. The Palestinian Authority made little or no effort to rein in these attacks. In June Palestinian armed groups abducted and killed an Israeli settler in the West Bank and captured Corporal Shalit, who at this writing continued to be held as a hostage in violation of the laws of war.

The number of Palestinian suicide bombings targeting civilians inside Israel in 2006 was lower than at any time since the beginning of the current *intifada* in 2000, but such attacks continued. The Islamic Jihad carried out a lethal suicide bombing in Tel Aviv in April 2006, killing 11 Israelis. Armed groups also carried out several attacks in the OPT, killing seven Israeli civilians. Human Rights Watch has repeatedly pointed out that there is no justification under any circumstances for attacks on civilians, which violate the most basic principles of international human rights and humanitarian law. As in previous years, the Palestinian Authority failed to take decisive action to apprehend those who had ordered or organized the attacks.

Violence against women and girls inside the family is a serious problem in the OPT, but the PA has done far too little in response. Law enforcement and health officials lack adequate training, guidelines, and commitment to report and investigate the problem. Even in the rare instances where the authorities pursue cases, perpetrators benefit from outdated and lenient laws that provide a reduction in penalty to men who kill or attack female relatives committing adultery, relieve rapists who agree to marry their victims from any criminal prosecution, and allow only male relatives to file incest charges on behalf of minors.

Key International Actors

International financial support, and withholding of such support, played an ever greater role in Israel in 2006. Israel remained the largest recipient of US aid, receiving US$2.28 billion in military aid and $280 million in financial aid. At the same time, the US cut all ties with the Hamas-led PA, pushed the other members of the Quartet (the United Nations, Russia, and the European Union) to cut direct aid to the PA, and, in October 2006, announced that it would spend US$43 million to bolster Fatah and other groups opposing Hamas.

The EU suspended its direct budgetary support to the PA following the election of Hamas, but funneled some money through the Temporary International Mechanism (TIM), established in June, to provide urgent humanitarian aid to the Palestinian people without funding the PA. Both the US and the EU continue to fund UN agencies and nongovernmental agencies working in the OPT.

On September 20, the Quartet stressed the urgent need for implementation of the Agreement on Movement and Access, signed by the parties in November 2005, to allow for continuous opening of Rafah and other crossing points into and out of Gaza. The Quartet also called for increased international donor funding through the TIM. Finally, the Quartet indicated that "the resumption of transfers of tax and customs revenues collected by Israel on behalf of the PA would have a significant impact on the Palestinian economy," but fell short of calling on Israel to immediately hand over the money.

At this writing, the newly created UN Human Rights Council already had held three special sessions in 2006, one to consider the situation in the OPT (July 5-6), one to consider the situation in Lebanon (August 11), and one to consider the situation in Gaza after Israeli artillery shelling killed 19 civilians in Beit Hanoun (November 15). All resolutions focused primarily on Israeli actions and violations, and failed to consider, let alone condemn, abuses committed by armed groups in the OPT or by Hezbollah in Lebanon.

JORDAN

Jordan made little progress in changing law or practice restricting the exercise of basic rights such as freedom of expression, association, and assembly. The National Agenda, a project initiated by King Abdullah II in 2005, recommended reforms but the government and parliament have not yet passed any of the promised legislation to enact them, such as a political parties bill, an election law, and amendments to the public assemblies, welfare societies, and journalism and publication laws.

The king appointed a new prime minister and cabinet in November 2005 and a new intelligence chief in December. The lower house of parliament, which must ratify laws and international agreements, approved four international human rights treaties in 2006, but did not initiate legislation or exercise effective government oversight.

A new counterterrorism law that maintains provisions allowing a military prosecutor to detain a suspect for up to seven days without charge, and expands prosecutorial powers to freeze bank accounts and restrict suspects' international travel, came into force November 1. The government withdrew its proposal in an early draft of the law to extend the time suspects could be held without charge to two weeks.

Arbitrary Detention, Torture, and the Death Penalty

The General Intelligence Department (GID) arrests suspects mostly in the name of counterterrorism and detains them at its own detention facility for prolonged periods (in excess of the permitted seven days), often without charge or on baseless charges. The GID routinely denies detainees access to legal representation, and allows family visits with considerable delay, if at all. Most security detainees allege torture and ill-treatment to extract confessions, in the form of beatings and psychological abuse such as mock executions, sleep deprivation, and prolonged solitary confinement.

Provincial governors detain persons they deem a "danger to society" under the crime prevention law without proof of criminal action. Such persons, who usually

483

have committed prior offenses, remain in detention until they can meet a bail guarantee. If no guarantor comes forward, they remain imprisoned. In 2005 there were 513 such detentions.

2006 witnessed the most serious prison disturbances in recent years. An attempt in March to extract two convicts scheduled for execution, Yasir Furaihat and Salim Bin Suwaid, from their cells in Swaqa prison set Islamist inmates rioting in three prisons (the two were executed 10 days later). In Juwaida prison Islamists took prison officials hostage, but Islamic Action Front parliamentarians helped mediate a peaceful end. In April a search of a Qafqafa prison wing holding Islamists sparked violent clashes during which one prisoner died. Officials had rejected an offer of mediation. Following these incidents, prison officials put many Islamist detainees in prolonged solitary confinement and sharply limited the number and duration of visits as well as visitor eligibility and the items they could bring. In August Islamist prisoners in Swaqa prison went on hunger strike to demand better conditions, including an end to solitary confinement.

The execution of Furaihat and Bin Suwaid was for the 2002 killing of US diplomat Lawrence Foley. The State Security Court in 2006 passed death sentences on several other persons for involvement in terrorism, including Sajida al-Rishawi, an Iraqi woman who confessed to participating in the bombing of three hotels in Amman in November 2005.

In a positive move, the government in August amended four laws to reduce their penalties from death to hard labor.

Human Rights Defenders

Jordanian human rights organizations published reports highly critical of government policy and practice, and Jordan became the first Arab country to invite the UN special rapporteur on torture. The Arab Organization for Human Rights (AOHR) in July reported on torture, arbitrary detention, inhumane prison conditions, and a lack of judicial oversight. In response, the head of the Public Security Department sent the organization a private letter accusing it of slandering public officials. As a consequence of the prison riots, officials denied a request by the Public Liberties Committee of the lower house of parliament for access to prisons, as well as a request by the AOHR and the Engineers' Association's human rights committee (which had visited other prisons between October and December 2005) to visit Jafr prison. Only the National Center for Human Rights (NCHR) and the special rapporteur had access to Jafr prison and the GID detention facility. The NCHR and the AOHR called for the closure of Jafr—which the special rapporteur described as a "punishment centre"— and reported allegations of torture at the GID facility.

The government and parliament increasingly consulted human rights organizations on draft laws under discussion. The Adaleh Center for Human Rights Studies advised on changes to the welfare societies law; the Center for Defending Freedom of Journalists published detailed legal analysis regarding a draft journalism and publications law; and the NCHR presented its observations on the draft counterterrorism law. Parliament passed the counterterrorism law without taking these observations into account, however. The other two laws remain in draft, with parliamentarians so far rejecting the suggested changes that would make the laws compliant with international human rights standards.

Freedom of Expression and Assembly

Criticisms of the king and the intelligence forces are strictly taboo and carry serious penalties. Articles of the penal code criminalize speech slandering public officials, criticizing the king, and harming relations with other states. Although government officials said that these laws would no longer be enforced, and would eventually be cancelled, criminal charges against government critics remained frequent.

For example, the military prosecutor at the State Security Court (SSC) in November filed charges, later dropped, of insulting the king and of causing sectarian strife against Adnan Abu Odeh, a former head of the Royal Court, for remarks he made in an interview with Al Jazeera. In a highly irregular trial, the SSC in August also found members of parliament Muhammad Abu Faris and Ali Abu Sukkar guilty of stirring up sectarian strife for their visit to Abu Mus'ab al-Zarqawi's wake, where Abu Faris called al-Zarqawi (the Jordanian-born head of al Qaeda in Iraq), a martyr, but not the victims of his violence.

Security forces in April detained for six days *al-Sabeel* journalist 'Izz al-Din Ahmad as he was returning from interviewing a senior Hamas member in Syria. Security forces in June and again in August briefly arrested Yasir Abu Hilalah, Al Jazeera's Amman bureau chief, during interviews with relatives or supporters of al-Zarqawi. Intelligence officers detained Fahd al-Rimawi, chief editor of *al-Majd* newspaper, in May for several hours over an article the GID claimed contained false information. In September reporters covering a Human Rights Watch report on the intelligence forces' use of arbitrary arrests and torture received intimidating phone calls from the GID.

The governor of Amman in May twice refused permission for an Islamic Action Front demonstration, the first entitled "Yes to the Right of Return, No to an Alternative Homeland," and the second, on the occasion of Jordan's independence day. In September the governor banned an Islamic Action Front demonstration to protest Pope Benedict XVI's remarks regarding Islam. Jordanian law obliges organizers of public gatherings to seek permission from the relevant governor three days in advance. A governor can withhold permission without giving a reason.

Iraqi Refugees

Jordan hosts at least 500,000 Iraqi refugees, the majority of whom arrived after 2003 (only Syria hosts a comparable number of Iraqis). After Iraqis killed 57 people in the Amman hotel bombings of November 2005, Jordan's traditional tolerance toward Iraqis eroded. Jordan's government, which does not have an established mechanism to determine refugee status, shortened the length of tourist visas for Iraqis, deported visa overstayers, and prevented increasing numbers of Iraqis from entering. The office of the United Nations High Commissioner for Refugees in Jordan only exceptionally recognizes Iraqis as refugees, instead providing applicants with asylum seeker cards. Jordan does not always respect asylum seeker status and the protection it entails against deportation. In 2006 Jordan barred Iraqi refugee children without residency permits from attending Jordanian public and private schools.

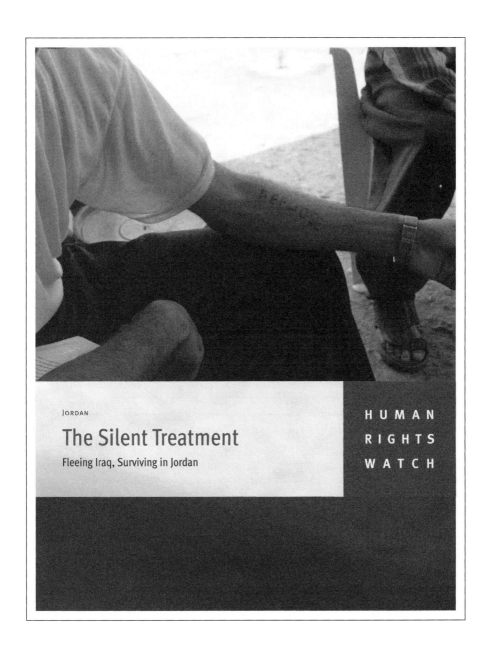

JORDAN

The Silent Treatment

Fleeing Iraq, Surviving in Jordan

HUMAN
RIGHTS
WATCH

Migrant Worker Rights

Reports documenting abuses of mostly Southeast Asian migrants working in Jordan's Qualified Industrial Zones induced the government to increase the number of inspectors and to install an emergency hotline. Reported abuse included beatings, long working hours, withholding of passports and paychecks, pay discrimination based on sex or nationality, preventing workers from leaving the work site at any time, and denying medical care. The provisions of Jordan's labor code, including the right to unionize, exclude non-Jordanians as well as agricultural and domestic workers. In early October the governor of Zarqa had Bangladeshi workers detained for striking.

Key International Actors

The United States gave Jordan US$510 million assistance in 2006 (compared to the European Union's €73 million). Jordan's dependence on US assistance led parliamentarians to approve a bilateral immunity agreement with the US in January that obligates Jordan not to surrender to the International Criminal Court US citizens (and non-citizens working for the US government) under Jordanian jurisdiction, even if the ICC seeks their extradition for genocide, war crimes, or crimes against humanity (US legislation in 2004 conditioned foreign economic assistance for ICC states parties on countries' ratifying such an agreement).

The United Kingdom concluded a memorandum of understanding with Jordan in 2005 under which Jordan undertook not to mistreat persons the UK deports to Jordan. Human Rights Watch has found that such promises do nothing to reduce the risk of torture or to satisfy the sending country's obligation not to deport people to the risk of torture. Jordanian officials have admitted that this agreement is not enforceable in court, leaving a rupture in UK-Jordanian relations as the highest sanction. The UK has not in the past strongly criticized human rights violations in Jordan. Abu Qatada, a Jordanian residing in the UK, has challenged his deportation to Jordan, claiming a risk of ill-treatment.

LEBANON

Lebanon's tentative steps towards reform and stability following the assassination of former Prime Minister Rafiq Hariri and the subsequent withdrawal of Syrian troops came to a halt after war broke out between Hezbollah and Israel on July 12. The 34-day conflict devastated the country and killed an estimated 1,000 civilians.

A UN investigation into the Hariri assassination and 14 other cases continues with the likelihood that that the Lebanese government and the UN will establish an international tribunal to try those responsible. However, accountability remains elusive for the families of the approximately 17,000 who "disappeared" during and after Lebanon's deadly civil war (1975-1990).

Palestinian refugees resident in Lebanon continue to face discrimination; Lebanese laws deny them access to adequate housing and certain categories of employment. Iraqis fleeing their war-torn country to Lebanon find themselves facing a real risk of deportation. Despite campaigning by civil society, Lebanese law continues to discriminate against women by, among other things, denying them the right to pass their nationality to their children or spouses. Migrant domestic workers remain particularly at risk of abuse and employers regularly violate their basic rights, with little possibility for legal remedy. Human rights groups operate freely in Lebanon, but some human rights defenders faced harassment in 2006.

War between Hezbollah and Israel

According to the Lebanese government, the Israel-Hezbollah war resulted in 1,189 killed (mostly civilians), 4,399 injured, and an estimated one million displaced. Children accounted for approximately one third of the casualties. Israeli attacks also did massive damage to infrastructure and the natural environment and destroyed at least 15,000 homes. Returnees faced shortages of water and electricity as well as reduced access to health care and other public services. The destruction harmed virtually all sectors of the country's economy, directly affecting the livelihood of hundreds of thousands of Lebanese. According to Oxfam, up to 85 percent of Lebanon's farmers lost some or all of their harvest.

In its conduct of hostilities, the Israel Defense Forces (IDF) repeatedly violated the laws of war by failing to distinguish between combatants and civilians. The IDF claims that the high proportion of civilian deaths in the war was due to Hezbollah hiding its rockets and fighters in villages and towns, but IDF attacks responsible for a majority of the civilian deaths took place at times when there was no evidence that Hezbollah fighters or weapons were even in the vicinity. While the IDF in certain cases gave advance warnings for civilians to evacuate areas likely to be attacked, such warnings do not relieve a warring party of its obligation to target only combatants. In southern Lebanon, many people remained even after warnings because of age, infirmity, responsibility for livestock and crops, inability to afford exorbitant taxi fares charged for evacuation, or fear of becoming another roadside casualty of IDF bombing. As a result, the IDF's indiscriminate bombardment had devastating consequences for civilians.

Israel's extensive use of cluster munitions also continues to be a pressing concern. The UN has estimated that Israel fired cluster munitions containing 2.6 to 4 million submunitions into Lebanon, leaving behind as many as one million hazardous duds that, at this writing, had resulted in more than 20 deaths and 100 injuries, many of them serious. According to the UN, Israel blanketed much of southern Lebanon with 90 percent of those submunitions in the last three days before the cease-fire.

For its part, Hezbollah launched thousands of rockets on cities, towns, and villages in northern Israel, using a variety of unguided surface-to-surface rockets. These rockets killed 39 Israeli civilians and injured hundreds more. Hezbollah packed some of these rockets with more than 4,000 anti-personnel steel spheres ("ball bearings") that shoot out upon impact, causing many of the civilian deaths and injuries. Hezbollah also fired Chinese-made cluster rockets, each containing 39 explosive submunitions as well as deadly steel spheres. At least 113 such cluster rockets hit Israel, causing one death and 12 injuries, according to Israeli police. The rockets also caused damage to civilian homes, businesses, the natural environment, and the economy. While Hezbollah appeared to target some of its rockets at military objectives, in some cases hitting them, many of its rockets hit civilian areas, far from any apparent military target. Such attacks—at best indiscriminate attacks on civilian areas and, at worst, deliberate attacks against civilians—violated the laws of war.

LEBANON

Fatal Strikes
Israel's Indiscriminate Attacks Against Civilians in Lebanon

HUMAN
RIGHTS
WATCH

Investigation into Killing of Rafiq Hariri

The UN-appointed International Independent Investigation Commission continues its investigation into the killing of former Prime Minister Hariri. The UN Security Council adopted Resolution 1686 in June 2006, which expanded the mandate of the commission to include assisting Lebanese authorities with investigations into other politically motivated assassinations, assassination attempts, and explosions since October 2004.

Lebanese and UN officials made progress toward establishing a tribunal to try those responsible for the Hariri killing, but no final agreement has been reached at this writing. Four former heads of Lebanese intelligence and security services— General 'Ali al-Hajj, General Raymond Azar, Brigadier General Jamil al-Sayyed and Mustafa Hamdan—remained in detention following their arrest on August 30, 2005.

"Disappearances"

No progress was made in 2006 to uncover the fate of the Lebanese, Palestinians and other nationals who were "disappeared" during and after the 1975-1990 Lebanese civil war. The Lebanese government estimates that there were a total of 17,415 such cases, but no criminal investigations or prosecutions had been initiated at this writing. Since April 2005, relatives and friends of the "disappeared" have been holding sit-ins in front of the UN offices in Beirut demanding information on the fate of people still unaccounted for.

According to Lebanese human rights groups, Syria detained at least 640 victims of forced disappearances in Syrian prisons, but an official joint Syrian-Lebanese committee established in May 2005 to investigate the cases had not published any findings at this writing.

Refugees

Palestinians are the largest refugee group in Lebanon with approximately 400,000 Palestinians registered with the United Nations Relief and Works Agency (UNRWA). They are subject to wide-ranging restrictions on housing and work, and their living conditions are poor. In June 2005, the Lebanese government began allowing Palestinian refugees born in Lebanon to work in manual and clerical jobs, but a ban on professional employment remains in place. Non-registered Palestinian refugees in Lebanon—a group estimated to number between 3,000 and 5,000—are particularly vulnerable as they do not possess valid identification documents and do not receive any assistance from UNRWA or the Lebanese government.

An estimated 20,000 Iraqis are now living in Lebanon. Lebanon provides no services for them and no process for regularizing their status. It also has failed to date to institute a temporary protection regime for Iraqi asylum seekers, as advocated by the UN High Commissioner for Refugees, and it regularly deports Iraqis who may well have valid persecution claims.

Human Rights Defenders

Human rights groups operate freely in Lebanon, but Lebanese authorities harassed some human rights defenders and groups in 2006. In April, a military court finally dropped all charges against human rights defender and lawyer Dr. Muhamad Mugraby. Military prosecutors had charged Mugraby with the crime of "defaming the military establishment and its officers" after he delivered a speech in November 2003 criticizing the Lebanese government's practice of using military courts to prosecute civilians for dissent. At this writing, Samira Trad, whose organization Frontiers Center promotes the rights of refugees, continued to face ill-defined defamation charges dating from 2003, apparently related to her work on behalf of refugees.

The offices of *Soutien aux Libanais detenus arbitrairement* (SOLIDA), an organization fighting against the practice of torture, were broken into in October 2006; a computer hard-drive and work files were stolen. The burglary took place the night before the launch of SOLIDA's report documenting torture practices in the Ministry of Defense's detention center. The Lebanese police are investigating the burglary.

Discrimination against Women

Despite women's active participation in all aspects of Lebanese society, discriminatory provisions continue to exist in personal status laws, nationality laws, and criminal laws relating to violence in the family. Current Lebanese law does not allow Lebanese women to confer nationality on either their spouses or children.

Women migrants employed as domestic workers face exploitation and abuse by employers, including excessive hours of work and non-payment of wages. Journalists and social activists report that many women migrants suffer physical and sexual abuse at the hands of employers. The UN Special Rapporteur on trafficking in persons stated in her February 2006 report that Lebanon is a transit and destination country for large numbers of domestic migrant workers, a considerable number of whom are trafficked into exploitative labor situations.

Key International Actors

The UN Security Council remains actively involved in Lebanese issues. The passage of Resolution 1701 in August 2006 paved the way for a ceasefire between Israel and Hezbollah and created an expanded UNIFIL force in Southern Lebanon. Thousands of UN peacekeepers were deployed to monitor Lebanon's southern border and its territorial waters. Meanwhile, the Security Council continues to follow-up on the implementation of Resolution 1559, which called among other things for the Lebanese government to extend its control over all Lebanese territory, and on the progress of the international investigation into the Hariri assassination.

France and the United States retain a strong role in Lebanon; both countries send senior officials to visit the country regularly. France took the lead in heading the UNIFIL expanded force, and it remains a main driver of Security Council resolutions on Lebanon. The US role in Lebanon became more controversial as a result of the war between Hezbollah and Israel. The US government rejected efforts for an early ceasefire during the war and large segments of the Lebanese population considered the US a party to the war due to its military support of Israel.

Despite the withdrawal of Syrian troops from Lebanon in April 2005, Lebanese-Syrian relations remain tense and complicated. Contentious issues include Syria's continued refusal to establish diplomatic ties with Lebanon and its ongoing influence on Lebanese affairs. During the war between Hezbollah and Israel, Syria welcomed more than 140,000 Lebanese fleeing areas under attack.

As Hezbollah's main foreign ally, Iran also plays an important role in Lebanon and is seen by many as key to any long-term solution to the conflict between Hezbollah and Israel.

LIBYA

Human rights conditions in Libya improved somewhat in 2006 as the country continued its slow international reintegration, but serious violations remain. The government still restricts freedom of expression, and bans political parties and independent organizations. It continues to imprison individuals for criticizing Libya's political system, the government, or its leader Mu`ammar al-Qadhafi. Due process violations and torture remain concerns, as do disappearances unresolved from past years.

Political Prisoners

Dozens and perhaps hundreds of individuals are in prison for engaging in peaceful political activity. Many were imprisoned for violating Law 71, which bans any group activity based on a political ideology opposed to the principles of the 1969 revolution that brought al-Qadhafi to power. Violators of Law 71 can be put to death. In a positive development, in March 2006 the government announced the release of 132 political prisoners, including 86 members of the Muslim Brotherhood, a non-violent political and social organization, who had been in prison since 1998 after trials that violated Libyan and international law.

Fathi al-Jahmi remains Libya's most prominent political prisoner, detained since 2004. He faces a possible death sentence for slandering al-Qadhafi and talking with a foreign official, believed to be a United States diplomat. According to the Libyan government, al-Jahmi's trial began in late 2005, but the authorities have not announced the charges. His court-appointed lawyer told Human Rights Watch that al-Jahmi faces counts under penal code article 206, which imposes the death penalty on those who call "for the establishment of any grouping, organization or association proscribed by law," and on those who belong to or support such an organization.

The fate of dozens of political prisoners remains unknown: according to one Libyan group based abroad, more than 250 political prisoners have disappeared.

Freedom of Association and Freedom of Expression

Libya has many professional organizations and associations but no truly independent nongovernmental organizations. Law 19, On Associations, requires that organizations get approval from a political body to operate, and there is no right to appeal a negative decision. The government has refused to allow an independent journalists' organization, and reportedly does not allow the official lawyers' union to appoint its own leadership. Law 71, mentioned above, and other restrictive legislation severely limit the right to establish independent groups.

Two human rights groups exist in Libya, the more prominent being the human rights program at the quasi-official Qadhafi Development Foundation, run by Mu`ammar al-Qadhafi's influential son, Seif al-Islam. It was instrumental in the release of the 132 political prisoners in March 2006, and is the most vocal domestic critic of the government; in August Seif al-Islam al-Qadhafi gave a speech in which he criticized government corruption and the lack of representative government and free press, and called for the drafting of a constitution.

Freedom of expression is severely curtailed, although Libyan lawyers, academics, and journalists are slowly beginning to address previously taboo topics. The security service extensively monitors the population, and self-censorship is rife. There are no private radio or television stations, and government authorities or the Revolutionary Committees Movement (a powerful ideological organization) control the country's main newspapers. The only access to uncensored news comes via the internet and satellite television, which is widely viewed.

The internet continues to spread in Libya, with dozens of opposition or independent websites based abroad. The government has occasionally blocked some websites. In a positive step, in March the government released `Abd al-Raziq al-Mansuri, a writer for a website based in the United Kingdom who had been arrested in January 2005, apparently because of his critical work.

Abu Salim Prison

2006 marked 10 years since large-scale killings in Tripoli's Abu Salim prison, run by the Internal Security Agency. According to an ex-prisoner interviewed by Human Rights Watch, prisoners revolted on June 28, 1996, over prison conditions.

The prison held between 1,600 and 1,700 prisoners at the time, and the security forces killed "around 1,200 people," said the witness, who worked in the prison kitchen. Human Rights Watch could not verify the ex-prisoner's claim, but the government acknowledges that security forces killed prisoners in Abu Salim, saying they responded properly to a revolt. In 2005 the government said it had established a committee to investigate the incident, but it remains unclear how the committee will conduct its work or when it will produce its findings. Human Rights Watch has called for an independent inquiry to investigate the deaths. To date the government has failed to announce the number of people killed 10 years ago or the names of the dead.

On October 4, 2006, a group of prisoners in Abu Salim again staged a protest. As the situation escalated, guards opened fire. The Libyan prosecutor general issued a statement after an investigation that confirmed one inmate dead and three others injured (press and opposition reports said at least nine injured), as well as eight police officers who were hurt. The statement said several inmates were to blame for the violence and that prison guards had acted in accordance with the law.

Benghazi HIV Case

Libyan authorities have held five Bulgarian nurses and a Palestinian doctor since 1999 for allegedly infecting 426 Libyan children with HIV, despite credible claims that they were tortured to extract confessions. The Supreme Court in 2005 overturned their initial conviction, which had resulted in death sentences, and ordered the case returned to the lower court. The retrial has been repeatedly delayed, and as this writing no judgment has been reached. The state prosecutor is again calling for the death penalty.

Detention of Women and Girls in "Social Rehabilitation"

Women and girls suspected of transgressing moral codes may be detained indefinitely in "social rehabilitation" facilities—portrayed as "protective" homes for wayward women and girls or those whose families reject them. There, the government routinely violates women's and girls' human rights, including those to due process, liberty, freedom of movement, personal dignity, and privacy. Many

LIBYA

Stemming the Flow
Abuses Against Migrants, Asylum Seekers and Refugees

PART III OF A THREE-PART SERIES

HUMAN
RIGHTS
WATCH

women and girls detained in these facilities have committed no crime, or have already served a sentence. Some are there because they were raped and are now ostracized for staining their family's honor. There is no way out of these facilities unless a male relative takes custody of the woman or girl or she consents to marriage. Various government officials have promised to investigate these abuses after a report by Human Rights Watch, though announced changes to date have been cosmetic at best.

Treatment of Foreigners

Libya has not signed the 1951 Refugee Convention and has no formal working agreement with the United Nations High Commissioner for Refugees (UNHCR). In a positive development, in 2006 the secretary of justice created a committee to draft a law on asylum, which Libya currently lacks, and cooperation with UNHCR improved.

Throughout the year the government continued to deport thousands of foreigners who were without proper documentation, mostly sub-Saharan Africans, sometimes back to countries where they could face persecution or torture. Foreigners reported beatings and other abuse during their detention and deportation.

In an April 2006 memorandum to Human Rights Watch, the government said that some police officers "overindulge in the use of force" against foreigners, but that "the failings in these cases are nothing more than the isolated actions of individuals." In such cases, "legal action was taken," although the government did not provide details.

Promises of Reform

In 2006, the government continued its long-standing review of many Libyan laws, including proposals for a new penal code and code of criminal procedure. Under the new penal code, the secretary of justice told Human Rights Watch in 2005, the death penalty would remain only for the "most dangerous crimes" and for "terrorism." At this writing, however, the government had presented neither the draft penal code nor the code of criminal procedure to Libya's main legislative body, the General People's Congress.

While the most recent version of the penal code draft is unknown, a review of a 2004 draft suggests the government will accept a very broad definition of terrorism, which it might then use to criminalize people who are expressing peaceful political views.

Key International Actors

The United States and European governments continued to slowly improve their relations with Libya throughout 2006. In addition to renouncing weapons of mass destruction in 2003, Libya maintained its cooperation in the global "war on terror" and provided valuable intelligence on militant Islamic individuals and groups. Libya has also signed the International Atomic Energy Agency Additional Protocol and has become a State Party to the Chemical Weapons Convention. In return for Libya's cooperation, on June 30, 2006, the US rescinded Libya's designation as a state sponsor of terrorism.

In May the US and Libya resumed full diplomatic relations, and both countries upgraded their diplomatic offices to embassies (although at this writing neither country had appointed an ambassador). Despite warmer relations, the US government occasionally criticized human rights violations in Libya, saying "the Government continued to commit numerous, serious abuses." In public, the US government has called for the release of Fathi al-Jahmi and the 5 Bulgarian nurses and Palestinian doctor on trial in the Benghazi HIV case.

Libya's relations with the European Union progressed more slowly, largely due to the ongoing Benghazi HIV case. Cooperation continued in controlling illegal migration from Libya to southern Europe, often without adequate regard for the rights of migrants or the need to protect refugees and others at risk of abuse on return to their home countries.

MOROCCO/WESTERN SAHARA

Morocco continues to present a mixed picture on human rights. It has made great strides in addressing past abuses and allowed considerable space for public dissent and protest in recent years. But authorities, aided by complaisant courts, continue to use repressive legislation to occasionally punish peaceful opponents and the police use excessive force to break up demonstrations, especially in outlying areas.

Controls were particularly tight in the restive and disputed Western Sahara region, which Morocco administers as if it were part of its national territory. A pro-independence movement known as the Polisario Front (Popular Front for the Liberation of the Saguia el-Hamra and Rio de Oro) contests Moroccan sovereignty and demands implementation of a stalled UN plan for a referendum on self-determination for the Sahrawi people.

Several hundred suspected Islamist extremists arrested in the weeks after the Casablanca bombings of May 2003 continue to serve prison terms, despite a series of royal pardons that freed a few hundred Islamist prisoners. The remaining prisoners held hunger strikes during the year to demand their freedom or a review of their convictions, and improvements in prison conditions. Many of those rounded up in 2003 had been held in secret detention for days or weeks and subjected to mistreatment, and sometimes torture, while under interrogation, and then convicted in unfair trials.

Reforms to the family law, enacted in 2004, raised the minimum age of marriage for women from fifteen to eighteen, made the family the joint responsibility of both spouses, rescinded the wife's duty of obedience to her husband, and placed the practice of polygamy under strict judicial control. Concerns remain that these reforms are being implemented at a slow pace.

Child labor is widespread, despite the Labor Code's ban on children under 15 working. Young girls working as live-in servants in private homes are especially vulnerable to abuse, including sexual abuse, and frequently work one hundred hours a week without access to education or adequate food and medical care. Authorities rarely punish employers who abuse child domestics, and labor inspectors are not authorized to enter private homes. The government introduced draft legislation in 2006 to regulate employment conditions for domestic workers but, as of early November, the draft did not provide an adequate enforcement mechanism accessible to children.

The Justice System and Legal Reforms

Police are rarely held accountable for human rights violations. However, authorities told a visiting UN delegation in May 2006 that two policeman were awaiting trial for having caused the death of Hamdi Lembarki, a Sahrawi who died from blows to the head on October 30, 2005, during a turbulent period in el-Ayoun. A new law on torture entered into force in February, providing prison terms for state agents guilty of torturing or ill-treating persons in custody.

In cases with a political color, courts routinely denied defendants a fair trial, ignoring requests for medical examinations lodged by defendants who claim to have been tortured, refusing to summon exculpatory witnesses, and convicting defendants solely on the basis of apparently coerced confessions.

For example, in December 2005, a court in El-Ayoun convicted seven Sahrawi human rights activists in connection with the sometimes-violent protests that had broken out sporadically in the region since the previous May. The evidence linking the seven to acts of violence was dubious and in some cases appeared fabricated. Authorities appear to have targeted these Sahrawis because of their human rights activism and outspoken pro-independence views. The seven got prison terms of up to two years but by April all had been released.

In another instance of justice denied—one that seems to involve personal score-settling rather than political repression—Casablanca businessman Mourad Belmâachi entered his third year in pretrial detention on charges of stealing documents and altering them illegally in an effort to evade creditors. After emerging from police interrogation in June 2004, Belmâachi immediately demanded a medical examination, claiming his confession had been obtained under torture, but judicial authorities did not act on this request. Since then, judges have refused to release him pending trial, without justifying this refusal.

Freedom of Association and Assembly and Movement

Authorities generally tolerate the work of the many human rights organizations active in Rabat and Casablanca. They also generally do not hamper foreign human rights organizations visiting Morocco, and often respond to their letters of concern. However, in the Western Sahara, surveillance is tighter, and harassment of domestic and foreign rights workers more common.

Most types of public assemblies require authorization from the Interior Ministry, which can refuse permission if it deems them liable to "disturb the public order." This discretion is exercised more often when the demonstrators' agenda is critical of government policies. Although many of the frequent public protests in Rabat run their course undisturbed, baton-wielding police have broken up others with brutality. For example, they used force to disperse a small sit-in on July 6, 2006, in front of parliament in Rabat called to protest recent violations of the right of assembly.

Police repression of public protests was fiercer in the Western Sahara than elsewhere, and involved a pattern of excessive force against demonstrators, some of whom threw rocks and Molotov cocktails.

Authorities continued to restrict foreign travel for some Sahrawi activists, although such measures have decreased overall in recent years. As of early November, authorities had yet to return the passports they confiscated from nine activists whom they had blocked from traveling to Geneva in 2003 to participate in UN human rights activities.

Press Freedom

Media criticism of the authorities is often quite blunt, but is nevertheless circumscribed by a press law that provides prison terms for libel and for expression critical of "Islam, the institution of the monarchy, or the territorial integrity." A 2004 law liberalized broadcast media but requires foreign media seeking licenses for stations inside Morocco to "scrupulously respect the values of the monarchy and its heritage in terms of Islam and territorial integrity." Authorities blocked access to certain pro-Polisario websites, explaining to a visiting UN delegation that they controlled online material to prevent attacks on "territorial integrity."

Since mid-2005, a series of prosecutions of independent weeklies, the most outspoken and critical sector of the Moroccan news media, showed the continuing limits on press freedom. Courts convicted at least four weeklies, or their journalists, on criminal charges of libel, publishing "false news," or "insulting" a foreign head of state, and were trying a fifth for "undermining" the institution of the monarchy. An appeals court on April 18 confirmed a record 3.1 million dirham (US $356,500) libel judgment against *Le Journal Hebdomadaire* ("The Weekly Journal"). A Brussels-based research institute said *Le Journal* had defamed it by saying that its report on the Western Sahara was so one-sided that it gave the impression of having been commissioned by the Moroccan government. The weekly said it would have to close if forced to pay the fine.

Counterterrorism Measures

There were persistent but unconfirmed media reports throughout the year that Morocco had agreed to receive detainees secretly transferred by Western countries, for harsh interrogations by Moroccan intelligence agents. Moroccan authorities denied these reports categorically.

On September 14, 2006, Francesca Longhi, lawyer for Italian citizen Abou el-Kassim Britel, testified before a temporary committee of the European Parliament that her client had been arrested in Pakistan in 2002 and then secretly flown in a private plane "under CIA aegis" to his native Morocco, where police tortured him under interrogation. Britel was freed after nine months in detention without charge but then rearrested in 2003 and sentenced to a long prison term on terrorism charges. Binyam Mohammed, an Ethiopian-born detainee at the US-run Guantanamo facility, claimed through his lawyer that American agents transferred him in 2002 from Pakistan to Morocco, where interrogators tortured him, before he was transported to US custody in Afghanistan and then Guantanamo.

Acknowledging Past Abuses

On November 30, 2005, Morocco's Equity and Reconciliation Commission (ERC), launched in 2004 by King Mohamed VI, issued its report into grave human rights violations committed between 1956 and 1999, stimulating taboo-breaking discussions of past repression. The ERC provided an official acknowledgement of past repression, gave a long-overdue voice to victims, and elucidated many individual cases. However, non-cooperation by public officials prevented it from resolving other cases. And despite ERC recommendations on ending impunity, authorities took no steps to bring to trial those implicated in past abuse, including some who continue to hold high government posts. During 2006, in accordance with its mandate, the ERC worked on determining the level of compensation that the state would pay to past victims.

Key International Actors

Morocco is an important ally of the United States because of its cooperation in fighting terrorism, the 2004 signing of a bilateral free-trade agreement, and its generally pro-West policies. In June 2004, the United States designated Morocco "a major non-NATO ally," thus easing restrictions on arms sales. In public comments, US officials emphasized these facets of the bilateral alliance and spoke rarely about human rights problems, even though the State Department reports on human rights accurately reflected the range of rights violations in Morocco and the Western Sahara.

An association agreement has been in effect between Morocco and the European Union since 2000. Morocco is the leading beneficiary of MEDA funds, the EU's main aid program for its Mediterranean partner countries. Morocco received 1.25 billion euros in grants over the past decade; the program for 2005-2006 was budgeted at 275 million euros. EU public comments on Morocco's human rights situation are rare. A bilateral subcommittee on human rights, governance, and democratization, was due to convene for the first time in November.

France is Morocco's leading trade partner and the leading provider of investments and public development aid. French officials made almost no public comments on human rights in Morocco during 2006.

The UN High Commissioner for Human Rights dispatched a delegation in May to examine human rights conditions in the Moroccan-administered Western Sahara and the Polisario-administered Sahrawi refugee camps in Tindouf, Algeria. After negotiating the easing of a tight Moroccan security presence, the delegation was able, in its own words, "to meet with whomever they deemed useful." It concluded, "The Sahrawi people are not only denied their right to self-determination but equally are severely restricted from exercising a series of other rights, and especially rights of particular importance to the right of self-determination, such as the right to express their views about the issue, to create associations defending their right to self-determination and to hold assemblies to make their views known." The delegation said it was unable to collect sufficient information about human rights conditions in the Tindouf camps, but called closer monitoring of rights conditions there and in the Moroccan-controlled areas "indispensable."

SAUDI ARABIA

Overall human rights conditions remain poor in Saudi Arabia, an absolute monarchy. Despite international and domestic pressure to implement reforms, King Abdullah has not met expectations of improvements following his succession to the throne in August 2005. The government undertook no major human rights reforms in 2006, and there were signs of backsliding on issues of human rights defenders, freedom of association, and freedom of expression.

Saudi law does not protect many basic rights and the government places strict limits on freedom of association, assembly, and expression. Arbitrary detention, mistreatment and torture of detainees, restrictions on freedom of movement, and lack of official accountability remain serious concerns. Saudi women continue to face serious obstacles to their participation in society. Many foreign workers, especially women, face exploitative working conditions.

The United States in 2006 transferred 29 Saudi detainees at Guantanamo Bay to Saudi custody. Nine of the 29 were released after three months, in addition to three other former Guantanamo detainees who had been transferred in July 2005.

Political and Social Reform

Nascent political reform stalled in 2006. The government did not take up the recommendations of the fifth and most recent National Dialogue session of December 2005, or of previous Dialogue sessions, such as considering women for judgeships.

Conservative views hardened in response to small steps in social liberalization. In February 2006 conservatives including the religious police harassed visitors and authors, especially women, at the Riyadh International Book Fair, which displayed a Bible and works by the banned author Turki al-Hamad for the first time. In March conservatives rallied against proposals to reform the education curriculum, which had received strong US support.

Several court decisions raised concern over a lack of standardized canon law to rein in biased judges. In February a judge barred a Saudi Shia from bearing legal witness to the marriage of his Sunni boss's son. Another judge annulled a marriage, finding the husband "inadequate" because he followed the Ismaili (Shia) creed and not the prevailing Wahhabi (Sunni) creed like his wife. A third judge annulled a marriage, finding in favor of a man who claimed the inferior tribal lineage of his sister's husband made the latter ineligible to marry into their family, although Saudi sharia law places no conditions of heritage on couples who intend to marry.

Arbitrary Detention, Torture and Ill-Treatment, and the Death Penalty

Dr. Saud al-Musaibih, the head of a special consultative committee of the Ministry of Interior and the Ministry of Islamic Affairs, said 700 detainees "who were not involved in terrorist acts," but suspected of "harboring extremist thoughts," had been released, the newspaper *Okaz* reported on October 12.

Dammam secret police (*mabahith*) moved Shia activist Kamil 'Abbas Al Ahmad from the General Prison to their own prison one week before his five-year sentence was due to expire in July. *Mabahith* officials denied all knowledge of Al Ahmad when Human Rights Watch telephoned giving the date of his transfer. After the governmental Human Rights Commission intervened, the *mabahith* released Al Ahmad in September.

A former prisoner in Mecca General Prison alleged to Human Rights Watch that prison guards regularly beat him, burned his back on a hot metal block, and kept him in solitary confinement for six months. He said such abuse was routine during his time as an inmate between 2002 and 2006. Thirty-six inmates of al-Ha'ir prison in Riyadh in late 2005 issued a "Cry for Help to Global Rights Organizations" detailing their "despondence" due to beatings in prison and public lashings.

Saudi judges routinely issue sentences of thousands of lashes as punishment, often carried out in public. The beatings lead to severe mental trauma and physical pain, and the victims do not receive medical treatment.

The kingdom carried out some 22 executions as of November 2006, around one-fourth the figure for 2005.

Freedom of Expression, Assembly, and Association

In February 2006 Saudi authorities briefly closed *al-Shams* newspaper for republishing cartoons of the Prophet Muhammad deemed offensive. In March 2006 the *mabahith* arrested Muhsin al-'Awaji for several days for openly criticizing the king's alleged heavy reliance on the advice of liberals. In April the *mabahith* arrested Rabbah al-Quwa'i for "harboring destructive thoughts" displayed in his internet writings critiquing al Qaeda. The judge extracted an unspecified pledge from al-Quwa'i, who described himself as "half-free" to Human Rights Watch following his release. In June the *mabahith* arrested Sa'd bin Zu'air for 20 days for saying in an interview on *al-Arabiya* television that the death of Abu Mus'ab al-Zarqawi (the head of al Qaeda in Iraq) was "sad for most Muslims."

In February 2006 the authorities arrested several Shia publicly celebrating their religious holiday *'Ashura'* in Safwa. In August security forces stopped Shias who had begun to demonstrate against Israeli attacks in Lebanon. In October security forces arrested four Shia in the Eastern Province for several days for displaying Hezbollah emblems.

In September 2006 around 300 Ismailis demonstrated peacefully and undisturbed in Najran against discrimination, amidst a heavy security presence.

In March the appointed national Shura (Advisory) Council did not pass a draft law regulating nongovernmental organizations that would have further restricted freedom of association, including by giving a governmental National Commission extensive and excessively intrusive supervisory powers over nongovernmental organizations (NGOs).

Human Rights Defenders

More than one year after the king pardoned three prominent reformers, Ali al-Dumaini, Abdullah al-Hamid, and Matruk al-Falih, and their lawyer, Abd al-

Rahman al-Lahim, the government has not responded to their demands to lift a ban on their traveling abroad.

In September the *mabahith* detained women's rights activist Wajeha al-Huwaider, forcing her to pledge to refrain from speaking to the media and to cease her human rights advocacy as a condition for release. Saudi non-judicial authorities often extract such pledges from regime critics.

In August 2006 the government failed to reply to a request to open a new human rights organization. The government also continued to refuse to license Human Rights First in Saudi Arabia, an independent group that nonetheless continued to monitor violations.

The government-approved National Society for Human Rights (NSHR) became more active and outspoken in 2006. It proposed an HIV patients bill of rights, and publicly criticized the draft NGO law. The NSHR also called for judicial reforms to ensure equal sentences for the same crime.

The Ministry of Interior approved the long-delayed governmental Human Rights Commission's 24-member board, but has yet to announce the members who reportedly include several Shia (including one Ismaili), but no women. The king has instructed all government bodies to cooperate with the commission.

Women's Rights

Women in Saudi Arabia continue to suffer from severe discrimination in the workplace, home, and the courts, and from restrictions on their freedom of movement and their choice of partners. The religious police enforce strict gender segregation and a women's public dress code of head-to-toe covering. Women are excluded from the weekly *majlis* (council), where senior members of the royal family listen to the complaints and proposals of citizens.

Women need permission from their male guardian to work, study, or travel. In February 2006 the Transport Committee of the Shura Council declined a motion to discuss the possibility of allowing women to drive. Minister of Information Iyad al-Madani, however, said there was no obstacle to women applying for driver's licenses.

A directive to replace male staff in lingerie shops with Saudi women under a new provision in the labor law allowing women to work in jobs "suitable to their nature" met with strong conservative objections. In December 2005 women could cast ballots for women running for local chamber of commerce boards; women won seats in Jeddah, Lama al-Sulaiman, and Nashwa al-Taher.

Migrant Worker Rights

Many of the estimated 8.8 million foreign workers face exploitative working conditions, including 16-hour workdays, no breaks or food and drink, and being locked in dormitories during their time off. The government promised to publish in November 2006 a special annex to the new labor law that regulates domestic migrant workers' rights. Women domestic workers, whom the labor law currently does not protect, are often at risk of serious abuse in private homes.

In September the government began to ease its discriminatory ban of August 2004 on all Chadians renewing their residency permits, attending school, and accessing emergency medical care. Security forces in October rounded up 7,000 mostly illegal immigrants around the Bukhariya quarter of Ta'if, the Hindawiya and Karantina quarters of Jeddah, and elsewhere. The authorities deported tens of thousands of illegal immigrants in 2006 without assessing whether they have a well founded fear of persecution in their home country.

Key International Actors

Saudi Arabia is a key United States ally. The US-Saudi Strategic Dialogue, initiated in 2005, held its second round of working meetings in March 2006, but human rights discussions in the working group on "Education, Exchange and Human Resources" produced no results.

The 2006 US State Department's international religious freedom report maintained Saudi Arabia's designation as "a country of particular concern," but no longer claimed that "freedom of religion does not exist." Citing a Saudi undertaking in July to reform school textbooks, curb the religious police's powers of arrest, and strengthen the Human Rights Commission, the US government did not impose sanctions for religious freedom violations.

The United Kingdom in August reportedly agreed to sell Saudi Arabia 72 advanced Eurofighter "Typhoon" war planes worth around $10 billion. The UK Foreign and Commonwealth Office's *Human Rights Report 2006* continued to list Saudi Arabia as a "major country of concern."

SYRIA

Syria's poor human rights situation deteriorated further in 2006. The government strictly limits freedom of expression, association, and assembly. Emergency rule, imposed in 1963, remains in effect, despite public calls by Syrian reformers for its repeal. The authorities continue to harass and imprison human rights defenders and non-violent critics of government policies.

Following the May 2006 Beirut-Damascus Declaration, which called for improved relations between Lebanon and Syria, security forces apprehended some dozen activists who had signed the petition, including prominent writer Michel Kilo and human rights lawyer Anwar al-Bunni. On August 15, 2006, a military court sentenced Habib Saleh, a regular contributor to online forums, to three years for "spreading false and exaggerated information." Saleh had earlier served a three-year sentence for his involvement in the Damascus Spring initiatives of 2001.

Thousands of political prisoners, many of them members of the banned Muslim Brotherhood and the Communist Party, remain in detention. Syrian Kurds, the country's largest ethnic minority, continue to protest their treatment as second-class citizens. Women face legal as well as societal discrimination and have little means for redress against sexual abuse or domestic violence.

Arbitrary Detention, Torture, and "Disappearances"

In January 2006 the government released five of the eight remaining Damascus Spring prisoners, including former members of parliament Ma'mun al-Humsi and Riad Seif, as well as Fawaz Tello, Walid al-Bunni, and Habib Issa, but all five continue to face harassment. The authorities briefly detained Riad Seif twice following his release. Rights activist Ali al-Abdullah, who was released after six months in prison in November 2005, was detained again in March 2006 along with two of his sons. Syrian authorities disavowed any knowledge of their whereabouts for over a month. Al-Abdullah and one son were convicted in October 2006 for spreading false news and undermining the state but were released as they had already served their six-month sentences.

The authorities brought additional charges against activist Kamal al-Labwani, who has been detained since November 2005 after meeting abroad with European and US officials. He now stands accused of "communicating with a foreign country and prompting it to direct confrontation," which carries a sentence of life imprisonment or death.

Dr. `Arif Dalila, a prominent economics professor and a proponent of political liberalization, continues to serve a 10-year prison term imposed in July 2002 for his non-violent criticism of government policies. His health deteriorated sharply in 2006; reports indicate that he suffered a stroke.

The London-based Syrian Human Rights Committee (SHRC) estimates that about 4,000 political prisoners remain in detention in Syria. The authorities refuse to divulge information regarding numbers or names of people in detention on political or security-related charges.

The government also targets university students and other youths who exercise their right to freedom of expression and assembly. In early 2006 Syrian Air Force Intelligence arrested eight young men who tried to establish a youth movement. The authorities referred all eight—Husam Melhem, Ali Nazir al-Ali, Tariq al-Ghourani, Ayham Saqr, 'Ulam Fakhour, Maher Ibrahim Asbar, Omar al-Abdullah, and Diab Siriya—to the Supreme State Security Court, but as of mid-November 2006 the charges against them were still unknown.

Torture remains a serious problem in Syria, especially during interrogation. The September 2006 report of the official Canadian Commission of Inquiry into the 2002 US deportation to Syria of Maher Arar, a Syrian-born Canadian, concluded that "the SMI [Syrian Military Intelligence] tortured Mr. Arar while interrogating him during the period he was held incommunicado at the SMI's Palestine Branch facility." The report also concluded that Arar had come under Canadian and US suspicion on the basis of information the SMI extracted by torture from two other Canadian nationals of Arab origin, Abdullah al-Malki and Ahmad El Maati.

Syrian human rights organizations reported a number of cases of torture in 2006. One such case involved 26-year-old Mohammad Shaher Haysa, who reportedly died in a Damascus interrogation center as a result of severe torture.

2006 passed without any government acknowledgement that its security forces had "disappeared" an estimated 17,000 persons. The "disappeared" were mostly Muslim Brotherhood members and other Syrian activists who were detained in the late 1970s and early 1980s as well as hundreds of Lebanese and Palestinians who were detained in Syria or abducted from Lebanon by Syrian forces or Lebanese and Palestinian militias.

Human Rights Defenders

Human rights activists continue to be targets of government harassment and arrest. Among those arrested in 2006 and still in detention is human rights lawyer Anwar al-Bunni, arrested May 17 on charges of "belonging to a secret organization intending to topple President Bashar al-Assad." Fatih Jamus, arrested May 1, was released on October 12, 2006, but awaits trial for "spreading false information."

The government continues to prevent human rights activists from traveling and in 2006 expanded its list of those banned from leaving the country. The Syria-based Committees for the Defense of Democratic Liberties and Human Rights has published a list of over 110 activists banned from traveling; the actual number is considerably higher. Among those banned from traveling in 2006 are Radwan Ziadeh, director of the Damascus Centre for Human Rights Studies; Suheir Atassi, head of the Jamal al-Atassi Forum for Democratic Dialogue, which Syrian authorities shut down in 2005; and Walid al-Bunni, a physician who helped found the Committees for the Revival of Civil Society.

Syrian officials consistently have denied registration requests by human rights organizations. For instance, in August 2006 the Ministry of Social Affairs refused the request of the Syria-based National Organization for Human Rights to register, without providing any explanation.

Discrimination and Violence against Kurds

Kurds are the largest non-Arab ethnic minority in Syria, comprising about 10 percent of the population of 18.5 million. They remain subject to systematic discrimination, including the arbitrary denial of citizenship to an estimated 300,000 Syria-born Kurds.

Tensions have remained high since serious clashes between Kurdish demonstrators and security forces in Qamishli in 2004 that left more than 30 dead and 400 injured. Despite a general presidential pardon for those involved in the March 2004 clashes, dozens of Kurds still face trials in the criminal court of Al-Hasake, reportedly on charges of inciting disturbances and damaging public property.

Syrian authorities also suppress expressions of Kurdish identity. On March 20, 2006, security services arrested dozens of Kurds for participating in a candle-lit night procession in celebration of the Kurdish new year, Nowruz, and used tear gas and batons to break up the march.

Discrimination against Women

Syria's constitution guarantees gender equality, and many women are active in public life, but personal status laws as well as the penal code contain provisions that discriminate against women and girls. The penal code allows a judge to suspend punishment for a rapist if the rapist chooses to marry his victim, and provides leniency for so-called "honor" crimes, such as assault or killing of women and girls by male relatives for alleged sexual misconduct. Wives require the permission of their husbands to travel abroad, and divorce laws remain discriminatory.

Situation of Refugees Fleeing Iraq

An estimated 450,000 Iraqis are now living in Syria. While Syria initially welcomed Iraqi refugees and provided them with access to public hospitals and schools, Syrian attitudes and policies towards these refugees hardened in 2006 with the implementation of increasingly restrictive national immigration rules. Access to public hospitals has also become more limited. This has created difficulties for an increasing number of Iraqis, some of whom have started to leave the country seeking asylum elsewhere.

Syria has also hardened its position towards Palestinians fleeing Iraq. Since May 2006 Syria closed its border to Iraqi Palestinians and several hundred remain now at a makeshift camp in the no-man's land between the Iraqi and Syrian border checkpoints.

Key International Actors

Syria's relationship with the United States, United Kingdom, and France remained strained in 2006 over Syria's role in Lebanon and its ties to Iran. On May 17, 2006, the UN Security Council adopted Resolution 1680, which called on Syria to cooperate in the implementation of Resolution 1559 requiring the complete withdrawal of all foreign—that is, Syrian—troops from Lebanon. Following the war between Israel and Hezbollah in July 2006, a number of European countries began to question the policy of ostracizing Syria and started thinking about how best to reengage dialogue with al-Assad's regime.

Syria remains under pressure to cooperate with the ongoing international investigation into the assassination of former Lebanese Prime Minister Rafik Hariri. In his September 2006 interim report, Serge Brammertz, the head of the UN International Independent Investigation Committee, wrote that Syria's cooperation "remained generally satisfactory, and the Commission continues to require its full support in providing information and facilitating interviews with individuals located on Syrian territory." At this writing, four senior pro-Syrian Lebanese intelligence and security officers remained in detention in Lebanon on suspicion of involvement in the Hariri assassination.

Iran continued to be Syria's main regional ally and in June 2006 the two countries signed an agreement for military cooperation aiming at consolidating their defense efforts.

The Association Agreement between Syria and the European Union, initialed in October 2004, contains a clause requiring respect for human rights. At this writing, the agreement remained suspended at the final approval stage as European countries remained divided over how to engage with Syria.

Tunisia

President Zine el-Abidine Ben Ali and the ruling party, the Constitutional Democratic Assembly, dominate political life in Tunisia. The government uses the threat of terrorism and religious extremism as a pretext to crack down on peaceful dissent. There are continuous and credible reports of torture and ill-treatment being used to obtain statements from suspects in custody. Sentenced prisoners also face deliberate ill-treatment.

In March President Ben Ali pardoned or conditionally released some 1,650 prisoners, including 70 members of the banned Islamist party an-Nahdha. In November the president pardoned or conditionally released about 50 more political prisoners, most of them an-Nahdha members. Some were party leaders who had been imprisoned since their mass trial in 1992 on dubious charges of plotting to topple the state. However, the number of political prisoners remained above 350, as authorities arrested scores of young men in sweeps around the country and charged them under the 2003 anti-terror law. Authorities made life difficult for released political prisoners, monitoring them closely, denying them passports and most jobs, and threatening to re-arrest some who spoke out on human rights or politics.

Human Rights Defenders

Authorities have refused to grant legal recognition to every truly independent human rights organization that has applied over the past decade. They then invoke the organization's "illegal" status to hamper its activities. On July 21, 2006, police encircled the Tunis office of the non-recognized National Council on Liberties in Tunisia and, as they had done many times before, prevented members from meeting, using force against those who did not disperse quickly enough. Police also blocked meetings by the non-recognized International Association of Solidarity with Political Prisoners.

The independent Tunisian Human Rights League, a legally recognized group, continued to face lawsuits filed by dissident members. The broader context shows that these suits are part of a larger pattern of repression; the courts ruled systematically in favor of these plaintiffs, providing a legal veneer for large-scale police operations to prevent most League meetings. On May 27 the police blocked the League's congress by turning back members from several cities as they sought to reach the national headquarters. On May 18 police prevented a small memorial service at the headquarters for veteran rights activist Adel Arfaoui. Authorities blocked foreign grants to the League, including support from the European Union.

Police conspicuously trail most foreign human rights workers who visit the country. On May 21 authorities expelled Yves Steiner of the Swiss section of Amnesty International, a day after he criticized Tunisia's rights record before Amnesty members. Authorities stated that Steiner had "violated the laws of the country in a way that disturbed the public order," but provided no details.

The Tunisian Association of Magistrates remained under the control of a pro-government leadership that authorities installed in 2005, after using dubious legal maneuvers to oust a newly elected executive committee that had urged more judicial independence.

In May 2006 parliament adopted a law requiring future lawyers to pass a training program at a new institute that the justice minister said was necessary to prepare them for an increasingly globalized environment. Lawyers protested that the law undermined the independence of the profession by tightening state control over the training and certification of lawyers.

Human rights defenders and dissidents are subject to heavy surveillance, arbitrary travel bans, dismissal from work, interruptions in phone service, physical assaults, harassment of relatives, suspicious acts of vandalism and theft, and slander campaigns in the press. Lawyer Mohamed Abou continued to serve a three-year sentence imposed in 2005, after he published harsh critiques of President Ben Ali in online forums. Police harassed his wife Samia during her prison visits and as she publicized her husband's plight.

The Justice System

The judiciary lacks independence. Investigative judges often question defendants without their lawyers present. Prosecutors and judges usually turn a blind eye to torture allegations, even when the subject of formal complaints submitted by lawyers. Trial judges convict defendants solely or predominantly on the basis of coerced confessions, or on the testimony of witnesses whom the defendant does not have the opportunity to confront in court.

The International Committee of the Red Cross (ICRC) continued its program of visiting Tunisian prisons. However, authorities refuse to allow access by independent human rights organizations. They refused to honor an explicit commitment made in April 2005 to allow visits by Human Rights Watch on "its next visit" to Tunisia, explaining that Tunisia was preoccupied with organizing the ICRC visits.

Media Freedom

None of the print and broadcast media offers critical coverage of government policies, apart from a few low-circulation independent magazines that are subject to occasional confiscation. The private dailies are all loyalist, often slandering government critics in a manner that is deemed too base for the official media. Tunisia now has privately-owned radio and television stations, but here too private ownership is not synonymous with editorial independence. The government blocks certain political or human rights websites featuring critical coverage of Tunisia.

Counterterrorism Measures

Tunisian authorities claim that they have long been in the forefront of combating terrorism and extremism. The 2003 Law in Support of "International Efforts to Fight Terrorism and the Repression of Money-Laundering" contains a broad definition of terrorism that could be used to prosecute persons for a peaceful exercise of their right to dissent, and erodes defendants' rights in terror cases.

Since 2005, the government has charged more than 200 mostly young Tunisians—who were arrested in cities around the country, or who were extradited by Algeria or other governments—with planning to join jihadist movements abroad or planning terrorist activities. In many instances, plainclothes police carried out these arrests without identifying themselves or providing the reason for arrest, and families were unable to learn the persons' whereabouts for days or weeks. During their trials, these defendants overwhelmingly claimed the police had extracted their statements under torture or threat of torture. The courts sentenced many of these defendants to long prison terms on broad terrorism charges but, to Human Rights Watch's knowledge, convicted none of committing a specific act of violence or of possessing arms or explosives.

The presidential pardon in February 2006 freed six defendants in one of the best-known such cases, known as the "Zarzis" group, after they had served three years of sentences ranging up to 19 years. The court had convicted them on the basis of allegedly coerced confessions and also on evidence that they had downloaded bomb-making instructions from the internet. In another internet-related case, Ali Ramzi Bettibi continued to serve the four-year sentence he received in 2005 for cutting and pasting on an online forum a statement by an obscure group threatening bomb attacks if President Ben Ali hosted a visit by the Israeli prime minister.

Since 1991, there has been one deadly terrorist attack in Tunisia: an April 2002 truck bomb that targeted a synagogue on the island of Djerba. Al-Qaeda claimed responsibility for the attack.

Key International Actors

The United States enjoys good relations with Tunisia, while urging human rights progress there more vocally than in most other countries in the region. The embassy frequently sends diplomats to observe political trials and to meet civil society activists.

While the US gives minimal financial aid to Tunisia, the Department of Defense provides counterterrorism training and exchange programs for the military. Defense Secretary Donald Rumsfeld, after meeting with President Ben Ali in Tunis on February 11, 2006, declared, "Tunisia has long been an important voice of moderation and tolerance ... and has played a key role in confronting extremists not just within this country, but in the area as well." Rumsfeld did not suggest that Tunisia should stop using "extremism" to stifle all forms of non-violent opposition, saying only that "political and economic freedom go hand in hand, and each depends on the other for long-term stability."

On March 1 the State Department spokesman welcomed the president's pardon of prisoners but urged Tunisia to "accelerate reforms that create a more open and vibrant political space in which all parties, civil society organizations, and released prisoners can operate more freely." The State Department Report on Supporting Human Rights and Democracy for 2005-2006 said, "The Government continued to invoke a variety of laws and regulations to obstruct implementation of US and internationally funded reform projects and initiatives, including those promoting media freedom and opinion in the political process."

The EU-Tunisia Association Agreement continues to be in force, despite the government's human rights record and its blocking of EU grants to some NGOs. EU officials occasionally criticized their partner's rights record, while taking pains to praise the state of bilateral relations overall. The EU presidency criticized the last-minute refusal of Tunisia to host an international conference on employment and the right to work, scheduled for September 8-9, calling it one of "a series of negative signals which have been given by Tunisia in the area of human rights and governance over the last few years." The European Parliament on June 15, 2006, adopted a resolution deploring the repression of human rights activists in Tunisia.

France remained Tunisia's leading trade partner and foreign investor, and President Jacques Chirac remained a staunch supporter of President Ben Ali. Public statements about human rights on the part of France were exceedingly rare and cautious.

United Arab Emirates (UAE)

While the economy of the UAE continues its impressive growth, civil society continues to stagnate and human rights progress has been slow. Authorities have blocked the formation of independent human rights organizations and exerted censorial pressure on a wide range of social activists, impeding the kind of vigorous monitoring and reporting that can draw attention to and help curb human rights abuses.

The UAE is a federation of seven emirates: Abu Dhabi, 'Ajman, Al Fujayrah, Sharjah, Dubai, Ra's al- Khaymah, and Umm al-Qaywayn. The rulers of each emirate, sitting as the Federal Supreme Council, elect the president and vice president from among their number. The government announced in August 2006 that it would hold its first-ever elections for 20 of the 40 members of the Federal National Council, an advisory body to the president, in December 2006. The emir of each emirate chooses the candidates who can stand for election and the president of the UAE appoints the remaining council members.

The UAE has not signed most international human rights and labor rights treaties. Migrant workers, comprising nearly 90 percent of the workforce in the private sector, are particularly vulnerable to serious human rights violations.

Freedom of Association and Expression

The government approved the formation of the first human rights organization in the country, the Emirates Human Rights Association, in February 2006, but disputes among its board members kept the association from being fully functional at year's end.

The government actively discouraged the creation of other human rights organizations. In July 2004 a group led by lawyer Muhammad al-Roken applied to the Ministry of Labor and Social Welfare for permission to establish the Emirates Human Rights Society. In April 2005 another group of 30 activists headed by human rights campaigner Khalifa Bakhit al-Falasi applied to the ministry to set up another human rights association. According to the Associations Law, the Ministry of Labor and Social Welfare is to reply to such requests within a month of their filing, but as of November 2006 the ministry had not responded to either application.

Since 2000, the government has barred 12 prominent UAE commentators and academics from disseminating their views. In 2006 the government increased its persecution and prosecution of human rights defenders. In June 2006 the Federal High Court issued an arrest warrant for Muhammad al-Mansoori, president of the independent Jurists Association, for allegedly "insulting the public prosecutor." Security agents detained Muhammad al-Roken, a former president of the Jurists Association, for 24 hours in July and again in August for three days. On both occasions officials questioned him about his human rights activities and his public lectures. Security officials confiscated his passport and barred him from leaving the country. The government has also not recognized City of Hope, the country's only shelter for abused women, children, and domestic workers. The organization's director, Sharla Musabih, currently faces potential criminal prosecution in what she alleges to be a politically motivated case.

Migrant Labor

Nearly 80 percent of the UAE's population are foreigners, and foreigners account for 90 percent of the workforce in the private sector, including domestic workers. As of May 2006, according to the Ministry of Labor, there were 2,738,000 migrant workers in the country. The UAE's economic growth has attracted large domestic and foreign investments and the current construction boom is one of the largest in the world. Exploitation of migrant construction workers by employers, especially low-skilled workers in small firms, is particularly severe. Immigration sponsorship laws that grant employers extraordinary power over the lives of migrant workers are in part responsible for the continuing problem.

Abuses against migrant workers include nonpayment of wages, extended working hours without overtime compensation, unsafe working environments resulting in deaths and injuries, squalid living conditions in labor camps, and withholding of passports and travel documents.

The government failed in 2006 to put in place a minimum wage as required by the UAE Labor Law of 1980. 2006 saw an increasing number of public demonstra-

UNITED ARAB EMIRATES

Building Towers, Cheating Workers

Exploitation of Migrant Construction Workers
in the United Arab Emirates

HUMAN
RIGHTS
WATCH

tions by migrant workers protesting nonpayment of wages. Twenty-five hundred construction workers rioted in Dubai on March 21, 2006, demanding better working conditions and higher wages. In May 2006 thousands of construction workers working for Besix, a Brussels-based company, went on strike to demand an increase in their wage of US$4 a day and better working conditions. The government deported 50 strikers.

In March the government announced that it would legalize trade unions by the end of 2006, but as of November 2006 it had taken no steps to do so. Instead, in September the government introduced a law banning any migrant worker who participates in a strike from employment in the country for at least one year.

Following a surge in heat-related illnesses and injuries at construction sites in July 2005, the Labor Ministry directed construction companies to give their workers a break from 12:30 p.m. to 4:30 p.m. during July and August. However, in July 2006, after intense lobbying by construction companies, the government reduced the afternoon break to the hours of 12:30 p.m. to 3 p.m. When asked about the reason for this change, Minister of Labor Ali bin Abdullah al-Kaabi told reporters, "The contractors should be asked about the reduction in the hours, as they are the ones who have decided the timings."

Women domestic workers are often confined to their places of work, and are at particular risk of abuse, including unpaid wages, long working hours, and physical or sexual abuse.

Trafficking

According to the US State Department, human trafficking to the UAE is an endemic problem. Large numbers of young boys are annually trafficked to the UAE to be trained as camel jockeys, and in 2005 the UAE government estimated the number of children working as camel jockeys to be between 1,200 and 2,700; international organizations have put the numbers at 5,000-6,000. Responding to international criticism, UAE President Sheikh Khalifa bin Zayed al-Nahyan decreed in July 2005 that all camel jockeys must be age 18 or older. The law penalizes violators with jail terms of up to three years and/or fines of at least Dh50,000 (US$13,600). In 2006 the government cooperated with UNICEF to identify and return 1,071 children to their home countries. The government also provided funds for their reset-tlement.

Key International Actors

The UAE has emerged as a major business and trading hub in the Middle East, attracting substantial foreign investments. The US, Japan, and the European Union are among the UAE's main trading partners. In April 2004 the UAE signed a Trade and Investment Framework Agreement (TIFA) with the US, and the two coun-tries in November 2004 began negotiations toward a Free Trade Agreement. The UAE is also negotiating free trade agreements with the European Union and Australia.

In its 2006 annual report on human trafficking, the US State Department placed the UAE on its Tier 2 Watch List for its "failure to show increased efforts to combat trafficking over the past year, particularly in its efforts to address the large-scale trafficking of foreign girls and women for commercial sexual exploitation."

In October 2004 the UAE acceded to the Convention on the Elimination of All Forms of Discrimination against Women. However, it is not a signatory to other major international human rights instruments such as the International Covenant on Civil and Political Rights, the International Covenant on Economic, Social and Cultural Rights, the Convention on the Protection of the Rights of All Migrant Workers and Members of Their Families, and the Convention against Torture.

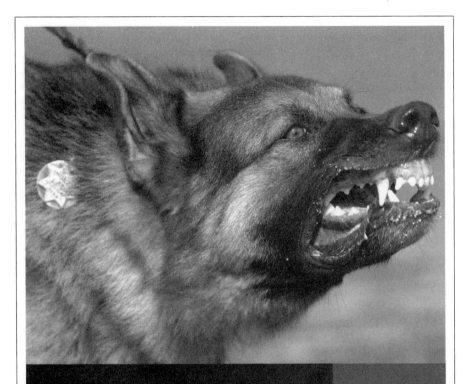

UNITED STATES

Cruel and Degrading

The Use of Dogs for Cell Extractions in U.S. Prisons

HUMAN

RIGHTS

WATCH

WORLD REPORT

2007

UNITED STATES

United States

In our World Report 2004, Human Rights Watch noted with alarm in an essay titled "Above the Law" the Bush administration's efforts post 9/11 to dramatically expand executive power at the expense of judicial or legislative protection for individual rights. It now appears we underestimated the extent and tenacity of those efforts.

In the past five years the administration has authorized torture and other abusive interrogation techniques, "disappeared" dozens of suspected terrorists into secret prisons, twisted domestic law to permit indefinite detention without charge of persons suspected of links to terrorism, and confined hundreds at Guantanamo Bay without charge while denying them information about the basis for their detention and meaningful opportunity to contest it. The administration has sought to exempt its actions from court oversight.

Wholly outside the counterterrorism arena, the executive branch has continued to slight its obligation to protect the human rights of US residents, particularly those who are accused or convicted of crimes, or who are immigrants.

In 2006 the Supreme Court provided an important check on some of the administration's counterterrorism policies, striking down the military commissions originally authorized by President George W. Bush to try Guantanamo detainees and calling into question the legality of the administration's secret detention program. The president, in response, asked Congress to authorize a system of military commissions akin to those that had been struck down, and to redefine the humane treatment requirements of the Geneva Conventions so that the CIA's "enhanced"—and abusive—interrogation program could continue. The legislation Congress ultimately passed did not give the administration everything it wanted. Congress left intact the humane treatment requirements and insisted abusive interrogation techniques such as waterboarding (mock drowning), induced hypothermia, and extended sleep deprivation remain prosecutable war crimes. But the legislation also endorsed deeply troubling provisions that violate international human rights protections. These include provisions that curtail the fundamental right of non-citizens to contest their detention and define "combatant" in a way that allows for the military detention and trial of civilians who did not participate in armed hostilities.

The United States appeared in 2006 before the United Nations Committee against Torture and Human Rights Committee regarding its compliance with the Convention against Torture and the International Covenant on Civil and Political Rights. With regard to US counterterrorism policies, both committee of experts rejected most of the administration's justifications, issuing strong and thorough critiques of the US record on torture, detention without charge, and lack of accountability for abuse. The Human Rights Committee also issued a robust critique of US criminal justice, detention, and immigration policies, including the practice of sentencing juveniles to life without parole and the overbroad "material support to terrorism" bars on admission that put asylum seekers at risk of being returned to countries where they fear persecution.

Guantanamo Bay, Indefinite Detention, and Military Commissions

Approximately 450 men remain in long-term, indefinite, and largely incommunicado detention at Guantanamo Bay. The United States continues to assert its authority to hold these men as "unlawful enemy combatants" without charge and without regard to the laws of armed conflict.

In late 2005 Congress passed a law preventing non-citizen Guantanamo detainees from bringing any future court challenges to their detention, their treatment by US officials, or their confinement conditions. In September 2006 Congress extended and made these provisions retroactive—applying them to pending cases and to non-citizens in US custody anywhere in the world. Unless found unconstitutional, this measure could result in courts dismissing the more than 200 pending habeas corpus cases brought on behalf of Guantanamo detainees, as well as the pending habeas challenge brought by Ali Saleh Kahleh al-Marri, the only so-called unlawful enemy combatant still detained in the United States, and a handful of habeas cases brought on behalf of detainees in Afghanistan.

In response to litigation brought by the Associated Press, the US publicly disclosed in early 2006 the names of the Guantanamo detainees and transcripts of administrative proceedings regarding their continued detention. These documents suggest that, contrary to the claims of the Bush administration, only a small proportion of the detainees are alleged to have engaged in armed conflict against the United States.

The Department of Defense has been working through a second round of administrative reviews to determine whether individual Guantanamo detainees are still a "threat" or of intelligence value that warrants their continued detention. At this writing, the military Administrative Review Boards have slated 166 detainees for transfer or release, although fewer than a third have actually left Guantanamo. Some countries have refused to take back nationals declared "enemy combatants" by the US or to accept US requirements for their monitoring or continued detention. In other cases, detainees had substantial grounds for believing they might be tortured if returned. Rather than allowing some of these detainees into the United States—including men who have been cleared of any wrongdoing—the Bush administration continues to hold them in Guantanamo.

Alleged "enemy combatant" Ali Saleh Kahleh al-Marri remains in custody in the United States. A Qatari who had been living in the US on a student visa, he was charged in 2002 with credit card fraud, but just weeks before his trial the US administration declared him an "enemy combatant," and sent him to a military brig in South Carolina, where he has been held in solitary confinement for three years, essentially incommunicado; his only contact is with his lawyers, who had to sue in US court for access to him. The charges against al-Marri are based on a single hearsay declaration relying heavily on accusations by a man widely reported to have been tortured in a secret Central Intelligence Agency (CIA)-run detention center. The government has filed to dismiss al-Marri's habeas challenge to the lawfulness of his detention—citing the court-stripping provisions in the Military Commissions Act. As of this writing, the court had not ruled on the government's request.

In June 2006 the US Supreme Court, in *Hamdan v. Rumsfeld*, struck down the military commissions set up to try non-citizens accused of participating in or supporting terrorist acts against the United States. In response to *Hamdan*, in

September Congress legislated a new system of military commissions (the Military Commissions Act of 2006). The new commissions contain important improvements over the previous ones. For example, Congress has specified that the accused have access to the same evidence as is considered by the fact-finder, and that they may appeal convictions to a civilian appellate court (though such review is limited to legal findings, not factual ones, so actual innocence would not be a basis for overturning a verdict). But the new rules still contain troubling provisions: for example, statements obtained through "cruel, inhuman or degrading treatment" prior to December 30, 2005, are admissible so long as a judge finds they have probative value and are "reliable" (a contradiction in terms).

Perhaps the most disturbing aspect of these new commissions is their expansive jurisdiction. The commissions are authorized to try any non-US citizen, including longtime US residents, who falls within a definition of "unlawful enemy combatant" that is far broader than the definition ordinarily used under the laws of war. Because the definition includes anyone who "purposefully and materially supported" hostilities against the United States, it potentially turns ordinary civilians—such as an individual who sends money to a banned group—into "combatants" who can be placed in military custody and hauled before a military commission.

At this writing no charges have been brought against detainees under the new military commission rules, and the first trials were not expected until summer 2007 at the earliest.

Torture Policy

In late 2005 Congress—over the Bush administration's objections—passed the Detainee Treatment Act, which prohibits the use of cruel, inhuman, or degrading treatment by any US personnel operating anywhere in the world. The Supreme Court stepped in here as well, ruling in *Hamdan* that the US is bound to treat al Qaeda detainees in accordance with the minimal provisions of the Geneva Conventions' Common Article 3.

In response, in July 2006 the Pentagon ordered the military to ensure that all of its practices complied with these standards, and in September it announced new interrogation rules that repudiated many of the abusive techniques reportedly used by US interrogators in the past, including waterboarding, painful stress positions, and prolonged sleep deprivation or exposure to cold. Ironically, that same day the Bush administration proposed legislation effectively rewriting the humane treatment standards of Common Article 3, permitting the CIA to continue using the abusive interrogation techniques now banned by the Pentagon.

Congress rejected the administration's proposal, but with mixed results. It retains most of the War Crimes Act, which exposes interrogators to criminal prosecution for both torture and "cruel and inhuman treatment" (defined as conduct that causes serious physical or mental pain or suffering). As two of the primary authors of the legislation, Senators McCain and Warner, have stated that the definition of prohibited conduct is intended to criminalize a wide range of abusive interrogation techniques. However, the law narrowed prosecutable offenses under the War Crimes Act by creating a higher threshold for inflicting serious physical pain or suffering, preventing prosecution for non-prolonged mental abuse occurring prior to the new law, and eliminating as a war crime the punishing of a person after an unfair trial.

Most seriously, the legislation prohibits any detainee the US government has labeled an "unlawful enemy combatant" from ever challenging in court his treatment while in US custody, even after his release.

Secret Prisons

In early September 2006 President Bush admitted for the first time that the CIA had maintained secret detention centers abroad to interrogate terrorism suspects. He announced that his administration was shutting them down and had moved the 14 people still being held in those centers to Guantanamo Bay (where they have since been visited by the International Committee of the Red Cross). Bush was unrepentant when he announced the existence of the secret prisons, and his administration kept open the option of restarting the program of enforced disappearances of terrorist suspects.

The administration has not identified the other people whom it held in the secret prisons, nor has it disclosed their current whereabouts. Human Rights Watch has identified at least 15 other people we believe were held in those prisons. Those persons remain "disappeared" under international law until the US can account for them.

Accountability for Detainee Abuse

Despite a number of official investigations into abuse of detainees in US custody in Afghanistan, Iraq, and Guantanamo Bay, the United States has done little to hold those involved accountable. Joint research conducted by New York University Law School, Human Rights First, and Human Rights Watch documented over 330 cases in which US military and civilian personnel were credibly alleged to have abused or killed detainees. While these cases involved at least 600 US personnel and over 460 detainees, only a small percentage have been prosecuted: approximately 90 military personnel, no CIA agents, and one civilian contractor. Only 10 of the convicted abusers were sentenced to a year or more in prison.

The US persisted in thwarting efforts by victims of abuse to seek redress in court. Asserting claims of "state secrets" and "national security," the government moved to dismiss claims brought by Khaled el-Masri, a German citizen who was seized in Macedonia, transferred to a CIA-run prison in Afghanistan, beaten, and held incommunicado for several months, and by Maher Arar, a dual Canadian-Syrian citizen detained by US authorities on his way home to Canada and sent to Syria, where he was imprisoned for 10 months and tortured. Lower courts dismissed both cases on the grounds that the court should not second-guess—or even investigate—the government's actions. Both Arar and el-Masri have appealed. A Canadian commission of inquiry into Arar's case found that the US deported him to Syria based on Canadian authorities' erroneous claims that he was linked to terrorism. The inquiry concluded "categorically" that there was "no evidence to indicate that Arar has committed any offense."

The US continues to assert that it may lawfully send detainees to countries that regularly engage in torture, so long as it has obtained "diplomatic assurances"—i.e. promises by the receiving government not to mistreat the detainee. But these promises cannot be enforced and, indeed, there is little incentive for the governments involved to uncover any breach of the assurances. The US has stated that it will rely on such assurances in moving detainees from Guantanamo Bay.

Incarceration

With more than 2.2 million men and women in US jails and prisons, a preponderance of whom are low-level nonviolent offenders, the United States has the highest incarceration rate in the world. The burden of incarceration falls disproportionately on the poor and members of racial and ethnic minorities.

Many prisons and jails are dangerous, plagued by high rates of violence and illness, and devoid of productive programs and activities for prisoners. The private bipartisan Commission on Safety and Abuse in America's Prisons released a report in June 2006 concluding that overcrowding and prisoner idleness promotes disorder and tension that can escalate into violence. Staff members engage in unnecessary as well as excessive use of force to respond to minor prisoner misbehavior.

As of the beginning of the year, prison policies in six states permitted use of aggressive unmuzzled dogs to intimidate and even attack prisoners who did not obey orders to leave their cells – four of those states used dogs for this purpose. This practice was virtually secret, even within the corrections community, until Human Rights Watch revealed it in October. Advocacy by Human Rights Watch helped persuade three states to change their policies. At this writing, only one state continues to use dogs to help prison officers remove prisoners from their cells.

In July 2006 a Department of Justice Bureau of Statistics (BJS) report found that formal complaints of sexual violence filed in adult prisons and jails increased nearly 16 percent between 2004 and 2005, from 5,386 to 6,241; more than half concerned staff sexual misconduct or harassment. As the BJS acknowledges, these numbers underestimate the level of sexual violence in prison because inmates are reluctant to make complaints for fear of retaliation, among other reasons. The National Prison Rape Elimination Commission held four public hearings this year during which witnesses testified to the causes and consequences of staff and inmate-on-inmate rape and sexual abuse.

In an investigation of two high-security juvenile facilities for girls in New York state, Human Rights Watch and the American Civil Liberties Union found that young girls were subjected to excessive use of a face-down "restraint" procedure

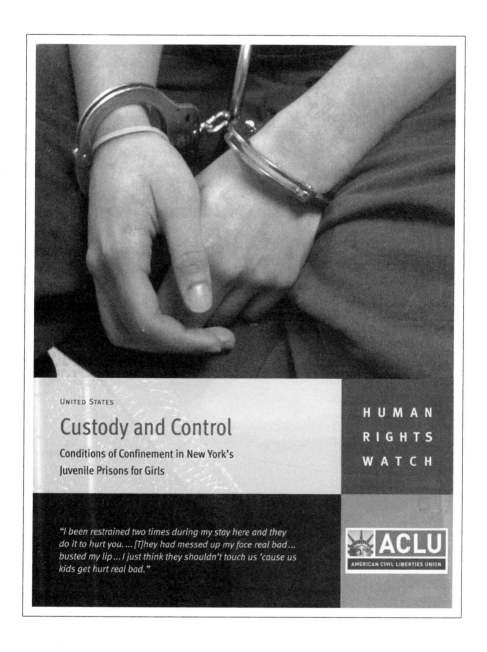

in which girls were thrown to the floor, often causing injury, as well as incidents of sexual abuse, and inadequate educational and mental health services.

Prisons struggle to provide quality medical care without adequate resources or qualified staff. A federal judge put the entire California prison medical system under receivership because care was so abysmal that one prisoner died from medical malpractice or neglect every six to seven days. In Florida, over 300 inmates who have been found mentally incompetent to stand trial had been left to languish in jail, despite a law requiring the state to move them to hospitals or other mental health facilities where they can get the treatment they need.

The Death Penalty and Other Cruel Sentences

State and federal governments executed 51 prisoners between January and November 2006, bringing the total number of men and women executed in the country to 1055 since 1977. Almost all were killed by lethal injection. Mounting evidence indicates that contrary to public belief, lethal injection may be a very painful way to die. Execution logs from six recent executions in California and toxicology reports from executions in Missouri and North Carolina suggest that some prisoners may have been conscious and suffering at the time of their executions. Despite being used for almost 30 years, state lethal injection protocols were never subjected to scientific, medical, or public scrutiny until recent litigation prompted some judges and officials to examine them.

In the United States, youth who were below the age of 18 at the time of their crimes may be tried and sentenced as adults. Courts in the US continue to impose life sentences without the possibility of parole on many such youthful offenders. The more than 2,225 youthful offenders serving life without parole are disproportionately African American or Hispanic. The UN Committee against Torture, the Human Rights Committee, and the Secretary-General in his study on violence against children worldwide all rebuked the United States in 2006 for imposing life without parole sentences on young offenders. On the legislative front, the Colorado legislature eliminated the sentence, although it substituted a mandatory term of 40 years' imprisonment. A package of bills to eliminate the sentence remained under serious consideration in Michigan.

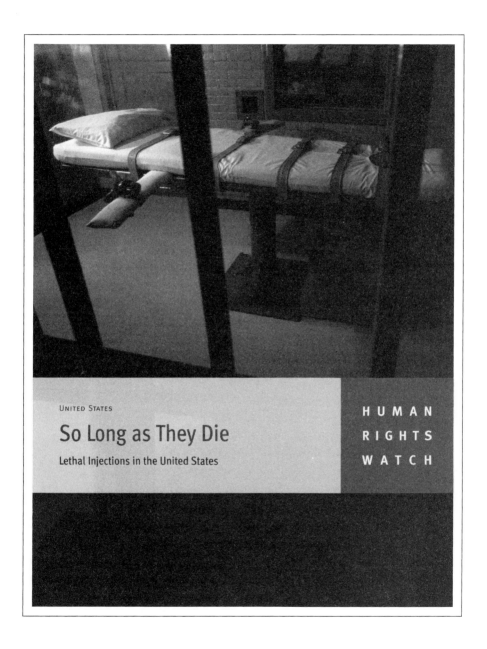

UNITED STATES

So Long as They Die

Lethal Injections in the United States

HUMAN
RIGHTS
WATCH

Immigrants and Other Non-Citizens

The two houses of Congress remained in a stalemate over the correct approach to immigration reform, with the Senate embracing the concept of a guest worker program, and the House focusing solely on immigration restrictions and enforcement. Just before the November 7, 2006 elections, Republican Party leaders in the House re-introduced previously failed legislation that would allow fencing of 700 miles of the US-Mexico border, give state and local officials the authority to enforce immigration law while shielding them from accountability for errors, and reverse two Supreme Court decisions that had found indefinite detention of non-citizens unconstitutional. None of these measures were considered in committees, and instead were rushed to a vote and passed by the House, though only the border fence legislation had passed the Senate and won the approval of President Bush at this writing.

As of late 2006 hundreds of asylum seekers faced return to their countries of origin by the United States and thousands of refugees are being denied resettlement inside the US due to overbroad definitions of terrorism and terrorism-related activity in the Immigration and Nationality Act. Anyone who associated with, or provided any "material support" to any armed group is denied asylum, including civilians caught up in civil wars who are forced at gunpoint to provide food to rebel forces.

HIV/AIDS

Massachusetts, Delaware, and New Jersey made progress toward ensuring injection drug users' access to sterile syringes, recognizing their human right to obtain lifesaving HIV/AIDS information and services without fear of punishment. Massachusetts enacted legislation permitting non-prescription sale of syringes; Delaware approved its first needle exchange program; and the New Jersey legislature considered legislation to increase access to clean needles, including by establishing needle exchange programs.

California Governor Arnold Schwarzenegger vetoed legislation that would have permitted condom distribution to prevent the spread of HIV/AIDS in state prisons, rejecting the example of jurisdictions in the US and abroad that have taken such measures to protect inmate health.

VIETNAM

No Sanctuary

Ongoing Threats to Indigenous Montagnards
in Vietnam's Central Highlands

**HUMAN
RIGHTS
WATCH**

2006
HUMAN RIGHTS WATCH
PUBLICATIONS

BY COUNTRY

Afghanistan

Lessons in Terror: Attacks on Education in Afghanistan, 07/06, 145pp.

Angola

Still Not Fully Protected: Rights to Freedom of Expression and Information under Angola's New Press Law, 11/06, 25pp.

Bosnia and Herzegovina

A Chance for Justice? War Crime Prosecutions in Bosnia's Serb Republic, 03/06, 42pp.

Looking for Justice: The War Crimes Chamber in Bosnia and Herzegovina, 02/06, 44pp.

Burundi

"We Flee When We See Them": Abuses with Impunity at the National Intelligence Service in Burundi, 10/06, 33pp.

A High Price to Pay: Detention of Poor Patients in Hospitals, 09/06, 75pp.

A Long Way from Home: FNL Child Soldiers in Burundi, 06/06, 13pp.

Warning Signs: Continuing Abuses in Burundi, 02/06, 11pp.

Canada

Funding the "Final War": LTTE Intimidation and Extortion in the Tamil Diaspora, 03/06, 48pp.

Chad

Violence Beyond Borders: The Human Rights Crisis in Eastern Chad, 06/06, 28pp.

Darfur Bleeds: Recent Cross-Border Violence in Chad, 02/06, 17pp.

Chile

Probable Cause: Evidence Implicating Fujimori, 12/05, 24pp.

China

"A Great Danger for Lawyers": New Regulatory Curbs on Lawyers Representing Protesters, 12/06, 60pp.

"Race to the Bottom": Corporate Complicity in Chinese Internet Censorship, 08/06, 141pp.

Côte d'Ivoire

"Because They Have the Guns … I'm Left With Nothing": The Price of Continuing Impunity in Cote d'Ivoire, 05/06, 36 pp.

Croatia

A Decade of Disappointment: Continuing Obstacles to the Reintegration of Serb Returnees, 09/06, 43pp.

Democratic Republic of Congo

What Future? Street Children in the Democratic Republic of Congo, 04/06, 73pp.

Elections in Sight: "Don't Rock the Boat"? 12/05, 20pp.

European Union

European Union: Managing Migration Means Potential EU Complicity in Neighboring States' Abuse of Migrants and Refugees, 10/06, 22pp.

Georgia

Undue Punishments: Abuses against Prisoners in Georgia, 09/06, 102pp.

Guinea

"The Perverse Side of Things": Torture, Inadequate Detention Conditions, and Excessive Use of Force by Guinean Security Forces, 08/06, 30pp.

India

"Everyone Lives in Fear": Patterns of Impunity in Jammu and Kashmir, 09/06, 152pp.

Indonesia

Condemned Communities: Forced Evictions in Jakarta, 09/06, 111pp.

Too High a Price: The Human Rights Cost of the Indonesian Military's Economic Activities, 06/06, 136pp.

Iran

Denying the Right to Education, 10/06, 15pp.

Ministers of Murder: Iran's New Security Cabinet, 12/05, 15pp.

Iraq

"The Silent Treatment": Fleeing Iraq, Surviving in Jordan, 11/06, 108pp.

Judging Dujail: The First Trial before the Iraqi High Tribunal, 11/06, 93pp.

Nowhere to Flee: The Perilous Situation of Palestinians in Iraq, 08/06 42pp.

"No Blood, No Foul": Soldiers' Accounts of Detainee Abuse in Iraq, 07/06, 53pp.

Israel/Occupied Palestinian Territories

A Question of Security: Violence against Palestinian Women and Girls, 11/06, 101pp.

Fatal Strikes: Israel's Indiscriminate Attacks Against Civilians in Lebanon, 08/06, 51pp.

Jordan

"The Silent Treatment": Fleeing Iraq, Surviving in Jordan, 11/06, 108pp.

Suspicious Sweeps: the General Intelligence Department and Jordan's Rule of Law Problem, 09/06, 64pp.

Kyrgyzstan

RECONCILED TO VIOLENCE: STATE FAILURE TO STOP DOMESTIC ABUSE AND ABDUCTION OF WOMEN IN KYRGYZSTAN, 09/06, 144pp.

Lebanon

FATAL STRIKES: ISRAEL'S INDISCRIMINATE ATTACKS AGAINST CIVILIANS IN LEBANON, 08/06, 51pp.

Liberia

TRYING CHARLES TAYLOR IN THE HAGUE: MAKING JUSTICE ACCESSIBLE TO THOSE MOST AFFECTED, 06/06, 15pp.

Libya

STEMMING THE FLOW: ABUSES AGAINST MIGRANTS, ASYLUM SEEKERS AND REFUGEES, 09/06, 136pp.

A THREAT TO SOCIETY? THE ARBITRARY DETENTION OF WOMEN AND GIRLS FOR "SOCIAL REHABILITATION," 02/06, 39pp.

WORDS TO DEEDS: THE URGENT NEED FOR HUMAN RIGHTS REFORM, 01/06, 83pp.

Malaysia

CONVICTED BEFORE TRIAL: INDEFINITE DETENTION UNDER MALAYSIA'S EMERGENCY ORDINANCE, 08/06, 38pp.

Mexico

LOST IN TRANSITION: BOLD AMBITIONS, LIMITED RESULTS FOR HUMAN RIGHTS UNDER FOX, 05/06, 150pp.

THE SECOND ASSAULT: OBSTRUCTING ACCESS TO LEGAL ABORTION AFTER RAPE IN MEXICO, 03/06, 92pp.

Morocco

PROSECUTION OF INDEPENDENT NEWSWEEKLIES, 05/06, 17pp.

Nigeria

"They Do Not Own This Place": Government Discrimination Against "Non-Indigenes" in Nigeria, 04/06, 66pp.

North Korea

North Korea: Workers' Rights at the Kaesong Industrial Complex, 10/06, 19pp.

A Matter of Survival: The North Korean Government's Control of Food and the Risk of Hunger, 05/06, 37pp.

Pakistan

"With Friends Like These..." Human Rights Violation in Kashmir, 09/06, 73pp.

Papua New Guinea

Still Making Their Own Rules: Ongoing Impunity for Police Beatings, Rape and Torture in Papua New Guinea, 10/06, 50pp.

Peru

Probable Cause: Evidence Implicating Fujimori, 12/05, 24pp.

Romania

"Life Doesn't Wait": Romania's Failure to Protect and Support Children and Youth Living with HIV, 08/06, 107pp.

Russia

Widespread Torture in the Chechen Republic: Human Rights Watch Briefing Paper for the 37th Session UN Committee against Torture, 11/06, 16pp.

Serbia

NOT ON THE AGENDA: THE CONTINUING FAILURE TO ADDRESS ACCOUNTABILITY IN KOSOVO POST-MARCH 2004, 05/06, 74pp.

Sri Lanka

IMPROVING CIVILIAN PROTECTION IN SRI LANKA: RECOMMENDATIONS FOR THE GOVERNMENT AND THE LTTE, 09/06, 58pp.

FUNDING THE "FINAL WAR": LTTE INTIMIDATION AND EXTORTION IN THE TAMIL DIASPORA, 03/06, 48pp.

South Africa

UNPROTECTED MIGRANTS: ZIMBABWEANS IN SOUTH AFRICA'S LIMPOPO PROVINCE, 07/06, 52pp.

Sudan

LACK OF CONVICTION: THE SPECIAL CRIMINAL COURT ON THE EVENTS IN DARFUR, 06/06, 32pp.

DARFUR: HUMANITARIAN AID UNDER SIEGE, 05/06, 30pp.

THE IMPACT OF THE COMPREHENSIVE PEACE AGREEMENT AND THE NEW GOVERNMENT OF NATIONAL UNITY ON SOUTHERN SUDAN, 03/06, 28pp.

DARFUR BLEEDS: RECENT CROSS-BORDER VIOLENCE IN CHAD, 02/06, 17pp.

IMPERATIVES FOR IMMEDIATE CHANGE: THE AFRICAN UNION MISSION IN SUDAN, 01/06, 55pp.

ENTRENCHING IMPUNITY: GOVERNMENT RESPONSIBILITY FOR INTERNATIONAL CRIMES IN DARFUR, 12/05, 91pp.

Timor-Leste (formerly East Timor)

TORTURED BEGINNINGS: POLICE VIOLENCE AND THE BEGINNINGS OF IMPUNITY IN EAST TIMOR, 04/06, 59pp.

Ukraine

RHETORIC AND RISK: HUMAN RIGHTS ABUSES IMPEDING UKRAINE'S FIGHT AGAINST HIV/AIDS, 03/06, 86pp.

United Arab Emirates

BUILDING TOWERS, CHEATING WORKERS: EXPLOITATION OF MIGRANT CONSTRUCTION WORKERS IN THE UNITED ARAB EMIRATES, 11/06, 71pp.

United Kingdom

DANGEROUS AMBIVALENCE: UK POLICY ON TORTURE SINCE 9/11, 11/06, 45pp.

FUNDING THE "FINAL WAR": LTTE INTIMIDATION AND EXTORTION IN THE TAMIL DIASPORA, 03/06, 48pp.

United States

CRUEL AND DEGRADING: THE USE OF DOGS FOR CELL EXTRACTIONS IN US PRISONS, 10/06, 20pp.

CUSTODY AND CONTROL: CONDITIONS OF CONFINEMENT IN NEW YORK'S JUVENILE PRISONS FOR GIRLS, 09/06, 136pp.

"NO BLOOD, NO FOUL": SOLDIERS' ACCOUNTS OF DETAINEE ABUSE IN IRAQ, 07/06, 53pp.

BY THE NUMBERS: FINDINGS OF THE DETAINEE ABUSE AND ACCOUNTABILITY PROJECT, 04/06, 27pp.

SO LONG AS THEY DIE: LETHAL INJECTIONS IN THE UNITED STATES, 04/06, 65pp.

Uzbekistan

THE ANDIJAN MASSACRE: ONE YEAR LATER, STILL NO JUSTICE, 05/06, 10 pp.

MYTHS AND REALITY: AN ANALYSIS OF THE UZBEK GOVERNMENT'S JUNE 30, 2006 AIDE-MEMOIRE, "SITUATION OF HUMAN RIGHTS IN UZBEKISTAN," RESPONDING TO UN GENERAL ASSEMBLY RESOLUTION 60/174 OF DECEMBER 16, 2005, 10/06, 16 pp.

Vietnam

"Children of the Dust": Abuse of Hanoi Street Children in Detention, 11/06, 77pp.

No Sanctuary: Ongoing Threats to Indigenous Montagnards in Vietnam's Central Highlands, 06/06, 128pp.

Zimbabwe

"You Will Be Thoroughly Beaten": The Brutal Suppression of Dissent in Zimbabwe, 11/06, 28pp.

No Bright Future: Government Failures, Human Rights Abuses and Squandered Progress in the Fight against AIDS in Zimbabwe, 07/06, 72pp.

Evicted and Forsaken: Internally Displaced Persons in the Aftermath of Operation Murambatsvina, 12/05, 63pp.

Worldwide

Swept Under the Rug: Abuses against Domestic Workers Around the World, 07/06, 93pp.

Universal Jurisdiction in Europe: The State of the Art, 06/06, 101pp.

Human Rights Council: No More Business as Usual, 05/06, 11pp.

BY THEME

Arms Issues

Landmine Monitor Report 2006: Toward a Mine-Free World, 09/06, 1,230pp.

Business and Human Rights Issues

North Korea: Workers' Rights at the Kaesong Industrial Complex, 10/06, 19pp.

"Race to the Bottom": Corporate Complicity in Chinese Internet Censorship, 08/06, 141pp.

Too High a Price: The Human Rights Cost of the Indonesian Military's Economic Activities, 06/06, 136pp.

Children's Rights Issues

"Children of the Dust": Abuse of Hanoi Street Children in Detention, 11/06, 77pp.

Still Making Their Own Rules: Ongoing Impunity for Police Beatings, Rape and Torture in Papua New Guinea, 10/06, 50pp.

Custody and Control: Conditions of Confinement in New York's Juvenile Prisons for Girls, 09/06, 136pp.

"Life Doesn't Wait": Romania's Failure to Protect and Support Children and Youth Living with HIV, 08/06, 105pp.

Lessons in Terror: Attacks on Education in Afghanistan, 07/06, 145pp.

A Long Way from Home: FNL Child Soldiers in Burundi, 06/06, 13pp.

What Future? Street Children in the Democratic Republic of Congo, 04/06, 73pp.

Counterterrorism Issues

Dangerous Ambivalence: UK Policy on Torture since 9/11, 11/06, 45pp.

"No Blood, No Foul": Soldiers' Accounts of Detainee Abuse in Iraq, 07/06, 53pp.

By the Numbers: Findings of the Detainee Abuse and Accountability Project, 04/06, 27pp.

HIV/AIDS Issues

"Life Doesn't Wait": Romania's Failure to Protect and Support Children and Youth Living with HIV, 08/06, 107pp.

No Bright Future: Government Failures, Human Rights Abuses and Squandered Progress in the Fight against AIDS in Zimbabwe, 07/06, 72pp.

Rhetoric and Risk: Human Rights Abuses Impeding Ukraine's Fight against HIV/AIDS, 03/06, 86pp.

International Justice Issues

JUDGING DUJAIL: THE FIRST TRIAL BEFORE THE IRAQI HIGH TRIBUNAL, 11/06, 93pp.

TRYING CHARLES TAYLOR IN THE HAGUE: MAKING JUSTICE ACCESSIBLE TO THOSE MOST AFFECTED, 06/06, 15pp.

LACK OF CONVICTION: THE SPECIAL CRIMINAL COURT ON THE EVENTS IN DARFUR, 06/06, 32 pp.

"BECAUSE THEY HAVE THE GUNS … I'M LEFT WITH NOTHING": THE PRICE OF CONTINUING IMPUNITY IN COTE D'IVOIRE, 05/06, 36pp.

NOT ON THE AGENDA: THE CONTINUING FAILURE TO ADDRESS ACCOUNTABILITY IN KOSOVO POST-MARCH 2004, 05/06, 74pp.

A CHANCE FOR JUSTICE? WAR CRIME PROSECUTIONS IN BOSNIA'S SERB REPUBLIC, 03/06, 42pp.

Refugees/Displaced Persons Issues

"THE SILENT TREATMENT": FLEEING IRAQ, SURVIVING IN JORDAN, 11/06, 108pp.

A DECADE OF DISAPPOINTMENT: CONTINUING OBSTACLES TO THE REINTEGRATION OF SERB RETURNEES, 09/06, 43pp.

STEMMING THE FLOW: ABUSES AGAINST MIGRANTS, ASYLUM SEEKERS AND REFUGEES, 09/06, 136pp.

NOWHERE TO FLEE: THE PERILOUS SITUATION OF PALESTINIANS IN IRAQ, 08/06, 42pp.

UNPROTECTED MIGRANTS: ZIMBABWEANS IN SOUTH AFRICA'S LIMPOPO PROVINCE, 07/06, 52pp.

DARFUR: HUMANITARIAN AID UNDER SIEGE, 05/06, 30pp.

EVICTED AND FORSAKEN: INTERNALLY DISPLACED PERSONS IN THE AFTERMATH OF OPERATION MURAMBATSVINA, 12/05, 63pp.

Women's Rights Issues

A QUESTION OF SECURITY: VIOLENCE AGAINST PALESTINIAN WOMEN AND GIRLS, 11/06 101pp.

CUSTODY AND CONTROL: CONDITIONS OF CONFINEMENT IN NEW YORK'S JUVENILE PRISONS FOR GIRLS, 09/06, 136pp.

RECONCILED TO VIOLENCE: STATE FAILURE TO STOP DOMESTIC ABUSE AND ABDUCTION OF WOMEN IN KYRGYZSTAN, 09/06, 144pp.

SWEPT UNDER THE RUG: ABUSES AGAINST DOMESTIC WORKERS AROUND THE WORLD, 07/06, 93pp.

THE SECOND ASSAULT: OBSTRUCTING ACCESS TO LEGAL ABORTION AFTER RAPE IN MEXICO, 03/06, 92pp.

A THREAT TO SOCIETY? THE ARBITRARY DETENTION OF WOMEN AND GIRLS FOR "SOCIAL REHABILITATION", 02/06, 40pp.